The
European Cinema
Reader

Edited by

Catherine Fowler

London and New York

First published 2002
by Routledge
11 New Fetter Lane, London EC4P 4EE

Simultaneously published in the USA and Canada
by Routledge
29 West 35th Street, New York, NY 10001

Routledge is an imprint of the Taylor & Francis Group

© 2002 Catherine Fowler

Typeset in Bell Gothic and Perpetua by M Rules
Printed and bound in Great Britain by
TJ International Ltd, Padstow, Cornwall

British Library Cataloguing in Publication Data
A catalogue record for this book is available from the British Library

Library of Congress Cataloging in Publication Data
A catalog record for this book has been requested

ISBN 0-415-24091-3 (hbk)
ISBN 0-415-24092-1 (pbk)

The European Cinema Reader

The Europ
tice of nati
such as Se
to Peter V
examine ke
tionship be
in Europe.
context, an

- Europ
- Mome
  includi
- Europ
  film th
- The B
  tries a

Includes e:
Byg, '*Cahi*
Eisenstein
Johnston,
Rivette, E

Editor: Catherine Fowler is Reader and Course Leader of the MA in Independent Film and Film-making at Southampton Institute of Higher Education. She has published in *Screen* and *The Historical Journal of Radio, Film and Television*, and is currently writing a book on Belgian cinema.

For their help in creating this book, I wish to thank
The Media Arts Faculty at the Southampton Institute of Higher Education,
Andrew Lockett and Katherine Ahl at Routledge
and Martin and the grandparents

Contents

Acknowledgements

Ricciotto Canudo, 'The Birth of the Sixth Art' from *Framework* Issue 13 Autumn 1980, pp. 3–7. © 1980 *Framework*

Sergei Eisenstein 'The Montage of Film Attractions' from *Eisenstein's Writings 1922–34*, ed. Richard Taylor (London: BFI, 1988), pp. 39–48. © 1988 BFI

Dziga Vertov 'Provisional Instructions to Kino-Eye Groups' from *Kino-Eye: The Writings of Dziga Vertov*, trans./ed. Annette Michelson (Berkeley: University of California Press, 1984), pp. 67–76. © 1984 Regents of the University of California

John Grierson 'First Principles of Documentary' in Forsyth Hardy (ed.) *Grierson on Documentary* (1946). © John Grierson Archive, University of Stirling

Luis Buñuel, 'Cinema Instrument of Poetry' from *The Shadow and its Shadow*, ed. Paul Hammond (London: BFI, 1978), pp. 66–9. © 1978 BFI

André Bazin 'An Aesthetic of Reality: neo-realism' from *What is Cinema?*, ed./trans. Hugh Gray (Berkeley: University of California Press, 1967). © 1967 The Regents of the University of California

André Bazin, Jacques Doniol-Valcroze, Pierre Kast, Roger Leenhardt, Jacques Rivette, Eric Rohmer 'Six Characters in Search of Auteurs: A Discussion about the French Cinema' from *Cahiers du Cinéma Vol. 1 1950s neo-realism, Hollywood, New Wave*, trans. Liz Heron, ed. Jim Hillier (London: BFI, 1985). © BFI 1985

'The Oberhausen Manifesto' from '*West German Filmmakers on Film: Visions and Voices*, ed. Eric Rentschler (New York: Holmes & Meier, 1988). © 1988 by Holmes and Meier Publishers Inc.

Peter Wollen 'Godard's Cinema and Counter-Cinema: *Vent D'Est*' from *Afterimage* no. 4 Autumn 1972, pp. 6–16. © Afterimage/Visual Studies Workshop 1972.

'The Vow of Chastity' © Dogme 95, Nimbus Film and Zentropa Ent

David Bordwell, 'The Art Cinema as a Mode of Film Practice' in *Film Criticism*, vol. IV, no. 1 Fall 1979. © 1979 Film Criticism

Steve Neale 'Art Cinema as Institution' in *Screen*, vol. 22, no. 1 1981, pp. 11–39. © Screen 1981

Sheila Johnston 'The Author as Public Institution, the "New" Cinema in the Federal Republic of Germany' *Screen Education*, vol. 32–3 1979–80, pp. 67–78. © *Screen* 1979–80

Andrew Higson 'National Cinema' in *Screen*, vol. 30, no. 4 Autumn, 1989. © *Screen* 1989

David Gillespie 'Identity and the Past in Recent Russian Cinema' first published in *European Identity in Cinema*, ed. Wendy Everett (Exeter: Intellect, 1999). © Intellect 1999 (updated version here)

Barton Byg 'DEFA and the Traditions of International Cinema' from *DEFA – East German Cinema, 1946–1992*, ed. Sean Allan and John Sandford (Oxford: Berghahn Books, 1999). © 1999 Berghahn

Marvin D'Lugo 'Catalan Cinema: Historical Experience and Cinematic Practice' in *Quarterly Review of Film and Video*, vol. 13, nos 1–3 1991, pp. 131–46. © 1991 Taylor and Francis

Richard Maltby and Ruth Vasey 'Temporary American Citizens – Cultural Anxieties and Industrial Strategies in the Americanisation of European Cinema' in Andrew Higson and Richard Maltby (eds.) *Film Europe and Film America: Cinema Commerce and Cultural Exchange 1920–39* (Exeter University Press), pp. 32–55. © 1999 Exeter University Press

Janet Thumim 'The "Popular", Cash and Culture in the Post-War British Cinema Industry' *Screen*, vol. 32, no. 3 Autumn, pp. 245–85. © 1991 Oxford University Press

Angus Finney 'Support Mechanisms across Europe' from *A New Dose of Reality* (London: Cassell, 1996), pp. 114–33. © 1996 Continuum

Peter Besas 'The Financial Structure of Spanish Cinema' from *Refiguring Spain – Cinema/Media/Representation*, ed. Marsha Kinder (Durham, NC: Duke University Press, 1997), pp. 241–59. © 1997 Duke University Press

Martin Danan 'From the "Prenational" to a "Postnational" French Cinema' first published in *Film History*, vol. 8 1996, pp. 72–84. © John Libbey and Co., 1996 (updated version here)

Catherine Fowler

INTRODUCTION

Films need to be carped at . . . Need an awfully firm hand. Need
snobbism. Need to be sneered at, that is to say, need standards of
value.

(Ken Macpherson, 1931)[1]

IN HIS WORDS ABOVE Ken Macpherson seems to be playing the role of what
Peter Wollen has referred to as a 'gate-keeper of taste' (Wollen, 1993: 27);
someone, then, who tells us what films are worth preserving for all time, and who
therefore plays a part in creating 'the canon'. The role of critics in relation to
European cinemas has been so great we could almost say that without critics such as
Macpherson there would be no canon, and no 'great' directors; there would be no
'masterpieces' and no 'golden age', no 'avant-gardes' and no revolutionary cinema, no
classic moments and no significant movements; in short, without critics there would
be no 'European Cinemas'. The first observation of this *European Cinema Reader* is
that outside of the critical field there is no 'European cinema'. Like the notion of
'Europe', that of 'European cinema' must refer to a space which relies on discourse
to create its identity, to decide which nations should and should not be included (and
this can change at any one time), and then which films 'need standards of value' or
critical appraisal. This introduction will explore how critics have filled the space of
'European cinema', it will offer some suggestions as to why this is so and it will indicate through this the aims of the Reader.

Since the idea of a pan-European film industry producing films which bring together
all, most, or even some of the nations which make up 'Europe' has rarely been realised
in any sustained sense, the phrase 'European cinema' has usually been used to refer to
national cinemas in Europe. However, we should start not with these national cinemas,
but rather with the term 'European': to what does it refer – geographically, culturally
and (in a cinematic context) aesthetically? Since in these terms it does own an agreed
meaning, even if that meaning is subject to change.

Mapping the boundaries of the European

First, geographically, what is the territory of Europe? Which countries have been excluded and included and why? Second, how has this agreed territory impacted on what has been studied as European cinema? As a descriptive term 'Europe' can be used to designate a territory whose borders shift according to how it is applied: thus a 'European Union' application would be different from a 'historical' one or even a more popular (and inclusive) one decided according to those countries which play in football's European cup. For the purposes of this Reader, we will begin with a 'traditional' reading of Europe as:

> rooted in Judeo-Christian religion, Roman law, Greek ideas on politics, philosophy, art and science, and all refracted through the Renaissance and the enlightenment
>
> (Petrie, 1992: 1)

Through these traditions the boundaries of Europe are drawn in three different directions. First, a north–south line separating the Christian world from Islam and White Europe from non-white. Second, an east–west line separating the democratic from the totalitarian or communist and, finally, a line which excludes America, a boundary which divides the historical, cultured, elite European from the modern, populist and popular American.

Writers have largely kept within these boundaries when casting their critical eye over Europe and cinema. However, other considerations must come into play when we consider that geographically, European cinema studies favours Britain, France, Germany, Italy and Spain with far less work (in the English language anyway) on Scandinavia – though the Dogme movement has obviously raised the profile here – and on smaller countries such as Belgium, Portugal, the Netherlands and Greece. How do we explain these favouritisms when clearly all these countries fall within the boundaries ascribed above?

The first explanation could be seen as the amount of film production, from which follows the point of how much national product is exported to other countries. A second explanation for this could be the ways in which film history has been written to prioritise movements, moments and auteurs, this excludes certain countries (on an international scale Belgium and Portugal have had no sustained movements, and while moments of innovation and auteurs do exist, a more local approach is needed in order to grasp their significance). Finally, we might suggest that given that the critical field is largely created from within academia, language has a part to play in which countries are taught the most. After English, the dominant languages studied (and indeed languages spoken in Europe) are French, German, Italian and Spanish[2] – which might explain the exclusion of Portugal and the Netherlands.

European film criticism can be seen here to have accepted the north–south and west boundaries above as a limit of study, yet the boundary to the east is more contentious. A political boundary would at one time have excluded the GDR, Poland, Czechoslovakia, Hungary and Yugoslavia, and would therefore have closed off 'Western' Europe from Russia. Since the fall of the Berlin Wall and the spread of

democracy through Poland, Czechoslovakia and Russia it is harder to draw the boundary on this side, though most critics would argue that film makers such as Eisenstein,
Vertov and Pudovkin have always been part of a 'European film culture'. On this subject David Gillespie writes:

> For centuries Russia has toyed with its relationship with the West with its intellectual elite
> torn between the pull of the Slavophiles, emphasizing Russia's uniqueness and moral supe-
> riority over the West, and the Westerners, who see Russia's only path to the future through
> adoption of Western social-democratic structures and institutions. We find these polarities,
> and these same parameters, prevalent in Russian culture, and in particular film, of the past
> few decades.
>
> (Gillespie: Chapter 15 this volume)

Gillespie's observation suggests that Russia's relationship with European cinemas is
something about which there will always be discussion and debate, however, the place
of cinema up to the end of the 1930s seems to be less contentious.

A European (film) culture

The 'European' of 'European cinema' can be used to describe a number of critical
spaces: the *geographic boundaries* of the 'European', the *conceptual space* to which
the study of films and film makers in Europe refers; and the *methodologies* which
have been used to analyse and theorise European films and film makers. With some
understanding of what has been defined as 'European culture' now in place, we can
return to the subject of the cinema in order to ask what has been defined as
European film culture. While the notion of a collective European identity is a contentious one, most critics seem to agree that there are memories that nations in
Europe share, thus:

> Today we can claim the capability and self-confidence to create in European cinema a cul-
> tural factor which can make good the ravages wrought by the average American film's lack
> of taste. Beyond all national variations, racial distinctions and differences in national char-
> acter we can claim a foundation upon which European culture is based and that the different
> cultural streams of Europe can be united in a single current: in short, there is such a thing
> as European identity. This also applies to cinema.
>
> (Felix Henseleit, 1926)[3]

> European culture is marked by its diversity of climate, countryside, architecture, language,
> beliefs, taste and artistic style . . . but underlying this variety there is an affinity, a family like-
> ness, a common European identity.
>
> (Morley and Robins, 1990)

> when I think of European cinema I think of the masters: Pudovkin, Eisenstein, Fellini, Antonioni . . . the cinema became mature through these people
>
> (Istvan Szabo)[4]

And Jan Nederveen Pieterse talks of stations such as 'Greece, Rome, Christendom, the Renaissance, the Enlightenment, Industrialisation and colonialism' (Pieterse, 1991). To these we might want to add the twentieth-century experiences of the two world wars. It is these experiences, though configured differently for different nations, which have shaped European tradition, heritage and culture. Yet what of European *film culture*? How have critics constructed its stations, or shared memory? And are these constructions informed by the European tradition, heritage and culture above?

Two versions of *European film culture* are already at hand: Szabo's list of 'great' directors above and those writings included in this Reader's first section – Canudo, Buñuel, Eisenstein, Vertov, and Grierson. These two versions depict European film culture as being about the canon, and key preoccupations: around the specificity of cinema, cinema's ability to transport us to the land of dreams, theories of montage and a politically and socially engaged film practice. Whilst these are simply some of the first ideas engaged with by European film culture and there were many more to follow, it is fair to say that they represent an agreed notion of European cinema: as *experimental* (thus with practice informing theory, theories constantly changing, and an emphasis on formal experimentation) *serious* (none of the writer/practitioners above wants to 'satisfy' his audience, instead each wants to challenge them) and *an art form* (this follows from the first two notions). It is this version of European film culture that critics have chosen to preserve; and in foregrounding experiment, seriousness and art they have produced a European film history written to include:

- a liking for 'high culture' – films/film makers working with an 'art cinema' model, films which are elitist appealing to critics rather than real audiences;
- a tendency to divide national cinema history into 'moments' (of innovation, change or difference);
- an equal tendency to collect films and film makers into movements – usually aesthetically defined;
- the privileging of the director as the key creator of a film over other personnel (script-writer, editor, producer, cinematographer).

This history therefore:

- excludes 'low culture', genre cinema and those films produced to be popular at the box-office;
- is written as a history which has little continuity, which makes it difficult to see how different forms of cinema have coexisted at the same time;
- fails to acknowledge the collective nature of film making and has therefore produced a distorted view of the creative process, also fails to pay attention to directors who do not work within the strict *auteurist* form (such as women directors, or those who work with popular forms).

In order to answer the question: 'why has European film history been written to prioritise in this way?' we must return to the boundaries of Europe as originally described.
Thus, criticism has been used to distinguish European cinema from its others, and in
a cinematic context for all European countries the dominant other has been America.
The dominance of America can be applied in terms of both film production and film
studies, since America obviously dominated world film production all other cinemas
have been forced to define themselves against it; equally, film studies were dominated
by work on American cinema, with European film study until the last ten years being
far less well defined.

Once this need to define against America is factored into the version of European
film history above, the reason for some of the exclusions become evident. The tactic
has consequently been to emphasise those aspects which distinguish European films
and film makers from Hollywood. Thus, because Hollywood films were aimed at the
box-office, European critics emphasised cultural remit and artistic content; in place
of the classical continuity system and the studio make-up, they offered sporadic
moments and movements and over stability they inadvertently favoured instability. It
is this emphasis of difference which has created the series of familiar oppositions
already cited: art not entertainment, *auteur* not genre or stars, movements and
moments not one continuity system.

> American culture repositions frontiers – social, cultural, psychic, linguistic, geographical.
> America is now within. America is now part of a European cultural repertoire, part of
> European identity.
>
> (Morley and Robins, 1989: 21)

Before exploring the Europe versus America boundary further, it is necessary to
add that, as with most conceptual boundaries, whilst its conception allowed the
European to take on a certain identity, it also repressed some of the intermingling
of the European and the American which actually goes on, as noted by Morley and
Robins above. European audiences consume American films to such an extent that
'in their own cultures . . . audiences imagined America, imitated Hollywood, and
irritated their native bourgeois nationalists' (Maltby and Vasey, Chapter 18 this
volume). Janet Thumim's article also assumes the impact of American cinema in a
British context (Chapter 19 this volume). Formal and aesthetic influence has been
discussed by Peter Lev (1993) who has used the term 'Euro-American' cinema to
suggest the influence of European art cinema on the generation of Scorsese,
Coppola and others. There has also been work on Euro-American genres, the influence of American cinema on Eisenstein, for example, has never been questioned,
but we have had to wait until recently to encounter work which compares the
American and Italian Westerns (Wagstaff, 1992). Whilst this work does not completely destroy the boundaries between Europe and America, it at least exposes
them as a strategic creation.

The European versus the American

In general terms European film culture has been able to define itself against America in two ways – as the land of history and heritage against a land with no history, and as the land of high culture against the land of popular culture. Cinematically this has manifest itself in first, a reverence for European cinema's past and, second (and consequently), the emphasis on the auteur, the canon, art cinema and an elitist strain.

Reverence for the past

The two tendencies above are intertwined, as reverence for the past is largely represented by the canon of European cinema, which most frequently prizes the old masters over the young and new apprentices. It is figured in phrases such as 'the golden age' and talk of 'masterpieces' which might stand the test of time. This preference covertly favours art over commerce, since box-office popularity is assumed to be tied to such things as 'public taste' which are highly changeable; the popular is seen as transitory, rooted in its context (since it is dependent on this context for meaning) and therefore unworthy of greatness, whilst art cinema (most frequently referring to auteur films) is seen as everlasting, transcending time and place to occupy some sort of independent space of genius. The impact of this critical agenda is evident in Janet Thumim's article here in which her painstaking exploration of 'popularity' is waged against the ephemeral nature of all evidence which might affirm such a notion. Two further critical prejudices are evident in this situation, both of which will be explored further in this introduction: the exclusion of the audience from European film history and film theory and the implementation of an aesthetic agenda which foregrounds text over context.

Reverence for the new

The emphasis on the preservation of the past (largely through canonisation) mimics the sense of heritage found elsewhere in European history and culture, we should note, however, that this has been accompanied by a discourse which turns its back on the past in order to embrace the new. This second discourse operates largely on a national level, it derives from a dissatisfaction with cinema of the moment (whatever that moment) and it is frequently expressed as the need for a change of (old) guard for new (or avant) g(u)arde. The 'cure' for the instability of a national cinema was that it could be saved by a 'new generation' of film makers. This new generation has taken many forms, from the 'advance' guard, to the vital sons who will overthrow various 'cinéma du papa' to those who are simply young enough to be untainted by previous regimes.

It should be immediately apparent that this second cure belies a certain escapism from the realities of film making and assumes a disconnection with one's past. The new generation will inevitably do things differently, they will oppose the cinema of now in order to create the cinema of the future, if realism has dominated they will foster modernism, if dialogue has reigned they will free cinema from the tyranny of the word, for the scriptwriter they will substitute the *auteur*, for studio sets, the city streets and so on. Instead of endorsing the urgency for an infrastructure for film practice, this tendency glosses this with the need for new blood, new voices, new styles – in other words, a new generation.

We can see this narrative played out again and again – from Truffaut's rejection of the tradition of quality which signalled the onslaught of the French New Wave, through the explicit references in the Oberhausen Manifesto to the belief in 'the new German feature film' and 'young authors'. The Manifesto finishes with 'the old film is dead. We believe in the new one.' This impulse can also be traced back to the first avant-gardes, with Vertov declaring: 'We affirm the future of cinema by rejecting its present' (Vertov, 'WE: A variant of a manifesto' (1922), in Michelson, 1984: 7).

Vertov's words above also remind us that this endorsement of new generations is essentially a rejection of the past and therefore goes against the promotion of heritage mentioned earlier. The difference between European cinemas needs to be recognised here as it is evident that some countries may have more pressing reasons for rejecting the past than others. German cinema stands as a case in point, following the rise of fascism which led to the Second World War, all cinema produced during that period needed to be suppressed. The impact of this, however, was restricted largely to the Federal Republic as Barton Byg notes: 'there was less of a rupture in cultural identity in 1945 in the East than in the West [as] . . . [t]he official anti-fascism of the GDR played a role in this tolerance for continuity with Nazi institutions' (Chapter 16 this volume).

The European film industry

The aesthetic imperative of European film historians has produced a film history written as a succession of New Waves, which is therefore characterised by *instability,* in which the moments of innovation and the new are embraced as the most important moments. The consequence of this is that less attention has been given to the question of why particular preceding cinemas were created as 'the bad other' enabling the new to seem favourable and any sense of what a European film industry might be has been sporadic, interrupted by this national, less practical, aesthetic agenda.

Where a European film industry has been discussed though, the suggestion has always been that Europe must mimic the American model. A tone of lamentation and criticism also prevails: whereas European film culture has been celebrated, a European film industry is seen as something to be criticised, and a discourse of 'sickness' prevails. Examples abound: in the introduction to 'A Dose of Reality: The State of European Cinema' (Finney, 1993: 4–5) Oscar Moore (editor of *Screen International*) writes:

[we] have a common purpose: the *strengthening* of European Cinema at every level . . . a common desire to help nurture a diversity of cinema from a diversity of sources playing to a diversity of audiences . . . the *lifeblood* of a *revived* industry will be creatively *robust* films reaching *healthily* large audiences . . . but the industry's ability to face this challenge becomes *weaker* by the day. [my emphases]

and even in a national context, writing on French cinema under Jack Lang's rule, Susan Hayward suggests:

> The 1990s could see the renaissance of French cinema in the best sense of the word. That is, that it be both popular and creative. That is, also, that Lang's policies might in the end prove to have been bold, innovative and to have given the French film industry (which almost since its birth has complained of *ill-health*) a financial structure and a framework for creative *vitality*. [my emphasis]
>
> (Hayward, 1993: 391)

This extended metaphor of sickness suggests a dissatisfaction with performance, which compares the 'healthy' American film industry with the 'weak', 'ill' European film industry. Thus, whilst the 'European' part of 'European film culture' has been defined as a point of difference from the American; when it comes to a European film industry, the American model prevails to be copied. We can see this from a very early stage, for example in the 'Film Europe' movement which lasted from 1924–29 and which was alleged to:

> describe . . . the ideal of a vibrant pan-European cinema industry, making international co-productions for a massively enhanced 'domestic' market, and thereby in a position to challenge American distributors for control of that market – an industry fit for what some politicians envisaged as a united states of Europe.
>
> (Maltby and Higson, 1999: 2)

As we can see on a 'pan-European' level, the 'cure' for this sickness usually involved facing the realities of industrial organisation and collaborating towards an American model of consolidated production, distribution and exhibition. However, the continuity of effort, stability of context and international collaboration, which are pre-requisites for the creation of a pan-European film industry, have been denied: we can look to the lack of co-operation between countries as one reason for this and European rivalry is detailed in pieces by Maltby and Vasey, Thumim, and Finney in Part 4. More importantly, we might suggest that the aesthetic agenda of European film criticism, coupled with the constant rejection of the past on a national level and endorsement of 'the next New Wave', have deterred the need to face reality. If we return to the 'gate-keepers of taste' who were at our starting point, we might want to add that their 'standards of value' may have created a European film culture, but they have fallen short of producing a European film industry whether on a pan-European or a national scale.

Following this account of how the field of 'European cinema' has been defined, that is, the competing agendas, influencing factors and discourses, it is possible to turn to this present Reader and its aims. The main aim is to represent some of the ways in which film studies has conceptualised European cinemas. It collects together both hard to find and more accessible work, and through its juxtaposition of articles hopes to cover some of the key contributions which studies of European cinemas have made to film studies.

The first section, 'European Film Culture', records some of the ways in which cinema was first received in Europe. The essays pose the questions: how might we analyse the specificity of the cinema? (Canudo, Eisenstein, Vertov), what is the relationship between cinema and reality? and should the cinema be popular or elitist? of broad appeal or an art form? With four of the five being written by practitioners they are also examples of 'manifesto's, and provide insights into a variety of film practices, film texts and contexts.

The second section, 'Moments from European Film History', offers essays which serve as historical documents: witnesses from European cinema's past. Each has been chosen because it offers an insight into one of the canonised 'moments' or 'movements' of European film history: Italian neo-realism (Bazin), French New Wave (*Cahiers du Cinéma*) New German Cinema (Oberhausen), May '68 and its aftermath (Wollen) and the Dogme 95 movement. While the Oberhausen Manifesto and the Dogme Vow of Chastity have a direct bearing on the movements which followed them, *Cahiers*', discussion, though carried out before the signs of the New Wave were apparent, should be seen as calling for the cinema which followed. Meanwhile, Bazin and Wollen's essays serve as examples of the ways in which theory has made use of movements and moments. For Bazin, out of Italian neo-realism comes a new use of reality in the cinema. For Wollen, Godard's turn to a political cinema in the aftermath of May '68 heralds a new attitude to the mainstream.

The third section, 'European Films and Theory' follows on from Wollen and Bazin and asks: to what use have European films been put in theory and analysis? Whilst American cinema has most frequently been characterised as a genre cinema, the one indigenous European genre could be said to be 'art cinema' and Bordwell and Neale attempt to define the art cinema as mode and institution. Equally, while American cinema markets its films as star vehicles, the European equivalent could be said to be the auteur, marketing tool, voice of meaning and signifier of value in the cultural gatekeeping sense. As art cinema and *auteur* approaches have been questioned, so theory has turned its attention to 'the national' and this section closes with four examples of essays that address the concept of national cinema.

The fourth and final section of the Reader, 'The Boundaries of European Film Criticism', touches upon two areas which have been given less attention: the film industry and the audience.

Inevitably this Reader is shaped by the field which it represents, thus the priorities and prejudices of the field can be used to explain its omissions as well as decisions as to what has been included. The decision has been made where possible **not** to provide case studies of individual films, since these are widely available elsewhere, see for example Forbes and Street (2000), the BFI Classics and Modern Classics series, or the Cambridge Film Classics series and many of the excellent edited collections of work on specific national cinemas with essays around single films (Ezra and Harris, 2000; Silberman, 1995; Kinder, 1997).

The approach instead has been to offer articles which define a particular area without focusing on specific films (for example Bordwell and Neale on art cinema) or which, although they focus on specific national cinemas offer models which could be applied to other national contexts (D'Lugo on Catalan cinema which addresses linguistic issues or Thumim on postwar British cinema which examines possible models

for the study of the 'popularity' of certain films in a national context). As observed earlier European criticism seems to have organised itself around studying movements,
moments and individuals (*auteurs*) and the prevalence of the first two is present here
with writing which references neo-realism (Bazin) the French New Wave (Bazin et al.)
and new German cinema (Johnston). The omissions of the canon are also present here,
thus there are no articles on women directors and only brief mentions of smaller
European countries; however, the bibliography at the end of the book does offer
detailed refences to work in these areas.

Finally, since the field of European cinema studies is so vibrant the decision has been
made to leave some work to other publications, thus this reader will not attempt to
offer extensive work on Popular European cinema (see Dyer and Vincendeau, 1992),
on contemporary films (see Tamosunas and Jordan, 1998) or European film theory
(see Ian Aitken, 2001). Whilst it may not offer a *mise-en-scène* approach to European
cinema: dissecting in detail the concepts and contexts of each essay, this Reader will
make use of the 'montage' which is produced by the editing together of formerly disparate articles, hoping to create something new which enables us to see the old with
fresh eyes.

Notes

1   Ken Macpherson, 'As Is', *Close Up* vol. VIII no. 2, June 1931: 72.
2   A survey of language degrees in the UK reveals: French 89, German 88, Spanish (Latin
    American) 81 and Italian 58 (UCAS 2000 entry).
3   (Document 4: Felix Henseleit, '"A European Front," *Reichsfilmblatt* no. 10, 6 March
    1926, pp. 3–5 (translated by Thomas J. Saunders)', in Maltby and Higson, 1999: 334).
4   Documentary extract from unknown source, in the editor's collection.

PART ONE

European film culture

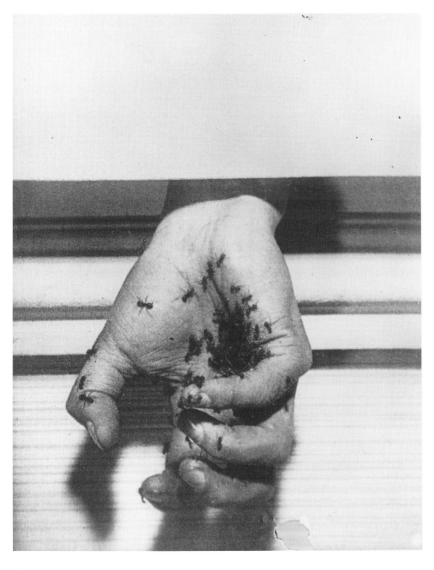

Chien Andalou: BFI collections

INTRODUCTION TO PART ONE

T HIS OPENING SECTION on 'European Film Culture' looks at some of the roots, the traditions and heritage of that which has been defined as 'European cinema'. Thus, first, a European canon of 'great' directors and films; second, key concerns that are represented in the work of all five writers here: the purpose of cinema, its relation to reality and how we might characterise its specificity; third, a variety of approaches to film practice; and fourth, the index each writer offers to a particular national context: France, Soviet Russia and Britain, each of which contributed to a sense of a pan-European film culture.

These were not the only writers, films and theories which were circulating in the first fifty years of European cinema; however, they have been singled out as representatives of questions, currents, concepts and contexts which would surface again and again over the course of European cinema's first century. Taken separately, they represent some of the differences between national cinemas and individual practices; through juxtaposition – whether against others in this section or in the wider context of the Reader – they can be used to extract common themes. Since these writers are some of the most celebrated figures in European film culture, this introduction will not reiterate their achievements, instead it will focus on some of the ideas that unite them. Whilst the name of Ricciotto Canudo may not be as well known as some in the pre-1920s period, many of his ideas have filtered down into key notions such as art cinema and he has been described as the 'first theoretician/aesthetician of the cinema'.[1] Born in Italy, Canudo undertook much of his writing in France surrounded by the early avant-gardes and the first evidence of a European film culture. Around him the first writings about film were appearing, as well as the first film journals and ciné-clubs which brought together those usually from the artist community, who believed that, due to its motion (for Canudo, its velocity), its distinct relation to reality, or its plastic qualities, cinema might offer something more than sculpture, painting, literature or theatre.

'The Birth of the Sixth Art' is caught up in this early moment, as it tries hard to compare cinema to the other arts, suggesting in the end that it is both unique and a synthesis of them. In 1923 Canudo was to write a second famous essay in which he suggested film was, in fact, the 'seventh art'. The main difference from his earlier piece is in his growing confidence in cinema's specific and unique qualities. 'The Birth of the Sixth Art' (1911) has been chosen over 'Reflections on the Seventh Art'[2] (1923) since its place as one of the earliest serious writings on the cinema lends it a prophetic qual-ity. The other four writers of this section can be read through Canudo: how do they, as practitioners, take up his challenge and explore his assertions? Most of all though, Canudo's writing can be taken as a key example of the three areas highlighted as the concern of this early period: the question of the purpose of cinema, the relation of cinema to reality and the specificity of the cinematic medium.

Film history has recorded distinct activity across Europe in the pre-sound period, but what have been less well documented are cross-cultural influences. To a certain extent these are inferred in the five pieces in this section and, through comparison, we can draw out developing themes and preoccupations. We can also extract signs of influence – thus Eisenstein mentions Griffith and Chaplin – yet there are further pas-sages to be reconstructed: the journey of *The Battleship Potemkin* (1926) for example, which had little impact until it was screened in Berlin, at which point the the-atre director Max Reinhardt is reputed to have said that it could bring about the death of theatre. In Paris it was to influence the surrealists including Buñuel, and in England the inter-titles would be created by none other than John Grierson[3] and then the film would be shown in a double bill with *Drifters* (1927).[4]

This international view of film culture is inevitably mediated through the lens of crit-icism and in the 1920s and 1930s this meant journals such as 'Close Up' (in Britain 1927–33) which claimed to be 'the only magazine devoted to films as an art'. Edited all over the world, *Close Up* championed, among other things, Soviet film making and French film theory, and firmly believed that in writing about alternative film practice they might influence what films were made. Thanks to critics such as these the canon of European film history was swiftly formed, and already the prejudices we can iden-tify today were evident. In preserving the modernist movements of Eisenstein and Vertov, French impressionism and surrealism, German Expressionism and Grierson's documentary film movement,[5] critics were excluding those cinemas whose impact was on a more national scale: for example the 'regional and local customs' emphasised in Spanish melodramas have gone unrecorded (Peter W. Evans in Vincendeau, 1995: 403). Also, we can see from the above that cultural, artistic or political impact becomes the key to critical attention and canonisation rather than box-office or pop-ular success.

Canudo's attempt to define cinema as an art form sets in motion the familiar 'art' versus 'commerce' opposition of European cinema. However, the other pieces in this section imply that we should not be so quick to erect this opposition and instead they suggest that what exists is a combination of art and commerce, or formal and aes-thetic experiment (as identified by critics) and an appeal to the broadest audience possible (the aim of some of the directors). This was certainly the intention of Vertov, with his democratisation of the production process and his attempt to make films that would appeal to the masses. Eisenstein's practice has a similiar intent, though in his use of montage there is a curious mix of inclusion and exclusion, as he challenges his audience to engage both emotionally and intellectually. Such contradictions are widespread in surrealism: its manifesto claimed to want to attack the bourgeoisie, yet it promoted films that were funded by and almost wholly exhibited to the monied classes, therefore never reaching the audience they were supposedly made for. Finally, Grierson has been identified as displaying both progressive and conservative elements. Alongside this alleged attention to the audience goes an awareness on the behalf of Grierson and Vertov of the responsibilities of the director to the audience. For Vertov, 'we have come to serve a particular class', 'to explain to the worker the bourgeois structure'; and for Grierson, documentary must be a committed film making not just about 'form'.

Cinema and the real

For Canudo, it is the photographic basis of the film which deters it from being recognised in an unqualifed way as 'art': 'Arts are the greater the less they imitate.' This is also seen as a problem for the writers here, though one which constitutes a challenge rather than an obstacle. For Eisenstein, film's reference to reality is what brings it close to theatre, within which he first worked; for Vertov and Grierson, it is important that film begins with reality and that that reality is then preserved throughout, rather than smothered. Buñuel is the only one here to refer to the sense of dreaming which is evoked by the conditions of cinema: the darkened room, our static position, our head looking up at the bright light. It is from this analogy that he extends his theory that cinema can offer the surrealist joining of realities. In all these cases, then, film *adds to reality*. Before being filmed, produced, or edited, reality is poorer and film therefore enriches our understanding of it, our perception and representation of it.

Only ten years later Bazin will draw from these intentions in order to define his own theory of how realism works in the cinema. What he shares with these early practitioners is a sense that the manipulation of the image takes one away from 'reality'; possibly towards filmed drama, possibly towards the director who has put it together, or even towards an observation of style. In his thinking Bazin falls between the schools of manipulation and transparency, insisting on a narrative which originates in reality, yet is then translated via a particular film style.

Cinema and wonder

What Canudo also exhibits in his piece (Chapter 1) is a preoccupation with the 'wonder' of the cinematic apparatus. For him, the apparatus is still something that cannot be fully explained, that has not fulfilled its potential, and which might 'enrich the poetic and painterly imagination' and 'increase the sum total of our sensations'. In the context of early film the paradigm of this wonder at the cinema can perhaps be seen as the mini narrative which surrounds the showing of the Lumière's film *L'arriveé d'un train en gare de La Ciotat* (1895), during which it is reported people ran screaming from the cinema convinced that the train, filmed from the platform, was about to crash into them.

We might want to suggest here that of course such tales of 'wonder' are common to the experience of the cinema across the world, and therefore have only a small place in European film culture. However, 'wonder' becomes a more important part of this context once we consider Jean Epstein's suggestions that it was the development of narrative codes which destroyed this wonder (Michelson, 1984: xliii). Whilst the 'mysterious, indefinable something' of cinema (Willemen 1981: 40) is essential to Epstein's work, it is still possible to extend a sense of 'mystery' to our other writers. Thus, one might want to question the relation between Epstein's 'mystery' and Eisenstein's 'third something' that is produced by montage and that liberates film from plot, and from script (Chapter 2). Buñuel's 'cinema of poetry' (Chapter 5) seems to retain some of Epstein's mystery of the apparatus which is also present in Vertov's use of film form in order to 'show the world as it is' (Chapter 3). All writers here are united, then, in insisting that the potential of cinema is not solely to be narrative, and instead we must explore its ability to 'exercise emotional influence over the masses' (Eisenstein), 'penetrate deeper into the invisible world to explore and record' (Vertov), 'express the subconscious life' (Buñuel) and to 'reveal the reality' (Grierson Chapter 4).

Also evident here is a wariness of the power of narrative, in particular the dominance of the story and the pull of illusionism to drain cinema of everything they held as its potential. For Eisenstein, this necessitated the use of the model actor; for Vertov, the avoidance of scripted, plot-based films; for Buñuel, it meant the need to 'open up the marvellous world of the unknown'; and for Grierson, the avoidance of the kind of organisation found in the 'symphony film', in which form dominates over content. The struggle waged here was not simply seen in terms of America, for narrative, melodramatic film making was strong in Sweden and Denmark, and was also the project of such figures as Jacques Feyder in France and Ernst Lubitsch in Germany. Equally, not all countries had the same relationship with America, America was greatly interested in and impressed by France's output in the 1920s, Germany was challenged as much by Russia as America and for smaller countries such as Belgium, their bordering neighbours – France, Germany, the Netherlands were their first cinematic colonisers. Equally so in terms of film practice, as we can see that both Eisenstein and the surrealists greatly admired the work of such directors as Chaplin and Griffith, yet wanted to put their technique of montage and command of film form to different uses.

The five pieces which make up this section on European film culture should be read, then, as examples of the concerns of those who were witnesses to the early days of cinema, as explorations of the potential of silent cinema, and, finally, as manifestos for a cinema which retains its elements of wonder, which enriches the real and which had far fewer boundaries than the European cinema that we now know.

Notes

1 From *Framework*'s introduction to the piece which is reprinted here.
2 Riccioto Canudo, 'Reflections on the seventh art', trans. Claudia Gorbman from 'Réflexions sur le septième art' (1923) *L'Usine aux images* (Paris: Etienne Chiron, 1926): 29–47 as reprinted in Richard Abel, 1988: 291–303.
3 Information taken from the documentary 'Films that shook the world: *Battleship Potemkin*', BBC2 28/04/01, 50 mins.
4 Ian Aitken, 1998: 10, he says *Drifters* premiered in November 1929 alongside *The Battleship Potemkin*.
5 Though it should be noted that *Close Up* itself did not favour the documentary film movement, preferring instead avant-garde work.

References and further reading

Abel, Richard. (ed.) (1988) *French Film Theory and Criticism 1907–1939, Vol 1: 1907–1929*, Princeton, NJ: Princeton University Press.
——(ed.) (1988) *French Film Theory and Criticism 1907–1939, Vol 2: 1929–39*, Princeton, NJ: Princeton University Press.
——(ed.) (1996) *Silent Film*, London: Athlone.
Aitken, Ian. (1990, 1992) *Film and Reform: John Grierson and the British Documentary Film Movement*, London and New York: Routledge.
——(ed.) (1998) *The Documentary Film Movement – An Anthology*, Edinburgh: Edinburgh University Press.
Breakwell, Ian and Paul Hammond. (eds) (1990) *Seeing in the Dark*, London: Serpent's Tail.
Buñuel, Luis. (1985) *My Last Breath*, London: Fontana.
Christie, Ian and Richard Taylor. (eds) (1993) *Eisenstein Re-discovered*, London and New York: Routledge.
Colina, José de la and Tomas Pérez Turrent. (1992) *Objects of Desire*, New York: Marsilio.
Donald, James, Anne Friedberg and Laura Marcus. (eds) (1998) *Close Up – (A Quarterly in the Art of Films) 1927–1933, Cinema and Modernism*, London: Cassell.
Eisenstein, Sergei. (1943) (trans. and ed. Jay Leda) *The Film Sense*, London: Faber and Faber.
——(1970) *Notes of a Film Director*, New York: Dover Publications.
——(1987) (trans. Herbert Marshall) *Nonindifferent Nature – Film and the Structure of Things*, Cambridge: Cambridge University Press.
Evans, Peter William. (1995) *The Films of Luis Buñuel*, Oxford: Oxford University Press.
Flitterman-Lewis, Sandy. (1990) 'Dulac in context: French film production in the twenties' in Sandy Flitterman-Lewis. *To Desire Differently – Feminism and the French Cinema*, Urbana and Chicago: University of Illinois Press, pp. 78–97.
Forsyth, Hardy. (ed.) (1946) *Grierson on Documentary*, London: Faber and Faber.
——(ed.) (1981) *John Grierson on the Movies*, London: Faber and Faber.
Gillespie, David. (2000) *Early Soviet Cinema – Innovation, Ideology and Propaganda*, London: Wallflower Press.
Goodwin, James. (1993) *Eisenstein, Cinema and History*, Urbana and Chicago: University of Illinois Press.
Hogenkamp, Bert. (1986) *Deadly Parallels – Film and the Left in Britain 1929–39*, London: Lawrence and Wishart.

Jacobs, Lewis. (ed.) (1971) *The Documentary Tradition*, New York: Hopkinson and Blake.

Kenez, Peter. (1992) 'The films of the golden age, 1925–29', in Peter Kenez. *Cinema and Soviet Society 1917–1953*, Cambridge: Cambridge University Press: pp. 50–77.

Lawder, Standish. (1975) 'Eisenstein and Constructivism', in P. Adams Sitney (ed.) *The Essential Cinema*, New York: Anthology Film Archives/New York University Press.

Leyda, Jay. (1960) *Kino*, London: George Allen & Unwin.

Lodder, Christina. (1983) *Russian Constructivism*, New Haven, CT: Yale University Press.

Michelson, Annette. (ed.) (1984) *Kino-Eye: The Writings of Dziga Vertov*, Berkeley and London: University of California Press.

Murray, Bruce. (1990) *Film and the German Left in the Weimar Republic from Caligari to Kuhle Wampe*, Austin: University of Texas Press.

Nichols, Bill. (1991) *Representing Reality: Issues and Concepts in Documentary*, Bloomington and Indianapolis: Indiana University Press.

Petric, Vlada. (1993) *Constructivism in Film – The Man with a Movie Camera A Cinematic Analysis*, Cambridge: Cambridge University Press.

Sussex, Elizabeth. (1975) *The Rise and Fall of British Documentary – the Story of the Film Movement Founded by John Grierson*, Berkeley and London: University of California Press.

Swann, Paul. (1989) *The British Documentary Film 1926–46*, Cambridge: Cambridge University Press.

Taylor, Richard. (ed.) (1988) *Eisenstein Writings 1922–1934*, London: BFI.

——(1996)' The double-headed eagle: Russia – East or West', in Richard Taylor (ed.). *Eisenstein Writings 1934–47*, London: BFI.

——(1998a) *Film Propaganda: Soviet Russia and Nazi Germany*, London and New York: I.B. Tauris.

——(ed.) (1998b) *The Eisenstein Reader*, London: BFI.

——and Michael Glenny. (1991) *Eisenstein Writings, Vol 2: Towards a Theory of Montage*, London: BFI.

Thompson, Kristin. (1993a) 'Early alternatives to the Hollywood mode of production', *Film History* 5: 4 December.

——(1993b) 'Eisenstein's Early Films Abroad', in Ian Christie and Richard Taylor. (eds) *Eisenstein Rediscovered*, London: Routledge.

Tsivian, Yuri. (1990) 'Some Historical Footnotes to the Kuleshov Experiment', in Thomas Elsaesser. (ed.) *Early Cinema – Space Frame Narrative*, London: BFI.

Vaughan, Dai. (1999) *For Documentary – Twelve Essays*, Berkeley and London: University of California Press.

Vincendeau, Ginette. (ed.) (1995) *The Encyclopedia of European Cinema*, London: BFI/Cassell.

Willemen, Paul. (1981) 'On reading Epstein on *Photogénie*', *Afterimage*, 10 Autumn.

Winston, Brian. (1995) *Claiming the Real: The Griersonian Documentary and Its Legitimations* London: BFI.

Wollen, Peter. (1982) 'Art in Revolution', in Peter Wollen. *Readings and Writings*, London: Verso.

Yampolsky, Mikhail. (1996) 'Kuleshov's Experiments and the New Anthropology of the Actor', in Richard Abel. (ed.) *Silent Film*, London: Athlone.

Chapter 1

Ricciotto Canudo

THE BIRTH OF THE SIXTH ART (1911)

IT IS SURPRISING TO FIND how everyone has, either by fate or some universal telepathy, the same aesthetic conception of the natural environment. From the most ancient people of the east to those more recently discovered by our geographical heroes, we can find in all peoples the same manifestations of the aesthetic sense; Music, with its complementary art, Poetry; and Agriculture, with its own two complements, Sculpture and Painting. The whole aesthetic life of the world developed itself in these five expressions of Art. Assuredly, a sixth artistic manifestation seems to us now absurd and even unthinkable; for thousands of years, in fact, no people have been capable of conceiving it. But we are witnessing the birth of such a sixth art. [. . .] It will be a superb conciliation of the Rhythms of Space (the Plastic Arts) and the Rhythms of Time (Music and Poetry).

II

The theatre has so far best realised such a conciliation, but in an ephemeral manner because the plastic characteristics of the theatre are identified with those of the actors, and consequently are always different. The new manifestation of Art should really be more precisely *a Painting and a Sculpture developing in Time*, as in music and poetry, which realise themselves by transforming air into rhythm for the duration of their execution.

The Cinematograph, so vulgar in name, points the way. [. . .]

III

The Cinematograph is composed of significant elements, 'representative' in the sense used by Emerson rather than the theatrical sense of the term, which are already classifiable.

There are two aspects of it: the *symbolic* and the *real*, both absolutely modern; that is to say only possible in our era, composed of certain essential elements of modern spirit and energy.

The *Symbolic aspect* is that of velocity. Velocity possesses the potential for a great series of combinations, of interlocking activities, combining to create a spectacle that is a series of visions and images tied together in a vibrant agglomeration, similar to a living organism. This spectacle is produced exactly by the excess of movement to be found in film, those mysterious reels impressed by life itself. The reels of the engraved celluloid unroll in front of and within the beam of light so rapidly that the presentation lasts for the shortest possible time. [. . .]

Yet more than the motion of images and the speed of representation, what is truly symbolic in relation to velocity are the actions of the characters. We see the most tumultuous, the most inverisimilitudinous scenes unfolding with a speed that appears impossible in real life. [. . .] The cinematograph can satisfy the most impatient racer. The motorist who has just finished the craziest of races and becomes a spectator at one of these shows will certainly not feel a sense of slowness; images of life will flicker in front of him with the speed of the distances covered. The cinematograph, moreover, will present to him the farthest countries, the most unknown people, the least known of human customs, moving, shaking, throbbing before the spectator transported by the extreme rapidity of the representation. Here is the second symbol of modern life constituted by the cinematograph, an 'instructive' symbol found in its rudimentary state in the display of 'freaks' at the old fairgrounds. It is the symbolic destruction of distances by the immediate connaissance of the most diverse countries, similar to the real destruction of distances performed for a hundred years now by monsters of steel.

The *real aspect* of the cinematograph is made up of elements which arouse the interest and wonder of the modern audience. It is increasingly evident that present day humanity actively seeks its own show, the most meaningful re-presentation of its self. [. . .] Suddenly, the cinematograph has become popular, summing up at once all the values of a still eminently scientific age, entrusted to Calculus rather than to the operations of Fantasy (*Fantasia*), and has imposed itself in a peculiar way as a new kind of theatre, a scientific theatre built with precise calculations, a mechanical mode of expression. Restless humanity has welcomed it with joy. It is precisely this theatre of plastic Art in motion which seems to have brought us the rich promise of the *Festival* which has been longed for unconsciously, the ultimate evolution of the ancient *Festival* taking place in the temples, the theatres, the fairgrounds of each generation. The thesis of a plastic Art in motion has recreated the *Festival*. [. . .]

IV

The careful observer who seeks in every movement of the masses a meaning that is in some way eternal, simultaneously traditional and new, cannot fail to register the following considerations of a general psychological order.

[. . .]

At the cinematograph theatre, everything is done to retain the attention, almost in suspension, to retain an iron hold on the minds of the audience bolted to the animated screen. The quick gesture, which affirms itself with monstrous precision and clock-work regularity, exhalts the modern audience used to living at an ever-increasing velocity. 'Real' life is therefore represented in its quintessence, *stylised in speed*.

V

I move on now to a great aesthetic problem, which must be emphasised.

Art has always been essentially a stylisation of life into stillness; the better an artist has been able to express the greater number of 'typical' conditions, that is, the synthetic and immutable states of souls and forms, the greater the recognition he has attained. The cinematograph, on the contrary, achieves the greatest mobility in the representation of life. The thought that it might open the unsuspected horizon of a new art different from all pre-existing manifestations cannot fail to appeal to an emancipated mind, free from all traditions and constraints. The ancient painters and engravers of prehistoric caves who reproduced on reindeer bones the contracted movements of a galloping horse, of the artists who sculpted cavalcades on the Parthenon friezes, also developed the device of stylising certain aspects of life in clear, incisive moments. But the cinematograph does not merely reproduce one aspect; it represents the whole of life in action, and in such action that, even when the succession of its characteristic events unravel slowly, in life, it is developed with as much speed as possible.

In this way cinematography heightens the basic psychic condition of western life which manifests itself in action, just as eastern life manifests itself in contemplation. [. . .]

Now, it is necessary to ask of the cinematograph, is it to be accepted within the confines of the arts?

It is not yet an art, because it lacks the freedom of choice peculiar to plastic *interpretation*, conditioned as it is to being the *copy* of a subject, the condition that prevents photography from becoming an art. In executing the design of a tree on a canvas, the painter expresses without any doubt, unconsciously and in a particular and clear configuration, his global interpretation of the vegetative soul, that is of all the conceptual elements deposited deep in his creative spirit by an examination of all the trees he has seen in his life; as Poe said, with the 'eyes of dream'. [. . .]

Arts are the greater the less they *imitate*, and they *evoke* by means of synthesis. A photographer, on the other hand, does not have the faculty of choice and elaboration fundamental to Aesthetics; he can only put together the forms he wishes to reproduce, which he really is not reproducing, limiting himself to cutting out images with the aid of the luminous mechanism of a lens and a chemical composition. The cinematograph, therefore, cannot today be an art. But for several reasons, the cinematograph theatre is the first abode of the new art – an art which we can just barely conceive. Can this abode become a 'temple' for aesthetics?

[. . .]

VI

The cinematograph is not only the perfect outcome of the achievements of modern science, which it summarises wonderfully. It also represents, in a disconcerting but important way, the most recent product of contemporary theatre. [. . .]

Shakespeare, who synthesized for the theatrical art the wild and artistic vigour of the great talents of his race, by his own predecessors, was himself the precursor of our 'psychological' theatre. And above all he was the great dramatist of the theatre without music. This theatrical form is absurd when applied to tragedy (in this sense the very important, but not truly brilliant art of Racine and Corneille, undoubtedly more deeply tragic in a collective and religious sense, is an art of aberration). On the other hand, a theatre without music is not at all absurd if it represents an ephemeral life, everyday life, to capture some of its aspects without pretending, and in any case without being bale to fix its 'activity' in a profound sense. This is the reason, then, why comedy, from Aristophanes to Becque, or Porto-Riche to Hervieu, continues to exist and to be enjoyed, even in its altered form which has become 'serious', called drama. The basis of such dramas is the portrayal of common contemporary life, and for this very reason this type of theatre is realistic, or as the Italians would call it, *rivista*. All our playwrights writing for the indoor theatre (as against the small band of new poets of the open-air theatre) mean to portray life as accurately as possible by copying it. Impresarios, theatre directors, take this principle to extremes, to the point of attributing more importance to a painstakingly photographic scenography than to the works themselves.

Now, all the cinematograph does is to exalt the principle of the representation of life in its total and exclusively exterior 'truth'.

It is the triumph of that artistic view called by Cézanne with sacred disdain: '*l'oeil photographique*'.

VII

The cinematograph, on the other hand, adds to this type of theatre the element of *absolutely accurate* speed, in this way inducing a new kind of pleasure that the spectator discovers in the extreme precision of the spectacle. In fact, none of the actors moving on the illusory stage will betray his part, nor would the mathematical development of the action lag for a fraction of a second. All movement is regulated with clockwork precision. The scenic illusion is therefore less engaging, in a sense less physical, but terribly absorbing. And this life, regulated as if by clockwork, makes one think of the triumph of modern scientific principle as a new Alviman, master of the mechanics of the world in Manichean doctrine.

The rapid communion of vital energies between the two opposite poles of the *very touching* and the *very comical* produces in the spectator a sense of relaxation. Everything which in real life presents itself as an obstacle, the inevitable slowness of movements and actions in space, is as if suppressed in the cinematograph. Moreover, the *very comical* soothes the mind, lightening existence of the weight of the sombre social cape, imposed by the thousand conventions of the community and representing all kinds of hierarchies. The comic can suppress hierarchies, it can join together the most different beings, give an extraordinary impression of the mixture of the most separate universes, which in real life are irreducibly distinct from one another. Since the comic is essentially irreverent, it gives a deep sense of relief to individuals oppressed in every moment of their real lives by social discriminations, so emphatically present. This sense of relief is one of the factors of that nervous motion of contraction and expansion called laughter. Life is *simplified* by the grotesque which is nothing other than a deformation *per excessum* or *per defectum* of the established forms. The grotesque, at least in this sense, relieves life of its inescapable grimness and releases it into laughter.

Caricature is based on the display and masterful combination of the most minimal facets of the human soul, its weak spots, which gush forth from the irony of social life, which is itself, after all, somewhat ironical and insane. With irony, in the convulsive motion of laughter, caricature provokes in man this feeling of extreme lightness, because irony throws over its raised shoulders Zarathustra's 'dancing and laughing' cape of many colours.

The ancients were able to perceive in irony the roots of Tragedy. They crowned their tragic spectacles in laughter, in the farce. Conversely, we precede rather than follow the dramatic spectacle Farce, immediately upon the raising of the curtain, because we have forgotten the significance of some of the truths discovered by our forebears. Yet the need for an *ironic spectacle* persists. And the Farce of the Orestes Tetrology of Aeschylus, the Farce which could not be found, must have been originally immensely rich in humour to have been able to lighten the spirit of the elegant Athenian women oppressed by the sacred terror of Cassandra. Now I do not know of anything more superbly grotesque than the antics of film comics. People appear in such an extravagant manner that no magician could pull anything like them out of a hat; movements and vision change so rapidly that no man of flesh and blood could present so many to his fellows, without the help of that stunning mixture of chemistry and mechanics, that extraordinary creator of emotions that is the cinematograph. A new comic type is thus created. He is the man of blunders and metamorphoses who can be squashed under a wardrobe of mirrors, or fall head-first breaking through all four floors of a four-storey building, only to climb up out of the chimney to reappear on the roof in the guise of a genuine snake.

The complexity of this new kind of spectacle is surprising. The whole of human activity throughout the centuries has contributed to its composition. When artists of genius bestow rhythms of Thought and Art on this spectacle, the new Aesthetics will show the cinematographic theatre some of its most significant aspects

In fact the cinematographic theatre *is the first new theatre*, the first authentic and fundamental theatre of our time. When it becomes truly aesthetic, complemented with a worthy musical score played by a good orchestra, even if only representing life, real life, momentarily fixed by the photographic lens, we shall be able to feel then our first *sacred* emotion, we shall have a glimpse of the spirits, moving towards a vision of the temple, where Theatre and Museum will once more be restored for a new religious communion of the spectacle and Aesthetics. The cinematograph as it is today will evoke for the historians of the future the image of the first extremely rudimentary wooden theatres, where goats have their throats slashed and the primitive 'goat song' and 'tragedy' were danced [. . .]

It is desire for a new *Festival*, for a new joyous *unanimity*, released at a show, in a place where together, all men can forge, in greater or lesser measure, their isolated individuality. This forgetting, soul of any religion and spirit of any aesthetic, will one day be superbly triumphant. And the Theatre, which still holds the vague promise of something never dreamt of in previous ages: *the creation of a sixth art, the plastic Art in motion*, having already achieved the rudimentary form of the modern pantomime.

[. . .]

Summing up, then, painting consists of the still representation of a gesture, an attitude, or a whole body of gestures and attitudes, or yet again of certain significant representations of living beings and of objects. But who could have dreamt of *successive series of pictures* strung together? A successive series of paintings, that is of certain moods of living beings and objects put together in an event – that is what life is, without doubt. Each passing minute composes, decomposes, transforms an incalculable number of pictures before our eyes. The successful cinematograph film can fix and reproduce them *ad infinitum*. In fixing them, it performs an action previously reserved to painting, or to that weak, merely mechanical copy of painting which is photography. By presenting a succession of gestures, or represented attitudes, just as real life does in transporting the picture from space, where it existed immobile and enduring, into time, where it appears and is immediately transformed, the cinematograph can allow us a glimpse of what it could become if a real, valid, directing idea could co-ordinate the pictures it produces along the ideal and profoundly significant line of a central aesthetic principle. We are able, therefore, to think of a plastic Art in motion, the sixth art. Who could have done it before now? No-one, because the spiritual development of mankind had not yet succeeded in experiencing such a strong desire for the conciliation of Science and Art, for the complex representation of life as a whole. The cinematograph renews more strongly every day the promise of such a great conciliation, not only between Science and Art, but between the Rhythms of Time and the Rhythms of Space.

Chapter 2

Sergei Eisenstein

THE MONTAGE OF FILM ATTRACTIONS[1] (1924)

THESE THOUGHTS DO NOT ASPIRE TO BE MANIFESTOS or declarations but they do represent an attempt to gain at least some understanding of the bases of our complex craft.

If we regard cinema as a factor for exercising emotional influence over the masses (and even the Cine-Eyes,[2] who want to remove cinema from the ranks of the arts at all costs, are convinced that it is) we must secure its place in this category and, in our search for ways of building cinema up, we must make widespread use of the experience and the latest achievements in the sphere of those arts that set themselves similar tasks. The first of these is, of course, theatre, which is linked to cinema by a common (identical) *basic* material – the *audience* – and by a common purpose – *influencing this audience in the desired direction* through a series of calculated pressures on its psyche. I consider it superfluous to expatiate solely on the intelligence of this ('agit') kind of approach to cinema and theatre since it is obvious and well-founded from the standpoint both of social necessity (the class struggle) and of the very nature of these arts that deliver, because of their former characteristics, a series of blows to the consciousness and emotions of the audience. Finally, only an ultimate aspiration of this sort can serve to justify diversions that give the audience *real* satisfaction (both physical and moral) as a result of *fictive* collaboration with what is being shown (through motor imitation of the action by those perceiving it and through psychological 'empathy'). If it were not for this phenomenon which, incidentally, alone makes for the magnetism of theatre, circus and cinema, the thoroughgoing removal of accumulated forces would proceed at a more intense pace and sports clubs would have in their debt a significantly larger number of people whose physical nature had caught up with them.

Thus cinema, like theatre, makes sense only as 'one form of pressure'. There is a difference in their methods but they have one basic device in common: the montage of attractions, confirmed by my theatre work in Proletkult and now being applied by me to cinema. It is this path that liberates film from the plot-based script and for the

first time takes account of film material, both thematicaly and formally, in the construction. In addition, it provides criticism with a method of objective expertise for
evaluating theatre or film works, instead of the printed exposition of personal impres-
sions and sympathies spiced with quotations from a run-of-the-mill political report
that happens to be popular at a particular moment.

An attraction is in our understanding any demonstrable fact (an action, an object,
a phenomenon, a conscious combination, and so on) that is known and proven to exercise a definite effect on the attention and emotions of the audience and that, combined
with others, possesses the characteristic of concentrating the audience's emotions in
any direction dictated by the production's purpose. From this point of view a film
cannot be a simple presentation or demonstration of events: rather it must be a ten-
dentious selection of, and comparison between, events, free from narrowly
plot-related plans and moulding the audience in accordance with its purpose. (Let us
look at *Cine-Pravada*[3] in particular: *Cine-Pravada* does not follow this path – its construction takes no account of attractions – but 'grabs' you through the attraction of its
themes and, purely superficially, through the formal mastery of its montage of separate sequences, which by their short footage conceal the 'neutral' epic 'statement of
facts'.)

The widespread use of all means of influence does not make this a cinema of pol-
ished style but a cinema of action that is useful to our class, a class cinema due to its
actual formal approach because attractional calculation is conceivable only when the
audience is known and selected in advance for its homogeneity.

The application of the method of the montage of attractions (the comparison of
facts) to cinema is even more acceptable than it is to theatre. I should call cinema 'the
art of comparisons' because it shows not facts but conventional (photographic) representations (in contrast to 'real action' in theatre, at least when theatre is employing
the techniques we approve of). For the exposition of even the simplest phenomena
cinema needs comparison (by means of consecutive, separate presentation) between
the elements which constitute it: montage (in the technical, cinematic sense of the
word) is fundamental to cinema, deeply grounded in the conventions of cinema and
the corresponding characteristics of perception.

Whereas in theatre an effect is achieved primarily through the physiological perception of an actually occurring fact (e.g. a murder), in cinema it is made up of the
juxtaposition and accumulation, in the audience's psyche, of associations that the film's
purpose requires, associations that are aroused by the separate elements of the stated (in
practical terms, in 'montage fragments') fact, associations that produce, albeit tan-
gentially, a similar (and often stronger) effect only when taken as a whole. Let us take
that same murder as an example: a throat is gripped, eyes bulge, a knife is brandished,
the victim closes his eyes, blood is spattered on a wall, the victim falls to the floor, a
hand wipes off the knife – each fragment is chosen to 'provoke' associations.

An analogous process occurs in the montage of attractions: it is not in fact phenomena that are compared but chains of associations that are linked to a particular
phenomenon in the mind of a particular audience. (It is quite clear that for a worker
and a former cavalry officer the chain of associations set off by seeing a meeting
broken up and the corresponding emotional effect in contrast to the material which

frames this incident, will be somewhat different.) I managed to test quite definitively the correctness of this position with one example where, because what I should call this law had not been observed, the comic effect of such a well-tried device as the alogism[4] fell flat. I have in mind the place in *The Extraordinary Adventures of Mr West in the Land of the Bolsheviks*[5] where an enormous lorry is pulling a tiny sledge carrying Mr West's briefcase. This construction can be found in different variants in any clown's act – from a tiny top hat to enormous boots. The appearance of such a combination in the ring is enough. But, when the whole combination was shown on the screen in one shot all at once (even though it occurred as the lorry was leaving the gates so that there was a short pause – as long as the rope joining the lorry to the sledge), the effect was very weak. Whereas a real lorry is immediately perceived in all its immensity and compared to a real briefcase in all its insignificance and [for comic effect] it is enough to see them side by side, cinema requires that a 'representation' of the lorry be provided first for long enough to inculcate the appropriate association – and then we are shown the incongruous light load. As a parallel to this I recall the construction of an analogous moment in a Chaplin film where much footage is spent on the endlessly complicated opening of the locks on a huge safe* and it is only later (and apparently from a different angle) that we are shown the brooms, rags and buckets that are hidden inside it. The Americans use this technique brilliantly for characterisation – I remember the way Griffith 'introduced' the 'Musketeer', the gang-leader in *Intolerance*,[6] he showed us a wall of his room completely covered with naked women and then showed the man himself. How much more powerful and more cinematic this is, we submit, than the introduction of the workhouse supervisor in *Oliver Twist* in a scene where he pushes two cripples around: i.e. he is shown through his deeds (a purely theatrical method of sketching character through action) and not through provoking the necessary associations.

From what I have said it is clear that the centre of gravity of cinema effects, in contrast to those of theatre, lies not in directly *physiological* effects, although a purely *physical* infectiousness can sometimes be attained (in a chase, with the montage of two sequences with movements running against the shot). It seems that there has been absolutely no study or evaluation of the purely physiological effect of montage irregularity and rhythm and, if it has been evaluated, this has only been for its role in narrative illustration (the tempo of the plot corresponding with the material being narrated). 'We ask you not to confuse' the montage of attractions and its method of comparison with the usual montage parallelism used in the exposition of a theme such as the narrative principle in *Cine-Pravda* where the audience has first to guess what is going on and then become 'intellectually' involved with the theme.

The montage of attractions is closer to the simple contrasting comparisons [. . .] that often produce a definitely powerful emotional effect [. . .]

The method of the montage of attractions is the comparison of subjects for thematic effect. I shall refer to the original version of the montage resolution in the finale of my film *The Strike*: the mass shooting where I employed the associational comparison with a slaughterhouse. I did this, on the one hand, to avoid overacting among the extras

* And a large number of bank premises are shown first.

from the labour exchange 'in the business of dying' but mainly to excise from such a serious scene the falseness that the screen will not tolerate but that is unavoidable in even the most brilliant death scene and, on the other hand, to extract the maximum effect of bloody horror. The shooting is shown only in 'establishing' long and medium shots of 1,800 workers falling over a precipice, the crowd fleeting, gunfire, etc., and all the close-ups are provided by a demonstration of the real horrors of the slaughterhouse where cattle are slaughtered and skinned. One version of the montage was composed roughly as follows:

1 The head of a bull. The butcher's knife takes aim and moves upwards beyond the frame.
2 Close-up. The hand holding the knife strikes downward below the frame.
3 Long shot: 1,500 people roll down a slope. (Profile shot.)
4 Fifty people get up off the ground, their arms outstretched.
5 The face of a soldier taking aim.
6 Medium shot. Gunfire.
7 The bull's body (the head is outside the frame) jerks and rolls over.
8 Close-up. The bull's legs convulse. A hoof beats in a pool of blood.
9 Close-up. The bolts of the rifles.
10 The bull's head is tied with a rope to a bench.
11 A thousand people rush past.
12 A line of soldiers emerges from behind a clump of bushes.
13 Close-up. The bull's head as it dies beneath unseen blows (the eyes glaze over).
14 Gunfire, in longer shot, seen from behind the soldiers' backs.
15 Medium shot. The bull's legs are bound together 'according to Jewish custom' (the method of slaughtering cattle lying down).
16 Closer shot. People falling over a precipice.
17 The bull's throat is cut. Blood gushes out.
18 Medium close-up. People rise into the frame with their arms outstretched.
19 The butcher advances towards the (panning) camera holding the blood-stained rope.
20 The crowd rushes to a fence, breaks it down but is met by an ambush (two or three shots).
21 Arms fall into the frame.
22 The head of the bull is severed from the trunk.
23 Gunfire.
24 The crowd rolls down the precipice into the water.
25 Gunfire.
26 Close-up. Teeth are knocked out by the shooting.
27 The soldiers' feet move away.
28 Blood flows into the water, colouring it.
29 Close-up. Blood gushes from the bull's throat.
30 Hands pour blood from a basin into a bucket.
31 Dissolve from a platform with buckets of blood on it . . . in motion towards a processing plant.
32 The dead bull's tongue is pulled through the slit throat (one of the devices used in

a slaughterhouse, probably so that the teeth will not do any damage during the convulsions).

33 The soldiers' feet move away. (Longer shot.)
34 The head is skinned.
35 One thousand eight hundred dead bodies at the foot of the precipice.
36 Two dead skinned bulls' heads.
37 A human hand in a pool of blood.
38 Close-up. Filling the whole screen. The dead bull's eye.

Final title.

The downfall of the majority of our Russian films derives from the fact that the people who make them do not know how to construct attractional schemas consciously but only rarely and in fumbling fashion hit on successful combinations. The American detective film and, to an even greater extent, the American comedy film (the method in its pure form) provide inexhaustible material for the study of these methods (admittedly on a purely formal level, ignoring content). Griffith's films, if we had seen them and not just known them from descriptions, would teach us a lot about this kind of montage, albeit with a social purpose that is hostile to us. It is not, however, necessary to transplant America, although in all fields the study of methods does at first proceed through imitation. It is necessary to train ourselves in the skill of selecting attractions from our own raw material.

[. . .]

When, in the process of constructing, shooting and moulding the montage elements, we are selecting the filmed fragments, we must fully recall the characteristics of cinema's effect that we stated initially and that establish the montage approach as the essential, meaningful and sole possible language of cinema, completely analogous to the role of the word in spoken material. In the selection and presentation of this material the decisive factor should be the immediacy and economy of the resources expended in the cause of associative effect.

The first practical indication that derives from this is the selection of an angle of vision for every element, conditioned exclusively by the accuracy and force of impact of the necessary presentation of this element. If the montage elements are strung together consecutively this will lead to a constant movement of the angle of vision in relation to the material being demonstrated (in itself one of the most absorbing purely cinematic possibilities).

Strictly speaking, the montage elision of one fragment into another is inadmissible: each element can most profitably be shown from just one angle and part of the film fact that proceeds from, let us say, an inserted close-up, already requires a new angle that is different from the fragment that preceded the close-up. Thus, where a tightly expounded fact is concerned, the work of the firm director, as distinct from the theatre director, requires, in addition to a mastery of production (planning and acting), a repertoire of montage-calculated angles for the camera to 'capture' these elements. I almost managed to achieve this kind of montage in the fight scene in *The Strike* where the repetition of sequences was almost completely avoided.

These considerations play a decisive role in the selection of camera angles and the arrangement of the lights. No plot 'justification' for the selection of the angle of vision or the light sources is necessary. (Apart, that is, from a case where the task involves a particularly persistent emphasis on reality. For instance, *contre-jour* lighting is by no means 'justified' in American interior shots.)

On a par with the method of staging a scene and taking it with a camera there exists what I should call the Futurist method of exposition, based on the pure montage of associations and on the separate depiction of a fact: for example, the impression of that fight may be represented through the montage of the separate elements that are not joined by any logical sequence in the staging of the scene. The accumulation of the details of conflicting objects, blows, fighting methods, facial expressions and so on produces just as great an impression as the detailed investigation by the camera of all the phases in a logically unfolding process of struggle: I contrast both kinds of montage, done separately, in the scene of the shooting. (I do not, for example, use the chain: the gun is cocked – the shot fired – the bullet strikes – the victim falls, but: the fall – the shot – the cocking – the raising of the wounded, etc.)

If we move on to the persistently posed question of the 'demonstration of real life' as such, we must point out that this particular instance of demonstration is covered by our general position on the montage of attractions: but the assertion that the essence of cinema lies only in the demonstration of real life must be called into question. It is, I think, a matter of transposing the characteristics of a '1922/3 attraction' (which was, as is always the case, a response to social aspirations – in this instance, the orientation towards 'construction' as the raw material for these aspirations and towards a 'presentation' that advertised this construction, e.g. an important event like the Agricultural Exhibition) to the entire nature of cinema as a whole. The canonisation of this material and of this approach as the only acceptable ones deprive cinema of its flexibility in relation to its broadly social task and, by deflecting the centre of gravity of public attention to other spheres (which is already noticeable), it leaves only a single aesthetic 'love for real life' [. . .]

I maintain my conviction that the future undoubtedly lies with the plot-less actor-less form of exposition but this future will dawn only with the advent of the conditions of social organisation that provide the opportunity for the general development and the comprehensive mastering of their nature and the application of all their energy in action, and the human race will not lack satisfaction through fictive energetic deeds, provided for it by all types of spectacle, distinguished only by the methods by which they are summoned forth. That time is still a long way off but, I repeat, we must not ignore the enormous effectiveness of the work of the model actor [*naturshchik*][7] on the audience. I submit that the campaign against the model actor is caused by the negative effect of the lack of system and principle in the organisation of his work.

This 'play' is either a semi-narcotic experience with no account of time or space (and really only a little off the 'place where the camera is standing'), or a stereometric spread in three-dimensional space of the body and the extremities of the model actor in different directions, remotely recalling some forms of human action (and perceived by the audience thus: 'Aha, apparently he's getting angry') or consecutive local contractions of facial muscles quite independent of one another and their system as a whole, which are considered as mime. Both lead to a superb division of space in the shot and the surface of the screen that follows strict rhythmic schemas, with no single 'daubing' or unfixed place. But . . . a rhythmic schema is arbitrary, it is established according to the whim or 'feeling' of the director and not according to periods dictated by the mechanical conditions of the course of a particular motor process; the disposition of the extremities (which is precisely not 'movement') is produced outside any mutual mechanical interaction such as the unified motor system of a single organism.

The audience in this kind of presentation is deprived of the emotional effect of perception which is replaced by guesswork as to what is happening. Because emotional perception is achieved through the motor reproduction of the movements of the actor by the perceiver, this kind of reproduction can only be caused by movement that adheres to the methods that it normally adheres to in nature. [. . .]

The circle of effective arts is closed by the open essence of the agitational spectacle and a 'union' with the primary sources is established: I think that the celebrated dances in animal skins of the primitive savages 'whence theatre derived' are a very reasonable institution of the ancient sorcerers directed much less towards the realisation of figurative tendencies ('for what purpose?') than towards the very precise training of the hunting and fighting instincts of the primitive audience. The refinement of imitative skill is by no means a matter of satisfying those same figurative tendencies but of counting on the maximum emotional effect on the audience. This fundamental orientation towards the role of the audience was later forfeited in a purely formal refinement of methods and it is only now being revived to meet the concrete requirements of the day. This pure method of training the reflexes through performance effect deserves the careful consideration of people organising educational films and theatres that quite unconsciously cram children with an entirely unjustified repertoire.

We shall move on to analyse a particular, but very important, affective factor: the work of the model actor. Without repeating in brief the observations I have already made as to what that work is and what it should be, we shall set out our system of work, endeavouring somehow to organise this branch of our labour (reforging someone else's psyche is no less difficult and considerable a task than forging iron and the term 'playing' is by no means appropriate).

The basic premiss

1   The value lies not in the figurativeness of the actions of the model actor but in the degree of his motor and associatively infectious capabilities vis-à-vis the audience (i.e. the whole process of the actor's movement is organised with the aim of facilitating the imitative capacities of the audience).

2   Hence the first direction concerns the *selection* of versions presented to the audience: a reliance on invention, i.e. on the *combination* of the movement, required by the purpose, from the versions that are most characteristic of real circumstances (and consequently automatically imitated by the audience) and simplest in form. The development and complication of motivations in the matter of 'delays' (as literature treats them). NB Cinema makes very frequent use, apart from

delays, of montage methods and this method too. I can cite an example of a moment that is constructed cinematically in this way from my theatre production of *Can You Hear Me, Moscow?*,[8] when the *agent provocateur* is handed an empty envelope that purports to contain evidence of his provocations. (There will be no reference in this section to the film I am working on in so far as the film as a whole is not orientated in its construction towards this group of actions whereas the work of the model actor is a matter of investigating the methods of 'free work'.) Here the de-texturisation [*rasfakturennost'*] of the elements taken from the simplest versions of the movement of handing the envelope over and attempting to take it so excites the emotion of the audience with its delay that the 'break' (the transition to the murder) makes the same impression as a bomb exploding. (In a film treatment you would add a montage section following the same rhythmic module.)

3   The refinement of this version of movement: i.e. the real ascertainment of the purely mechanical schema of its normal course in real life.

4   Breakdown of movement into its pseudo-primitive primary component elements for the audience – a system of shocks, rises, falls, spins, pirouettes, etc. – for the director to convey to the performer the precise arrangement of the motor version and to train these inherently neutral expressive (not in terms of plot but in terms of production) motor units.

5   Assembly (montage) and co-ordination into a temporal scheme of these neutral elements of the movements in a combination that produces action.

6   Obfuscation of the schema in the realisation of the difference in execution that exists between the play of a virtuoso with his own individual reordering of rhythm [*pereritmovka*] and the play of a pupil metrically tapping out the musical notation. (NB The completion of the minor details in fixing the version also enters into this obfuscation.)

The realisation of the movement does not proceed in a superficially imitative and figurative manner vis-à-vis a real action (murder, drunkenness, chopping wood, etc.) but results in an organic representation that emerges through the appropriate mechanical schema and a real achievement of the motor process of the phenomena being depicted.

Notes

1 Source: 'Montazh kinoattraktsionov', a typescript, dated October 1924, held in the Eisenstein archive, TsGALI, Moscow, as yet unpublished in Russian in its complete form and reproduced by kind permission of the USSR Union of Film-Makers. [. . .]

2 The Cine-Eyes (*Kinoki*, singular: *Kinoglaz*) were the documentary film-makers grouped around Dziga Vertov (pseudonym of Denis A. Kaufman, 1896–1954). The group published two major, and numerous minor, attacks on fictional film and on the concept of 'art' as a manifestation of bourgeois culture to be torn down 'like the Tower of Babel. [. . .]

3 *Cine-Pravda* (*Kinopravda*) meaning 'Cinema Truth' and pointing the analogy with the name of the Party newspaper *Pravda*, was the name of the newsreel produced by the Cine-Eye group in twenty-three issues between June 1922 and 1925.

4 *Alogizm*: a neologism coined by E to denote an action or event that had no logical explanation in its particular context.
5 *The Extraordinary Adventures of Mr West in the Land of the Bolsheviks* (*Neobychainye priklyucheniya
   Mistera Vesta v strane bol'shevikov*) (USSR, 1924) was directed by Lev Kuleshov (1899–1970)
   and satirised Western notions of the Bolsheviks. It was Kuleshov who first developed the
   notion of montage as the essence of cinema specificity.
6 *Intolerance* (USA, 1916) was made by D. W. Griffith (1875–1948).
7 *Naturshchik*: a 'model' or 'mannequin', the word used by E. Kuleshov and others to
   denote an actor who functioned as a mere tool of the director and expressed his emotions
   through specific physical actions.
8 During E's production of *Can You Hear Me, Moscow (Slyshish', Moskva?)* squibs were let off
   under the seats in the auditorium. The play was written by E's collaborator Sergei M.
   Tretyakov.

Chapter 3

Dziga Vertov

PROVISIONAL INSTRUCTIONS TO KINO-EYE GROUPS (1926)

1 Introduction

OUR EYE SEES VERY POORLY AND VERY LITTLE – and so men conceived of the microscope in order to see invisible phenomena; and they discovered the telescope in order to see and explore distant, unknown worlds. The movie camera was invented in order to penetrate deeper into the visible world, to explore and record visual phenomena, so that we do not forget what happens and what the future must take into account.

But the camera experienced a misfortune. It was invented at a time when there was no single country in which capital was not in power. The bourgeoisie's hellish idea consisted of using the new toy to entertain the masses, or rather to divert the workers' attention from their basic aim: the struggle against their masters. Under the electric narcotic of the movie theatres, the more or less starving proletariat, the jobless, unclenched its iron fist and unwittingly submitted to the corrupting influence of the masters' cinema. The theater is expensive and seats are few. And so the masters force the camera to disseminate theatrical productions that show us how the bourgeoisie love, how they suffer, how they 'care for' their workers, and how these higher beings, the aristocracy, differ from lower ones (workers, peasants, etc.).

In prerevolutionary Russia the masters' cinema played a precisely similar role. After the October Revolution the cinema was faced with the difficult task of adapting itself to the new life. Actors who had played tsarist civil servants began to play workers; those who had played ladies of the court are now grimacing in Soviet style. Few of us yet realize, however, that all this grimacing remains, in many respects, within the framework of bourgeois technique and theatrical form. We know many enemies of the contemporary theater who are at the same time passionate admirers of cinema in its present form.

Few people see clearly as yet that nontheatrical cinema (with the exception of newsreel and some scientific films) does not exist.

Every theatrical presentation, every motion picture is constructed in exactly the same way: a playwright or scriptwriter, then a director or film director, then actors, rehearsals, sets, and the presentation to the public. The essential thing in theater is acting, and so *every motion picture constructed upon a scenario and acting is a theatrical presentation*, and that is why there are no differences between the productions by directors of different nuances.

All of this, both in whole and in part, applies to theater regardless of its trend and direction, regardless of its relationship to theater as such. *All of this lies outside the genuine purpose of the movie camera — the exploration of the phenomena of life.*

Kinopravda has clearly shown that *it is possible to work outside theater and in step with the revolution. Kino-eye is continuing the work, begun by kinopravda, of creating Red Soviet cinema.*

2 The work of kino-eye

On the basis of reports by film-observers a plan for the orientation and offensive of the movie camera in life's ever-changing environment is being worked out by the Council of Kino-Eye. The work of the movie camera is reminiscent of the work of the agents of the GPU who do not know what lies ahead, but have a definite assignment to separate out and bring to light a particular issue, a particular affair.

1   The kinok-observer closely watches the environment and the people around him and tries to connect separate, isolated phenomena according to generalized or distinctive characteristics. The kinok-observer is assigned a theme by the leader.

2   The group leader or film [reconnaissance] scout distributes themes to the observers and, in the beginning, helps each observer to summarize his observations. When the leader has collected all the summaries, he in turn classifies them and rearranges the individual data until a sufficiently clear construction of the theme is achieved. Themes for initial observation can be split into roughly three categories:

   a *Observation of a place* (for example, a village reading room, a cooperative)
   b *Observation of a person or object in motion* (examples: your father, a young Pioneer, a postman, a streetcar, etc.)
   c *Observation of a theme irrespective of particular persons or places* (examples: water, bread, footwear, fathers and children, city and country, tears, laughter, etc.)
   The group leader must teach them to use a camera (later, a movie camera) in order to photograph the more striking moments of observation for a bulletin-board newspaper.
   A bulletin-board newspaper is issued monthly or every two weeks and uses photographs to illustrate the life of a factory, plant, or village; it participates in campaigns, reveals surrounding life as fully as possible, agitates, propagandizes, and organizes. The group leader submits his work for approval by the Goskino cell of the Red *kinoks* and is under the immediate supervision of the Council of Kino-Eye.

3   The *Council of Kino-Eye* heads the entire organization. It is made up of one representative from each group of kinok-observers, one representative of the unorganized kinok, and, provisionally, three representatives of the kinok production workers.

In its practical, everyday work the Council of Kino-Eye relies upon a technical staff – the Goskino cell of Red kinoks.

The Goskino kinoks' cell should be regarded as one of the factories in which the raw material supplied by the kinok-observers is made into film-objects.

The Goskino kinoks' cell should also be regarded as an educational, model workshop through which Young Pioneers and Komsomol film groups will be drawn into production work.

Specifically, all groups of kinok-observers will be drawn into the production of future kino-eye series. They will be the author-creators of all subsequent film-objects.

This departure from authorship by one person or a group of persons to mass authorship will, in our view, accelerate the destruction of bourgeois, artistic cinema and its attributes: the poser-actor, fairy-tale script, those costly toys – sets, and the director-high priest.

3 Very simple slogans

1   Film-drama is the opium of the people.
2   Down with the immortal kings and queens of the screen! Long live the ordinary mortal, filmed in life at his daily tasks!
3   Down with the bourgeois fairy-tale script! Long live life as it is!
4   Film-drama and religion are deadly weapons in the hands of the capitalists. By showing our revolutionary way of life, we will wrest that weapon from the enemy's hands.
5   The contemporary artistic drama is a vestige of the old world. It is an attempt to pour our revolutionary reality into bourgeois molds.
6   Down with the staging of everyday life! Film us as we are.
7   The scenario is a fairy tale invented for us by a writer. We live our own lives, and we do not submit to anyone's fictions.
8   Each of us does his task in life and does not prevent anyone else from working. The film workers' task is to film us so as not to interfere with our work.
9   Long live the kino-eye of the proletarian revolution!

4 The kinoks and editing

By editing, artistic cinema usually means the *splicing together of individual filmed scenes* according to a scenario, worked out to a greater or lesser extent by the director.

The kinoks attribute a completely different significance to editing and regard it as the *organization of the visible world*.

The kinoks distinguish among:

1   *Editing during observation* – orienting the unaided eye at any place, any time.
2   *Editing after observation* – mentally organizing what has been seen, according to characteristic features.
3   *Editing during filming* – orienting the aided eye of the movie camera in the place inspected in step 1. Adjusting for the somewhat changed conditions of filming.

4   *Editing after filming* – roughly organizing the footage according to characteristic features. Looking for the montage fragments that are lacking.

5   *Gauging by sight (hunting for montage fragments)* – instantaneous orienting in any visual environment so as to capture the essential link shots. Exceptional attentiveness. A military rule: gauging by sight, speed, attack.

6   *The final editing* – revealing minor, concealed themes together with the major ones. Reorganizing all the footage into the best sequence. Bringing out the core of the film-object. Coordinating similar elements, and finally, numerically calculating the montage groupings.

When filming under conditions which do not permit preliminary observation – as in shadowing with a movie camera or filming unobserved – the first two steps drop away and the third or fifth step comes to the fore.

When filming short moments, or in rush filming, the combining of several steps is possible.

In all other instances, when filming one or several themes, all the steps are carried out and the editing is uninterrupted, *beginning with the initial observation and ending with the finished film-object*.

5 The kinoks and the scenario

It is entirely appropriate to mention the script here. Once added to the above-mentioned editing system, a literary scenario immediately cancels its meaning and significance. Because our objects are constructed by editing, by organizing the footage of everyday life, unlike artistic dramas that are constructed by the writer's pen.

Does this mean that we work haphazardly, without thought or plan? Nothing of the kind.

If, however, we compare our *preliminary plan* to the plan of a commission that sets out, let us say, to investigate the living quarters of the unemployed, then we must compare the scenario to a short story of that investigation *written before* the investigation has taken place.

How do artistic cinema and the kinoks each proceed in the present case?

The kinoks organize a film-object on the basis of the factual film-data of the investigation.

After polishing up a scenario, *film directors* will shoot some entertaining film-illustrations to go with it: a couple of kisses, a few tears, a murder, moonlit clouds rushing above, and a dove. At the end they write 'Long live . . .!' and it all ends with 'The Internationale.'

Such, with minor changes, are all film-art-agitdramas.

When a picture ends with 'The Internationale,' the censors usually pass it, but the viewers always feel a bit uneasy hearing the proletarian hymn in such a bourgeois context.

A scenario is the invention of an individual or a group of people; it is a short story that these people desire to transfer to the screen.

We do not consider this desire criminal, but presenting this sort of work as cinema's main objective, ousting real film-objects with these little film short stories, and suppressing all the movie camera's remarkable possibilities in worship of the god of art-drama – this we cannot understand and do not, of course, accept.

We have not come to cinema in order to feed fairy tales to the Nepmen and Nepwomen lounging in the loges of our first-class movie theatres.

We are not tearing down artistic cinema in order to soothe and amuse the consciousness of the working masses with new rattles.

We have come to serve a particular class, the workers and peasants not yet caught in the sweet web of art-drama.

We have come to show the world as it is, and to explain to the worker the bourgeois structure of the world.

We want to bring clarity into the worker's awareness of the phenomena concerning him and surrounding him. To give everyone working behind a plow or a machine the opportunity to see his brothers at work with him simultaneously in different parts of the world and to see all his enemies, the exploiters.

We are taking our first steps in cinema, and that is why we are called kinoks. Existing cinema, as a commercial affair, like cinema as a sphere of art, has nothing in common with our work.

Even in technique we only partially overlap with so-called artistic cinema, since the goals we have set for ourselves require a different technical approach.

We have absolutely no need of huge studios or massive sets, just as we have no need for 'mighty' film directors, 'great' actors, and 'amazing,' photogenic women.

On the other hand, we must have:

1   quick means of transport,
2   more sensitive film,
3   small, lightweight, hand-held cameras,
4   lighting equipment that is equally lightweight,
5   a staff of lightning-fast film reporters,
6   an army of kinok-observers.

In our organization we distinguish amongst:

1   kinok-observers,
2   kinok-cameramen,
3   kinok-constructors [designers],
4   kinok-editors (women and men),
5   kinok laboratory assistants.

We teach our methods of cinema work only to Komsomols and Young Pioneers; we pass on our skill and our technical experience to the rising generation of young workers in whom we place our trust.

We venture to assure both respectable and not-so-respectable film directors that the cinema revolution is only beginning.

We will hold out without yielding a single position until the iron shift of young people eventually arrives, and then, all together, we will advance, over the head of bourgeois art-cinema, toward the cinematic October of the whole Soviet Union, of the whole world.

Chapter 4

John Grierson

FIRST PRINCIPLES OF
DOCUMENTARY (1932)

D OCUMENTARY IS A CLUMSY DESCRIPTION, but let it stand. The French who first used the term only meant travelogue. It gave them a solid high-sounding excuse for the shimmying (and otherwise discursive) exoticisms of the Vieux Colombier. Meanwhile documentary has gone on its way. From shimmying exoticisms it has gone on to include dramatic films like *Moana*, *Earth*, and *Turksib*. And in time it will include other kinds as different in form and intention from *Moana*, as *Moana* was from *Voyage au Congo*.

So far we have regarded all films made from natural material as coming within the category. The use of natural material has been regarded as the vital distinction. Where the camera shot on the spot (whether it shot newsreel items or magazine items or discursive 'interests' or dramatised 'interests' or educational films or scientific films proper or *Changs* or *Rangos*) in that fact was documentary. This array of species is, of course, quite unmanageable in criticism, and we shall have to do something about it. They all represent different qualities of observation, different intentions in observation, and, of course, very different powers and ambitions at the stage of organizing material. I propose, therefore, after a brief word on the lower categories, to use the documentary description exclusively of the higher.

The peacetime newsreel is just a speedy snip-snap of some utterly unimportant ceremony. Its skill is in the speed with which the babblings of a politician (gazing sternly into the camera) are transferred to fifty million relatively unwilling ears in a couple of days or so. The magazine items (one a week) have adopted the original 'Tit-Bits' manner of observation. The skill they represent is a purely journalistic skill. They describe novelties novelly. With their money-making eye (their almost only eye) glued like the newsreels to vast and speedy audiences, they avoid on the one hand the consideration of solid material, and escape, on the other, the solid consideration of any material. Within these limits they are often brilliantly done. But ten in a row would bore the average human to death. Their reaching out for the flippant or popular touch is so completely far-reaching that it dislocates something. Possibly taste; possibly common sense. You may take your choice at those little theatres where you are invited to gad around the world in fifty minutes. It takes only that long – in these days of great invention – to see almost everything. Consider, however, the very frequent beauty and very great skill of exposition in such Ufa shorts as *Turbulent Timber*, in the sports shorts from Metro-Goldwyn-Mayer, in the *Secrets of Nature* shorts from Bruce Woolfe, and the Fitzpatrick travel talks. Together they have brought the popular lecture to a pitch undreamed of, and even impossible in the days of magic lanterns.

These films, of course, would not like to be called lecture films, but this, for all their disguises, is what they are. They do not dramatize, they do not even dramatize an episode: they describe, and even expose, but in any aesthetic sense, only rarely reveal. Herein is their formal limit, and it is unlikely that they will make any considerable contribution to the fuller art of documentary. This indeed is a particularly important limit to record, for beyond the newsmen and the magazine men and the lecturers (comic or interesting or exciting or only rhetorical) one begins to wander into the world of documentary proper, into the only world in which documentary can hope to achieve the ordinary virtues of an art.

First principles. (1) We believe that the cinema's capacity for getting around, for observing and selecting from life itself, can be exploited in a new and vital art form. The studio films largely ignore this possibility of opening up the screen on the real world. They photograph acted stories against artificial backgrounds. Documentary would photograph the living scene and the living story. (2) We believe that the original (or native) actor, and the original (or native) scene, are better guides to a screen interpretation of the modern world. They give cinema a greater fund of material. They give it power over a million and one images. They give it power of interpretation over more complex and astonishing happenings in the real world than the studio mind can conjure up or the studio mechanician recreate. (3) We believe that the materials and the stories thus taken from the raw can be finer (more real in the philosophic sense) than the acted article. Spontaneous gesture has a special value on the screen. Cinema has a sensational capacity for enhancing the movement which tradition has formed or time worn smooth. Its arbitrary rectangle specially reveals movement; it gives it maximum pattern in space and time. Add to this that documentary can achieve an intimacy of knowledge and effect impossible to the shimsham mechanics of the studio, and the lily-fingered interpretations of the metropolitan actor.

In an earlier reference to Flaherty, I have indicated how one great exponent walked away from the studio. The main point of the story was this. Hollywood wanted to impose a ready-made dramatic shape on the raw material. It failed in the case of *Moana;* it succeeded (through Van Dyke) in the case of *White Shadows of the South Seas*, and (through Murnau) in the case of *Tabu*. In the last examples it was at the expense of Flaherty, who severed his association with both.

With Flaherty it became an absolute principle that the story must be taken from the location, and that it should be (what he considers) the essential story of the location. His drama, therefore, is a drama of days and nights, of the round of the year's seasons, of the fundamental fights which give his people sustenance, or make their community life possible, or build up the dignity of the tribe.

Such an interpretation of subject-matter reflects, of course, Flaherty's particular philosophy of things. A succeeding documentary exponent is in no way obliged to chase off to the ends of the earth in search of old-time simplicity, and the ancient dignities of man against the sky. Indeed, if I may for the moment represent the opposition, I hope the Neo-Rousseauism implicit in Flaherty's work dies with his own exceptional self. Theory of naturals apart, it represents an escapism, a wan and distant eye, which tends in lesser hands to sentimentalism. However it be shot through with vigour of Lawrentian poetry, it must always fail to develop a form adequate to the more immediate material of the modern world. [. . .]

Question of theory and practice apart, Flaherty illustrates better than anyone the first principles of documentary. (1) It must master its material on the spot, and come in intimacy to ordering it. Flaherty digs himself in for a year, or two maybe. He lives with his people till the story is told 'out of himself'. (2) It must follow him in his distinction between descriptions and drama. I think we shall find that there are other forms of drama or, more accurately, other forms of film, that the one he chooses; but it is important to make the primary distinction between a method which describes only the surface values of a subject, and the method which more explosively reveals the reality of it. You photograph the natural life, but you also, by your juxtaposition of detail, create an interpretation of it.

This final creative intention established, several methods are possible. You may, like Flaherty, go for a story form, passing in the ancient manner from the individual to the environment, to the environment transcended or not transcended, to the consequent honours of heroism. Or you may not be so interested in the individual. You may think that the individual life is no longer capable of cross-sectioning reality. You may believe that its particular belly-aches are of no consequence in a world which complex and impersonal forces command, and conclude that the individual as a self-sufficient dramatic figure is outmoded. When Flaherty tells you that it is a devilish noble thing to fight for food in a wilderness, you may, with some justice, observe that you are more concerned with the problem of people fighting for food in the midst of plenty. When he draws your attention to the fact that Nanook's spear is grave in its upheld angle, and finely rigid in its down-pointing bravery, you may, with some justice, observe that no spear, held however bravely by the individual, will master the crazy walrus of international finance. Indeed you may feel that in individualism is a yahoo tradition largely responsible for our present anarchy, and deny at once both the hero of decent heroics (Flaherty) and the hero of indecent ones (studio). In this case, you will feel that you want your drama in terms of some cross-section of reality which will reveal the essentially co-operative or mass nature of society: leaving the individual to find his honours in the swoop of creative social forces. In other words, you are liable to abandon the story form, and seek, like the modern exponent of poetry and painting and prose, a matter and method more satisfactory to the mind and spirit of the time.

Berlin or the Symphony of a City initiated the more modern fashion of finding documentary material on one's doorstep: in events which have no novelty of the unknown, or romance of noble savage on exotic landscape, to recommend them. It represented, slimly, the return from romance to reality.

Berlin was variously reported as made by Ruttmann, or begun by Ruttmann and finished by Freund: certainly it was begun by Ruttmann. In smooth and finely tempo'd visuals, a train swung through suburban mornings into Berlin. Wheels, rails, details of engines, telegraph wires, landscapes and other simple images flowed along in procession, with similar abstracts passing occasionally in and out of the general movement. There followed a sequence of such movement which, in their total effect, created very imposingly the story of a Berlin day. The day began with a processional of workers, the factories got under way, the streets filled; the city's forenoon became a hurly-burly of tangled pedestrians and street cars. There was respite for food: a various respite with contrast of rich and poor. The city started work again, and a shower of rain in the afternoon became a considerable event. The city stopped work and, in further more hectic processional of pubs and cabarets and dancing legs and illuminated sky-signs, finished its day.

In so far as the film was principally concerned with movements and the building of separate images into movements, Ruttmann was justified in calling it a symphony. It meant a break away from the story borrowed from literature, and from the play borrowed from the stage. In *Berlin* cinema swung along according to its own more natural powers: creating dramatic effect from the tempo'd accumulation of its single observations. Cavalcanti's *Rien que les Heures* and Léger's *Ballet Mécanique* came before *Berlin*, each with a similar attempt to combine images in an emotionally satisfactory sequence of movements. They were too scrappy and had not mastered the art of cutting sufficiently well to create the sense of 'march' necessary to the genre. The symphony of Berlin City was both larger in its movements and larger in its vision.

There was one criticism of *Berlin* which, out of appreciation for a fine film and a new and arresting form, the critics failed to make; and time has not justified the omission. For all its ado of workmen and factories and swirl and swing of a great city, Berlin created nothing. Or rather if it created something, it was that shower of rain in the afternoon. The people of the city got up splendidly, they tumbled through their five million hoops impressively, the turned in; and no other issue of God or man emerged than that sudden besmattering spilling of wet on people and pavements.

I urge the criticism because *Berlin* still excites the mind of the young, and the symphony form is still their most popular persuasion. In fifty scenarios, presented by the tyros, forty-five are symphonies of Edinburgh or of Ecclefechan or of Paris or of Prague. Day breaks – the people come to work – the factories start – the street cars rattle – lunch hour and streets again – sport if it is Saturday afternoon – certainly evening and the local dance hall. And so, nothing have happened and nothing positively said about anything, to bed; though Edinburgh is the capital of a country and Ecclefechan, by some power inside itself, was the birthplace of Carlyle, in some ways one of the greatest exponents of this documentary idea.

The little daily doings, however finely symphonized, are not enough. One must pile up beyond doing or process to creation itself, before one hits the higher reaches of art. In this distinction, creation indicates not the making of things but the making of virtues.

And there's the rub for tyros. Critical appreciation of movement they can build easily from their power to observe, and power to observe they can build from their own good taste, but the real job only begins as they apply ends to their observation and their movements. The artist need not posit the ends – for that is the work of the critic – but the ends must be there, informing his description and giving finality (beyond space and time) to the slice of life he has chosen. For that larger effect there must be power of poetry or of prophecy. Failing either or both in the highest degree, there must be at least the sociological sense implicit in poetry and prophecy.

[. . .]

This sense of social responsibility makes our realist documentary a troubled and difficult art, and particularly in a time like ours. The job of romantic documentary is easy in comparison: easy in the sense that the noble savage is already a figure of romance and the seasons of the year have already been articulated in poetry. Their essential virtues have been declared and can more easily be declared again, and no one will deny them. But realist documentary, with its streets and cities and slums and markets and exchanges and factories, has given itself the job of making poetry where no poet has gone before it, and where no ends, sufficient for the purposes of art, are easily observed. It requires not only taste but also inspiration, which is to say a very laborious, deep-seeing, deep-sympathizing creative effort indeed.

The symphonists have found a way of building such matters of common reality into very pleasant sequences. By uses of tempo and rhythm, and by the large-scale integration of single effects, they capture the eye and impress the mind in the same way as a tattoo or a military parade might do. But by their concentration on mass and movement, they tend to avoid the larger creative job. What more attractive (for a man of visual taste) than to swing wheels and pistons about in ding-dong description of a machine, when he has little to say about the man who tends it, and still less to say about the tin-pan product it spills? And what more comfortable if, in one's heart, there is avoidance of the issue of underpaid labour and meaningless production? For this reason I hold the symphony tradition of cinema for a danger and *Berlin* for the most dangerous of all film models to follow.

Unfortunately, the fashion is with such avoidance as *Berlin* represents. The highbrows bless the symphony for its good looks and, being sheltered rich little souls for the most part, absolve it gladly from further intention. [. . .]

The objection remains, however. The rebellion from the who-gets-who tradition of commercial cinema to the tradition of pure form in cinema is no great shakes as a rebellion. Dadaism, expressionism, symphonics, are all in the same category. They present new beauties and new shapes; they fail to present new persuasions.

The imagist or more definitely poetic approach might have taken our consideration of documentary a step further, but no great imagist film has arrived to give character to the advance. By imagism I mean the telling of story or illumination of theme by images, as poetry is story or theme told by images: I mean the addition of poetic references to the 'mass' and 'march' of the symphonic form.

Drifters was one simple contribution in that direction, but only a simple one. Its subject belonged in part to Flaherty's world, for it had something of the noble savage and certainly a great deal of the elements of nature to play with. It did, however, use steam and smoke and did, in a sense, marshal the effects of a modern industry. Looking back on the film now, I would not stress the tempo effects which it built (for both *Berlin* and

Potemkin came before it), nor even the rhythmic effects (though I believe they outdid the technical example of *Potemkin* in that direction). What seemed possible of development in the film was the integration of imagery with the movement. The ship at sea, the men casting, the men hauling, were not only seen as functionaries doing something. They were seen as functionaries in half a hundred different ways, and each tended to add something to the illumination as well as the description of them. In other words the shots were massed together, not only for description and tempo but for commentary on it. One felt impressed by the tough continuing upstanding labour involved, and the feeling shaped the images, determined the background and supplied the extra details which gave colour to the whole. I do not urge the example of *Drifters*, but in theory at least the example is there. If the high bravery of upstanding labour came through the film, as I hope it did, it was made not by the story itself, but by the imagery attendant on it. I put the point, not in praise of the method but in simple analysis of the method.

Chapter 5

Luis Buñuel

CINEMA, INSTRUMENT OF POETRY (1953)

THE GROUP OF YOUNG PEOPLE who form the Dirección de Difusión Cultural approached me to ask me to give a lecture. Although duly grateful for the attention, my reply was negative: I have none of the qualities which a lecturer requires and have a special bashfulness about speaking in public. Fatally, the speaker attracts the collective attention of his listeners, only to feel intimidated by their gaze. In my case I cannot avoid a certain embarrassment in face of the dread of what can make me somewhat, let us say, exhibitionist. Although this idea of mine about the lecturer may be exaggerated or false, the fact of feeling it as true obliges me to ask that my period of exhibition will be as brief as possible, and I propose the constitution of a Round Table, in which as a number of friends belonging to distinct artistic and intellectual activities, we can discuss *en famille* the problems pertaining to the so-called seventh art: hence it is agreed that the theme shall be 'The Cinema as Artistic Expression', or more concretely, as an instrument of poetry, with all that that word can imply of the sense of liberation, of subversion of reality, of the threshold of the marvellous world of the subconscious, of nonconformity with the limited society that surrounds us.

Octavio Paz has said: 'An imprisoned man has only to close his eyes to be able to blow up the world.' I would add, in paraphrase: it would suffice for the white pupil of the cinema screen to reflect the light which is proper to it, to blow up the universe. But for the moment we can sleep in peace, because the cinematographic light is carefully drugged and imprisoned. None of the traditional arts reveals so massive a disproportion between the possibilities it offers and its achievements. Because it acts in a direct manner upon the spectator in presenting to him concrete people and objects, because it isolates him by virtue of the silence and darkness from what might be called his 'psychic habitat', the cinema is capable of putting him into a state of ecstasy more effectively than any other mode of human expression. But more effectively than any other, it is capable of brutalising him. And unhappily the great part of present-day cinema production seems to have no other mission: the screens rejoice in the moral and intellectual emptiness in which the cinema prospers; in effect it limits itself to imitating the novel or the theatre with the difference that its means are less rich to express psychology: it repeats to satiety the same stories which the nineteenth century was already tired of telling and which still continue in contemporary fiction.

A moderately cultivated individual would reject with scorn any book with one of the arguments that serve the film. However, sitting comfortably in a dark room, dazzled by the light and the movement which exert a quasi-hypnotic power over him, fascinated by the interest of human faces and the rapid changes of place, this same almost cultivated individual placidly accepts the most appalling themes.

The cinema spectator, through this kind of hypnotic inhibition, loses an important percentage of his intellectual capacity. I will give a concrete example, the film called *Detective Story*. The structure of its subject is perfect, the director excellent, the actors extraordinary, the realisation brilliant, etc. But al this talent, all this ability, all the complications which the making of a film involve, have been put at the service of an idiotic story, of a remarkable moral wretchedness. This reminds me of the extraordinary machine of *Opus 11*, a vast machine made of the best steel, with a thousand complex gears, with tubes, manometers, dials, precise as a watch, as big as a liner, whose sole use was to gum postage-stamps.

Mystery, the essential element of every work of art, is in general lacking in films. Authors, directors, and producers are at pains not to disturb our peace, by leaving the window on to the liberating world of poetry tightly closed. They prefer to make the screen reflect subjects which could compose the normal continuation of our daily life, to repeat a thousand times the same drama or to make us forget the painful hours of daily work. And all this naturally sanctioned by habitual morality, government, and international censorship, religion, dominated by good taste and enlivened by white humour and other prosaic imperatives of reality.

If we hope to see good cinema, we shall rarely achieve it through bit productions and those which are accompanied by the sanction of the critics and the approval of the public. The private story, the individual drama cannot, in my view, interest anyone worthy of living in his times; if the spectator shares the joys, the sorrows, the anxieties of a personage on the screen, this can be only because he sees reflected in it the joys, sorrows, anxieties of a whole society, and therefore his own. Strikes, social insecurity, fear of war, etc., are the things which affect everyone today, and also affect the spectator; but that Mr X. is unhappy at home and seeks a girl-friend to console him, and finally abandons her to return to his wife all penitent, is no doubt very moral and edifying, but leaves us completely indifferent.

Sometimes the essence of cinema spurts unexpectedly from an anodine film, from a farce or a crude novelette. Man Ray said something very significant: 'The worst films which I have seen, those which send me into a deep sleep, always contain five marvellous minutes, while the best films, the most praised, have scarcely more than five worthwhile minutes.' This is to say that in all films, good or bad, beyond and despite the intentions of the makers, cinema poetry struggles to come to the surface and manifest itself.

The cinema is a magnificent and perilous weapon when wielded by a free spirit. It is the best instrument to express the world of dreams, of emotions, of instinct. The creative mechanism of cinema images, through its manner of functioning, is among all the means of human expression the one which comes nearest to the mind of man, or, even more, which best imitates the functioning of the mind in the state of dreaming. Jacques B. Brunius has pointed out that the night which bit by bit invades the cinema is equivalent to closing the eyes. Then begins, on the screen and within the man, the incursion into the night of the unconscious; the images, as in dream, appear and disappear through 'dissolves' and fade-outs; time and space become flexible, retrace or extend at will; chronological order and relative values of duration no longer respond to reality; cyclic action is accomplished in a few minutes or in several centuries; movements accelerate their speed.

The cinema seems to have been invented to express the subconscious life, whose roots penetrate so deeply into poetry; but it is almost never used for that end. Among modern tendencies of cinema, the best known is what is called 'neo-realism'. Its films present to the eyes of the spectator slices of real life, with people taken from the street, and with real buildings and exteriors. With a few exceptions, among which I would especially instance *Bicycle Thieves*, neo-realism has done nothing to produce in its films what is proper to the cinema, that is to say, the mysterious and fantastic. What use is all this visual drapery if the situations, the motives which animate the people, their reactions, the very subjects are taken from the most sentimental and conformist literature? The one interesting innovation, not of neo-realism but of Zavattini personally, is to have elevated the anodine action to the status of dramatic action. In *Umberto D*, one of the most interesting products of neo-realism, an entire reel of ten minutes shows a little maid performing actions which, a little while before, would have appeared unworthy of the screen. We see the servant enter the kitchen, light the stove, put a pan on the gas, throw water on a line of ants who advance on the wall in indian file, give the thermometer to an old man who feels feverish and so on. Despite the trivial nature of the situation, these activities are followed with interest and there is even a certain 'suspense'.

Neo-realism has introduced into cinematographic expression certain elements which enrich its language, but nothing more. The reality of neo-realism is incomplete, official and above all rational; but poetry, mystery, all that completes and enlarges tangible reality, is completely lacking in its working. It confuses ironic fantasy with the fantastic and black humour.

'What is most admirable in the fantastic,' André Breton has said, 'is that the fantastic doesn't exist; all is real.' In a conversation with Zavattini, I explained to him a few months ago my disagreement with neo-realism. As we dined together the first example which offered itself to me was that of the glass of wine. For a neo-realist, I said to him, a glass is a glass and nothing more; you see it taken from the sideboard, filled with drink, taken to the kitchen where the maid washes it and perhaps breaks it, which will result in its return or otherwise, etc. But this same glass, contemplated by different beings, can be a thousand different things, because each one changes what he sees with *affectivity*; no one sees things as they are, but as his desires and his state of soul make him see. I fight for the cinema which will show me this kind of glass, because this cinema will give me an integral vision of reality, will broaden my knowledge of things and people, will open up to me the marvellous world of the unknown, of all that which I find neither in the newspaper nor in the street.

Don't think from what I have just said that I am for a cinema consecrated solely to the fantastic and to mystery, for a cinema which, fleeing or scorning daily reality, would aim to plunge us into the unconscious world of the dream. Although I have just now indicated very briefly the capital importance which I attach to the film which treats the fundamental problems of a modern man, I do not consider man in isolation, as a particular case, but in his relationship to other men. I take for mine the words of Engels, who defined the function of the novelist (understood in this case as that of the film-maker): 'The novelist will have accomplished his task honourably when, through a faithful depiction of authentic social relations, he will have destroyed the conventional representation of the nature of these relations, shaken the optimism of the bourgeois world and obliged the reader to question the permanence of the existing order, even if he does not directly propose a conclusion to us, even if he does not openly take sides.'

PART TWO

Moments from European film history

Tout Va Bien: BFI collections

INTRODUCTION TO PART TWO

1n 1960 enough was enough! The movie was dead and called for
resurrection. The goal was correct but the means were not! The
New Wave proved to be a ripple that washed ashore and turned to
muck . . . The wave was up for grabs, like the directors themselves.[1]

THE DECLARATION ABOVE, which introduces Dogme 95's 'Vow of Chastity', is
both typical and unique when it comes to the discourse which forms around
moments and movements in European cinema history. On the one hand, it character-
istically sets up a 'bad other', in this case a 'wave' of innovation that had failed in
certain ways in which it (Dogme) will succeed. On the other hand, the bad other
chosen comes from a different national context and a historical context which is far
from adjacent to that of Dogme 95; both these facts go against the usual national
insularity and historical linearity of New Waves. These points are indicative of the
postmodern nature of Dogme, as it indiscriminately dips into the pool of film history
for its rules, in the process juxtaposing different theories from different nations and
eras.

A survey of the pieces in this section of the Reader reveals the Dogme magpies have
raided gems from all cinema's represented: from Italian neo-realism they have taken
what Bazin characterises as 'the predisposition toward reality', visited here in their
aim to 'force truth out of my characters and settings' and 'avoid superficial action';
and from the French New Wave the aim for their films to take place in the 'here and
now'. They seem to be referencing the politicisation which followed May 1968 through
their call for collectivisation and subsequent rejection of authorship: 'To Dogme 95
cinema is not individual'[2] and despite the *auteur*-laden nature of the New German
cinema, Dogme shares with them the sense of a group of film makers, subscribing to
the same manifesto.

If, in Part 1 of this Reader, Canudo led the way by raising questions which the
writers who followed often explored, the same is true, though in reverse, for Dogme
95. In not leading but following, Dogme have the benefit of viewing several failed
movements, learning from them and then, as we see above, playing around with
them. Despite this, Thomas Vinterberg admitted of the movement in 2000: 'It
started as an attempt to avoid mediocrity and to create energy, a riot; and it slowly

becomes accepted, and thereby dies. Which is, I think, natural, but a bit sad.'[3] His words are prescient for all movements, explaining why they take up only a moment in the pages of film history.

Unlike film genres, which are constantly changing and reinventing themselves, or *auteur* film making which asserts itself as universal and above its context, European film movements are typically defined around a key aesthetic, a common 'conception of the new world' (as Rivette puts it in the *Cahiers du Cinéma* discussion here) or a reaction to a national and historical context. But styles, worldviews and contexts change, and cinema moves on to the next wave leaving the old one 'washed ashore and turned to muck'.

Whilst European film history has been heavily weighted towards New Waves, it has until recently failed to account for how waves have been produced and why they crash, equally there is little sense given here of inter-national influence. Recent re-writings have made more evident the institutional, political and economic factors that govern the appearance of the new. In her essay on the New German cinema in Part 3, Sheila Johnston is keen to show how a movement which championed the autonomy of the *auteur* was actually highly dependent on a network of changes in the West German film industry, which thereby 'allowed' New German cinema to exist.

Johnston's essay shifts the emphasis on directors as authors of movements, which we find in the Oberhausen and Dogme Manifestos. The three other essays in this section then foreground critics and theory as playing a part in interpreting the significance of the new. Bazin's extract (Chapter 6) is an example of his long-term project – to analyse film style. It was written before the *Cahiers* school of thought and it signalled a return to talking about form in detailed terms. It is reproduced here because it offers one way of reading Italian neo-realism as a film style, and as such it suggests some of the lasting importance of that movement. The *Cahiers* discussion, which follows (and includes) Bazin, can be taken both as an example of the debates around the composition of a 'national' cinema (which can usefully introduce Andrew Higson's essay, Chapter 14), and of the critical arguments which could be said to have induced the birth of the French New Wave, as only two years afterwards (in 1959) *A bout de souffle, Les quatre cents coups* and *Hiroshima mon amour* would be let loose upon the world's screens. *Cahiers'* discussion clearly sets out the factors that may be at work in bringing about the new. Initially, discussion revolves around who or what is to blame for the current state of French film making. Is it the state that does not allow first-time film makers to receive money for their work? Is it distributors who will not take up new work? Or is it personnel who are either making the wrong type of films, are unambitious, or making them in the wrong way? Then attention seems to move to the instability of French cinema, though this is expressed in a contradictory manner – either in terms of the lack of a 'school' that might lean on auteur models, or the lack of a sustained 'tradition', with American genre cinema serving as the example here. Underlying these claims seems to be the suggestion that there is no French 'industry'. This is soon dispelled as attention shifts on to 'subject matter', thus it is not that France is not making films, it is instead that, according to *Cahiers*, they are not making the right types of films on the right subjects.

In what ways did the French New Wave respond to the demands of this discussion?

On the one hand, in its time it was both critically respectable and successful at the box-office. It put France on the international map as a country that was inspired and original. It offered fresh voices as demanded, and while those voices on the one hand had much to say about their generation, yet on the other hand, they largely ignored political issues (such as the Vietnam War and conflicts in Algeria). It also allowed a 'French school' and a tradition on which the films that followed it could build. *Cahiers'* discussion therefore helps us to see the factors that had to converge in order to bring about the new and the dissatisfactions from a critical perspective, which the French New Wave answered.

Peter Wollen's theory of counter-cinema encapsulates a moment in European film history. Very briefly, in May 1968 a protest by French students over the authoritarian structures of the university soon garnered support from the labour unions and led to mass strikes. The reverberations of this unrest were far-reaching and the effect on the cinema of the time was to produce a brief return to the leftist avant-garde which we saw in the Soviet montage and Surrealist groups, when film had a political purpose and, indeed, duty. Whilst a rejection of the past – past politics, culture and cinema – is inevitable, here Wollen's definition of counter-cinema disallows a completely clean break, as it relies upon a knowledge of the 'Hollywood mos-film' in opposition to which it defines itself. This gesture of opposition is also evident in the Oberhausen and Dogme Manifestos, both of which set out the boundaries which they will not cross: 'the conventional German film', which is controlled by commerce, and superficial action 'genre movies' respectively. Despite the calls in each of these three essays (Chapters 8–10) for 'liberty' and the suggestion that these new cinemas are more 'truthful' (apparent, for example, in Dogme's aim 'to force the truth out of my characters and settings'), the rather idealistic nature of such claims is captured by Wollen when he concludes:

> The cinema cannot show truth, or reveal it, because the truth is not out there in the real world, waiting to be photographed. What the cinema can do is produce meanings and meanings can only be plotted . . . in relation to other meanings.

In setting themselves up in such stark opposition to their bad other and in dealing in such ambitious terms (truth, authenticity, liberty), these movements are propelling not only their own demise – since their high standards prevent change – but also critical approbation as those such as Wollen and Johnston show their alleged transparency to be opaque. An awareness of these conflicts and contradictions can, however, be found in Dogme 95, since, while the vow of chastity suggests a pared down aesthetic in which the hand-held camera is an index to the 'immediate' reality of the shooting process, untainted by technology, the narratives of the eventual films foreground artifice and performance in an extremely playful manner.

The moments and movements represented here are the bones in film history's corset; as such they do not need detailed explanation. However, the juxtaposition of the pieces does allow us to address some key areas of importance. First, the new can be seen as a rejection of something that has gone before, but it too can soon find itself as 'the old'. Besides Dogme 95, this is evident in the Oberhausen Manifesto and in

Wollen's 'counter-cinema', both of which were set up in opposition to commercial cinema. New German cinema pitted its artistry and its new production structure against the formula of the commercial cinema that had gone before; however, its demise was brought about by the rise of a more popular national cinema. Meanwhile, the political cinema of Godard was halted by his own change in direction – as he began working with video.

As already noted, there has also been a tendency to present movements as if they originated in the minds of directors or critics, when in fact they came about due to an intersection of industrial, technological, social, cultural and political factors. Typically, they arise at a time of national change and they often take part in the process of nation building. For neo-realism, the aftermath of the Second World War was a time when Italy was trying to re-form its national identity. The reaction of cinema is to turn inward, to capture as much of live reality as possible so that the cinema offered a mirror for Italy. It did this through its use of real people, and its focus on contemporary problems such as poverty, the after-effects of the war and family tensions.

We should note the ways in which, again and again, those cinemas which offer a frame for reality (in all its guises) are more likely to be canonised than those which offer an escape – through entertainment or spectacle. It is for this reason that Bazin picks on neo-realism – through the inclusion of as much reality as possible and the use of a style which prioritises this (leaving aside of course the heavy use of melodrama), he finds it helps him focus his mind on the cinema's relation to reality. In relation to the essays in the first part of this book, Bazin's work here clearly shows the increasingly sophisticated use of film language which was part of sound cinema, and the still enduring desire to do something else besides tell as story.

Occurring at a time of social and political change, movements also function as a hub around which all sorts of contextual issues form and this could be the reason why they have been so frequently studied. It is evident from the *Cahiers* discussion that many factors might converge at one moment to bring about the new. What can also be seen here is the fact that movements are ideal teaching tools, functioning as they do as a nexus for the study of text and context, and an accessible condensation of a particular moment in a particular national cinema.

Having suggested some of the uses of movements and moments when studying European cinema, we might want to ask why European film history has been so consistently organised in this way. Given that American cinema's history has been written through accounts that favour stability, consistency and developing styles and genres, why has Europe emphasised innovation and change? As the introduction to this Reader notes, we could look to the European–American boundary as our reason; however, it is also important to register the international elements involved here. All national cinemas experience the world wars, the rise of new generations, new political regimes and industrial practices, and each moment or movement is a way of registering the reaction of text to context in a way that jostles for international dominance. Film history has until lately rested on models written vertically through national cinema history rather than horizontally across European cinema, and it is such an opportunity to take the horizontal view – across history and nation – that is offered in this section.

Notes

1 As printed on the web pages of Dogme 95: www.tvropa.com/tvropa1.2/ dogme95/the_vow/index.htm
2 Ibid.
3 Thomas Vinterberg in an interview in London's *Time Out* as cited by Richard Coombs (2000).

References and further reading

Andrew, Dudley. (1990) *André Bazin*, New York: Columbia University Press.
Cardullo, Bert. (ed.) (1997) *Bazin at Work: Major Essays and Reviews from the Forties and Fifties*, London and New York: Routledge.
Coombs, Richard. (2000) 'Rules of the Game', *Film Comment* September.
Harvey, Sylvia. (1974) *May'68 and Film Culture*, London: BFI.
Hillier, Jim. (ed.) (1985) *Cahiers du Cinéma – the 1950s: neo-realism, Hollywood, New Wave*, London: BFI.
MacCabe, Colin. (1980) *Godard: Images, Sounds, Politics*, London: BFI.
Milne, Tom. (ed.) (1972) *Godard on Godard*, New York: Da Capo Press.
Corrigan, Timothy. (1983, 1994) *New German Film – The Displaced Image*, Bloomington and Indianapolis: Indiana University Press.
Davidson John E. (1996) *Deterritorializing the New German Cinema*, Minneapolis and London: University of Minnesota Press.
Elsaesser, Thomas. (1996) *Fassbinder's Germany: History, Identity, Subject*, Amsterdam: Amsterdam University Press.
Franklin, James. (1983) *New German Cinema from Oberhausen to Hamburg*, Boston, MA: Twayne Publishers.
Hess, John. 'La Politique des auteurs, Part One, World View as Aesthetic', *Jump Cut* no. 1, pp. 19–22.
Knight, Julia. (1992) *Women and the New German Cinema*, London: Verso.
Marcus, Millicent. (1986) *Italian Film in the Light of neo-realism*, Princeton, NJ: Princeton University Press.
Orr, John and Olga Taxidou. (eds) (2000) *Post-War Cinema and Modernity*, Edinburgh: Edinburgh University Press.

Chapter 6

André Bazin

AN AESTHETIC OF REALITY
Neo-realism (1948)

From *Citizen Kane* to *Farrebique*

RECENT YEARS HAVE BROUGHT a noticeable evolution of the aesthetic of cinema in the direction of realism. The two most significant events in this evolution in the history of the cinema since 1940 are *Citizen Kane* and *Paisà*. Both mark a decisive step forward in the direction of realism but by different paths. If I bring up the film of Orson Welles before I analyze the stylistics of the Italian film, it is because it will allow us to place the latter in its true perspective. Orson Welles restored to cinematographic illusion a fundamental quality of reality – its continuity. Classical editing, deriving from Griffith, separated reality into successive shots which were just a series of either logical or subjective points of view of an event. A man locked in a cell is waiting for the arrival of his executioner. His anguished eyes are on the door. At the moment the executioner is about to enter we can be quite sure that the director will cut to a close shot of the door handle as it slowly turns. This close-up is justified psychologically by the victim's concentration on the symbol of his extreme distress. It is this ordering of the shots, this conventional analysis of the reality continuum, that truly goes to make up the cinematographic language of the period.

The construction thus introduces an obviously abstract element into reality. Because we are so used to such abstractions, we no longer sense them. Orson Welles started a revolution by systematically employing a depth of focus that had so far not been used. Whereas the camera lens, classically, had focused successively on different parts of the scene, the camera of Orson Welles takes in with equal sharpness the whole field of vision contained simultaneously within the dramatic field. It is no longer the editing that selects what we see, thus giving it an *a priori* significance, it is the mind of the spectator which is forced to discern, as in a sort of parallelepiped of reality with the screen as its cross-section, the dramatic spectrum proper to the scene. It is therefore to an intelligent use of a specific step forward that *Citizen Kane* owes its realism. Thanks to the depth of focus of the lens, Orson Welles restored to reality its visible continuity.

We clearly see with what elements of reality the cinema has enriched itself. But from other points of view, it is also evident that it has moved away from reality or at least that it gets no nearer to it than does the classical aesthetic. In ruling out, because of the complexity of his techniques, all recourse to nature in the raw, natural settings,* exteriors, sunlight, and nonprofessional actors, Orson Welles rejects those qualities of the authentic document for which there is no substitute and which, being likewise a part of reality, can themselves establish a form of realism. Let us contrast *Citizen Kane* and *Farrebique* – in the latter, a systematic determination to exclude everything that was not primarily natural material is precisely the reason why Rouquier failed in the area of technical perfection.

Thus, the most realistic of the arts shares the common lot. It cannot make reality entirely its own because reality must inevitably elude it at some point. Undoubtedly an improved technique, skillfully applied, may narrow the holes of the net, but one is compelled to choose between one kind of reality and another. The sensitiveness resembles the sensitiveness of the retina. The nerve endings that register color and intensity of light are not at all the same, the density of one being ordinarily in inverse ratio to that of the other. Animals that have no difficulty in making out the shape of their quarry in the dark are almost color blind.

Between the contrasting but equally pure kinds of realism represented by *Farrebique* on the one hand and *Citizen Kane* on the other, there is a wide variety of possible combinations. For the rest, the margin of loss of the real, implicit in any realist choice, frequently allows the artist, by the use of any aesthetic convention he may introduce into the area thus left vacant, to increase the effectiveness of his chosen form of reality. Indeed we have a remarkable example of this in the recent Italian cinema. In the absence of technical equipment, the Italian directors have been obliged to record the sound and dialogue after actual filming. The net result is a loss of realism. However, left free to use the camera unfettered by the microphone, such directors have thereby profited by the occasion to enlarge the camera's field of action and its mobility with, consequently, an immediate raising of the reality coefficient.

Future technical improvements which will permit the conquest of the properties of the real (color and stereoscopy for example) can only increase the distance between

---

* Matters become complicated when we are dealing with urban settings. Here the Italians are at an undoubted advantage. The Italian city, ancient or modern, is prodigiously photogenic. From antiquity, Italian city planning remained theatrical and decorative. City life is a spectacle, a *commedia dell'arte* that the Italians stage for their own pleasure. And even in the poorest quarters of the town, the coral-like groupings of the houses, thanks to the terraces and balconies, offer outstanding possibilities for spectacle. The courtyard is an Elizabethan set in which the show is seen from below, the spectators in the gallery being the actors in the comedy [. . .] Add to this the sunshine and the absence of clouds (chief enemy of shooting on exteriors) and you have explained why the urban exteriors of Italian films are superior to all others.

the two realist poles which today are situated in the area surrounding *Farrebique* and *Citizen Kane*. The quality of the interior shots will in fact increasingly depend on a complex, delicate and cumbersome apparatus. Some measure of reality must always be sacrificed in the effort of achieving it.

Paisà

How do you fit the Italian film into the realist spectrum? After trying to trace the geographical boundaries of this cinema, so penetrating in its portrayal of the social setting, so meticulous and perceptive in its choice of authentic and significant detail, it now remains for us to fathom its aesthetic geology.

We would clearly be deluding ourselves if we pretended to reduce recent Italian production to certain common, easily definable characteristics applicable to all directors. We will simply try to single out those characteristics with the widest application, reserving the right when the occasion arises to limit our concern to the most significant films. Since we must also make a choice, we will arrange, by implication, the major Italian films in concentric circles of decreasing interest around *Paisà*, since it is this film of Rossellini's that yields the most aesthetic secrets.

Narrative technique

As in the novel, the aesthetic implicit in the cinema reveals itself in its narrative technique. A film is always presented as a succession of fragments of imaged reality on a rectangular surface of given proportions, the ordering of the images and their duration on the screen determining its import.

The objective nature of the modern novel, by reducing the strictly grammatical aspect of its sytlistics to a minimum, has laid bare the secret essence of style. Certain qualities of the language of Faulkner, Hemingway, or Malraux would certainly not come through in translation, but the essential quality of their styles would not suffer because their style is almost completely identical with their narrative technique – the ordering in time of fragments of reality. The style becomes the inner dynamic principle of the narrative, somewhat like the relation of energy to matter or the specific physics of the work, as it were. This it is which distributes the fragmented realities across the aesthetic spectrum of the narrative, which polarizes the filings of the facts without changing their chemical composition. A Faulkner, a Malraux, a Dos Passos, each has his personal universe which is defined by the nature of the facts reported, but also by the law of gravity which holds them suspended above chaos. It will be useful, therefore, to arrive at a definition of the Italian style on the basis of the scenario, of its genesis, and of the forms of exposition that it follows. Unfortunately the demon of melodrama that Italian film makers seem incapable of exorcising takes over every so often, thus imposing a dramatic necessity on strictly foreseeable events. But that is another story. What matters is the creative surge, the special way in which the situations are brought to life. The necessity inherent in the narrative is biological rather than dramatic. It burgeons and grows with all the verisimilitude of life.* One must not conclude that this method, on the face of it, is less aesthetic than a slow and meticulous preplanning. But the old prejudice that time, money, and resources have a value of their own is so rooted that people forget to relate them to the work and to the artist. Van Gogh repainted the same picture ten times, very quickly, while Cézanne would return to a painting time and again over the years. Certain genres call for speed, for work done in the heat of the moment, but surgery could not call for a greater sureness of touch, for greater precision. It is only at this price that the Italian film has the air of documentary, a naturalness nearer to the spoken than to the written account, to the sketch rather than to the painting. It calls for the ease and sure eye of Rossellini, Lattuada, Vergano, and de Santis. In their hands the camera is endowed with well-defined cinematographic tact, wonderfully sentitive antennae which allow them with one stroke to get precisely what they are after. In *Il Bandito*, the prisoner, returning from Germany, finds his house in ruins. Where a solid building once stood there is now just a pile of stones surrounded by broken-down walls. The camera shows us the man's face. Then, following the movement of his eyes, it travels through a 360-degree turn which gives us the whole spectacle. This panning shot is doubly original. First, because at the outset, we stand off from the actor since we are looking at him by way of a camera trick, but during the traveling shot we become identified with him to the point of feeling surprised when, the 360–degree pan having been completed, we return to his face with its expression of utter horror. Second, because the speed of this subjective panning shot varies. It starts with a long slide, then it comes almost to a halt, slowly studies the burned and shattered walls with the same rhythm of the man's watching eye, as if directly impelled by his concentration.

I have had to dwell at some length on this minor example to avoid making a purely abstract affirmation concerning what I regard, in an almost psychological sense of the word, as cinematic 'tact.' A shot of this kind by virtue of its dynamism belongs with the movement of a hand drawing a sketch, leaving a space here, filling in there, here sketching round the subject, and there bringing it into relief. I am thinking of the slow motion of the documentary on Matisse which allows us to observe, beneath the continuous and uniform arabesques of the stroke, the varying hesitations of the artist's hand. In such a case the camera movement is important. The camera must be equally as ready to move as to remain still. Traveling and panning shots do not have the same god-like character that the Hollywood camera crane has bestowed on them. Everything is shot from eye-level or from a concrete point of view, such as a roof top

---

* Nearly all the credits of an Italian film list under the heading 'scenario' a good dozen names. This imposing evidence of collaboration need not be taken too seriously. It is intended to provide the producers with a naïvely political assurance. It usually consists of one Christian Democrat and one Communist (just as in the film there is a Marxist and a priest); the third screenwriter has a reputation for story construction; the fourth is a gag man; the fifth because he is a good dialogue writer; the sixth because he has a fine feeling for life. The result is no better or no worse than if there had been only one screen writer, but the Italian notion of a scenario fits in with their concept of a collective paternity according to which everyone contributes an idea without any obligation on the part of the director to use it. Rather than the assembly line of American screenwriters, this interdependence of improvisation is like that of *commedia dell'arte* or jazz.

or window. Technically speaking, all the memorable poetry of the children's ride on the white horse in *Sciuscià* can be attributed to a low-level camera angle which gives the riders on their mounts the appearance of an equestrian statue. In *Sortilège*, Christian Jacques went to a great deal more trouble over his phantom horse. But all that cinematic virtuosity did not prevent his animal from having the prosaic look of a broken-down cab horse. The Italian camera retains something of a human quality of the Bell and Howell newsreel camera, a projection of hand and eye, almost a living part of the operator, instantly in tune with his awareness.

As for the photography, the lighting plays only a minor expressive role. First, because lighting calls for a studio, and the greater part of the filming is done on exteriors or in real-life settings. Second, because documentary camera work is identified in our minds with the grey tones of newsreels. It would be a contradiction to take any great pains with or to touch up excessively the plastic quality of the style.

As we have thus far attempted to describe it, the style of Italian films would appear to belong with a greater or less degree of skill and mastery of technique or feeling to the same family as quasi-literary journalism, to an ingenious art, pleasing, lively, and even moving, but basically a minor art. This is sometimes true even though one may actually rank the genre fairly high in the aesthetic hierarchy. It would be unjust and untrue to see such an assessment as the final measure of this particular technique. Just as, in literature, reportage with its ethic of objectivity (perhaps it would be more correct to say with its ethic of seeming objectivity) has simply provided a basis for a new aesthetic of the novel, so the technique of the Italian film makers results in the best films especially in *Paisà*, with its aesthetic of narrative that is both complex and original.

Paisà is unquestionably the first film to resemble closely a collection of short stories. Up to now we had only known the film composed of sketches – a bastard and phony type of film if ever there was one. Rossellini tells us, in succession, six stories of the Italian Liberation. This historical element is the only thing they have in common. Three of them, the first, the fourth, and the last, are taken from the Resistance. The others are droll or pathetic or tragic episodes occurring on the fringes of the Allied advance. Prostitution, the black market, and a Franciscan convent alike provide the story material. There is no progression other than a chronological ordering of the story beginning with the landing of an Allied force in Sicily. But their social, historical, and human foundation gives them a unity enough to constitute a collection perfectly homogeneous in its diversity. Above all, the length of each story, its form, contents, and aesthetic duration gives us for the first time precisely the impression of a short story. The Naples episode of the urchin – a black-market expert, selling the clothes of a drunk Negro soldier – is an excellent Saroyan story. Another makes us think of Hemingway, yet another (the first) of Faulkner. I am not merely referring to the tone or the subject, but in a profound way to the style. Unfortunately one cannot put a film sequence in quotation marks like a paragraph, and hence any literary description of one must of necessity be incomplete. However, here is an episode from the final story which reminds me now of Hemingway, now of Faulkner:

1. A small group of Italian partisans and Allied soldiers have been given a supply of food by a family of fisher folk living in an isolated farmhouse in the heart of the

marshlands of the Po delta. Having been handed a basket of eels, they take off. Some while later, a German patrol discovers this, and executes the inhabitants of the farm. 2. An American officer and a partisan are wandering at twilight in the marshes. There is a burst of gunfire in the distance. From a highly elliptical conversation we gather that the Germans have shot the fishermen. 3. The dead bodies of the men and women lie stretched out in front of the little farmhouse. In the twilight, a half-naked baby cries endlessly.

Even with such a succinct description, this fragment of the story reveals enormous ellipses – or rather, great holes. A complex train of action is reduced to three or four brief fragments, in themselves already elliptical enough in comparison with the reality they are unfolding. Let us pass over the first purely descriptive fragment. The second event is conveyed to us by something only the partisans can know – distant gunfire. The third is presented to us independently of the presence of the partisans. It is not even certain that there were any witnesses to the scene. A baby cries besides its dead parents. There is a fact. How did the Germans discover that the parents were guilty? How is it that the child is still alive? That is not the film's concern, and yet a whole train of connected events led to this particular outcome. In any case, the film maker does not ordinarily show us everything. That is impossible – but the things he selects and the things he leaves out tend to form a logical pattern by way of which the mind passes easily from cause to effect. The technique of Rossellini undoubtedly maintains an intelligible succession of events, but these do not mesh like a chain with the sprockets of a wheel. The mind has to leap from one event to the other as one leaps from stone to stone in crossing a river. [. . .] In the usual shooting script (according to a process resembling the classical novel form) the fact comes under the scrutiny of the camera, is divided up, analyzed, and put together again, undoubtedly without entirely losing its factual nature; but the latter, presumably, is enveloped in abstraction [. . .] For Rossellini, facts take on a meaning, but not like a tool whose function has predetermined its form. The facts follow one another, and the mind is forced to observe their resemblance; and thus, by recalling one another, they end by meaning something which was inherent in each and which is, so to speak, the moral of the story – a moral the mind cannot fail to grasp since it was drawn from reality itself. In the Florentine episode, a woman crosses the city while it is still occupied by a number of Germans and groups of Italian Fascists; she is on her way to meet her fiancé, a leader of the Italian underground, accompanied by a man who likewise is looking for his wife and child. The attention of the camera following them, step by step, though it will share all the difficulties they encounter, all their dangers, will however be impartially divided between the heroes of the adventure and the conditions they must encounter. Actually, everything that is happening in a Florence in the throes of the Liberation is of a like importance. The personal adventures of the two individuals blend into the mass of other adventures, just as one attempts to elbow one's way into a crowd to recover something one has lost. In the course of making one's way one sees in the eyes of those who stand aside the reflections of other concerns, other passions, other dangers alongside which one's own may well be merely laughable. Ultimately and by chance, the woman learns, from a wounded partisan, that the man she is looking for is dead. But the statement from which she learned the news was not aimed straight at her – but hit her like a stray bullet. The impeccable line followed by this recital owes nothing to classical forms that are standard for a story of this kind. Attention is never artificially focused on the heroine. The camera makes no pretense at being psychologically subjective. We share all the more fully in the feelings of the protagonists because it is easy for us to sense what they are feeling; and also because the pathetic aspect of the episode does not derive from the fact that a woman has lost the man she loves but from the special place this drama holds among a thousand others, apart from and yet also part of the complete drama of the Liberation of Florence. The camera, as if making an impartial report, confines itself to following a woman searching for a man, leaving to us the task of being alone with her, of understanding her, and of sharing her suffering.

In the admirable final episode of the partisans surrounded in the marshlands, the muddy waters of the Po Delta, the reeds stretching away to the horizon, just sufficiently tall to hide the man crouching down in the little flat-bottomed boat, the lapping of the waves against the wood, all occupy a place of equal importance with the men. This dramatic role played by the marsh is due in great measure to deliberately intended qualities in the photography. This is why the horizon is always at the same height. Maintaining the same proportions between water and sky in every shot brings out one of the basic characteristics of this landscape. It is the exact equivalent, under conditions imposed by the screen, of the inner feeling men experience who are living between the sky and the water and whose lives are at the mercy of an infinitesimal shift of angle in relation to the horizon. This shows how much subtlety of expression can be got on exteriors from a camera in the hands of the man who photographed *Paisà*.

The unit of cinematic narrative in *Paisà* is not the 'shot,' an abstract view of a reality which is being analyzed, but the 'fact.' A fragment of concrete reality in itself multiple and full of ambiguity, whose meaning emerges only after the fact, thanks to other imposed facts between which the mind establishes certain relationships. Unquestionably, the director chose these 'facts' carefully while at the same time respecting their factual integrity. The closeup of the door knob referred to earlier was less a fact than a sign brought into arbitrary relief by the camera, and no more independent semantically than a preposition in a sentence. The opposite is true of the marsh or the death of the peasants.

But the nature of the 'image facts' is not only to maintain with the other image facts the relationship invented by the mind. These are in a sense the centrifugal properties of the images – those which make the narrative possible. Each image being on its own just a fragment of reality existing before any meanings, the entire surface of the scene should manifest an equally concrete density. Once again we have here the opposite of the 'door-knob' type of scene, in which the color of the enamel, the dirt marks at the level of the hand, the shine of the metal, the worn-away look are just so many useless facts, concrete parasites of an abstraction fittingly dispensed with.

In *Paisà* (and I repeat that I imply by this, in varying degrees, all Italian films) the closeup of the door knob would be replaced, without any loss of that peculiar quality of which it is part, by the 'image fact' of a door whose concrete characteristics would be equally visible. For the same reason the actors will take care never to dissociate their performance from the decor or from the performance of their fellow actors.

Man himself is just one fact among others, to whom no pride of place should be given *a priori*. That is why the Italian film makers alone know how to shoot successful scenes in buses, trucks, or trains, namely because these scenes combine to create a special density within the framework of which they know how to portray an action without separating it from its material context and without loss of that uniquely human quality of which it is an integral part. The subtlety and suppleness of movement within these cluttered spaces, the naturalness of the behavior of everyone in the shooting area, make of these scenes supreme bravura moments of the Italian cinema.

The realism of the Italian cinema and the technique of the American novel

The absence of any film documentation may have operated against a clear understanding of what I have so far written. I have arrived at the point of characterizing as similar the styles of Rossellini in *Paisà* and of Orson Welles in *Citizen Kane*. By diametrically opposite technical routes each arrives at a scenario with roughly the same approach to reality – the depth of focus of Welles and the predisposition toward reality of Rossellini. In both we find the same dependence of the actor relative to the setting, the same realistic acting demanded of everyone in the scene whatever their dramatic importance. Better still, although the styles are so different, the narrative follows basically the same pattern in *Citizen Kane* and in *Paisà*.

In short, although they use independent techniques, without the least possibility of a direct influence one on the other, and possessed of temperaments that could hardly be less compatible, Rossellini and Welles have, to all intents and purposes, the same basic aesthetic objective, the same aesthetic concept of realism.

Chapter 7

André Bazin, Jacques Doniol-Valcroze, Pierre Kast, Roger Leenhardt, Jacques Rivette, Eric Rohmer

SIX CHARACTERS IN SEARCH OF *AUTEURS*
A discussion about the French cinema (1957)

SO FAR CAHIERS HAS SAID A LOT, and at the same time very little, about French cinema. A lot about the directors we like and very little about the others — out of politeness, a sense of futility, lack of energy . . . This could have resulted in the impression that our only concern is with foreign cinema (either across the Alps or the Atlantic). Yet our writers talk more often about Saint-Maurice or Billancourt than about Cinecittà or Beverly Hills. But the discussions in our editorial offices aren't always quite right for publication.

So the question came up, as we were preparing this issue: who would be responsible, and in what form, for an appraisal of our cinema that would be fair and at the same time refrain from setting up Aunt Sallies? Our film-makers have enough licensed sycophants to permit themselves the luxury of doing without the approval of our humble scribes; and who is there to deny that there is something rotten in our cinematographic kingdom? But why? That's what needs lengthy discussion and argument. The easiest way was simply to reproduce one of those conversations where people say what they think more freely than when they put pen to paper. And that's what we did. So André Bazin, Jacques Doniol-Valcroze, Pierre Kast, Roger Leenhardt, Jacques Rivette and Eric Rohmer got together around a tape-recorder.

André Bazin: 'The present situation of French cinema.' That implies both its evolution and the present conjuncture. In my view Rivette should begin. He's the one with the most radical and decided opinions on the subject.

Jacques Rivette: It's not exactly an opinion, more a way of formulating the subject. I think that French cinema at the moment is unwittingly another version of British cinema, or to put it another way, it's a British cinema not recognized as such,

---

*'Six personnages en quête d'auteurs: débat sur le cinéma français', Cahiers du Cinéma 71, May 1957 (extracts)

because it's the work of people who are none the less talented. But the films seem no more ambitious and of no more real value than what is exemplified in the British cinema. I imagine we all agree on that.

Bazin: What in your opinion defines the mediocrity of British cinema?

Rivette: British cinema is a *genre* cinema, but one where the genres have no genuine roots. On the one hand there are no self-validating genres as there are in American cinema, like the Western and the thriller (run-of-the-mill Westerns have a value independent of the great Westerns). There are just false, in the sense of imitative, genres. Anyway, most of them are only imitations of American imitations. And on the other hand it isn't an *auteur* cinema either, since none of them have anything to say. It's a cinema that limps along, caught between two stools, a cinema based on supply and demand, and on false notions of supply and demand at that. They believe that that's the kind of thing the public wants and so that's what they get, but in trying to play by all the rules of the game they do it badly, without either honesty or talent.

[. . .]

Roger Leenhardt: We could perhaps throw some light on the debate by drawing an analogy, which may seem pointless but could prove fruitful. Let's imagine that instead of talking about the current state of French cinema, we are literary critics talking about the current state of the novel or literature in France and comparing it with English or American literature. We would perceive that this year or for the years ahead there is very little one can say about French literature, and that wouldn't surprise anyone. What we have to establish is whether we are speaking as literary critics from a position above culture, or from the position of professionals in the industry. They are two very different things. The distinction to be made is much less between *auteur* films and genres and much more between run-of-the-mill cinema and the efforts of those new creators who represent new tendencies. I feel that this is a fundamental distinction that could be made from the outset.

Kast: Unfortunately, such a distinction is completely useless as far as cinema is concerned, given that the very existence of a cinema that would fit the second category in terms of production depends in reality on the first category. *Auteur* films are produced in exactly the same conditions and for the same reasons as commercial films.

[. . .]

Bazin: [. . .] I feel I should point out that the essential characteristic of American cinema is that unexceptional films, those commercial films which are its principal ingredient, are precisely genre films. American cinema thrives financially if the genres thrive. Production can keep going at an average or even above average rate as long as there are good genres. The weakness of the European film industries is that they are incapable of relying on genres for current production. In French prewar cinema, even if there wasn't exactly a genre there was a style, the realist *film noir*. It's still around, but it's diversified, and I'm afraid that one of the problems of French cinema may arise from its inability to sustain good basic genres that thrive, the way they do in America. That's by the way, and of more concern to American than French cinema.

[. . .]

Kast: I'm very sorry to have to do duty as the Marxist – like the drunken Helot at the Spartan banquets – but it's certain that one of the issues facing French cinema (one that has to be recognized at the outset, or we risk getting everything the wrong way round) is the question of the conditions in which potential *auteurs* have the chance to express themselves.

Leenhardt: I don't like quoting authority to support an argument, but I remember a conversation I had with the *directeur général de la cinématographie* [Jacques Flaud] who told me (it was his personal opinion, given in what was a private and very free conversation) that, whatever may be argued to the contrary, the financial state of French cinema was relatively remarkably healthy. 'It's quite obvious,' he added, 'that what we are facing is almost solely a crisis on the level of subject matter in films.' My argument is that prewar French cinema (I mentioned Prévert, and we could add Aurenche, Cocteau and a few others) was decisively influenced, even in terms of quantity, by particular scriptwriters. In the same way, the Italian intelligentsia of the new generation of writers has shaped Italian cinema. And the American cinema itself has taken its direction from the thriller and the great sociological best-sellers.

Jacques Doniol-Valcorze: Yes, but contrary to the phenomenon you describe, i.e. the influence of the scriptwriters, what is recognizable in French cinema since the Liberation is the emergence of a number of directors who are more or less *auteurs* and who could have been the cinema's equivalent of the Paris School in painting. In 1946 or 1947 one might optimistically have thought that Messieurs Bresson, Becker, Clouzot and Clément were going to create, in terms of style, a new school of French cinema. That didn't happen, I think, because there was no agreement on its substance and no shared inspiration.

Rivette: That's indisputable. You could say that in spite of their great successes, Clouzot, Clément and Becker failed because they thought that finding a style was all it took to create a new soul for French cinema. It's quite clear, on the other hand, that Italian neo-realism wasn't first and foremost a search for a style. It became a style; but it was part of a conception of the new world. I defy anyone (and I think everyone would agree) to find any conception of the world in Clouzot's films, or Becker's or Clément's films. At very best it would be a conception of the world that is banal, literary, and twenty or thirty years out of date.

Kast: I agree that the failure to achieve what could have been a postwar school of French cinema is an accurate way of describing it. [. . .] However (and I'm sorry to have to insist on this point), I'd like us first to clear up the problems of the conditions of production. It's undeniable that if you look at how films are made in France you can see that it's relatively easy (assuming that you already have a subject and the desire to film it) to find a producer and a star who'll do the film. The real problems start when you have to deal with the true masters of production, the distributors. The distributor is far from being the odious beast people think: he's someone with a certain amount of capital to manage and he tries to make use of it in conditions that will give a maximum return. But he completely lacks imagination. The big distribution companies always want the follow up; they won't buy the first *Bread, Love and Dreams*, but they will buy the follow-up; they won't buy the first *Don Camillo* but they'll buy the second one. One of the key problems of production in France is finding a distributor who'll take the first film. The crisis facing subject matter isn't simply an *auteur* crisis, it's also the problem of having subjects accepted.

[. . .]

Rivette: I think we all implicitly agree on the name for the evolution of the great directors: it's called *academicism*. This academicism isn't serious in itself. For example, academicism is less of a serious problem in the American cinema – when King Vidor made *War and Peace* we were very clear beforehand about the limits imposed on him by Paramount, Dino de Laurentiis and the whole super-production system. What is serious in the latest films of Becker and Clément is that it's an academicism to which the directors acquiesced. And one even wonders whether they aren't actually seeking it out.

[. . .]

Leenhardt: Well, there I'll take up Kast's position, which is the economic point of view. What has characterized the evolution of French cinema over the last four years, in economic terms, that's to say in terms of financing, is that, for reasons which we don't need to go into here, the films that make money are the big productions and co-productions that are described as international – the ones that are essentially aiming at the foreign market. And it's very likely that a certain insipidness, a certain tendency towards what you call academicism, is connected with the fact that the directors concerned dare not throw themselves into a film whose perspective is essentially that of their own culture. In other words a French film. Instead they aim at making an international film. I'll always remember being struck by something said by the producer of Becker's last film but one, *Ali Baba*: 'You see', I told Becker, 'it doesn't have to be a big money spinner, but it does have to be a film that people will go to see in Berlin, in Peking and in Hollywood!'

Eric Rohmer: That's very important, because it's precisely its universal character that gives American cinema its value. American cinema gives a lead. What should be deplored is not so much that French cinema isn't producing worthwhile work, but that its work is shut off – I mean it doesn't influence work in other countries. There is no French school, at least not any more, while there is an American school and an Italian school.

[. . .]

Rivette: The ideal for French cinema would be to have on the one hand super-productions made by directors like Delannoy or Le Chanois (people who are suited to that kind of thing and who do it well, so that a film that costs 500 million brings in 800 million or even more, which is after all what everyone wants), and on the other hand talented directors who would refuse to involve themselves in such deals, which can in no way be profitable for them, and who have the kind of moral integrity to be satisfied with films – let's say costing 100 million which don't need foreign markets to avoid making a loss, but with which they could really create *auteur* works. These two spheres would have to coexist and would also have to be quite clearly separate. That's exactly what is happening in Italian cinema, which also has its crises but stays in better health

because there is never any confusion between *Ulysses*, or all the other super-productions, and the school of Rossellini, Zavattini, De Sica, Antonioni, all of whom,
although they disagree on a lot of issues, have never compromised. Never. The only
exception is Visconti, in making *Senso*, but it's quite clear that this is a purely formal
exception, since Visconti just got as much as he could out of the producer, like
Ophuls with *Lola Montès* and Renoir, to some extent, with *Eléna et les hommes*. But at
heart Italian cinema has never let itself be taken over, while in France what we've been
witnessing over the past two or three years is the disintegration of what we regarded
as the core of French cinema. People like Becker, Clément and Clouzot have successively let themselves be swallowed up by the all-devouring super-productions. I don't
know why: for love of either money or international fame. And now you might as
well say that there is nobody. There's only one film-maker left who hasn't sold out,
and that's Bresson. He's the only one. And there are some youngsters,[1] but there
hasn't exactly been time yet for temptation to come their way. Perhaps they'll give in
too when the time comes? There's no way of knowing.

[. . .]

Rivette: Why such a desire to conquer the world? That's precisely the cause of the disaster. On the contrary, we should be trying above all to maintain French audiences
and only conquer the world as an indirect consequence. From the moment we start
trying to manufacture international stars, from the moment we aim at making
international films, nine times out of ten we'll fall flat on our faces.

[. . .]

Leenhardt: I started this conversation by saying that the literary parallel was interesting. [. . .] If French cinema isn't interesting it's because at the moment there is
nothing interesting happening in the French novel.

[. . .]

Kast: . . . When you look at what we're reading in France every year, you can see that,
while you may not like the vast majority of the films that come out during the year,
there aren't many worthwhile novels, either. [. . .] There are several simultaneous
reasons for that. First, one which seems very clear to me: a lot of people who might
write novels have turned to the idea of making films. There's no doubt that in
Astruc's case, for instance, it explains both his qualities and his defects. He makes
films without the slightest conception of film-making as a technical craft, something
one does with one's hands, but exactly in the way that he would write the books he
doesn't write. That does away at a stroke with the distinction between scriptwriter
and director, which is a long-standing, traditional distinction in French cinema, and
now on it's way out. Professional scriptwriters were necessary when you had old-
style directors whose role was technical. There had to be someone to write the
story for them since they were only capable of doing the *mise en scène* – in fact, nothing! (*Laughter.*) When Vadim makes a film or when Astruc makes a film, whatever
the film is like or whatever reservations you may have about it, it's something
quite different from a film made by two people – a scriptwriter and a director.

Rivette: It's what we call an *auteur* film!

Doniol-Valcroze: We're falling back on our old 'Objectif 49' theories,[2] which are out-dated in principle but still correct. We've reached a point where the cinema is a medium of expression for saying something. And the staggering thing is that the cinema in France has nothing to say, and that French film says nothing.

Leenhardt: The notion of the total *auteur* is a myth all the same, because the director's craft requires specific capabilities which are not the same as those of a writer. It's possible that one man could have both, but the fact that at the moment directors who have no apparent talent for scriptwriting, like Becker for example, are doing it and risking disaster, means the degeneration of what is a major profession. It still exists in Italy (where there are usually five scriptwriters, not just one) and in the USA.

Kast: But it's obvious that however many people work on a Fellini scenario the film is Fellini's, including its subject.

Rivette: I think that what you're saying about Fellini could apply just as well to the American film-makers, in spite of the credits, for as we now know for sure there isn't a single one of the great American directors who doesn't work on the scenario himself right from the beginning, in collaboration with a scriptwriter who writes the screenplay for him and does the purely literary work that he himself couldn't do with the same formal skill but which is nevertheless in accordance with his own directives (not simply under his supervision but following the direction he gives to it). And that's why in *Cahiers* we've chosen to defend directors like Hitchcock rather than Wyler, and Mann rather than Zinnemann, because they are directors who actually work on their scenarios. And that's precisely the new element that they've introduced over these last ten years. So I agree with Kast in thinking that the question of the pure scriptwriter is out of date.

Bazin: It's out of date in psychological terms. It's possible that the evolution of the cinema (I know nothing about it, which I readily admit) is moving in the direction of the director-*auteur* working on the scenario with the scriptwriter or scriptwriters. But it matters very little to me whether there are scriptwriters as such – what does matter is that the scriptwriter should exist as a function. [. . .] What we come back to in fact isn't the problem of people, but the problem of inspiration and themes. American cinema is just about inexhaustible in the richness of its themes; that's just not the case in France. Before the war there were thematic continuities. Now we have to ask ourselves what they are. The great unity there was before the war has split in all sorts of directions. But one characteristic remains – of context though not of subject-matter: that is, beyond psychology, a particular novelistic vision of the world. Films like Becker's *Casque d'or* or *Edouard et Caroline* are films which, without any specific literary origins, to me seem very French and very 'postwar'. *Les Dernières Vacances* is also a very postwar film. Similarly Clément's *Jeux interdits* or Bresson's *Journal d'un curé de campagne*. While they vary widely in style, atmosphere and theme, they have in common a sharper sense of humanity than anything in prewar cinema, as well as a capacity for analysis which is close to literature. I'm afraid we're losing this, and it's the only capital we've got.

Doniol-Valcroze: [. . .] Why have adaptations from fiction failed? Because apart from a few isolated instances like Bresson, there is no adequate sociological or social *context* in the films to support them. The strength of American cinema is that it has this context. That's also the strength of the Italian cinema. When Antonioni made that extraordinary film *Le Amiche*, adapted from Pavese, he was able to keep the same context as Pavese's book. I think French cinema missed out for several reasons: the *auteurs* lacked confidence, but there were also financial prohibitions. I'm going to mention a word that applies very generally: censorship. I don't only mean the Board of Censors, but also pre-censorship, the censorship of the industry, individual censorship.

Rivette: That's right. There's no point in looking to comedy, which will always be a limited sphere; nor to films adapted from the novel, which was hopeful seven or eight years ago but is now out of date. The only possibility left for French cinema would be in films which although not social (I'm not happy with the word) at least take up a position, analogous to Italian postwar cinema. But why have people failed to recognize this possibility until now? I think it's too easy to blame it on censorship and the producers. It's only because the few French directors who have made statements to the press like 'I'd like to make social films' are, in reality, people who have been corrupted. [. . .] In a word I think that what is most lacking in French cinema is a *spirit of poverty*. Its only hope now lies in other directors – not those three any more (for if they once had the opportunity to say something they let it go by), but new directors taking those risks making films with 20 or 30 million, perhaps even less, and filming with whatever turns up, without putting their scripts forward for approval by the censors and perhaps without even putting them to the producers and the distributors. I think *that* is the only hope for French cinema.

Leenhardt: The true character of prewar French cinema (which, rightly or wrongly, was important) is that its fundamental non-conformism was positive in relation to humanity, in social and revolutionary terms. [. . .] It's the American and Italian cinema that's positive and invigorating. In France we are locked into reactionary values pure and simple, which make an art film a film about destiny, where everything is ill-fated and in the most stupid way imaginable. What constitutes success for Jeanson is to impose an unhappy ending where an inconclusive one or a happy one would have been good aesthetically. There's a kind of inverted censorship which means that nobody dares to attempt a positive film. The only ones that are positive are perhaps Bresson's films.

[. . .]

Kast: What's a positive film, what's a negative film? We would need to engage in a whole discussion which we'd never finish.

Rivette: A negative film is a cowardly film. And I think that the great problem of French cinema is now cowardice.

[. . .]

The only possibility that the cinema has of doing something important (and this is where I part company with Leenhardt) is in *not* following literature, whether it's the literature of fifty or fifteen years ago. [. . .] But it's not a question of following the literature of a few years ago. It's perhaps not even a question of trying to keep up with new literature: the real function of the cinema should be to go further than literature.

[. . .]

Rohmer: Rivette was saying that the cinema should be ahead of literature. Whether ahead or behind it's in any case on quite different territory. I wonder whether it's really the aim of the cinema to be in harmony with what Leenhardt calls 'the most contemporary literature', particularly in France where the literature seems to be going in quite a different direction. Cinema and literature are looking for different things. It's possible that this harmony could be achieved in some oblique way, but for the moment I can't easily see how. I find Bresson's latest film a very good example since it was taken from a non-literary work.

[. . .]

Doniol-Valcroze: I find it interesting to observe that in two films that have already been mentioned here several times, *Les Mauvaises Rencontres* and *Et Dieu . . . créa la femme*, two talented young film-makers have done exactly the opposite of what other dedicated film-makers would have done. Taking a very debatable novel, *Une Sacrée Salade*, as his source, Astruc has elevated his subject to a kind of personal meditation on youth, on a milieu that he knew, on ambition, etc. Vadim has done a very good essay on his conceptions of love and relationships with women. I observe with pleasure that two young film-makers of obvious talent are showing an inclination to put their current and future work entirely into a specific historical and social context. I think that this is apparent in all great literary or cinematic works. [. . .] The greatest possibility of doing good work that is open to young film-makers is to continue in the manner of Astruc and Vadim.

[. . .]

Bazin: There's no inevitability about a direct relationship between a given society and the cinema, although that's the case in American and in Italy. I don't think either that there's any direct relationship between the French novel and French society. It goes beyond just cinema. It's perhaps because at this stage in the development of society and of French art the connection can't be made. Should one seek themes related to contemporary reality at any price? That's what Le Chanois and Cayatte did. We can see the outcome of that. It isn't exemplary.

Doniol-Valcroze: I'm not saying that it's the golden rule. But it happens that in two films that we like there was this connection.

[. . .]

Kast: [. . .] For the moment there's nothing happening in France that's sufficiently decisive to provide the material for a narrative cinema based on a change in society. The only thing I can see is a series of impenetrable illusions created by the dominant mythology: the mythology of success, superiority, and the equation of worth with social function, all of which I see as the pillars of the bourgeoisie. For example monogamy and the family unit, as they exist in the *code civile,* no longer correspond to reality.

Bazin: Ninety-nine per cent of French drama, literature and cinema is based on it.

Rohmer: They are stereotypes as old as the world itself. French film-makers only know how to make endless versions of *La Garçonne*. If there are contradictions in modern society that's not where to look for them. If there's anything new it's that today's generation is not so much looking for freedom (at any rate a theoretical freedom which there's no shortage of) but for morality, whatever it might be.

Bazin: What's more, it's not enough just to have a good rich sociological foundation. There must be extremes. In Italy, unemployment fulfils the role of fate and destiny. Three-quarters of Italian neo-realism is founded on *fear*, social fear. American society is polarized by two things that figure importantly: money and luck. In France it's not material that's lacking, but the possibility of drama inherent in it. That doesn't mean that in France there aren't numerous problems: wars in Indochina or in Algeria, the housing shortage, etc.

Rivette: You certainly can't take up the housing shortage or racism or the war without relating them to a wider context. And you won't be able to do it so long as you go on believing (as Rohmer and Kast do, to my great amazement) that French society hasn't evolved in the last twenty years, which I think is absurd. The first duty of a French film-maker should be to try to see what are the most fundamental new elements in society over the last few years. And then he could handle any one of those issues, because he would have the key. Why haven't we found the key? Because we haven't even looked for it.

[. . .]

We started this debate without any expectation of reaching positive conclusions, but simply to raise certain problems and stir up every possible and imaginable issue. We do not hide from ourselves the fact that the impression people may finally take from it is that it's 'a lot of wind' — but the wind bloweth where it listeth; and maybe a few specks of dust will have stuck in your eye? We could not wish for more.

Translated by Liz Heron

Notes

1 The 'youngsters' referred to here would be, in particular, Alexandre Astruc and Roger Vadim, whose *Les Mauvaises Rencontres* (1955) and *Et Dieu . . . créa la femme* (1956), respectively, both important precursors of the *nouvelle vague*, have already been mentioned in sections of the discussion omitted here. On Vadim, cf. Godard on *Sait-on jamais?*, Ch. 3 below.

2 'Objectif 49': a polemical cine-club formed in 1948/9 from film-makers and film critics, generally opposing 'official' French cinema; the group included people like Jean Cocteau, Robert Bresson, Alexandre Astruc, Pierre Kast. 'Objectif 49' exerted significant influence on the formation of *Cahiers du Cinéma* [. . .]

Chapter 8

THE OBERHAUSEN MANIFESTO (1962)

THE COLLAPSE OF THE CONVENTIONAL GERMAN FILM finally removes the economic basis for the mode of filmmaking whose attitude and practice we reject. With it the new film has a chance to come to life.

German short films by young authors, directors, and producers have in recent years received a large number of prizes at international festivals and gained the recognition of international critics. These works and these successes show that the future of the German film lies in the hands of those who have proven that they speak a new film language.

Just as in other countries, the short film has become in Germany a school and experimental basis for the feature film.

We declare our intention to create the new German feature film.

This new film needs new freedoms. Freedom from the conventions of the established industry. Freedom from the outside influence of commercial partners. Freedom from the control of special interest groups.

We have concrete intellectual, formal, and economic conceptions about the production of the new German film. We are as a collective prepared to take economic risks.

The old film is dead. We believe in the new one.

Oberhausen, February 28, 1962.

Bodo Blüthner
Bovis v. Borresholm
Christian Doermer
Bernhard Dörries
Heinz Furchner
Rob Houwer
Ferdinand Khittl
Alexander Kluge
Pitt Koch

Walter Krüttner
Dieter Lemmel
Hans Loeper
Ronbald Martini
Hansjürgen Pohland
Raimond Ruehl
Edgar Reitz
Peter Schamoni
Detten Schleiermacher

Fritz Schwennicke
Haro Senft
Franz-Josef Spieker
Hans Rolf Strobel
Heinz Tichawsky
Wolfgang Urchs
Herbert Vesely
Wolf Wirth

Chapter 9

Peter Wollen

GODARD AND COUNTER-CINEMA
Vent d'Est (1972)

MORE AND MORE RADICALLY Godard has developed a counter-cinema whose values are counterposed to those of orthodox cinema. I want simply to write some notes about the mean features of this counter-cinema. My approach is to take seven of the values of the old cinema, Hollywood–Mosfilm, as Godard would put it, and contrast these with their (revolutionary, materialistic) counterparts and contraries. In a sense, the seven deadly sins of the cinema against the seven cardinal virtues. They can be set out schematically in a table as follows:

Narrative transitivity	Narrative intransitivity
Identification	Estrangement
Transparency	Foregrounding
Single diegesis	Multiple diegesis
Closure	Aperture
Pleasure	Unpleasure
Fiction	Reality

Obviously, these somewhat cryptic headings need further commentary. First, however, I should say that my overall argument is that Godard was right to break with Hollywood cinema and to set up his counter-cinema and, for this alone, he is the most important director working today. Nevertheless, I think there are various confusions in his strategy, which blunt its edges and even, at times, tend to nullify it – mainly, these concern his confusion over the series of terms: fiction/mystification/ideology/lies/deception/illusion/representation. At the end of these notes, I shall touch on some of my disagreements. First, some remarks on the main topics.

1. *Narrative transitivity v. narrative intransitivity*. (One thing following another v. gaps and interruptions, episodic construction, undigested digression.)

By narrative transivity, I mean a sequence of events in which each unit (each function that changes the course of the narrative) follows the one preceding it according to a chain of causation. In the Hollywood cinema, this chain is usually psychological and is made up, roughly speaking, of a series of coherent motivations. The beginning of the film starts with establishment, which sets up the basic dramatic situation – usually an equilibrium, which is then disturbed. A kind of chain reaction then follows, until at the end a new equilibrium is restored.

Godard began to break with this tradition very early. He did this, at first, in two ways, both drawn from literature. He borrowed the idea of separate chapters, which enabled him to introduce interruptions into the narrative, and he borrowed from the picaresque novel. The picaresque is a pseudo-autobiographical form which for tight plot construction substitutes a random and unconnected series of incidents, supposed to represent the variety and ups-and-downs of real life. (The hero is typically marginal to society, a rogue-errant, often an orphan, in any case without family ties, thrown hither and thither by the twists and turns of fortune.)

By the time he arrives at *Vent d'Est*, Godard has practically destroyed all narrative transitivity. Digression which, in earlier films, represented interruptions to the narrative have hypertrophied until they dominate the film entirely. The basic story, as much of it as remains, does not have any recognizable sequence, but is more like a series of intermittent flashes. Sometimes it seems to be following a definite order in time, but sometimes not. The constructive principle of the film is rhetorical, rather than narrative, in the sense that it sets out the disposition of an argument, point by point, in a sequence of 1–7, which is then repeated, with a subsidiary sequence of Theories A and B. There are also various figures of amplification and digression within this structure.

There are a number of reasons why Godard has broken with narrative transitivity. Perhaps the most important is that he can disrupt the emotional spell of the narrative and thus force the spectator, by interrupting the narrative flow, to reconcentrate and re-focus his attention. (Of course, his attention may get lost altogether.) Godard's cinema, broadly speaking, is within the modern tradition established by Brecht and Artaud, in their different ways, suspicious of the power of the arts – and the cinema, above all – to 'capture' its audience without apparently making it think, or changing it.

2. *Identification v. estrangement.* (Empathy, emotional involvement with a character v. direct address, multiple and divided characters, commentary.)

Identification is a well-known mechanism though, of course, in the cinema there are various special features which mark cinematic identification off as a distinct phenomenon. In the first place, there is the possibility of double identification with the star and/or the character. Second, the identification can only take place in a situation of suspended belief. Third, there are spatial and temporal limits either to the identification or, at any rate, to the presence of the imago. (In some respects, cinematic identification is similar to transference in analysis, though this analogy should not be taken too far.)

Again, the breakdown of identification begins early in Godard's films and then develops unevenly after that, until it reaches a new level with *Le Gai Savoir*. Early devices include non-matching of voice to character, introduction of 'real people' into the fiction, characters addressing the audience directly. All these devices are also used in *Vent d'Est*, which takes especially far the device of allowing voices to float off from characters into a discourse of their own on the soundtrack, using the same voice for different characters, different voices for the same character. It also introduces the 'real-life' company into the film itself and, in a rather complicated figure, introduces Gian Maria Volonte, not simply as an actor (Godard shows the actors being made up) but also as intervening in the process of 'image-building'. As well as this, there is a long and extremely effective direct address sequence in which the audience is described – somewhat pejoratively – from the screen and invited into the world of representation.

It is hardly necessary, after the work of Brecht, to comment on the purpose of estrangement-effects of this kind. Clearly, too, they are closely related to the breakup of narrative transitivity. It is impossible to maintain 'motivational' coherence, when characters themselves are incoherent, fissured, interrupted, multiple and self-critical. Similarly, the ruse of direct address breaks not only the fantasy identification but also the narrative surface. It raises directly the question, 'What is this film for?', superimposed on the orthodox narrative questions, 'Why did that happen?' and 'What is going to happen next?' Any form of cinema which aims to establish a dynamic relationship between film maker and spectator naturally has to consider the problem of what is technically the register of discourse, the content of the enunciation, as well as its designation, the content of the enunciate.

3. *Transparency v. foregrounding*. ('Language wants to be over-looked' – Siertsema v. making the mechanics of the film/text visible and explicit.)

Traditional cinema is in the direct line of descent from the Renaissance discovery of perspective and reformulation of the art of painting, expressed most clearly by Alberti, as providing a window on the world. The camera, of course, is simply the technological means towards achieving a perfect perspective construction. After the Renaissance the painting ceased to be a text which could be 'read,' as the iconographic imagery and ideographic space of pre-Renaissance painting were gradually rejected and replaced by the concept of pure representation. The 'language' of painting became simply the instrument by which representation of the world was achieved. A similar tendency can be seen at work with attitudes to verbal language. From the seventeenth century onwards, language was increasingly seen as an instrument which should efface itself in the performance of its task – the conveyance of meaning. Meaning, in its turn, was regarded as representation of the world.

In his early films Godard introduced the cinema as a topic in his narrative – the 'Lumière' sequence in *Les Carabiniers*, the film within a film in *Le Mépris*. But it was not until his contribution to *Loin du Vietnam* that the decisive step was taken, when he simply showed the camera on screen. In the post-1968 films the process of production is systematically highlighted. In *Vent d'Est* this shows itself not simply in taking the camera behind the scenes, as it were, but also in altering the actual film itself: thus the whole worker's control sequence is shown with the film marked and scratched, the first time that this has happened in Godard's work. In previous films, he had not gone further than using special film stock (*Les Carabiniers*) or printing sequences in negative (*Les Carabiniers, Alphaville*).

At first sight, it looks as if the decision to scratch the surface of the film brings Godard into line with other avant-garde film makers, in the American 'underground' especially. However this is not really the case. In the case of the American film makers, marking the film is best seen alongside developments in painting that have dominated, particularly in the USA, in recent years. Broadly speaking, this involves a reduction of film to its 'optical' substrate. Noise is amplified until, instead of being marginal to the film, it becomes its principal content. It may then be structured according to some calculus or algorithm or submitted to random coding. Just as, in painting, the canvas is foregrounded so, in cinema, the film is foregrounded.

Godard, however, is not interested in this kind of 'de-signification' of the image by foregrounding 'noise' and then introducing a new constructive principle appropriate to this. What he seems to be doing is looking for a way of expressing negation. It is well known that negation is the founding principle of verbal language, which marks it off both from animal signal-systems and from other kinds of human discourse, such as images. However, once the decision is made to consider a film as a process of writing in images, rather than a representation of the world, then it becomes possible to conceive of scratching the film as an erasure, a virtual negation. Evidently the use of marks as erasures, crossing-out an image, is quite different from using them as deliberate noise or to foreground the optical substrate. It presupposes a different concept of 'film-writing' and 'film-reading'.

Some years ago, Astruc, in a famous article, wrote about *le caméra-stylo*. His concept of writing – *écriture* – was closer to the idea of style. Godard, like Eisenstein before him, is more concerned with 'image-building' as a kind of pictography, in which images are liberated from their role as elements of representation and given a semantic function within a genuine iconic code, something like the baroque code of emblems. The sequences in which the image of Stalin is discussed are not simply – or even principally – about Stalin's politics, as much as they are about the problem of finding an image to signify 'repression'. In fact, the whole project of writing in images must involve a high degree of foregrounding, because the construction of an adequate code can only take place if it is glossed and commented upon in the process of construction. Otherwise, it would remain a purely private language.

4. *Single diegesis v. multiple diegesis.* (A unitary homogeneous world v. heterogeneous worlds. Rupture between different codes and different channels.)

In Hollywood films, everything shown belongs to the same world, and complex articulations within that world – such as flash-backs – are carefully signalled and located. The dominant aesthetic is a kind of liberalized classicism. The rigid constraints of the dramatic unities have been relaxed, but mainly because they were over-strict and limiting, whereas the basic principle remains unshaken. The world represented on the cinema must be coherent and integrated, though it need not observe compulsory, statutory constraints. Time and space must follow a consistent order. Traditionally, only one form of multiple diegesis is allowed – the play within a play – whereby the second, discontinuous diegetic space is embedded or bracketed within the first. (It should be added that there are some exemplary cases of transgression of single diegesis within literature, such as Hoffmann's *Life of Tomcat Murr*, which consists of Tomcat Murr's life – the primary diegesis – interleaved at random with pages from another text – the life of Kreisler – supposedly bound into the book by mistake by the book-binder. The pages from the secondary diegesis begin and end in the middle of sentences and are in the wrong order, with some missing. A novel like Sterne's *Tristram Shandy,* however, simply embeds a number of different diegeses on the play-within-a-play model. Of course, by recursion this principle can be taken to breaking point, as Borges has often pointed out.)

Godard uses film-within-a-film devices in a number of his early works. At the same time the primary diegesis begins to develop acute fissures and stresses. In *Le Mépris*, for example, there is not only a film-within-a-film, but many of the principal characters speak different languages and can only communicate with each other through an interpreter (an effect entirely lost in some dubbed versions, which have to give the interpreter meaningless remarks to speak). The first radical break with single diegesis, however, comes with *Weekend*, when characters, from different epochs and from fiction are interpolated into the main narrative: Saint-Just, Balsamo, Emily Brontë. Instead of a single narrative world, there is an interlocking and interweaving of a plurality of worlds.

At the same time that Godard breaks down the structure of the single diegesis, he also attacks the structure of the single, unitary code that expressed it. Not only do different characters speak different languages, but different parts of the film do too. Most strikingly, there is a rupture between soundtrack and images: indeed, the elaboration of this rupture dominates both *Le Gai Savoir* and *Pravda*. The text becomes a composite structure, like that of a medieval macaronic poem, using different codes and semantic systems. Moreover, these are not simply different, but also often contradictory. *Vent d'Est*, for instance, presents alternative ways of making a film (the Glauber Rocha sequence) only to reject them. It is one of the assumptions of contemporary linguistics that a language has a single, unitary semantic component, just as it has a single syntax. In fact, this is surely not the case. The semantic component of a language is composite and contradictory, permitting understanding on one level, misunderstanding on another. Godard systematically explores the areas of misunderstanding.

5. *Closure v. Aperture*. (A self-contained object, harmonized within its own bounds, v. open-endedness, overspill, intertextuality – allusion, quotation and parody.)

It has often been pointed out that in recent years, the cinema has become 'self-conscious', in contrast to the 'innocent' days of Hollywood. In itself, however, 'self-consciousness' is quite compatible with closure. There is a use of quotation and allusion that simply operates to provide a kind of 'surplus' of meaning, as the scholastics used to say, a bonus for those who catch the allusion. The notorious 'Tell me lies' sequence in *Le Petit Soldat*, borrowed from *Johnny Guitar*, is of this kind: it does not make much difference whether you recognise it or not and, even if you do, it has no effect on the meaning of the sequence. Or else quotation can be simply a sign of eclecticism, primarily a stylistic rather than semantic feature. Or, as with Makavejev's use of quotation, the objective may be to impose a new meaning on material by inserting it into a new context: a form of irony.

Godard, however, uses quotation in a much more radical manner. Indeed, his fondness for quotation has always been one of the distinguishing characteristics of his films. At the beginning of his career, Godard used to give instructions to the cameraman almost entirely in terms of shots from previous films and, at a more explicit level, there are endless direct quotes, both from films and from painting and literature. Whole films contain obvious elements of pastiche and parody: *Une Femme est une Femme* is obviously derivative from the Hollywood musical, *Les Carabiniers* from Rossellini, *Le Mépris* is 'Hawks and Hitchcock shot in the manner of Antonioni' . . . it would be possible to go on endlessly.

However, as Godard's work developed, these quotations and allusions, instead of being a mark of ecclecticism, began to take on an autonomy of their own, as structural and significant features within the films. It becomes more and more impossible to understand whole sequences and even whole films without a degree of familiarity with the quotations and allusions which structure them. What seemed at first to be a kind of jackdaw mentality, a personality trait of Godard himself, begins to harden into a genuine polyphony, in which Godard's own voice is drowned out and obliterated behind that of the authors quoted. The film can no longer be seen as a discourse with a single subject, the film maker/auteur. Just as there is multiplicity of narrative worlds, so too there is a multiplicity of speaking voices.

Again, this takes us back to the period before the rise of the novel, the representational painting, to the epoch of the battle of the books, the logomachia. Perhaps the author who comes most to mind is Rabelais, with his endless counter-position of quotations, his parodies, his citation of authorities. The text/film can only be understood as an arena, a meeting-place in which different discourses encounter each other and struggle for supremacy. Moreover these discourses take on an independent life of their own. Instead of each being corked up in its bottle with its author's name on it as a label, the discourses escape, and like genies, are let out to intermingle and quarrel.

In this sense, Godard is like Ezra Pound or James Joyce who, in the same way, no longer insist on speaking to us in their own words, but can be seen more as ventriloquist's dummies, through whom are speaking – or rather being written – palimpsests, multiple *Niederschriften* (Freud's word) in which meaning can no longer be said to express the intention of the author or to be a representation of the world, but must like the discourse of the unconscious be understood by a different kind of decipherment. In orthodox logic and linguistics, context is only important as an arbiter between alternative meanings (amphibologies, as they are called in logic). In Godard's films, the opposite process is at work: the juxtaposition and re-contextualization of discourses leads not to a separating-out of meanings but to a confrontation.

6. *Pleasure v. unpleasure.* (Entertainment, aiming to satisfy the spectator v. provocation, aiming to dissatisfy and hence change the spectator.)

The attack on 'entertainment' cinema is part of a broader attack on the whole of 'consumer society'. Cinema is conceived of as a drug that lulls and mollifies the militancy of the masses, by bribing them with pleasurable dreams, thus distracting them from the stern tasks which are their true destiny. It is hardly necessary to insist on the asceticism and Puritanism – repressiveness – of this conception that unflinchingly seeks to put the reality-principle in command over the pleasure-principle. It is true that the short-term (cinematic) dream is sometimes denounced in the name of a long-term (millenarian) dream, and short-term (false, illusory, deceptive) satisfactions contrasted with long-term (real, genuine, authentic) satisfaction, but this is exactly the kind of argument which is used to explain the accumulation of capital in a capitalist society by the saving principle and postponement of consumption.

Brecht was careful never to turn his back on entertainment and, indeed, he even quotes Horace in favour of pleasure as the purpose of the arts, combined, of course, with instruction. This is not to say that a revolutionary cinema should distract its spectators from realities, but that unless a revolution is desired (which means nothing less than coinciding with and embodying collective fantasies) it will never take place. The reality-principle only works together with the pleasure-principle when survival itself is at stake, and though this may evidently be the case in a revolutionary situation, it is not so in the advanced capitalist countries today. In a situation in which survival is – at least relatively – nonproblematic, the pleasure-principle and the reality-principle are antagonistic and, since the reality-principle is fundamentally adaptive, it is from the pleasure-principle that change must stem. This means that desire, and its representation in fantasy, far from being necessary enemies of revolutionary politics – and its cinematic auxiliary – are necessary conditions.

The problem, of course, concerns the nature of the fantasies on the one hand, and the way in which they are presented in the text/film on the other hand, the way in which fantasy scenarios are related to ideologies and beliefs and to scientific analysis. A revolutionary cinema has to operate at different levels – fantasy, ideology, science – and the articulation of these levels, which involve different modes of discourse and different positions of the subject, is a complicated matter.

In *Vent d'Est* the 'struggle against the bourgeois notion of representation' certainly does not rule out the presence of fantasy: fantasy of shooting the union delegate, fantasies of killing shoppers in a supermarket. Indeed, as long as there are images at all, it is impossible to eliminate fantasy. But the fantasies are almost entirely sado-masochistic in content, and this same fantasy content also seems to govern the relationship between film maker and spectator, rather on the lines of the relationship between the flute-player in the film and his audience. A great many of the devices Godard uses are designed to produce a collective working relationship between film maker and audience, in which the spectator can collaborate in the production/consumption of meaning. But Godard's view of collective work is conceived of in very imprecise terms. 'Criticism' consists of insults and interrogation. The fantasy content of the film is not articulated correctly with the ideology or political theory. This, in turn, seems to spring from a suspicion of the need for fantasy at all, except perhaps in the sado-masochistic form of provocation.

7. *Fiction v. reality*. ((Actors wearing make-up, acting a story v. real life, the breakdown of representation, truth.)

Godard's dissatisfaction with fiction cinema begins very early. Already in *Vivre sa vie* non-fiction is introduced – the chapter on the economics and sociology of prostitution. There is almost no costume drama in Godard's career, until – ironically enough – *Vent d'Est*. Even within the framework of fiction, he has stuck to contemporary life. His science fiction films (*Alphaville*, *Anticipation*) have all been set in a kind of future-in-the-present, without any paraphernalia of special effects or sets.

As with all the features I have described, the retreat from (and eventually attack on) fiction has proceeded unevenly through Godard's career, coming forward strongly in, for instance, *Deux ou trois choses*, then receding again. Especially since May 1968, the attack on fiction has been given a political rationale (fiction = mystification = bougeois ideology) but, at the beginning, it is much more closely connected with Godard's fascination (Cartesian, rather than Marxist) with the misleading and dissembling nature of appearances, the impossibility of reading an essence from a phenomenal surface, of seeing a soul through and within a body or telling the lie from the truth. At times Godard seems almost to adopt a kind of radical Romanticism, which sees silence (lovers' silence, killers' silence) as the only true communication, when reality and representation, essence and appearance, irreducibly coincide: the moment of truth.

Obviously, too, Godard's attitude to fiction is linked with his attitude to acting. This comes out most clearly in *Une Femme Mariée*, when the actor is interrogated about his true self, his relationship to his roles. Godard is obsessed with the problem of true speech, lying speech and theatrical speech. (In a sense, these three kinds of speech, seen first in purely personal terms, are eventually politicized and given a class content. The bourgeoisie lies, the revisionists lie, though they should speak the truth, the revolutionaries speak the truth, or, rather, stammer an approach to the truth.) Godard has long shown a horror of acting, based originally on a 'logocentric' antipathy to anybody who speaks someone else's words, ironic in the circumstances. Eventually, Godard seems to have reformulated his attitude so that actors are distrusted for speaking other people's words as if they were their own. This accompanies his growing recognition that nobody ever speaks in their own words, hence the impossibility of genuine dialogue and the reduction of dialogue to reciprocal – or often unilateral – interviewing. In *Vent d'Est* there is almost no dialogue at all (only a number of variants of monologue) and this must relate to the caricature of collective work Godard puts forward.

Interviewing is, of course, the purest form of linguistic demand, and the demand Godard makes is for the truth. Yet it never seems to be forthcoming, not surprisingly, since it cannot be produced on demand. It is as if Godard has a lingering hope that if people could find their own words, they might produce it miraculously in our presence, but if not, then it has to be looked for in books, which are the residues of real words. This kind of problematic has been tormenting Godard throughout his cinematic career. In *A Bout de souffle* for instance, there is the central contrast between Michel Poiccard/Laszlo Kovacs – an honest impostor – and Patricia, whose mania for honesty reveals her in the end as a deceiver.

The early films tend to explore this kind of problem as one between different levels, but in the post-1968 films, there seems to have been a kind of flattening out, so that fiction = acting = lying = deception = representation = illusion = mystification = ideology. In fact, as anybody reflecting on Godard's earlier films must surely know, these are all very different categories. Ideology, for instance, does not depend primarily on lies. It depends on the acceptance of common values and interests. Similarly mystification is different from deception: a priest does not deceive his congregation about the miracle of the mass in the same way that a conjurer deceives his audience, by hiding something from them. Again, the cinema is a form of representation, but this is not the same as illusion or 'trompe l'oeil'. It is only possible to obliterate these distinctions by defining each of them simply in terms of their departure from truth.

The cinema cannot show the truth, or reveal it, because the truth is not out there in the real world, waiting to be photographed. What the cinema can do is produce meanings, and meanings can only be plotted, not in relation to some abstract yardstick or criterion of truth, but in relation to other meanings. This is why Godard's objective of producing a counter-cinema is the right objective. But he is mistaken if he thinks that such a counter-cinema can have an absolute existence. It can only exist in relation to the rest of the cinema. Its function is to struggle against the fantasies, ideologies and aesthetic devices of one cinema with its own antagonistic fantasies, ideologies and aesthetic devices. In some respects this may bring it closer – or seem to bring it closer – to the cinema it opposes than *Vent d'Est* would suggest. *Vent d'Est* is a pioneering film, an avant-garde film, an extremely important film. It is the starting-point for work on a revolutionary cinema. But it is not that revolutionary cinema itself.

Chapter 10

DOGME 95 – THE VOW OF CHASTITY (1995)

'**I** SWEAR TO SUBMIT TO THE FOLLOWING set of rules drawn up and confirmed by DOGME 95:

1 Shooting must be done on location. Props and sets must not be brought in (if a particular prop is necessary for the story, a location must be chosen where the prop is to be found).
2 The sound must never be produced apart from the images or vice versa. (Music must not be used unless it occurs where the scene is being shot.)
3 The camera must be hand-held. Any movement or immobility attainable in the hand is permitted. (The film must not take place where the camera is standing; shooting must take place where the film takes place.)
4 The film must be in colour. Special lighting is not acceptable. (If there is too little light for exposure the scene must be cut or a single lamp be attached to the camera.)
5 Optical work and filters are forbidden.
6 The film must not contain superficial action. (Murders, weapons, etc. must not occur.)
7 Temporal and geographical alienation are forbidden. (That is to say that the film takes place here and now.)
8 Genre movies are not acceptable.
9 The film format must be Academy 35 mm.
10 The director must not be credited.

Furthermore I swear as a director to refrain from personal taste! I am no longer an artist. I swear to refrain from creating a 'work', as I regard the instant as more important than the whole. My supreme goal is to force the truth out of my characters and settings. I swear to do so by all the means available and at the cost of any good taste and any aesthetic considerations.

Thus I make my VOW OF CHASTITY.'

Copenhagen, Monday 13 March 1995

On behalf of DOGME 95

Lars von Trier   Thomas Vinterberg

European films and theory

Sjunde Injeslet (the Seventh Seal): BFI collections

INTRODUCTION TO PART THREE

IN THEIR DISCUSSION IN PART 2, *Cahiers* suggest that there have never been any French genres; many critics would now dispute this, but for our purposes here, *Cahiers'* lament serves to indicate why 'European Art Cinema' as identified by Bordwell and Neale has been so highly championed. As a *bona fide* European genre, art cinema has been the main culprit for European cinema's pigeon-holing as art and not commercial, and as serious and not entertainment. It is also around art cinema that the concepts to be discussed in this third section intersect: the national cinema promoted by countries frequently operates in an art cinema mode, which is also the mode within which most 'auteur' directors work.

Comparisons can be made between the three concepts, art cinema, authorship and national cinema:

- each of these concepts are both critical tools and national strategies (thus, marketing tools);
- all are concerned with negotiating national and international terrain (and all have been defined in relation to Hollywood);
- despite the above assertion, art and auteur have served as more 'European' concepts, which refer less to the national aspect; consequently the national differences between the use of art cinema and *auteur* film making have been less well explored.

The national is asserted as a critical tool just at the moment when boundaries and thus bounded identities are most fluid (following the fall of the Berlin Wall), thus it is not surprising that the use of the term 'national cinema' has been so quickly followed by terms such as trans-national or postnational (see Danan Chapter 22). However, though critics supplement 'the national' in this way, they do not replace it – it is re-defined, yet remains intact as the growth in studies shows (see Hayward, 1993; Elsaesser, 2000;

and Soilla et al. 1999). Before turning to the national we will introduce 'art' and 'auteur', European cinema's most enduring labels.

Art cinema

Canudo's writing testifies to the fact that 'art' has always been an ambition of European film makers and critics, who wanted to validate their own activity in the light of the lower-class, popular reputation of early cinema. In the 1910s and 1920s the art quota was assured by the involvement of personnel from art movements and thus the exhibition of film in salons, ciné clubs and generally to a bourgeois, high-brow audience.

The cinema to which Bordwell and Neale refer (Chapters 11 and 12) is largely a phenomenon of the 1960s and one that they are keen to construct in relation to Hollywood. For Bordwell and Neale a history of art cinema can be traced from the 1920s early avant-gardes and 'films d'art' through the 1930s, neo-realism, and the French New Wave. When comparing 1960s art cinema with the activities in the 1920s, clearly there are similarities but there are also differences. Thus, the emphasis on the director (here an artist) prevalent in the early moment is retained through the importance placed on individual expression. In the 1920s there is a suggestion that cinema is part of a national artistic style; however, as Bordwell characterises it, art cinema is a coherent style which does not refer to art movements. Gaps begin to emerge, then, between 'art films' of the 1920s onwards and the 'art cinema' which Bordwell and Neale diagnose as being connected to them.

One might wish to ask here, given the lack of reference to the other arts, in what way is this an 'art' cinema? Are we simply relying on the art versus commerce opposition without really thinking about what the application of 'art' might do to the films? Neale suggests that art cinema has been underanalysed, and there is certainly a sense in which it is almost allowed to exist as naturalised myth: taken for granted, a state apparatus, which, unlike counter-cinema, is respectable in a number of ways. Whereas Wollen's counter-cinema was *radically other*, art cinema presents itself more as an *alternative* to classical narrative cinema.

As Neale points out, art cinema is also tied up in commercial discourse, it is typically produced to be exported and it exists via a whole different, yet equally significant commercial circuit. What about using the terms 'cultural', 'creative', or simply 'quality' cinema then, rather than 'art' cinema? Clearly, 'art' is convenient because it evokes a tradition, it suggests respectability and a European heritage.

But beyond the fact that, first, 'many directors work in art cinema', second, it offers an alternative to American cinema, and third, its heritage has been traced back to early cinema, how is art cinema 'European'? In order to answer this question, we need to turn to studies of its difference, which do not rely on the European–American boundary. John Orr and Olga Taxidou's collection *Post-War Cinema and Modernity* is one such example, and in an essay in this collection Orr connects art cinema to Pasolini's notion of a 'cinema of poetry' in which, in particular, the 'linguistic' is substituted for the 'stylistic'.[1] This language (dialogue) versus style dialectic can be found at the heart of previous debates about European cinemas. We can find it in Truffaut's 'A certain tendency of French cinema' (Truffaut, 1968) where he criticises 'literary' translations of scripts, preferring 'men of the cinema'. Behind such criticism we could read a liking for the image over the spoken word, and *Les quatre cents coups* (1959), his manifesto, is clearly full of 'arresting images', not least the freeze frame which ends the film.

We can trace the stylistic–linguistic even further, to Bazin's endorsement of neo-realism's unscripted reality, to Eisenstein's insistence on the power of montage, to Vertov's condemnation of 'theatrical films', and in the emphasis that theories of authorship place on deciphering the *auteur*'s signature (through close attention to the visual). The stylistic over linguistic bias can even be seen in Kristin Thompson's comparative analysis of production methods between early European cinemas and Hollywood (Thompson, 1993).

Through the accumulation of examples above it would be fair to say that one pre-occupation of European cinemas is with an overemphasis on the visual and it is through its centring of this that art cinema can be connected to what has gone before. As the discussion around the emphasis on the visual suggests, art cinema is a form of cinema that needs to be talked of, thought and written about, thus assuming some translation. Art cinema is such a key part of the 'gate-keeping of taste', with which the introduction to this Reader began, that it is necessary to contemplate the fact that it may be more useful as a critical category, rather than as something defined by the director, institution or audience.

Authorship

Art cinema and the conception of the *auteur* come about at the same time and operate along the same European assumptions – the cult of individualism and romantic views of creativity. Unlike art cinema though, authorship has been the subject of much critical analysis and has undergone several transformations as a theory. The history of the term is beyond the reach of this Introduction, which will therefore focus on how authorship appears in the pieces reproduced here.

The *auteur* model of film making may seem to stretch across Europe's cinemas, yet it is more prevalent and configured differently in different contexts as Johnston (Chapter 13) shows in relation to West Germany. It is important to remember the origins of authorship, before turning to its rather diluted use today. 'La politique des auteurs' was a critical tool created by the writers of *Cahiers du Cinéma*, which, so Bordwell suggests, applied the standards of *mise-en-scène* analysis to Hollywood films. Looked at in such a way, we might want to conclude that this politique had more to do with a shift in the style of film criticism than with any difference in these films and film makers. It was not the case, then, that suddenly there existed *auteurs*, rather it was that the interest of film critics shifted towards *mise-en-scène*. Such a move had been signalled much earlier by Bazin's work, which focused on individual directors (Rossellini, Welles) and their film style.

When it comes to the prevalence of authorship in European cinema studies, the otherwise sustainable European–American opposition is complicated, since some of the first directors to be hailed as *auteurs* (Hawks, Ray, Preminger) worked in the 'foreign and enemy' American system. Whilst we can trace the *origins* of the *politique des auteurs* in European culture, its application obviously seems to go outside of its boundaries. Authorship clearly *is* a European notion, it originates in the minds of the writers of *Cahiers du Cinéma* in France, bears traces of such European traditions as romanticism, and European values of autonomy and liberty, and since its first application it has emphatically formed one of the criteria which the 'gate-keepers of taste' use to decide upon entry into the canon. So how do we explain its application to American films? We might put this down to *Cahiers'* personal taste; however, we could add to this the accusation by John Hess that:

> La politique des auteurs was, in fact, a justification, couched in aesthetic terms, of a culturally conservative, politically reactionary attempt to remove film from the realm of social and political concern, in which the progressive forces of the Resistance had placed all the arts in the years immediately after the war.
>
> (Hess, 1974a: 2)

In an attempt to escape from their postwar context the *Cahiers* writers turned to America, as did so many European audiences at the time and as have so many since. It is not surprising given their agenda mapped out so far that European cinema critics have since buried this need for the American, and firmly deposited *auteur*ship back in the hands of European film culture. However, this gesture of turning from, then returning to, Europe was not accompanied by a facing up to the realities which *Cahiers* had tried to escape. Instead, critics have allowed authorship to remain a tool that extracts films from a social, cultural, political and national context, thereby retaining *Cahiers'* initial intention. This embrace of authorship should be seen as one among many gestures by European critics, which emphasise the aesthetic over the industrial or economic.

Critics have seized *la politique des auteurs* for European cinema for several reasons. One might suggest that the first reason is because '*auteur*' film making can be relied upon as one of the few exportable European genres, and as such it has both a national and international quality. A second aspect, which is invested in the notion of the *auteur*, is the 'cultural' status of his work (and as we will see, the *auteur* is usually male). Thus, debates around 'national' cinemas – what form should they take? should they address the national audience or the international market? – usually rest on the decision that they should be both cultural (thus contributing to the nation's cultural output) and commercial (if not making a profit, at least recouping their costs). *Auteur* cinema manages to bridge these two aims.

The third reason for the place of *auteur* film making in European film history must be because it has provided a boundary of inclusion–exclusion. Thus, simplifying things: in order to be written about and thereby preserved, European cinema must be great; in order to be great, it must be made by an '*auteur*'; and, generally, in order to be an *auteur* one must be male and must make a particular type of cinema (which announces its greatness through ambiguity, through conforming to an art cinema style, through allowing a common thread of themes, imagery or autobiography to be read through one's work). Alongside the favouritism of this model has run a current which questions it and an example is Sheila Johnston's essay in which she explains that for the New German Cinema, 'the conditions for an *autor* cinema were deliberately cultivated (in conjunction with certain industrial, political and cultural developments) rather than accidentally propitious.'

In 'Theories of Authorship', still the most comprehensive collection of articles in this area, John Caughie begins his introduction with a quote from Fereydoun Hoveyda: 'The *politique des auteurs* has had its day: it was only a stage on the way to a new criticism.'[2]

This remark was made in 1961, and though 'la politique' which Hoveyda refers to has been transformed over the forty years since, essentially 'authorship' is still having its day as a key approach to European cinema. Generally, books on individual directors have accumulated; however, their increasing suspicion of the romanticism of author-ship can be measured by the efforts they take to recontextualise the author's work, thereby going against any 'universalising' effects of authorship. A recent example is the Manchester University Press series on French directors which prefaces its books with the following:

> throughout, the director will be treated as one highly significant element in a complex process of film production and reception which includes socio-economic and political deter-minants, the work of a large and highly skilled team of artists and technicians, the mechanisms of production and distribution, and the complex and multiply determined responses of spectators.
>
> (Robert Ingrams and Diana Holmes)[3]

The production of books on individual directors have grown; however, there has been a growing emphasis on 'context', which could be said to have brought about the next development in the vocabulary of European film theory: the national.

National cinema

As with '*auteur*' and 'art cinema', with the 'national' it is necessary to separate the use of the term as a critical tool – in which case French, German, Italian, British national cinema is used in the same way as the name of an *auteur*, to organise a group of films – from the national as a national strategy – with the state using policies around the national cinema industry to promote a particular form of cinema as the 'national' cinema. Examples of the latter given in the Reader include New German Cinema, Pilar Miló's policies in 1980s Spain, or the heritage genre in contemporary French cinema.

Although Andrew Higson's article (Chapter 14) is one of the first to use the term 'national cinema' for its polemical value, there have been discussions of a national cinema throughout the history of European film. The restoration of national context can lead to reflectionist accounts of film history, the most obvious example here being Siegfried Kracauer in his book *From Caligari to Hitler*, in which he reads the rise of fascism through a son–tyrant narrative, which he sees as prevalent in all German cinema from 1920–33. Critics have learnt from Kracauer's famous model and have since produced far more discerning contextualisations of national cinemas. If the textual study of European films has served to emphasise their difference from dominant cinemas (and thus their occupation of the margin rather than the mainstream), then the contextual has paid more heed to the differences *between* European cinemas.

All of the above deals mainly with the closing-down effect of the national when used in discourses of the cinema, and the pieces which follow Higson challenge this quality to offer studies of the national in crisis. Gillespie, Byg and D'Lugo (Chapters 15–17) show that although 'the national' is a critical term that can be applied equally to all nations, the results of its application will be very different. Results will depend on the status of national narratives; the foundations on which the national is constructed, such as language (D'Lugo) or ideology (Byg); and the attitude the nation holds to its past (addressed by all writers). What these essays also do is challenge some of the most established 'national cinema' histories (those of Russia, Germany and Spain).

Higson's intervention in debates around national cinema is to shift the emphasis from production to consumption and this suggestion is acted on in the essays by Thumim, and Maltby and Vasey in Part 4, as these writers consider the audience in the case of the former, and the influence of American culture in the latter. Equally, Martine Danan's essay (Chapter 22) furthers debate with her suggestion that the French state actually moved towards a film-making programme which can be thought of as 'post-national'. These most recent developments in the field of national cinemas emphasise competition and complexity, conceiving of the 'national' as something into which cinema comes, rather than something out of which cinema goes.

Notes

1 See John Orr, 'A Cinema of Poetry', pp. 133–41, in Orr and Taxidou (eds) (2000).
2 Fereydoun Hoveyda, 'Autocritique', *Cahiers du Cinéma*, no. 126, December 1961, p. 45, quoted in Caughie, 1981: 9
3 See for example Brigitte Rollet (1998) *Coline Serreau*, Manchester: Manchester University Press.

References and further reading

Balio, Tino. (1996) 'The Art Film Market in the new Hollywood', in Nowell-Smith and Ricci (eds) (1998), pp. 63–73.
Caughie, John. (ed.) (1981) *Theories of Authorship*, London: BFI.
Evans, Peter William. (ed.) (1999) *Spanish Cinema – the Auteurist Tradition*, Oxford: Oxford University Press.
Hayward, Susan. (1993) *French National Cinema*, London and New York: Routledge.
Hess, John. (1974a) 'La politique des Auteurs. Part One: world view as aesthetic', *Jump Cut* no. 1 Jan–Feb.
——(1974b) 'Part Two: Truffaut's manifesto', *Jump Cut* no. 2 May–June.

Hill, John. (1992) 'The Issue of National Cinema and British Film Production', in Duncan Petrie (ed.) *New Questions in British Cinema*, London: BFI Working Papers.

Hjort, Mette and Scott Mackenzie. (eds) (2000) *Cinema and Nation*, London: Routledge.

Kracauer, Siegfried. (1947) *From Caligari to Hitler: A Psychological History of German Film*, Princeton, NJ: Princeton University Press.

Morley, David and Kevin Robins. (1990) 'No Place Like *Heimat*: images of home(land) in European culture', *New Formations* no. 12 Winter.

Orr, John, and Olga Taxidou. (eds) (2000) *Post-War Cinema and Modernity – A Film Reader*, Edinburgh: Edinburgh University Press.

Soila, Tytti, Astrid Soderburgh Widding and Gunnar Iversen. (eds) (1998). *Nordic National Cinemas*, London and New York: Routledge.

Walsh, Michael. (1996) 'National Cinema, national imaginary', *Film History* vol. 8.

Staiger, Janet. (1992) 'With the compliments of the Auteur', in Staiger. *Interpreting Films,* Princeton,NJ: Princeton University Press.

—— (1994) 'The politics of film canons', in Diane Carson, Linda Dittmar and Janice R. Welsch. (eds) *Multiple Voices in Feminist Film Criticism*, Minnesota: University of Minnesota Press,.

Thompson, Kristin. (1993) 'Early alternatives to the Hollywood mode of production', *Film History* vol. 5, no. 4 December.

Truffaut, François. (1968) 'A certain tendency of the French cinema', in Peter Graham. (ed.) *The New Wave*, London: Martin Secker & Warburg.

Wollen, Peter. (1993) 'Films: why do some survive and others disappear?' *Sight and Sound* vol. 3, no. 5.

Chapter 11

David Bordwell

THE ART CINEMA AS A MODE OF FILM PRACTICE

*L**A STRADA, 8½, WILD STRAWBERRIES*, The Seventh Seal, Persona, Ashes and Diamonds, Jules et Jim, Knife in the Water, Vivre sa vie, Muriel*: whatever else one can say about these films, cultural fiat gives them a role altogether different from *Rio Bravo* on the one hand and *Mothlight* on the other. They are 'art films,' and, ignoring the tang of snobbishness about the phrase, we can say that these and many other films constitute a distinct branch of the cinematic institution. My purpose in this essay is to argue that we can usefully consider the 'art cinema' as a distinct mode of film practice, possessing a definite historical existence, a set of formal conventions, and implicit viewing procedures. Given the compass of this paper, I can only suggest some lines of work, but I hope to show that constructing the category of the art cinema is both feasible and illuminating.

It may seem perverse to propose that films produced in such various cultural contexts might share fundamentally similar features. Yet I think there are good reasons for believing this, reasons which come from the films' place in history. In the long run, the art cinema descends from the early *film d'art* and such silent national cinema schools as German Expressionism and Neue Sachlichkeit and French Impressionism.[1] (A thorough account of its sources would also have to include literary modernism, from Proust and James to Faulkner and Camus.) More specifically, the art cinema as a distinct mode appears after World War II when the dominance of the Hollywood cinema was beginning to wane. In the United States, the courts' divorcement decrees created a shortage of films for exhibition. Production films needed overseas markets and exhibitors needed to compete with television. In Europe, the end of the war re-established international commerce and facilitated film export and coproductions. Thomas Guback has shown how, after 1954, films began to be made for international audiences.[2] American films sponsored foreign production, and foreign films helped American exhibitors fill screen time. The later neo-realist films may be considered the first postwar instances of the international art cinema, and subsequent examples would include most works of the New Wave, Fellini, Resnais, Bergman, De Sica, Kurosawa, Pasolini, et al. While the art cinema is of little economic importance in the United States today, it evidently continues, as such international productions as *The Serpent's Egg* or *Stroszek* show.

Identifying a mode of production/consumption does not exhaustively characterize the art cinema, since the cinema also consists of formal traits and viewing conventions. To say this, however, is to invite the criticism that the creators of such films are too inherently different to be lumped together. Yet I shall try to show that whereas stylistic devices and thematic motifs may differ from director to director, the overall *functions* of style and theme remain remarkably constant in the art cinema as a whole. The narrative and stylistic principles of the films constitute a logically coherent mode of cinematic discourse.

Realism, authorship, ambiguity

The classical narrative cinema – paradigmatically, studio feature filmmaking in Hollywood since 1920 – rests upon particular assumptions about narrative structure, cinematic style, and spectatorial activity. While detailing those assumptions is a task far from complete,[3] we can say that in the classical cinema, narrative form motivates cinematic representation. Specifically, cause-effect logic and narrative parallelism generate a narrative which projects its action through psychologically-defined, goal oriented characters. Narrative time and space are constructed to represent the cause-effect chain. To this end, cinematic representation has recourse to fixed figures of cutting (e.g., 180 continuity, crosscutting, 'montage sequences'), mise-en-scene (e.g., three-point lighting, perspective sets), cinematography (e.g., a particular range of camera distances and lens lengths), and sound (e.g., modulation voice-over narration). More important than these devices themselves are their functions in advancing the narrative. The viewer makes sense of the classical film through criteria of verisimilitude (is x plausible?), of generic appropriateness (is x characteristic of this sort of film?) and of compositional unity (does x advance the story?). Given this background set, we can start to mark off some salient features of the art cinema.

First, the art cinema defines itself explicitly against the classical narrative mode, and especially against the cause-effect linkage of events. These linkages become looser, more tenuous in the art film. In *L'Avventura*, for example, Anna is lost and never found; in *A bout de souffle*, the reasons for Patricia's betrayal of Michel remain unknown; in *Bicycle Thieves*, the future of Antonio and his son is not revealed. It will not do, however, to characterize the art film solely by its loosening of casual relations. We must ask what motivates that loosening, what particular modes of unity follow from these motivations, what reading strategies the film demands, and what contradictions exist in this order of cinematic discourse.

The art cinema motivates its narratives by two principles: realism and authorial expressivity. On the one hand, the art cinema defines itself as a realistic cinema. It will show us real locations (Neorealism, the New Wave) and real problems (contemporary 'alienation,' 'lack of communication,' etc.). Part of this reality is sexual; the aesthetics and commerce of the art cinema often depend upon an eroticism that violates the production code of pre-1950 Hollywood. A *Stranger Knocks* and *And God Created Woman* are no more typical of this than, say *Jules et Jim* and *Persona* (whereas one can see *Le mépris* as consciously working upon the very problem of erotic spectacle in the art cinema). Most important, the art cinema uses: 'realistic' – that is, psychologically complex characters.

The art cinema is classical in its reliance upon psychological causation; characters and their effects on one another remain central. But whereas the characters of the classical narrative have clear-cut traits and objectives, the characters of the art cinema lack defined desires and goals. Characters may act for inconsistent reasons (Marcello in *La Dolce Vita*) or may question themselves about their goals (Borg in *Wild Strawberries* and the Knight in *The Seventh Seal*). Choices are vague or nonexistent. Hence a certain drifting episodic quality to the art film's narrative. Characters may wander out and never reappear; events may lead to nothing. The Hollywood protagonist speeds directly towards the target; lacking a goal, the art-film character slides passively from one situation to another.

The protagonist's itinerary is not completely random; it has a rough shape: a trip (*Wild Strawberries*, *The Silence*, *La Strada*), an idyll (*Jules et Jim*, *Elvira Madigan*, *Pierrot le fou*), a search (*L'avventura*, *Blow-up*, *High and Low*), even the making of a film (*8-1/2*, *The Clowns*, *Fellini Roma*, *Day for Night*, *The Last Movie*, *Le mépris*). Especially apt for the broken teleology of the art film is the biography of the individual, in which events become pared down toward a picaresque successivity (*La Dolce Vita*, *The Apu Trilogy*, *Alfie*). If the classical protagonist struggles, the drifting protagonist traces an itinerary, an encyclopedic survey of the film's world. Certain occupations (stockbroking in *Loeclisse*, journalism in *La Dolce Vita* and *The Passenger*, prostitution in *Vivre sa vie* and *Nights of Cabiria*) favor a survey form of narrative. Thus the art film's thematic of *la condition humaine*, its attempt to pronounce judgements on 'modern life' as a whole, proceeds from its formal needs: had the characters a goal, life would no longer seem so meaningless.

What is essential to any such organizational scheme is that it be sufficiently loose in its causation to permit characters to express and explain their psychological states. Slow to act, these characters tell all. The art cinema is less concerned with action than reaction; it is a cinema of psychological effects in search of their causes. The dissection of feeling is often represented explicitly as therapy and cure (e.g. *Through a Glass Darkly*, *Persona*), but even when it is not, the forward flow of causation is braked and characters pause to seek the aetiology of their feelings. Characters often tell one another stories: autobiographical events (especially from childhood), fantasies, and dreams. (A recurring line: 'I had a strange dream last night.') The hero becomes a supersensitive individual, one of those people on whom nothing is lost. During the film's survey of its world, the hero often shudders on the edge of breakdown. There recurs the realization of the anguish of ordinary living, the discovery of unrelieved misery: compare the heroines of *Europa 51*, *L'avventura*, *Deserto rosso*, and *Une Femme mariée*. In some circumstances the characters must attribute their feelings to social situations (as in *Ikiru*, *I live in Fear*, and *Shame*). In *Europe 51*, a communist tells Irene that individuals are not at fault: 'If you must blame something, blame our postwar society.' Yet there is seldom analysis at the level of groups or institutions; in the art cinema, social forces become significant insofar as they impinge upon the psychologically sensitive individual.

A conception of realism also affects the film's spatial and temporal construction, but the art cinema's realism here encompasses a spectrum of possibilities. The options range from a documentary factuality (e.g., *Il posto*) to intense psychological subjectivity (*Hiroshima mon amour*). (When the two impulses meet in the same film, the familiar 'illusion/reality' dichotomy of the art cinema results.) Thus room is left for two reading strategies. Violations of classical conceptions of time and space are justified as the intrusion of an unpredictable and contingent daily reality or as the subjective reality of complex characters. Plot manipulations of story order (especially flashbacks) remain anchored to character subjectivity as in *8-1/2* and *Hiroshima mon amour*. Manipulations of duration are justified realistically (e.g., the *temps morts* of early New Wave films) or psychologically (the jump cuts of *A bout de souffle* signalling a jittery lifestyle). By the same token, spatial representation will be motivated as documentary realism (e.g., location shooting, available light), as character revelation, or in extreme cases as character subjectivity. André Bazin may be considered the first major critic of the art cinema, not only because he praised a loose, accidental narrative structure that resembled life but also because he pinpointed privileged stylistic devices for representing a realistic continum of space and time (deep-focus, deep space, the moving camera, and the long take). In brief, a commitment to both objective and subjective verisimilitude distinguished the art cinema from the classical narrative mode.[4]

Yet at the same time, the art cinema foregrounds the *author* as a structure in the film's system. Not that the author is represented as a biographical individual (although some art films, e.g., Fellini's, Truffault's, and Pasolini's, solicit confessional readings), but rather the author becomes a formal component, the overriding intelligence organizing the film for our comprehension. Over this hovers a notion that the art-film director has a creative freedom denied to her/his Hollywood counterpart.[5] Within this frame of reference, the author is the textual force 'who' communicates (what is the film *saying?*) and 'who' expresses (what is the artist's *personal vision?*). Lacking identifiable stars and familiar genres, the art cinema uses a concept of authorship to unify the text.

Several conventions operate here. The competent viewer watches the film expecting not order in the narrative but stylistic signatures in the narration: technical touches (Truffaut's freeze frames, Antonioni's pans) and obsessive motifs (Buñuel's anticlericalism, Fellini's shows, Bergman's character names). The film also offers itself as a chapter in an *ouvre*. This strategy becomes especially apparent in the convention of the multi-film work (*The Apu Trilogy*, Bergman's two trilogies, Rohmer's 'Moral Tales,' and Truffaut's Doinel series). The initiated catch citations: references to previous films by the director or to works by others (e.g., the New Wave homages).

A small industry is devoted to informing viewers of such authorial marks. International film festivals, reviews and essays in the press, published scripts, film series, career retrospectives, and film education all introduce viewers to authorial codes. What is essential is that the art film be read as the work of an expressive individual. It is no accident, then, that the *politique des auteurs* arose in the wake of the art cinema, that *Cahiers du cinéma* admired Bergman and Antonioni as much as Hawks and Minnelli, that Robin Wood could esteem both Preminger and Satayajit Ray. As a critical enterprise, *auteur* analysis of the 1950s and 1960s consisted of applying art-cinema reading strategies to the classical Hollywood cinema.[6]

How does the author come forward in the film? Recent work in *Screen* has shown how narrational marks can betray the authorial code in the classical text, chiefly through gaps in motivation.[7] In the art-cinema text, the authorial code manifests itself as recurrent violations of the classical norm. Deviations from the classical canon – an unusual angle, a stressed bit of cutting, a prohibited camera movement, an unrealistic shift in lighting or setting – in short any breakdown of the motivation of cinematic space and time by cause-effect logic – can be read as 'Authorial commentary.' The credits for the film, as in *Persona* or *Blow-up*, can announce the power of the author to control what we see. Across the entire film, we must recognize and engage with the shaping narrative intelligence. For example, in what Normal Holland calls the 'puzzling film,'[8] the art cinema foregrounds the narrational act by posing enigmas. In the classic detective tale, however, the puzzle is one of *story*: who did it? how? why? In the art cinema, the puzzle is one of *plot*: who is telling this story? how is this story being told? why is this story being told this way? Another example of such marking of narration is the device of the flashforward – the plot's representation of a future story action. The flashforward is unthinkable in the classical narrative cinema, which seeks to retard the ending and efface the mode of narration. But in the art cinema, the flashforward functions perfectly to stress authorial presence: we must notice how the narrator teases us with knowledge that no character can have. Far from being isolated or idiosyncratic, such instances typify the tendency of the art film to throw its weight onto plot, not story; we play a game with the narrator.

Realism and authorial expressivity, then, will be the means whereby the art film unifies itself. Yet these means now seem contradictory. Verisimilitude, objective or subjective, is inconsistent with an intrusive author. The surest signs of authorial intelligibility – the flashforward, the doubled scene in *Persona*, the color filters at the start of *Le mépris* – are the least capable of realistic justification. Contrariwise, to push the realism of psychological uncertainty to its limit is to invite a haphazard text in which the author's shaping hand would not be visible. In short, a realistic aesthetic and an expressionist aesthetic are hard to merge.

The art cinema seeks to solve the problem in a sophisticated way: by the device of *ambiguity*. The art film is nonclassical in that it foregrounds deviations from the classical norm – there are certain gaps and problems. But these very deviations are *placed*, resituated as realism (in life things happen this way) or authorial commentary (the ambiguity is symbolic). Thus the art film solicits a particular reading procedure: Whenever confronted with a problem in causation, temporality, or spatiality, we first seek realistic motivation. (Is a character's mental state causing the uncertainty? Is life just leaving loose ends?) If we're thwarted, we next seek authorial motivation. (What is being 'said' here? What significance justifies the violation of the norm?) Ideally, the film hesitates, suggesting character subjectivity, life's untidiness, and author's vision.

Whatever is excessive in one category must belong to another. Uncertainties persist but are understood as such, as *obvious* uncertainties, so to speak. Put crudely, the slogan of the art cinema might be, 'When in doubt, read for maximum ambiguity.'

The drama of these tendencies can play across an entire film, as *Guiletta degli spiriti* and *Deserto rosso* illustrate. Fellini's film shows how the foregrounding of authorial narration can collapse before the attempt to represent character subjectivity. In the hallucinations of Guiletta, the film surrenders to expressionism. *Deserto rosso* keeps the elements in better balance. Putting aside the island fantasy, we can read any scene's color scheme in two registers simultaneously: as a psychological verisimilitude (Guiliana sees her life as a desert) or as authorial commentary (Antonioni-as-narrator says that this industrial landscape is a desert.)

If the organizational scheme of the art film creates the occasion for maximizing ambiguity, how to conclude the film? The solution is the open-ended narrative. Given the film's episodic structure and the minimization of character goals, the story will often lack a clear-cut resolution. Not only is Anna never found, but the ending of *L'avventura* refuses to specify the fate of the couple. At the close of *Les 400 coups*, the freeze-frame becomes the very figure of narrative irresolution, as does the car halted before the two roads at the end of *Knife in the Water*. At its limit, the art cinema creates an *8½* or a *Persona*, a film which, lacking a causally adequate ending, seems to conclude several distinct times. A banal remark of the 1960s, that such films make you leave the theatre thinking, is not far from the mark: the ambiguity, the play of thematic interpretation, must not be halted at the film's close. Furthermore, the pensive ending acknowledges the author as a peculiarly humble intelligence; s/he knows that life is more complex than art can ever be, and the only way to respect this complexity is to leave causes dangling, questions unanswered. With the open and arbitrary ending, the art film reasserts that ambiguity is the dominant principle of intelligibility, that we are to watch less for the tale than the telling, that life lacks the neatness of art and *this art knows it.*

The art cinema in history

The foregoing sketch of one mode of cinema needs more detailed examination, but in conclusion it may be enough to suggest some avenues for future work.

We cannot construct the art cinema in isolation from other cinematic practices. The art cinema has neighbors on each side, adjacent modes which define it. One such mode is the classical narrative cinema (historically, the dominant mode). There also exists a modernist cinema – that set of formal properties and viewing protocols that presents, above all, the radical split of narrative structure from cinematic style, so that the film constantly strains between the coherence of the fiction and the perceptual disjunctions of cinematic representation. it is worth mentioning that the modernist cinema is not ambiguous in the sense that the art cinema is; perceptual play, not thematic ambivalence, is the chief viewing strategy. The modernist cinema seems to me manifested (under various circumstances) in films like *October*, *La Passion de Jeanne d'Arc*, *Lancelot du lac*, *Playtime*, and *An Autumn Afternoon*. The art cinema can then be located in relation to such adjacent modes.

We must examine the complex historical relation of the art cinema to the classical narrative cinema. The art film requires the classical background set because deviations from the norm must be registered as such to be placed as realism or authorial expression. Thus the art film acknowledges the classical cinema in many ways, ranging from Antonioni's use of the detective story to explicit citations in New Wave films. Conversely, the art cinema has had an impact on the classical cinema. Just as the Hollywood silent cinema borrowed avant-garde devices but assimilated them to narrative ends, so recent American filmmaking has appropriated art-film devices. Yet such devices are bent to causally motivated functions – the jumpcut for violence or comedy, the sound bridge for continuity or shock effect, the elimination of the dissolve, and the freeze frame for finality. (Compare the narrative resolution of the freeze frame in *Les 400 coups* with its powerful closure in *Butch Cassidy and the Sundance Kid*.) More interestingly, we have seen an art cinema emerge in Hollywood. The open endings of *2001* and *Five Easy Pieces* and the psychological ambiguity of *The Conversation*, *Klute*, and *Three Women* testify to an assimilation of the conventions of the art film. (Simplifying brusquely, we might consider *The Godfather I* as a classical narrative film and *The Godfather II* as more of an art film.) Yet if Hollywood is adopting traits of the art cinema, that process must be seen as not simply copying but complex transformation. In particular, American film genres intervene to warp art-cinema conventions in new directions (as the work of Altman and Coppola shows).[9]

It is also possible to see that certain classical filmmakers have had something of the art cinema about them. Sirk, Ford, and Lang all come to mind here, but the preeminent instance is Alfred Hitchcock. Hitchcock has created a textual persona that is in every way equal to that of the art-cinema author's; of all classical films, I would argue, Hitchcock's foreground the narrational process most strikingly. A film like *Psycho* demonstrates how the classical text, with its psychological causality, its protagonist-antagonist struggle, its detective story, and its continuous time and homogeneous space, can under pressure exhibit the very negation of the classical system: psychology as inadequate explanation (the psychiatrist's account); character as only a position, an empty space (the protagonist is successively three characters, the antagonist is initially two, then two-as-one); and crucially stressed shifts in point-of-view which raise the art-film problem of narrational attitude. It may be that the attraction of Hitchcock's cinema for both mass audience and English literature professor lies in its successful merger of classical narrative and art-film narration.

Seen from the other side, the art cinema represents the domestication of modernist filmmaking. The art cinema softened modernism's attack on narrative casuality by creating mediating structures – 'reality,' character subjectivity, authorial vision – that allowed a fresh coherence of meaning. Works of Rossellini, Eisenstein, Renoir, Dreyer, and Ozu have proven assimilable to art-cinema reading strategies: each director has been assigned a distinct authorial world-view. Yet modernist cinema has responded in ways that make the art cinema in its turn, an important point of departure. By the 1960s, the art cinema enabled certain filmmakers to define new possibilities. In *Gertrud*, Dreyer created a perceptual surface so attenuated that all ambiguity drains away, leaving a narrative vacuum.[10] In *L'Année dernière à Marienbad*, Resnais dissolved causality altogether and used the very conventions of art cinema to shatter the premise of character subjectivity. In *Nicht Versöhnt*, Straub and Huillet took the flashback structure and *temps morts* of the art cinema and orchestrated empty intervals into a system irreducible to character psychology or authorial commentary. Nagisha Oshima turned the fantasy-structures and the narrational marks of the New Wave to political-analytical ends in *The Ceremony* and *Death by Hanging*. Most apparently, Godard, one of the figureheads of the 1960s art cinema, had by 1968 begun to question it. (*Deux ou trois choses que je sais d'elle* can be seen as a critique of *Deserto rosso*, or even of *Une femme mariée*.) Godard also reintroduced the issue of montage, a process which enabled *Tout va bien* and subsequent works to use Brechtian principles to analyze art-film assumptions about the unity of ideology. If, as some claim, a historical-materalist order of cinema is now appearing, the art cinema must be seen as its necessary background, and its adversary.

Notes

I am grateful to Edward Branigan, Noel Carroll, Bruce Jenkins, Bob Self, Janet Staiger, and Kristin Thompson for their helpful criticism of this essay.

1 More radical avant-garde movements, such as Soviet montage filmmaking, Surrealism, and *cinéma pur* seem to have been relatively without effect upon the art cinema style. I suspect that those experimental styles which did not fundamentally challenge narrative coherence were the most assimilable to the postwar art cinema.

2 See Thomas Guback, *The International Motion Picture Industry* (Bloomington: Indiana University Press, 1969), *passim*.

3 See, for example, Philip Rosen, 'Difference and Displacement in *Seventh Heaven*,' *Screen* XVIII, 2 (Summer 1977), 89–104.

4 This point is taken up by Christian Metz, 'The Modern Cinema and Narrativity,' *Film Language*, tr. by Michael Taylor (New York: Oxford University Press, 1974), 185–227.

5 Arthur Knight compares the Hollywood film to a commodity and the foreign film to an art work: 'Art is not manufactured by committees. Art comes from an individual who has something that he must express . . . This is the reason why we hear so often that foreign films are 'more artistic' than our own. There is in them the urgency of individual expression, an independence of vision, the coherence of a single-minded statement.' In Michael F. Mayer, *Foreign Films on American Screens* (New York: Arco, 1965), vii.

6 'The strategy was to talk about Hawks, Preminger, etc. as artists like Buñuel and Resnais' (Jim Hillier, 'The Return of *Movie*,' *Movie* no. 20 [Spring 1975], 17). I do not mean to imply that *auteur* criticism did not at times distinguish between the classical narrative cinema and the art cinema. A book like V. G. Perkins' *Film as Film* (Baltimore: Penguin, 1978) insists not only upon authorial presence but also upon the casual motivation and the stylistic economy characteristic of the classical cinema. Thus Perkins finds the labored directorial touches of Antonioni and Bergman insufficiently motivated by story action. Nevertheless, Perkins' interpretation of the jeep sequence in *Carmen Jones* in terms of characters' confinement and liberation (pp. 80–82) is a good example of how Hollywood cutting and camera placement can be invested with symbolic traces of the author.

7 See, for instance, Mark Nash, '*Vampyr* and the Fantastic,' *Screen* XVII, 3 (Autumn, 1976),

29–67, and Paul Willemen, 'The Fugitive Subject,' *Raoul Walsh*, ed. by Phil Hardy (London: Edinburgh Film Festival, 1974), 63–89.

8 Norman Holland, 'The Puzzling Movies: Three Analyses and a Guess at Their Appeal,' *Journal of Social Issues* XX, 1 (January 1964), 71–96.

9 See Steve Neal, 'New Hollywood Cinema,' *Screen* 17, 2 (Summer 1976), 117–133, and Paul Willemen, 'Notes on Subjectivity: On Reading Edward Branigan's "Subjectivity Under Siege" Screen XIX, 1 (Spring 1978), 59–64; cf. Robin Wood, 'Smart-Ass and Cutie Pie: Notes towards an Evaluation of Altman,' *Movie* no. 21 (Autumn 1975), 1–17.

10 See David Borwell, *The Films of Carl Theodor Dreyer* (Berkeley: University of California Press, forthcoming).

Chapter 12

Steve Neale

ART CINEMA AS INSTITUTION

T HE AIM OF THIS ARTICLE is to outline through contemporary and historical
examples the role played by what has come to be called 'Art Cinema' in the
attempts made by a number of European countries both to counter American domination of their indigenous markets in film and also to foster a film industry and a film
culture of their own. [. . .]

During the 1960s and early 1970s in particular, at a time when the polemics surrounding 'popular culture' and Hollywood were at their height, Art Cinema was
often defined as the 'enemy': as a bastion of 'high art' ideologies, as the kind of
cinema supported by *Sight and Sound* and the critical establishment, therefore, as the
kind of cinema to be fought. To parody the debate somewhat, it was a question of
Siegel, Fuller, Hitchcock, Hawks and Corman versus Antonioni, Bergman and Fellini,
of genre versus personal expression, of (in some extreme instances) trash versus
taste, hysteria versus restraint, energy versus decorum and quality, *Underworld USA*
(1960) and *Bringing up Baby* (1938) versus *Persona* (1966), *La Dolce Vita* (1960),
8½ (1963) and *The Red Desert* (1964).

This *is* a parody, a simplification. The debates were crossed by all kinds of
complexities [. . .].

What it is true to say is firstly that the debates and polemics were heavily dependent
upon the terms provided by literary ideologies and secondly that Art Cinema itself was
rarely defined. [. . .] There was never any systematic analysis of its texts, its sources
of finance, its modes and circuits of production, distribution and exhibition, its relationship to the state, the nature of the discourses used to support and promote it, the
institutional basis of these discourses, the relations within and across each of these elements and the structure of the international film industry.

All these elements are crucial to Art Cinema. Art Cinema is by no means simply a
question of films with particular textual characteristics, though there are a number of
such characteristics, recurring across its history. Art films tend to be marked by a

stress on visual style (an engagement of the look in terms of a marked individual point of view rather than in terms of institutionalised spectacle), by a suppression of action in the Hollywood sense, by a consequent stress on character rather than plot and by an interiorisation of dramatic conflict. A different textual weight is accorded the proairetic code,[1] whose units are inscribed and articulated in a manner that tends to be distinct from that marking Hollywood films. A different hierarchy is established between action and actant. Different orders of motivation sustain the relations between the two. If cinema has tended massively to exist hitherto as an institution for the perception of the novelistic, then it has historically been the case that it is within the institutional space of Art Cinema that film has most closely approximated that version of the novelistic that we associate with writers like Eliot, Mann, James and Tolstoy, shading at times into the hesitations of the modernist novel (Faulkner, Dostoievsky, the *nouveau roman*), while Hollywood has tended to produce and reproduce the version of the novelistic we associate with the genres of popular fiction. It is also true that Art films are marked at a textural level by the inscription of features that function as marks of enunciation – and, hence, as signifiers of an authorial voice (and look). The precise nature of these features has varied historically and geographically, as it were, since it derives in part from another, simultaneous function that these features perform: that of differentiating the text or texts in question from the texts produced by Hollywood. Hence they change in accordance with which features of Hollywood films are perceived or conceived as dominant or as basically characteristic at any one point in time. In neo-realist films, the features in question are those of location shooting, the absence of stars, a non-systematic laxity in the inscription of the codes involved in articulating spatial and temporal continuities. These features overall connote realism and function as the positive marks of Art both insofar as certain definitions and discourses of Art involve an ideology of realism and insofar as they simply contrast with features marking Hollywood films at this time. In an Antonioni film, on the other hand, the specific features that perform these functions are different. In this case they generally include an extreme de-dramatisation coupled, as a corollary, with a lack of spatio-temporal 'intensity', a problematisation of character motivation and a re-balancing of the weight of attention accorded the human figure on the one hand and landscape and decor on the other. These features are similar to those of neo-realism, however, in that they differ equally, so to speak, from the textual features of Hollywood films. They engage the other primary ideology of Art, the Romantic view that Art is subjective expression. They function both as the signs of such expression and, hence, as the marks of Art itself.

The function of differentiation is crucial. If Art films have tended to display the kinds of features noted above, then this has in part been because they are features that contrast with those of Hollywood. Simultaneously, and partly for this reason, they are features which circulate as the signs of art in established cultural institutions. The importance of this is that Art Cinema is bound to the definitions and value judgements these institutions produce. Their discourses are nearly always involved one way or another in articulating the criteria used to promote Art Cinema in countries seeking to counter American domination of their domestic market in film. Art is thus the space in which an indigenous cinema can develop and make its critical and economic mark.

Equally, to turn the equation around, in competing with Hollywood for a share in the market, or in seeking a space of its own within it, the films produced by a specific national film industry will have in any case to differentiate themselves from those produced by Hollywood. One way of doing so is to turn to high art and to the cultural traditions specific to the country involved. Either way, the films will be shown in different cinemas and be distributed by different distribution networks. And they will be marked by different textual characteristics. In constructing and sustaining such differences, the films will almost certainly tend to coincide with and to become supported by discourses functioning to define and perpetuate art and culture. The only reasons why they may not do so is if they transgress the social, sexual, political and aesthetic boundaries that these discourses construct. In which case they will find themselves in different institutional spheres of circulation: the avant-garde, agit-prop, pornography, and so on.

The discourses of Art and Culture are hostile to Hollywood on a variety of grounds and for a variety of reasons. Hence the variety of Art films themselves: from neo-realism to Felliniesque fantasy, from the austerity of Dreyer and Bergman to the plush visual spectacles of Bertolucci and Chabrol, from the relatively radical narrative experimentation of Antonioni, Godard and Resnais to the conventional story-telling of Visconti, De Sica and Truffaut, from the marxism of Bertolucci to the romantic humanism of Truffaut, and so on. Equally, however, that variety is contained both by the economic infrastructure of Art Cinema, its basis in commodity-dominated modes of production, distribution and exhibition, and by the repetitions that tend to mark cultural discourses in general and the discourses of high art and culture in particular. Hence the relative constancy of those features and elements noted above. Even where the marks of enunciation themselves are heterogeneous, they tend to be unified and stabilised within the space of an institution which reads and locates them in a homogenous way (each mark serving equally as the sign of the author) and which mobilises that meaning in accordance with commodity-based practices of production, distribution and exhibition (the mark of the author is used as a kind of brand name, to mark and to sell the filmic product).

In order to concretise the discussion of Art Cinema, and in order both to disentangle and to interrelate some of the factors and elements involved within it, I want to look in a little more detail at some of the instances and moments in its construction and perpetuation in three different countries: France, Germany and Italy. In each case I want to concentrate as a point of historical and theoretical departure upon the fact of Hollywood's increasing domination of the mass market in these countries after the First World War. From here it will be possible both to pull out a set of recurrent themes, issues and characteristics and to mark a set of differences and specificities, adding one or two important points not detailed in the sketches which follow, before relating them finally to the current situation here in Britain as it affects in particular the work and concerns of British independent cinema.

France

Although something in the nature of an Art Cinema existed in France before the war in the form of Le Film d'Art, a company producing stage classics designed specifically to appeal to a middle-class audience, it was after the war and the consolidation and spread of Hollywood's influence that, as in so many other European countries, a diversification in national production began in conjunction both with a sustained intellectual interest in film (an interest nearly always manifested as a theoretical concern with defining the nature of film as a specific art form) and with the beginnings of production of experimental forms.

Before the war, Pathé Frères had been one of the largest film companies in the world. During the course of the war, however, the German invasion diminished the home market and opened it up to German films, while America seized the opportunity to pour its films into France. [. . .] Ten years or so later Léon Moussinac was simply to write as follows: 'In 1914, 90 per cent of the films shown throughout the world were French; by 1928, 85 per cent of them were American.'[2]

If the industry in France collapsed during the war, it was the war period that saw the first sustained intellectual interest in cinema, with De Mille's *The Cheat* (1915) acting as a specific catalyst for many French intellectuals. Interest was sustained by Abel Gance's *La Roue* (1921), and, in common with many other countries at this time, books and magazines devoted to the 'art' of the cinema began to appear, alongside the establishment of non-commercial cinemas and cinema circuits and alongside the development of a cinematic avant-garde. The Club des Amis du Septième Art was started by the Italian-born art critic Riccioto Canudo in 1920. Canudo had been a supporter of the Italian futurists and cubists and was able to attract a considerable circle of artists and intellectuals to his Club. Louis Delluc, who edited a magazine called *Le Film*, which included Colette, Coceau, Aragon, Germaine Dulac and Marcel L'Herbier among its contributors, founded the Ciné Club de France (which merged with the *Club des Amis du Septième Art* on Canudo's death in 1923). Germaine Dulac founded the Fedération Française de Ciné-Clubs in 1925. Two specialised cinemas opened in Paris in 1924, the Vieux Colombier and the Studio des Ursulines.

All these cinemas were committed to the emerging French avant-gardes and all were also to show films from abroad, notably work from the Soviet Union, which was to have such an impact on Europe in the twenties. It is important that a number of the figures mentioned above not only promoted experimental films through their participation in exhibition, but also wrote about them and made them themselves. Between 1919 and 1923, Delluc wrote and directed six films and provided scripts for many others. Germaine Dulac directed *La Souriante Madame Beudet* in 1922 and *The Seashell and the Clergyman* in 1928. Jean Epstein made *La Daphnie* (1925), *Coeur Fidéle* (1923), *La Glace à Trois Faces* (1927) and *Finis Terrae* (1929). Marcel L'Herbier made *L'Inhumaine* (with sets designed by Léger, Mallet-Stevens, Autant-Lara and Cavalcanti) in 1924 and *Feu Mathias Pascal*, based on a novel by Pirandello, in 1925. Much of this work was privately financed. Germaine Dulac had her own production company and L'Herbier's work after 1924 was financed by himself. Renoir's first films were also privately financed. A number of these people also worked within the industry, however, and it is perhaps significant that L'Herbier, for example, started by making films for Gaumont. It was only at the point at which Gaumont was absorbed by Metro-Goldwyn in 1925, that he branched out on his own.

Overlapping, historically, with the 'first French avant-garde' Dadaist and Surrealist work in the cinema was similarly supported by the exhibition infrastructure of *ciné-clubs* [. . .]. Films by Man Ray, Buñuel and Dali, however, depended exclusively upon private financing and patronage, with the Comte de Noailles being particularly important in this respect: as well as financing *L'Age d'Or* in 1930, he also financed Cocteau's *Le Sang d'un Poète* (1930).

Although a number of these films produced in the 1920s fed into the notion of a national cinema of quality (especially and obviously those produced within the industry itself), it is important to stress both the influence and popularity of elements of Hollywood cinema among the intellectuals, writers and film-makers of the time (especially the Surrealists) and the extent to which all avant-garde activity was marked by an ideology of internationalism. [. . .]

The arrival of sound both markedly changed the structure of the French film industry and ensured the disappearance of the avant-garde. The extra cost of sound films eliminated many of the smaller film companies and made private sponsorship and patronage almost impossible. The early 1930s also saw the establishment of large-scale multi-language productions in Paris by Paramount and the German company, Tobis. Co-productions continued throughout the decade with UFA, but a number of German emigrés worked in the French industry during the same period.

Although small companies established in the 1920s disappeared with the coming of sound, others continued to proliferate, though they were generally under-capitalised and short-lived, and it was these which tended to provide the base for the films and the film-makers that became synonymous with 'Art cinema' in the 1930s: Renoir, Prévert and Carné, Jacques Feyder and Julien Duvivier; *Toni* (1934), *La Bête Humaine* (1938), *Le Kermesse Heroïque* (1935), *Le Jour se Lève* (1939), *Pépé Moko* (1936) and so on. The French market was dominated by foreign films. According to Roy Armes the native film industry never supplied any more than 25 per cent of the films distributed annually in France.[3] With the withdrawal of the two combines formed out of Pathé and Gaumont in the mid-1930s, film production became very unstable: out of this situation arose both the films mentioned above and the precariously-based production companies that made them.

In 1940, the industry fell under German control and in 1942 a new system of finance and control was set up with the Comité d'Organisation de l'Industrie Cinématographique. This was replaced after liberation by the Comité de Libération du Cinéma Française, itself dissolved and replaced in 1946 by the Centre National du Cinéma Française. The CNCF incorporated all the various production organisations involved in the French industry, and one of its immediate aims was to protect it against an influx of foreign – especially Hollywood – films by reinforcing its quota system. In 1949, the Loi d'Aide à l'Industrie Cinématographique was passed, giving aid on a non-selective basis to French producers through a tax of 25 per cent on receipts from foreign films. This law expired in 1953 and was replaced by the Loi de Développement de l'Industrie Cinématographique.

The importance of this law was that enormous stress was placed on art, culture and education both in drafting the law and in arguing and reporting it to the various state bodies involved. [. . .] The feature films benefiting from this system – in a sense the product of its ideology – included Marcel Camus' *Mort en Fraude* (1956), Chabrol's *Le*

Beau Serge (1958) and Louis Malle's *Ascenseur pour l'Echafaud* (1957). Short films, particularly important for directors like Franju (who made nine before moving into features) and Resnais (who made eleven), were also covered by the law. Again, the emphasis in distributing funds was on quality and culture [. . .].

Despite all this, it should be noted that the late 1950s (the period of the emergence of the New Wave), was a period of crisis, with a sharp decline in cinema attendance from 1957 on. The New Wave was partly a product of this crisis. What is interesting and important to note about it is, first, that it grew directly out of a school of critical writing, second, that it related itself to the re-construction of a national film-making tradition (with Vigo, Cocteau and Renoir especially prominent), third, that it consisted in large part of a re-inscription of elements of Hollywood cinema across the terms of the art film, and finally that its emergence was, to a considerable extent, due to the cheapness of the films and to the existence of 'enlightened' producers like De Beauregard and Braunberger.

Largely as a response to the crisis, there was a further reorientation of state intervention in 1958 and 1959. In 1958, the Assemblée Nationale increased the number of prizes for quality shorts from 80 to 120. The same year, tax concessions were granted to the *ciné-clubs* and the *cinémas d'art et d'essai*, contributing towards the development of a numerically powerful Art house circuit (that year over five million spectators attended the *ciné-clubs* alone). In 1959, with Malraux as Minister of Cultural Affairs, and as part of his policies for the encouragement of art and culture, the Centre National de la Cinématographie came under his ministerial aegis. And in June, following the expiry of the 1953 legislation, a whole series of measures was introduced to encourage the production, distribution and exhibition of 'quality' films, the most significant being the introduction of interest-free advances on box-office receipts, distributed in accordance with criteria laid down by a specially constituted committee. These measures led, directly and indirectly, to the funding of films like *Jules et Jim*, and *La Femme Infidèle*. [. . .]

The basic system continued through the 1960s and into the 1970s, though it was modified after the events and criticism of May '68 specifically to encourage 16mm production and the work of new film-makers. It continues to exist today after the essence of its modes of financing was re-adopted in 1976. If, however, these structures and practices continue to exist, so too does the problem of the domination of Hollywood and American distributors. As a final confirmation of this, it is worth noting that in 1977, the percentage of aid to distributors worked out so that the six companies distributing Hollywood films received 40%, the eleven commercial French distributors 44%, the 35 distributors of *films d'art et d'essai* only 4% and the 63 independents 12%. Even within the terms of the Art cinema problematic it can be seen there are considerable drawbacks, while the problematic itself, of course, remains open to criticism that it erects a false distinction between commerce and culture and that it tends to ghettoise the work of film-makers whose films circulate only in the Art house nexus:

The whole economic and aesthetic evolution of French cinema since 1958, in other words for the last twenty years, has served only to accentuate the gap between commercial and 'cultural'

*production . . . This conception [ie Malraux's] which in effect counterposes culture and educa-
tion is based on an overvaluation of the former and on the complete absence of consideration of
the cultural needs of the public in its broadest sense.*[4]

Germany

As in so many other countries during the period of the early 1910s, Germany partic-
ipated in the movement towards an early form of Art Cinema based largely in
'classical' literature and drama, both historical and contemporary. Following the
Kineform manifesto of 1910 (signed, among others, by Gerhart Hauptmann, Hermann
Sudermann, Arthur Schnitzler and Paul Lindau), Oskar Messter founded a subsidiary
to Messter Film GmbH called Autoren Film specifically to produce art films [. . .].

Foreign domination of the national market occurred very early in Germany, with
the number of German-produced films in distribution heavily outweighed by films
imported from American and (especially) Denmark and France. The 1914–18 war
aided and strengthened the domestic industry considerably, with the home market
closed to many foreign countries and the French industry suffering from German
occupation and war. It was towards the end of the war, in 1917, that UFA was
founded, funded in part by the state and in part by large banking and industrial interests. UFA was essentially an umbrella organisation, covering all three spheres of
production, distribution and exhibition, though for a long time its primary concern
was with distribution (it was only officially registered as a production company in
1924).

At the end of the war, the government was forced to relinquish its stake in UFA, but
its initial position of strength enabled it to weather the economic crisis of the early
1920s and to establish itself in the face of intense American competition. It was
responsible for the first significant international economic and intellectual successes
after the war [. . .] and played a significant part in the 'expressionist' films of the
period 1919 to 1926.

Germany passed the first quota legislation in film history on 29th May 1920 with
the Reich Film Act, restricting the number of foreign imports to 15% of its overall
annual total (a figure amended the following year). The act also imposed a municipal
entertainment tax on cinema seats, but, crucially, concessions were granted to those
exhibitors showing films recognised as having artistic and cultural value by a special
committee of cultural 'experts'.

Partly as a consequence of these legislative measures, partly as a consequence of
UFA's strategies and strengths both domestically and abroad [. . .] and partly as a consequence of the effects of domestic inflation on production, investment and export,
there was a postwar boom in German film production. The film produced included
a series of titles serving them, as subsequently, as the very indices of Art Cinema, from
the 'expressionist' cycle (*Caligari* (1919), *Waxworks* (1924), *Warning Shadows* (1922) et
al) through the *Kammerspiele* (from *Backstairs* (1921) to *The Last Laugh* (1924) to a series
of period spectacles (*Tartuffe* (1925), *Faust* (1926) and *Manon Lescaut* (1928)). What is
important to note about this phenomenon is not only that it was encouraged by the

1920 legislation, but also that it was pursued as a conscious policy by producers as a means of gaining international prestige and access to foreign markets.

[. . . A]part from features and its activities in distribution and exhibition, UFA produced a whole series of documentaries whose generic title was, precisely, the *Kulturfilm*, promoted by the slogan 'The world is beautiful; its mirror is the *Kulturfilm*.'[5]

UFA was by no means the only important film company in Germany at this time. The development of German Art Cinema owed its existence also to a multitude of small independent commercial production companies: Phoebus, Gloria, Helios, Luna, Terra, Nero, Rex, Neptune and so on. Because of its size and because of its presence in the sphere of distribution, however, UFA remained important, though it was forced in 1925 to sign away much of its autonomy in an agreement with Paramount and Metro-Goldwyn, following the Dawes plan and the stabilisation of the mark. With the introduction of a new monetary system, the previous currency could no longer be used to finance foreign trade. UFA was then cut off from its export market. The Parufamet Agreement, as it was called, gave Paramount and Metro-Goldwyn effective control of UFA's quota certificates and its movie theatres in exchange for loans. UFA, however, regained some of its former autonomy when Hugenberg stepped in in 1927 [. . .].

Richter, Balász and Ruttmann were all influential and important figures with the German cinematic avant-garde in the 1920s. What distinguished the German avant-garde at this time was that although, like elements within the French avant-garde, its activities had social and political dimensions, they were dimensions which were often institutionalised and formalised: through connections with the Bauhaus, through links with Piscator's theatre in Berlin, through the production of films by political parties, through organisations like the Popular Association for Film Art and the German League for Independent Film (which arranged screenings and discussions of avant-garde and Soviet films) and through the existence of links with the Soviet Union through Willi Muenzernberg's organisation, International Workers' Aid. [. . .] Alongside the use of private capital for avant-garde production, there also existed, then, some opportunities within the mainstream industry and a socially-radical infra-structure for the production, distribution, exhibition and (importantly) criticism and discussion of films.

The coming of sound radically curtailed the possibility of producing films outside of the industry proper – if only for reasons of cost. With the coming to power of the Nazis, many film-makers fled the country. The issue of Hollywood's domination of the national market came to be re-articulated within the terms provided by a specifically nationalist ideology. Relations between the state and industry were reorganised both by means of the establishment of a set of interlocking cultural apparatuses and by means of the establishment of the Filmkreditbank, the FKB.[6] The industry was finally nationalised in 1942, and it should be noted that throughout the period of Nazi rule, the cinema, like the other arts, was conceived of as having a specific role to play in the construction and re-construction of a German cultural heritage, encouraged by the existence of a system of prizes and awards based on criteria of artistic and cultural merit.

After the war, the German industry was heavily restructured in line with American foreign policy. Production was dispersed and American domination ensured, while the problems of the German industry were exacerbated by a determination to make it independent of imports and to regain for German production the whole of the home market. The result was a stream of insular and provincial commercial genres.

Various systems of state aid began to be introduced in the 1950s in the form of government-guaranteed credits and, later, subsidies through tax-relief. [. . .] However, as Thomas Elsaesser had pointed out, the systems worked either in favour of those already occupying a dominant position within the market and/or functioned as a means of censorship within the climate of the Cold War.[7]

The facts and details of state intervention following the Oberhausen Manifesto of 1962 are fairly well known: the setting up of the Kuratorium junger deutsche film in 1965, the Film Subsidy Bill of 1967, and the various interlocking systems of grants, subsidies and prizes since then, each feeding into the establishment of the 'New German Cinema'. What needs re-stating in this context is, firstly, that there was a very limited home market for these films. They achieved international acclaim (and international distribution) but lacked distribution and exhibition opportunities within Germany itself. Secondly, the cultural criteria involved in the distribution of the funds available were heavily linked to a romantic conception of authorship through the concept of the *Autorenfilm*,[8] with the result that the New German Cinema was a series of star films by star names, the films themselves almost obliged to contain marks of personal eccentricity (Herzog's perhaps are both the most extreme and the most typical, taking the logic to its limits).[9] Thirdly, and despite the role of television in providing a space both for production and exhibition, the contradictions and the political problems produced by the vicious circle of a continually declining commercial sector, a culturally privileged production divorced from a strong exhibition network, and a plurality of funding sources each geared within a narrowly defined set of cultural criteria have caused severe problems for film-makers lacking the adroit opportunism of someone like Fassbinder.

Italy

In rely to the vogue for French *Films d'Art* (inaugurated by *The Assassination of the Duke de Guise*), the Italian industry towards the end of the first decade of the 1900s produced its own *Série d'Or*, beginning with Luigi Maggi's *The Last Days of Pompeii* in 1908. The *Last Days of Pompeii*, a classical epic spectacle, was to inaugurate a specially important and successful cycle which included *Quo Vadis?* (in its numerous versions), *Spartacus* (1914), and above all, in 1914, *Cabiria*. As well as epics, Italy drew upon Shakespeare, Dante, Dumas and others in film versions of *The Three Musketeers*, *Hamlet*, *Macbeth*, *The Inferno* and *Joan of Arc*. Pathé, the producers of Film d'Art, were so worried that they established a subsidiary in Rome entitled the Film d'Arte Italiano (FAI), while one of the epics, *The Fall of Troy* (1911) became so well known internationally that it broke the American Motion Picture Patents company's blockade on European independent production.

The producers of these films, primarily Ambrosio, Cines and Itala, established a domestic position of great strength in the face of French and American productions thanks both to their *Série d'Or* and to the advantages they enjoyed by virtue of Italy's late entry into the First World War. The Italian futurists, meanwhile, were polemicising for an explicitly Italian avant-garde, and wrote extensively about the cinema. 1916 saw the publication of a manifesto entitled *The Futurist Cinema* published by Marinette, Corra, Emilio Settimelli, Arnaldo Ginna, Giacomo Balla and Remo Chiti, as well as the production of Arnaldo Ginna's *Vita futuristica* and three films by Anton Bragaglia *Il mio Cadavere*, *Il perfido Incanto* and *Thaïs*, each (presumably) privately financed.

Neither the futurists nor the international prestige and success of the Italian cinema much outlasted the war. A holding company, l'Unione Cinematografica Italiana (UCI) was founded with capital provided by the Banca Commerziale Italiana, Banca Italiano di Sconto and Credito Commerziale di Venezia under Giuseppe Barattolo in a move to strengthen the Italian industry, but foreign markets became gradually closed to Italian films following the invasion of Hollywood producers and distributors. UCI was dissolved in 1923 after making its last film (another version of *Quo Vadis?*) with the help of German capital.

These events fed into a series of measures, statements and discussions concerned with the Italian industry and Italian film culture that occurred during the period of fascist rule under Mussolini. On the 2nd April 1926 a royal decree instituted a commission of enquiry into the industry which led to establishment of L'Unione per la Cinematografica Educativa (LUCE) and the passing of a quota law in October decreeing that at least 10% of the films shown in the Italian cinema should be Italian. Meanwhile a group of young critics centred around the magazines *Cinematografo* and *Lo Schermo* (Umberto Barbaro, Francesco Pasinetti, Luigi Chianni and Alessandro Blasetti) began to articulate a demand for a new cinema 'inspired by genuine facts and social realities'.[10] They formed a production company, Augustus Film, and produced Blasetti's first film *Sole* in 1929.

With the coming of sound, the Italian state began to restructure the film industry even further, with the aim of stimulating Italian production. The Direzione Generale per la Cinematografica was founded in 1935, a year which also saw the opening of the Sezione Cinematografica of the Banca del Lavoro, the state bank. The Sezione Cinematografica was opened specifically as a means by which to encourage the production of culturally approved films on the basis of advances on box-office receipts. Meanwhile, Cinecitta studios, opened by Carlo Roncoroni, were taken over by the state on his death in 1937. The following year a system of rebates to producers was established which were paid in proportion to box-office takings. The result of all these measures was a steady increase in domestic production, which accelerated appreciably during the war, from 30 films in 1933 to 119 in 1942. As in the case of Germany during the fascist period, state intervention overall was clearly linked to a wish to produce a national (indeed nationalist) cinema marked by specific ideological and artistic features. Not an Art Cinema as such, but, rather, something like a nationalist popular cinema; not a cinema that was necessarily exportable, nor one that appealed to the values of 'art' and 'culture' as established in the capitalist democracies.

The end of the war saw both the emergence of the neo-realist movement and the swamping of the Italian market by American movies. Neo-realism became the very paradigm of Art Cinema in the period immediately following the war, from the late 1940s through to the early 1950s. It embodied [. . .] realism, humanism, lack of spectacle, lack of excesses in style and technique and so on.[11] It is important to note firstly that its unity as a movement was conjunctural insofar as it was dependent upon a particular political situation: 'the euphoria of liberation and the alliance of all political forces – Liberal, Catholic, Socialist and Communist – involved in the struggle against Fascism and German occupation'.[12] Secondly, many of the directors and critics involved in neo-realism had at some point been connected either with the Centro Sperimentale di Cinematografia, founded by the state in 1932, and, or with one of the two major film journals, *Bianco e Nero* and *Cinema*. Thirdly, as regards production, distribution and exhibition, neo-realism was a hybrid phenomenon, in part commercial, in part receiving state support (*Bicycle Thieves* (1949) was financed by the state distribution service, Italneggio, and exhibited in the state exhibition circuit), and in part linked to political organisations like the ANPI (Associazone Nazionale Partigiani Italiani). Fourthly, despite its international prestige, neo-realism came under strong attack from the government in 1949, partly because it was considered to lack commercial potential and partly because of its political overtones. Under the 'Andreotti Law' of December 1949, the Direzione Generale dello Spettacolo, a body empowered to subsidise films, was established, and it used its powers to stop, in effect, both the production and international distribution of neo-realist films.

The Andreotti Law was introduced in response to the flood of imported films and the concomitant crisis within the Italian film industry after the war. According to Thomas Guback, 600 American films were exported to Italy in 1946.[13] Over 800 films a year were imported to Italy over the next three years. Under Andreotti's proposals, a system of support for the industry was devised, consisting essentially of a tax on imported films to support domestic production. For each film imported, the distributor had to deposit 2,500,000 lire with the Banca del Lavoro. The money was channelled into a fund from which producers could draw at very low interest rates. There as thus no technical restriction on imported films (and exemptions were granted in return for import licences from foreign countries for more Italian films), but the number of American imports was reduced and Italian production was increased, aided still further by the signing of a co-production agreement with France. The agreement was signed in 1949, following calls from Italian producers themselves [. . .].

Like the Andreotti Law, the agreement with France was designed specifically to aid the production of 'quality' films, and thus to gain a niche within the world market [. . .].

During the period that followed, up until the next major Aid Law in 1965, the Italian Art Cinema flourished, with films by Antonioni, Fellini, Pasolini and Bertolucci, among others, making their critical and financial mark both nationally and internationally.

The Aid Law of 1965 largely strengthened both the systems of state aid and the cultural ideology lying behind it. The law, indeed, stated the importance of the social function of cinema as 'a means of artistic expression, cultural information and social communication'.[14] The production fund of the Banca del Lavoro was augmented by state funds, and producers were empowered to draw up to 30% of their production costs at an interest rate of 3%, the fund being specifically designated as support for films 'inspired by artistic and cultural aims'.[15] There was also a system of prizes offered for films of cultural merit.

The situation remains much the same today, with state funding channelled through the Banca del Lavoro (2 million lira in 1978 going to 'films of artistic and cultural merit'[16] and with a system of awards and prizes acting in conjunction with import restrictions and co-productions to sustain the Italian industry as a whole and its Art Film sector in particular.

There are one or two other points worth noting. One is the powerful and influential role played by producers like Dino de Laurentiis and Carlo Ponti. Another is the way in which a considerable portion of funding is reserved for promotional and cultural activities: festivals, conferences and the like. This is especially true of funding at a municipal level and is a result of inter-party rivalry; the Christian Democrats and the PCI compete with one another for cultural prestige. The third and final point to note is the crucial role played nowadays by Italian television (there are similarities with the role of television in France and Germany). RAI 2 has produced and shown films by Rossellini, Bertolucci, Olmi, Petri, Cavani and Pasolini, as well as films by Straub-Huillet and Jancso. Importantly, it pays high fees for showing Italian films and has engaged in a significant number of culturally prestigious co-productions. Once again, inter-party rivalry (articulated in the control of RAI 1 and RAI 2) has played an important part.

The rough pattern of the history of Art Cinema in these countries is thus as follows: following an early period in which the cinema appealed to and addressed what would seem to have been a largely proletarian audience, a number of countries, including Germany, France, Italy and the United States (through Zukor's distribution company Famous Plays by Famous Players) began developing a cinema which sought an address to the bourgeoisie. A process of change and differentiation was at work, but the shift was less towards a bourgeois audience and away from the proletariat than a shift towards an address to the two together. The war provided Hollywood with an opportunity to extend its share of the world market and to challenge the prominence hitherto enjoyed by France and Scandinavia in particular. Concomitantly, through the work of Griffith especially, Hollywood films themselves succeeded in allying proletarian and bourgeois genres with novelistic conventions of cinematic narration, thus producing a unified and unifying mode of textual address, a genuinely popular form of entertainment with a mass rather than a class-based audience.

The mode and terrain of Art Cinema thus shifted during the 1920s, emerging as a strategy through which to counter Hollywood's dominance in line with the first acts of legislation (quota laws and the like) designed to restrict the flood of Hollywood product. The 1920s in fact saw a considerable fragmentation and differentiation in production, distribution and exhibition with the beginnings of the emergence of those distinct spaces of cinematic activity we are used to today: entertainment, Art Cinema, the avant-garde, agit-prop and political cinema, and so on. [. . .]

The coming of sound consolidated these distinctions (in effect eclipsing avant-garde production until after the Second World War) and ensured the hegemony of Hollywood and novelistic entertainment. State support for indigenous European industries increased, especially in the fascist countries, but it was not until after the Second World War that state support became firmly linked to the promotion and development of national Art Cinemas under the aegis of liberal-democratic and social democratic governments and under the pressure of the presence of America and Hollywood in Europe. The result was an efflorescence of Art Cinema, the production of the films and the figures and the movements with which Art Cinema tends massively to be associated today. Before pulling some general and theoretical points from the historical sketches given above, it is worth, firstly, stressing the extent to which [. . .] historically, censorship and sexuality have figured as crucial elements in the emergence and consolidation of Art Cinema. The development of film clubs and *ciné-clubs* in the 1920s – the exhibition basis for the subsequent emergence of Art Cinema as a distinct sector within the cinematic institution – was due in large part to censorship restrictions on the showing of films from the Soviet Union. The Soviet films themselves became the models for notions of film as art and the fact that they were subject to political censorship meant that they could only be shown in private members' clubs. The conjunction of censorship with an intellectual interest in the aesthetics of the Soviet films and with the construction of a specific exhibition space not only for Soviet films but also for other films considered to have particular 'artistic' qualities set the seal on the construction of Art Cinema as a cinematic space distinct from that of the mainstream cinema of entertainment. Censorship continued to be an important factor from the 1930s on, though less in the area of politics than in the area of the representation of sexuality.

It could be argued that the cinematic tradition constructed and reconstructed over the years as the tradition of Art Cinema has always been concerned with the inscription of representations of the body that differ from those predominating in Hollywood. With the emergence of the star system at the point of the elaboration and stabilisation of novelistic modes of cinematic narration, the body, in Hollywood, became simultaneously the incarnation of the coherence of fictional characterisation and the nodal site of a fetishistic regime of eroticisation and sexual representation. Together with a reticence of gesture and (later) vocal delivery, these features came definitively to mark the representation of the body in Hollywood films. European Art Films from the 1920s on were marked by (major and minor) differences. German expressionism stresses the rhetoric of bodily movement and gesture; Soviet films were often marked by a refusal of the star system, the use of non-professional actors, and, in Eisenstein's case at least, the development of a system of 'typage'; Renoir's films stressed the artifice of acting, pushing the oscillation between body and role as far as it would go within the limits imposed by the novelistic;[17] neo-realism was marked by its refusal to use stars; Antonioni's films often stressed the plastic qualities of the body as a component part of an overall decor by refusing certain elements of character and narrative motivation; Fellini's films, from *La Dolce Vita* (1960) onwards, constructed an 'over-inscription' of the fetishised body of the star (especially the female star) through a rhetoric of systematic hyperbole; and so on.

Part and parcel of this process of differentiation has been, since the mid-1930s at least, a difference of the 'explicit' representation of sexuality and sexual activity in general and the female body in particular. It is a difference whose existence and significance for Art Cinema was importantly determined by the adoption of the Hays Code in Hollywood in 1934. Before the Hays Code, sexuality and censorship were issues and features common to both European and Hollywood cinema. From time to time the product of certain specific countries acquired a special notoriety (the Danish white slave trade cycle and the 'health and hygiene' films produced in Germany towards the end of the First World War are two examples), but, by and large, each country produced films which were equally 'explicit', equally notorious and equally subject to demands for censorship and propriety. Indeed, it seems there was a very specific regime of sexual representation tied to the epic and the historical spectacle that was common to the United States, Italy and France in particular, and included films by De Mille, Griffith, Gance and Von Stroheim. The adoption of the Hays Code arose partly as a consequence of vociferous demands for the censorship of films in the United States. It was a way in which Hollywood was able to ward off the threats (as much economic as ideological – censorship legislation in individual states would have made many films unmarketable on a national scale) and to standardise its own product as 'family entertainment'.

The Code prohibited representations of sexuality, the naked male and female body, and sexual relations and activities. On the continent, censorship systems and the debates around them drew heavily upon discourses around the 'adult' nature of art and around 'realism', linking it with debates around the representation of sexuality in the other arts. The consequence was that continental films differed – or were able to differ – from those of Hollywood with respect to representations of sexuality and the cultural status that those representations were able to draw upon. Hence films like *Une Partie du Campagne* (1936), *La Bête Humaine* (1938), and *Le Jour Se Lève* (1939). (The fact that these examples from the 1930s are French rather than German or Italian is a reflection of the fact that the latter at this time were fascist countries). However, since the Hays Code was in effect the instrument of the Motion Picture Producers and Distributors of America (MPPDA – later the MPPA, Motion Picture Association of America), and since the MPPDA controlled the entire industry in America, films from outside the United States which were considered to infringe the Code were denied distribution and exhibition. After the war though, as the anti-trust legislation began to divorce exhibition from production and distribution and thus to weaken the grip of the MPPA (as it was then) and the Hayes Code as it applied to imported films, alternative distribution and exhibition circuits began to be formed to show films from Europe including those which would previously have been denied access to American screens.

With the opening of a market in America, European films were able to trade more stably and commercially both upon their status as 'adult' art and upon their reputation for 'explicit' representations of sexuality. Hence the steady accumulation of these films through the 1950s and into the 1960s: *La Ronde* (1950), *Summer with Monika* (1952), *And God Created Woman* (1956), *La Notte* (1960), *L'Eclisse* (1962), *La Dolce Vita* (1960), *Les Amants* (1958), *Viridiana* (1961), *The Silence* (1963), *8½* (1963), *Une Femme Mariée* (1964) and so on. Indeed, it could be maintained that from the mid-1960s onward

Art Cinema has stabilised itself around a new genre: the soft-core art film. Hence *Last Tango in Paris* (1972), *Belle de Jour* (1967), Pasolini's trilogy of *The Arabian Nights* (1974), *The Decameron* (1970) and *The Canterbury Tales* (1971), as well as *Theorem* (1969) and *Salo* (1975), *L'Amour Fou* (1968), *La Bête* (1975), *Immoral Tales* (1974), *Casanova* (1977) *The Night Porter* (1973), *Private Vices, Public Virtues* (1976) and so on. Where previously the history of Art Cinema had been, apart from its authors, one of a series of unstable and short-lived movements (expressionism, Poetic Realism, neo-realism, the New Wave), the names of its authors, indeed, serving as the only conceptual means by which to categorise its output consistently, it now appears that there is a relatively permanent genre towards which Art Cinema internationally has begun to gravitate, assured as it is of an international market, notoriety and (generally) a degree of cultural and artistic prestige.[18]

It is at this point that I want to pull together some elements from the historical sketches of Art Cinema in France, Italy and Germany, pointing to a number of general characteristics and drawing some general conclusions [. . .]. I shall be concentrating largely on the limitations and problems of Art Cinema and of Art Cinema policies. But it is important to state firstly that Art Cinema has, historically, provided real – if limited –spaces for genuinely radical work, though the impact of that work has often been blocked and nullified by the overall institutional contexts in which it has found itself. Moreover, despite the generalisations I shall make, it is, certainly for those working towards a radical practice of cinema in the countries I have instanced, the differences, distinctions, specificities and opportunities that are important.

The first important general point to note about Art Cinema is that it always tends to involve balance between a national aspect on the one hand and an international aspect on the other: at the level of the market, at the level of the discourses of film theory and film criticism, at the level of the discourses involved in the articulation of policies (either within the industry or within the state) at the level of legislation, and at the level of the films themselves.

The production, distribution and exhibition of films always takes place within the context of predefined national boundaries, cultures, governments and economies. Because of the determinations exercised by this context, Hollywood's international dominance is nearly always conceived by the countries whose markets it dominates as a specifically *national problem*. Because of this, policies articulated as a solution to the problem nearly always involve the construction and reconstruction, firstly of a national industry to whose experiences they can refer and to whose structures, practices and problems their statements can be addressed, and secondly of national cultural and cinematic traditions which the measures embodied in such policies are expected to foster, through protection, encouragement and incentive. [. . .] Legislation – in the form of quotas, subventions, prizes or awards – can only apply across a national territory organised through a national state apparatus (though this may be modified with the development of EEC legislation) and almost always involves definitions of what constitutes an Italian (or French or German) film. It is only on the basis of such definitions that aid laws can function. Hence while the films made within any one country will tend inevitably, because of the overdetermined situation in which they are produced, to derive their intertextual affiliations from national cultures and traditions, the adoption of Art Cinema policies tends to re-mark such affiliation, encouraging their systematic inscription into the films produced under the aegis of such policies. The films themselves thus participate actively and systematically in the construction and reconstruction of particular national identities while the marks of nationality with which they are inscribed serve further to differentiate them from the films produced in Hollywood. [. . .]

There is also an important international dimension to Art Cinema. Art films are produced for international distribution and exhibition as well as for local consumption. Art Cinema is a niche within the international film market, a sector that is not yet completely dominated by Hollywood (though it is one that Hollywood has begun to take seriously, as its European co-productions and as films by Altman, Coppola and others perhaps start to illustrate). Art Cinema also, in its cultural and aesthetic aspirations, relies heavily upon an appeal to the 'universal' values of culture and art. And this is very much reflected in the existence of international film festivals, where international distribution is sought for these films, and where their status as 'Art' is confirmed and re-stated through the existence of prizes and awards, themselves neatly balancing the criteria of artistic merit and commercial potential. This international aspect of Art Cinema is one reason why the policies pursued by the fascist governments in Italy and Germany during the 1930s and 1940s cannot simply and easily be seen merely as extreme initial tendencies in what was to become a general trend. In these instances the international dimension was missing and the policies were elaborated within the context of very specific nationalist ideologies.

Art Cinema is always, then, a matter of balance between these two aspects. The nature of this balance can perhaps best be exemplified by the fact that during the course of their international circulation, Art films tend nearly always to retain a mark which serves simultaneously as a sign of their cultural status and a sign of their national origin. This mark is that of the national language. When they are shown outside of their country of origin, where their national status and their place within specific national traditions will be evident, Art films tend to be subtitled rather than dubbed. The international circulation of 'entertainment' films, by contrast, tends to involve the erasure of this mark. The balance between the two elements is, thus, a different one.

National Art Cinema policies involve, of necessity, mechanisms of selection, differentiation and evaluation in the allocation of funds through loans, guarantees, prizes and awards. To that extent, they also require the elaboration of a set of criteria as to what, in any one instance, constitutes 'art', 'culture' and 'quality' and, as a corollary, a set of marks is inscribed into the films, projects, scripts and scenarios to which these criteria are applied, differentiating them from conventional commercial projects and signifying their status as Art. There exists, then, a space for the intervention of a number of competing definitions of art, culture and quality and for the consequent funding of a range of practices differing from those of the mainstream commercial industry. Historically, however, that space has been foreclosed. What has tended to fill it has been an ideology of art as individual expression, manifest both in policies to support and to fund new film-makers (conceived as individuals who otherwise would be denied the means to express themselves) and in the prevalence of *auteurism* within the discourses circulating centrally across the institutions involved in Art Cinema as a whole. Hence the German *Autorenfilm*. Hence the dominance of *auteurist* ideologies in funding committees, awards panels and juries. And hence at a broader cultural level, the overwhelming association of Art Cinema as a whole with a set of individual names: Antonioni, Bergman, Bertolucci, Bresson, Buñuel, Chabrol, Dreyer, Fassbinder, Fellini, Herzog, Truffaut, Visconti, Wenders, etc.

There are a number of reasons for this. Concepts of art as individual expression are predominant within most cultural institutions and discourses. And they are readily mobilised in marking and conceptualising what is held up as a basic difference between Hollywood and Art Cinema: that the former is the realm of impersonal profit-seeking and entertainment where the latter is the realm of creativity, freedom and meaning. Authorship, moreover, can perform other functions. It can exist as a means of accounting for and unifying conceptually the multiplicity of differences that can exist between Art films and Hollywood films, reducing that plurality to a single homogeneous principle. The name of the author can function as a 'brand name', a means of labelling and selling a film and of orienting expectation and channelling meaning and pleasure in the absence of generic boundaries and categories. And as a means of categorisation itself the concept of the author is essential to aid policies geared to the funding of individual films rather than to funding specific practices. In giving a coherent rationale both to the policies and to the films they produce (they are all instances of 'self-expression' – hence their eclectic heterogeneity), authorship serves partly as a means by which to avoid coming to terms with the concept of film as social practice.

Overdetermining all these reasons and, indeed, most of the other features that mark Art Cinema and its films, is the fact that to varying degrees Art Cinema functions and has always functioned in terms of a conception of film as commodity. Art Cinema, fundamentally, is a mechanism of discrimination. It is a means of producing and sustaining a division within the field of cinema overall, a division that functions economically, ideologically and aesthetically. The terms of that division are constructed through a discrimination between art and industry, culture and entertainment, meaning and profit. However, the division and its discriminations do not, in general, function so as to challenge the economic, ideological and aesthetic bases of the cinematic institution as it currently exists. They function, instead, so as to carve out a space, a sector, *within it*, one which can be inhabited, so to speak, by national industries and national film-makers whose existence would otherwise be threatened by the domination of Hollywood. In the division of labour it sustains (with the ideology of authorship reinforcing a distinction between intellectual and manual labour); in the practices of production, distribution and exhibition it entails (with the relations between distribution and exhibition on the one hand and production on the other taking the form of commodity circulation); and in the forms and relations of representation with which it is associated, Art Cinema has rarely disturbed or altered fundamentally the commodity-based structures, relations and practices of what it likes nevertheless to label the 'commercial' film industry. It has merely modified them slightly. Certainly, radically avant-garde and insistently political practices have been persistently relegated either to its margins or else to a different social and cinematic space altogether.

Notes

1 See Roland Barthes. S/Z, Hill and Wang, New York, 1974.

2 Quoted in Eric Rhode, *A History of the Cinema*, Allen Lane, 1976, pp. 17–18.

3 Roy Armes, 'Images of France', *The Movie*, no 16, p. 301.

4 Michel Marie, 'L'Art du Film en France Depuis La "Nouvelle Vague"', *Cinema Aujourd'hui*, 12/13 Autumn/Winter 1977, p. 53.

5 See Siegfried Kracauer, *From Caligan to Hitler*, Princeton UP, 1971, p. 65.

6 For details see Julian Petley, *Capital and Culture, German Cinema 1933–1945*, BFI, London 1979, pp. 51–55.

7 Thomas Elsaesser, 'The Postwar German Cinema', in Tony Rayns (ed) *Fassbinder*, BFI, London 1976.

8 See Sheila Johnston 'The Author as Public Institution', *Screen Education*, nos 32/33 Autumn/Winter 1979/80.

9 Elsaesser, op. cit., pp. 13–14.

10 Quoted in Jean Mitry, *Histoire du Cinéma* vol. 2, Editions Universitaires, Paris 1967, p. 369.

11 John Ellis, 'Art, Culture and Quality – Terms for a cinema in the Forties and Seventies', *Screen*, vol 19 no 3, Autumn 1978.

12 Geoffrey Nowell-Smith, 'Voyage to Italy: Rossellini in Context', *Eye to Eye*, September/October 1979.

13 Thomas Guback, *The International Film Industry*, Indiana University Press 1969, p. 24.

14 Quoted in Goffredo Fofi, *Il Cinema Italiano: Serve e Padroni*, Feltrinelli, Milan 1973 p. 48.

15 Ibid., p. 48.

16 These figures are quoted in the *Report of the Committee on Culture and Education*, Council of Europe, Strasbourg, 1979.

17 See Jean-Louis Comolli, 'A Body Too Much', *Screen*, vol 19 no 2, Summer 1978. Comolli refers only to *La Marseillaise* but similar remarks apply also, in certain respects, to *Nana*, *La Règle du Jeu*, *La Grande Illusion*, *The Golden Coach* and *The Vanishing Corporal*.

18 It is in this context that Paul Willemen's remarks on the fourth look and voyeurism with respect to the art film and pornography acquire a particular significance. See 'Letter to John', *Screen*, vol 21 no 2, Summer 1980, esp pp. 57–58.

Chapter 13

Sheila Johnston

THE AUTHOR AS PUBLIC INSTITUTION

The 'New' Cinema in the Federal Republic of Germany

D URING KONRAD ADENAUER'S CHANCELLORSHIP (1949–1963) the international reputation of the West German cinema steadily declined until it was widely regarded as among the worst in Europe. It is perhaps hardly surprising that the subsequent revival should appear almost miraculous against this gloomy background. Certainly it was interpreted and presented as such by the popular media, which exploited the myth of the romantic visionary with relish – understandably so, for it is an appealing and picturesque myth. Journalists ascribed the change to the talents of three or four favoured directors, focusing attention on colourful personalities such as Werner Herzog or Rainer Werner Fassbinder. *Time* described how 'led by these two young visionaries, the New German wave has emerged with astonishing speed and surprise' and *Newsweek* enthused about 'a dedicated corps of young directors' who were 'putting Germany back on the cinematic map'. In this country the myth was disseminated by a BBC *Omnibus* report at the end of 1976.[1]

The German-speaking press took much the same line. A Swiss paper was typical in attributing the renaissance to 'not more than a dozen individuals working away on their own in a disorganised fashion'. Urs Jenny found a striking metaphor for the New Wave that obscurely hinted at an unresolved and slightly troubling paradox: 'Suddenly young film directors shot up like mushrooms after the rain – even though it hadn't rained'. A sense of malaise also pervades Ulrich Gregor's account of the crucial events in the early Sixties. At no less than three points in it he returns to the time-lag between the Oberhausen manifesto and the first spate of films, but without either explaining the delay or drawing the conclusion that no simple cause-and-effect relationship existed between the two events.[2] The picture mediated by these writers was overwhelmingly of a cinema more or less conjured into existence by a handful of young lobbyists and aspiring film-makers. And in some ways the movement *was* spontaneous, as a postwar generation deeply critical of what they contemptuously dubbed 'papa's cinema' came of age. But as Jenny's unresolved paradox seems to imply, it remains improbable that a small nucleus of directors, however determined or brilliant, could change the face of the West German cinema overnight and virtually single-handed.

This article sets out to trace the career of the concept of the *auteur* (or, in German, *Autor*) within the 'new' German cinema – a concept which may suggest an explanation for this mythology about its origins. The auteurist method implies understanding a film primarily as the personal statement of its creator and so has tended to leave out of consideration the institutional framework within which the work was produced. A popularised version of this approach can be discerned in the accounts I have quoted above: the economic, social and political circumstances of the films' inception are buried in their treatment as 'Wenders' or 'Fassbinder' works. But I should like to re-establish a link between the films as 'personal statements' and as 'products of an institutional framework'. My argument is not just that some highly individualistic West German films in the Sixties and Seventies seem to invite an auteurist reading, but that the conditions for an *Autor* cinema were deliberately cultivated (in conjunction with certain industrial, political and cultural developments) rather than accidently propitious.

Oberhausen and the Kuratorium

The origins of the movement are usually traced back to the Festival of Short Films at Oberhausen in February 1962, where twenty-six directors, writers and other film-makers issued a manifesto.

> The Oberhausen manifesto proclaimed the new German film that was to be free of the usual conventions of the industry, free of influence from commercial partners and free of the control of interested parties . . . The *Autor* film was henceforth to make history . . . The fundamental principle . . . was that the film-maker should have autonomy in giving shape to his film idea without having to take legal or serious financial risk. He was to retain control over the direction and the entire production process including the unrestricted commercial exploitation of his film. This concept was clear, but, in the situation of the German film at the time, highly unorthodox.[3]

This account of the manifesto is taken from the official history of the *Kuratorium junger deutscher Film* which was set up three years later in 1965 by the Federal Government with a mandate to fund the type of film 'proclaimed' by the Oberhausen group.

The concept of the *Autor* film implied both that it should clearly convey the vision of its creator and that the director should retain overall control without having any financial obligations. By the mid-Sixties much criticism and even popular journalism had taken up these two principles. But the most detailed rationale for the *Kuratorium* can be seen in an essay written in 1971 by Norbert Kückelmann,[4] founder member and, initially, the head of this funding agency. The question he addressed was how a 'subsidised institute of sponsorship' could safeguard the 'freedom of art'. Because administrators – even those committed to this principle – may define art inflexibly and so exclude a wide range of creative activities, Kückelmann rejected potentially 'restrictive' formal criteria in favour of St Augustine's dictum that 'art is what the artist creates'. An attempt to discern a work of art should be 'first and foremost guided by what is without a doubt the characteristic feature of all artistic creation, namely the expression of a commitment on behalf of its originator.' Kückelmann's shift of emphasis from the text to the author was in line with one of the *Kuratorium*'s main criteria in awarding aid: that film should be immediately recognisable as the avatar of its director's personality. But, he went on to argue, contemporary conditions posed a severe threat to such self-expression. Culture as commodity and, he implied, the mass media were seen as inimical to 'art', understood as a haven for the creative individual beleaguered by cupidity and philistinism.

[. . .]

In this context Kückelmann saw similarities between the demands of the Oberhausen manifesto and the article on *Les Etats Généraux du cinéma français* which was published by *Cahiers du Cinéma* in 1968 and which 'established that film-making today is dominated by the profit motive':

> Film remains a commodity . . . Film-making as understood by this generation of directors meant liberation from prescribed subject-matter and forms of dissemination and thus also the liberation of the public from the strangle-hold of a disastrous system of concentration of economic power characterised by the tendency to misuse film as a commodity and by state censorship geared to preserving the status quo.

The artist's 'engagement' with his or her position within the 'culture industry' and the reaffirmation of the primacy of art over the 'pressures of consumer society' were, argued Kückelmann, inextricably linked to a broader interrogation of existing social conditions.

Here, some of the contradictions inherent in the concept of the *Autor* are apparent: the artist opposed to 'economic and social power structures' yet 'liberated' from them and operating outside their ambit, the artist apparently critical of the debasement of art within a specific political system (capitalism) yet deeply pessimistic and mistrustful of 'modern industrial society' in general.

The project of the *Juratorium* was to reinstate the 'extremely underprivileged' director as 'true originator of the film work', an intervention seen as impossible within the existing structures of the industry.

> Within an industry that turns out 'off-the-peg' movies, the director cannot pass on his own independent ideas and there is no room for individual initiative or commitment; instead he increasingly becomes the mere executor of tried and tested stereotypical and schematised plots.

What was needed to stimulate artistic development, in Kückelmann's view, were new contractual relations for the director which would protect the needs of the

individual and free him or her from the lowly status of employee with all the limitations – and rights – that organised labour bestowed: [. . .]

The *Kuratorium* planned to do this by 'incorporating the independence of the director's activity as a condition of the contract' and by binding subsidies 'to the person of
the director'. Kückelmann regarded this approach to production as the sole hope for
Federal German film culture.

Auteurs and Autoren

In defining the particular inflection given to the concept of authorship in the ideology
of the *Kuratorium* and of the *Autor* film, it may be useful to distinguish it from the ways
in which it was used in the French *politique des auteurs* and in anglo-american auteur
theory. However deep and sometimes acrimonious the division within it may have
been, auteur criticism generally implied a principal criterion of directorial continuity
which was to be established by looking retrospectively at all the works of a particular
director. This feature was common to auteurists like Andrew Sarris who would 'look
at a film as the expression of a director's vision' and to 'auteur-structuralists' like Peter
Wollen who preferred to 'decipher, not a coherent message or world-view, but a
structure which underlies the film and shapes it', shifting attention away from the
directorial personality towards 'an unconscious, unintended meaning [which] can be
decoded in the film, usually to the surprise of the individual concerned'.[5] The
approach was also polemical, locating itself as a *re*-interpretation of work hitherto mis-
understood or undervalued. In many cases it was linked with an attempt to re-evaluate
popular cinema and Hollywood in particular, and was directed against the positions
embodied in John Simon's assertion that it is 'wrong to prefer Superman to Joseph
K . . . not morally wrong (though in some cases that too), but aesthetically wrong' and
Pauline Kael's censure of auteurism as a misguided justification of 'junk'.[6] Auteurs
therefore had to be rediscovered: Robin Wood, for example, set out to prove to
sceptical readers 'why [we should] take Hitchcock seriously' in the introduction to his
book on the director.[7]

In contrast to this project of showing that artistic self-expression was possible even
in an industrial system like Hollywood, the West German directors, writers and
administrators were arguing that the *Autor* film could only be made under conditions
which assured the director-producer absolute financial and artistic control. Moreover,
whereas the critical accolade of 'auteur' could only be awarded to a director on the
strength of an achieved body of work, the *Autoren* were defined as from the very
outset, often before they had even made a film – the vast majority of the Oberhausen
signatories had not made a feature at the time of the manifesto. It was to 'train young
directors for a cinema of *Autoren*' that the Department of Film-Making was established
at Ulm in 1963 under the aegis of Alexander Kluge.[8]

An essay written in 1967 by Franz Schöler reveals the same approach at the level of
criticism. Although acknowledging that 'an essential quality in the true *Autor* is the
consistency with which his personality is expressed in film', Schöler examined a
number of *début* films with a view to ascertaining whether 'the young German cinema

is a cinema of *Autoren*'. His criteria were 'the spiritual pervasion of the material', 'a distinctive vision of reality', 'a personal universe (one of the French auteur critics' favourite words)' and an ability to 'convey and reflect on ideas'. His conclusion, not altogether unexpectedly, was that 'the films of the first wave can, with slight reservations, definitely be regarded as *Autor* films'.[9] Indeed, in reading other discussions of the *Autor* film, one is immediately struck by the absence of controversy about who qualified for the kudos of authorship. A general consensus seemed to obtain in the unquestioning acceptance of the 'new' directors' designation of themselves as *Autoren*.

Schöler was concerned to establish the distinctiveness and instant recognisability of individual films rather than consistency across an oeuvre. And whereas the *Cahiers* approach called for an appreciation of visual properties and formal beauties, even in thematically banal Hollywood genre movies, Schöler stressed the primacy of thematic originality, the film as vector of ideas. It is around these questions of conventionality and popular cinema that the *Autoren* split most decisively from the auteurists, who followed Bazin's argument that the genre form could actually enable a director to draw on 'an artistic evolution that [had] always been in wonderfully close harmony with its public'.[10] Thus Robin Wood claimed that the genre form could build on 'strong and familiar foundations', the knowledge that the audience had acquired from countless similar films, so that its director's vision could 'find the fullest and freest expression'.[11] The polemical edge of Wood's argument was that pleasure and popular appeal in film were absolutely compatible with success as a work of art. So although the orthodox distinction between serious (European) cinema and popular (American) cinema was rejected, a comparison of Hitchcock with Shakespeare or (in the case of *Cahiers*) of D. W. Griffith with Bach implied that a new intake should be admitted into the 'pantheon' of high art whilst leaving the pantheon itself and all it stood for largely intact. But though the wall that separated commerce and art continued to stand, its foundations had been radically undermined. Aesthetic excellence was no longer automatically equated with the relative freedom from commercial pressures thought to be the sole prerogative of the European 'art' movie director: now value-judgements would have to be supported by the evidence of the actual films.

The supporters of the *Autor* film took quite a different line. Their strategy was to oppose 'formula movies' and to displace cinema as 'a factory of dreams and illusions'.[12] [. . .] Writing in 1965 about the Department of Film-Making in Ulm, Alexander Kluge contrasted the *Autor* film with the 'culinary film' (*Zatatenfilm*) for which 'the producer buys up stars, material, ideas, directors, specialists, script-writers, etc'.[13] In an article in a *Kuratorium* publication in 1968, Ulrich Gregor insisted that *Autoren* should not be 'confined within specific genres' but, liberated from 'economic and dramaturgical rules' and 'established forms of cinema aesthetics', should produce 'personal testimonies, structures of ideas, chains of association, reflections of feelings'.[14] These writers called for a completely fresh start. But whereas even the French 'New Wave' directors, who had been able to count on a cinematically literate audience, did not disdain the benefits of popular cinema, the West German enterprise was far more hazardous, for it aimed to create subjective, idiosyncratic and extremely demanding films in a context of minimal public interest and a desolate cinema culture.

One reason for this desire for an absolute break with the past was an acute shame at the heritage of the postwar German film industry. Yet the French reaction against a native 'tradition of quality' produced, in the turn towards American culture, very different results. The West German rejection of precedent, of whatever kind, suggested the conviction that the gifted *Autor* must be allowed to work untrammelled not only by material but also by formal constraints and that aesthetic merit could not be accommodated within a blatantly commercial cinema.[15] This hostility towards Hollywood may have been tinged with a growing disenchantment, by no means confined to the Federal Republic, with the American presence in Europe – and in Vietnam. And West German attitudes towards the United States were in any case complex. The double face of America as saviour from fascism but also as the former 'enemy' and occupying power reflected the ambivalence of West Germany's own self-image. American culture was experienced, according to Wim Wenders, as both a liberating impulse and a threat to national identity [. . .]

[. . .] The tenor of all this writing was of an emphatic denial that gifted *Autoren* could operate within any 'popular' context at all. Whereas Sarris hoped that the auteurist approach would draw attention to individual trees thriving within the Hollywood forest,[16] the purpose of the *Kuratorium* seemed to be the cultivation of tender young saplings in a specially protected nature reserve.

One of the first to point out the implications of this project was the critic Wilfred Berghahn.[17] He commented that the structure demanded in the Oberhausen manifesto was 'outmoded, because it was completely pre-industrial' – an atavism reflected in Volker Schlöndorff's preference for a 'small artisan-like workshop' or Werner Herzog's comparison of his production company to a 'market woman who sells vegetables'.[18] Their views clearly match a recent observation that literary thinking in the West Germany of the Sixties, although voiced in terms of 'politics and sociology', was 'energised by a romantic anti-capitalism expressive of a general contempt for modern industrial society'.[19] This 'obsession with whatever is thought to weaken or to disrupt the cohesion of individual and social existence' gives a new (and less radical) gloss to Kückelmann's view of art as 'an individual defence against pressures from economic and social power structures' – a shift of emphasis underlined by a comparison with a particularly vehement prophecy written from an antagonistic political position in 1964. The author was Berthold Martin, architect of the plan on which the 1967 Film Subsidy Bill was substantially based:

> The threat that all people experience today now affects culture itself because the incursion of technology is leaving less and less room for individual self-expression . . . The threat also emanates from the indisputable intention of communism to make Soviet man the future model of mankind. In both cases the danger is of collectivism: on the one hand as the result of technological civilisation and on the other as the product of ideology and power.[20]

Equally anachronistic were the ideas informing many of the debates about the purpose of the film academies. An important feature of the training at Ulm was that students should not become 'specialists stuck in the "culinary" thinking of the film industry' but *Autoren* 'who would differ from specialists in having a greater responsibility' and in

conceiving film as a 'general medium of expression of intelligence and human experience'.[21] [. . .]The journal *Filmkritik* likewise stressed the need for a 'universal film
education' and for an academy that would allow a talented élite to evolve 'without
being harnessed to and worn out by the commercial production industry'.[22] Even
Heinz Rathsack, who was to become head of the Berlin Film School, spoke in terms
of 'the education of the total personality' and of directors familiar with all aspects of
production so that they could 'draw on them as the responsible *Autor* of a film'; his
paradigm was the Bauhaus in whose programme the architect had the task of 'fusing
the work of the individual disciplines into a *Gesamtkunstwerk* of the visual arts'.[23] The
Autoren were supposed to synthesise and to impose order and meaning upon the fragmented elements of a highly technological society through the force of their
personalities and through the elimination of the division of labour usual in film-
making. Running through all these arguments about film academies is the idea of
Bildung, the traditional German notion of education not as specialised vocational
training nor even as education in all aspects of the production process, but as something closer to the classical ideal of the cultivation of multiple talents, refinement,
spiritual formation and the full development of personality and creative potential.

Television

For the auteur theorists authorship was a critical tool. The idea of the *Autor*, on the
other hand, was a programmatic principle which was to be achieved not just by arguing for a particular relation of director to film, but by setting up new legal, contractual
and institutional relations and special forms of training. The blossoming of the *Autor*
film was also favoured by the peculiar structure of the West German television companies. In the early Sixties these had already helped to foster a national cinema culture,
mainly by producing and commissioning new film material. But the companies were
predisposed not only towards film production but, especially, towards *Autor* film production. The reasons for this were partly economic, but were also connected with
their status as public corporations charged with mirroring 'the principle of a representative democracy'. As such, according to Friedrich Wilhelm von Sell (*Intendant* of
the *Westdeutscher Rundfunk*), they had to follow the principle of 'mediating a plurality
of opinions'. Von Sell argued that one way of ensuring that 'a variety of opinions on
all important subjects' could be conveyed was by purchasing material from freelance
sources,[24] a strategy which helped to create (and indeed depended for its success
upon) a large pool of independent workers. [. . .]

But as well as being representative, the television companies also had to be 'balanced'. (The concept was inscribed in the system of proportional representation
under which the party-political composition of supervisory boards and key programme staff in a particular station was to reflect that of the government of the *Land*
it serviced.) This balance was under constant scrutiny and frequent attack and some
critics even argued that it should be maintained within individual programmes as
well as across the whole output.[25] This is the context in which von Sell distinguished
'information/objectivity' from 'opinion/subjectivity': insistence on the *individual*

'recognisability of the bias of the commentator's opinion' could absolve the broad-casting station of institutional partiality. [. . .]

The concept of the *Autor* fitted neatly into this pattern. By attaching a programme to a 'name' director (particularly one whose autonomy was further validated by not being on the permanent staff), the television stations could both avoid the charge of 'excessive timidity' and at the same time acquire as an added bonus the prestige of a patron of the arts. [. . .]

Decline of the Autor

[. . .]n the Seventies changes both in the material conditions of film production and in critical attitudes undermined the status of the *Autor* film. In 1967 the *Kuratorium* was superseded as the main agency for awarding government aid to film by a new institu-tion, the Film Subsidy Board; the established industry had ensured that its funding criteria would be box-office success and a quick turnover. A year later the *Kuratorium*, the 'cultural' institution for public sponsorship, faced draconian cuts in its budget when it came up for renewal. As a result, independent directors found it increasingly difficult to finance their projects.

At the same time, the flow of funds from the television companies was drying up. Anthony Smith outlined the reasons to Annan:

> Many of the freelance producers had always been treated as if they were reg-ular employees for whom no established post existed . . . [But] in the period of inflation and economic strain which began in the early Seventies, the German freelance began to find that his standard of living was under threat . . . [and] began to become more militant; as the discussion about 'producers' rights' developed, it became apparent that the freelance, now working against market forces, was more vulnerable to institutional pressures than the staff man. The whole issue of the security of employment of free-lances became inseparable from the problem of freedom of expression for creative workers in broadcasting . . . Radio and television had existed for years by convincing large numbers of hard-working but humdrum employees that, in working without security, they were somehow 'artists'. That is what attracted them to the life of insecurity. In fact only a tiny minority of creative people in broadcasting were genuine 'artists' for whom complete detachment from an institution was essential. Under the pressure of the great inflation of 1973–75, the German freelance system discovered its weakest point and started to crumble.[26]

It may seem that in demanding both complete autonomy and a steady income the inde-pendents wanted to have their cake and eat it too – but the issues were not that simple. For one thing, the claims by the film-makers and their union that freelance fees were not keeping pace with the cost of living were later admitted in certain quarters by the television companies themselves.[27] At a deeper level, their plight can be traced back to the unresolved and always potentially explosive tensions latent in the concept of the *Autor* which, though itself multiply determined, called for a haven for creative activity supposedly immune to the very forces which had caused its own inception. By initially focusing on the 'crafted' and individualistic nature of their mode of production, the proponents of the *Autor* film blurred the contemporary economic framework within which, in spite of everything, they had to operate. Many knew themselves to be, like the travelling theatrical director (another uniquely West German phenomenon), subject to 'the laws of a capitalist economy [whose] supreme law is the saleability of the offered ware.'[28] But it was only when the financial cutbacks inevitable in the periods of recession reduced the demand for their 'commodities' that a shift of focus was effected to bring the economic conditions of existence of the film *Autor* into sharp relief.

A guaranteed income seemed particularly alluring as the shrinking market began to cause hardship for many independent film-makers and, backed by the union, some freelances successfully sued the television companies for permanent employment. The supreme irony of this was the fact that the terms on which this coveted security was granted – according to Harun Farocki,[29] economic dependence, regular employment and working under instruction (*Weisungsgebundenheit*) – were the very same aspects of film production from which Kückelmann had hoped to free the *Autor*. [. . .]

There can be little doubt that the *Autor* film as originally conceived by Kluge and Kückelmann is on the wane in the Federal Republic. Its career, which depended on the existence of an alternative production system, was largely a function of the growth and decline in the availability of resources for independent film-making. One decisive moment came in the late Sixties when the *Kuratorium* failed to achieve the commercial success necessary for its target of self-sufficiency. Another blow came from a 1969 survey, in which the psychologist and sociologist Ernst Dichter reported that cinemagoers could not understand the 'new' films and felt 'irritated and annoyed' by them. The trade press told the *Autorenfilmer* to 'stop sulking in their esoteric corner' and to make films 'that appealed to the public'. The same disenchantment gradually spread to other, more disinterested critics. In *Die Zeit* in 1972, a leading film journalist wrote that 'the group issuing from the Oberhausen manifesto' had been making films which became 'more and more esoteric and estranged from the public'. The following year *Der Spiegel* commented sceptically that the 'latest penchant' for 'good strong stories and picturesque landscapes' was 'a sorely needed attempt to escape from the art-ghetto . . . and to be popular – at any price'. In the same vein, *Stern* reported that 'Kluge and many of the others admitted that he and his colleagues had often produced *Autor* films for the museum and had neglected the cinema at the corner of the street'. When the journal *Filmfaust* was launched at the end of 1976 to provide a platform for newcomers, it regarded the *Autor* film-makers as belonging to the enemy camp just as much as the established industry and attacked the *Autor* film as a reified 'institution' estranged from the public. *Filmfaust*'s alternative was a 'spectator's film' more appropriate to the needs of West German audiences.

At this point the negative associations of the *Autor* film were firmly entrenched. The term almost invariably occurred in conjunction with the epithet 'esoteric' and the films were often compared unfavourably with a popular cinema – such as Hollywood. The path described by the concept of the *Autor* seemed to have come full circle. The initial rejection of genre forms, stereotypical plots, star names and all the other ingredients of a 'culinary film' geared to 'fulfilling market needs' had been abandoned and a director like Fassbinder was commended for using 'stars that invite identification' and the 'clichés of the culture industry', for his 'lack of inhibitions towards popular culture' and his ambition to make 'not esoteric *Autor* films, but films for a mass audience . . . films designed to entertain.' These changes show some of the central weaknesses (the dismissal of popular culture and the delusion of total autonomy) in the argument for the *Autor* film. But, despite its failings, the concept did raise important questions – about the place of 'the author' in the legal and economic relations of film production, for example, and about the intellectual formation of film-makers – which were never ultimately resolved.

Notes

1 Gerald Clark 'Seeking Planets That Do Not Exist' in *Time* 20/3/78; Carter S. Wiseman et al. 'The German Film Renaissance' in *Newsweek* 2/2/76. *Signs of Vigorous Life*, written and produced by Peter Adam, was first broadcast on 2/12/76.

2 Peter W. Engelmeier 'Nicht länger mehr ein Kino-Zwerg' in *National-Zeitung* (Basle) 21/8/76; Urs Jenny 'Nach einem Jahr: Der junge deutsche Film' in *Merkur* May 1967; Ulrich Gregor *Geschichte des Films ab 1960* Munich, Bertelsmann 1978 pp. 122, 123 and 128. (All translations from the German are mine unless otherwise noted.)

3 'Die Entwicklung der Kuratoriumsarbeit' in Hermann Gerber (ed) *Kuratorium junger deutscher Film 1965–1976* Munich 1977.

4 Norbert Kückelmann 'Filmkunstförderung unter sozialstaatlichem Aspekt' in *UFITA* v59 1971.

5 Andrew Sarris *The American Cinema* New York, Dutton 1968 p. 36; Peter Wollen *Signs and Meanings in the Cinema* (3rd edn) London, Secker & Warburg 1972 pp. 167–8 and 91–4.

6 John Simon *Movies into Films* New York, Dial Press 1971 p. 3; Pauline Kael 'Circles and Squares' in *Film Quarterly* Spring 1963.

7 Robin Wood *Hitchcock's Films* New York, Castle 1965 p. 7.

8 Alexander Kluge, 'Die Utopie Film' in *Film* n2 1965.

9 Franz Schöler 'Ist der junge deutsche Film ein Kino der Autoren?' in Constantin Film *Der junge deutsche Film* Munich, Wagner 1967.

10 André Bazin 'La Politique des Auteurs' in *Cahiers du Cinéma* n70 1957, translated by Peter Graham in *The New Wave* London, Secker & Warburg 1968.

11 Robin Wood *Howard Hawks* London, Secker & Warburg 1968 p. 12.

12 Hilali et al. *Dschungelbuch* Kassel, Gesamthochschule Department of Graphic Design 1977 p. 3.

13 Kluge op. cit.

14 Ulrich Gregor 'Autorenfilm im Wandel' in Norbert Kückelmann (ed) *Die ersten drei Jahre*, brochure published by the *Kuratorium* in 1968.

15 One of the major mediators of this conviction was the influential journal *Filmkritik*, which propagated a vulgarised version of the Frankfurt School's critique of mass culture. See the statement in the first issue of 1957, and the article 'Hollywoods Antwort' by the editor Enno Patalas in the sister publication *Film 58*, n.1.

16 Sarris op. cit. pp. 19ff.

17 Wilfred Berghahn 'Kino der Autoren – Kino der Produzenten' in *Die Zeit* 17/4/62.

18 See Barbara Bronnen and Corinna Brocher's collection of interviews *Die Filmemacher* Munich, Bertelsmann 1973 pp. 85, 12.

19 R. Hinton Thomas and Keith Bullivant *Literature in Upheaval* Manchester University Press 1974 pp. 182–3.

20 Berthold Martin 'Kultur als Politik und Politik als Kultur' in Martin (ed) *Jahrbuch der auswärtigen Kulturbeziehungen* Bonn, Akademischer Verlag 1964.

21 'Das Ulmer Projekt' in *Neue Zürcher Zeitung* 12/6/63; Hans-Jürgen Weber 'Ulm – Eine Schule für Regisseure' in *Filmecho/Filmwoche* nn101–102 1966.

22 Enno Patalas 'Die Chance 1' in *Filmkritik* n4 1962; Wilfried Berghahn & Enno Patalas 'Eine Filmakademie für Deutschland' in *Filmkritik* n4 1964.

23 Heinz Rathsack *Vier Filmhochschulen* Bonn, Schriftenreihe des Verbands der Film – und Fernsehgemeinschaften an den deutschen Hochschulen 1964.

24 Friedrich Wilhelm von Sell *Wie wird der Bürger vor einseitiger Meinungsvermittlung geschützt?*, conference paper, Bitburg 1977.

25 An article by von Sell's predecessor Klaus von Bismarck ('Wie zersetzend darf eine Sendung sein?' – in *Die Zeit* 4/2/66) gives a graphic account of the 'very diverse expectations' which an *Intendant* was expected to fulfil. The debates on 'balance' can be traced in the pages of *Medium*.

26 Anthony Smith paras 30, 32 'The German Television Producer and the Problem of Internal Democracy' in Annan op. cit.

27 Ernst W. Fuhr 'On the legal position of freelance workers in broadcasting organisations in the Federal Republic of Germany' in *European Broadcasting Union* vXXIX n5 September 1978.

28 Volker Canaris 'Style and the Director' in Ronald Haymann (ed) *The German Theatre* London, Oswald Wolff 1975 p. 252.

29 Harun Farocki 'Notwendige Abwechslung and Vielfalt' in *Filmkritik* n8 1975.

Chapter 14

Andrew Higson

THE CONCEPT OF NATIONAL CINEMA

ALTHOUGH THE TERM 'NATIONAL CINEMA' is often used to describe simply the films produced within a particular nation state, this is neither the only way in which the term has been used, nor is it, I want to argue, the most appropriate way of using the term. This article is not, however, intended as an examination of any historically concrete national cinema. It is intended instead as an exploration of some of the implications of using the term 'national' in discourse about cinema (the film industry, film culture), moving towards an argument that the parameters of a national cinema should be drawn at the site of consumption as much as at the site of production of films; an argument, in other words, that focuses on the activity of national audiences and the conditions under which they make sense of and use the films they watch. In so far as reference is made to historically specific national cinemas, most of my examples would relate to British cinema (and, of course, Hollywood), but I would hope that much of what I have to say is generalisable to other national cinemas – at least those of Western Europe – as well.[1]

The concept of national cinema has been appropriated in a variety of ways, for a variety of reasons: there is not a single universally accepted discourse of national cinema. In general terms, one can summarise these various mobilisations of the concept as follows. First, there is the possibility of defining national cinema in economic terms, establishing a conceptual correspondence between the terms 'national cinema' and 'the domestic film industry', and therefore being concerned with such questions as: where are these films made, and by whom? Who owns and controls the industrial infrastructures, the production companies, the distributors and the exhibition circuits? Second, there is the possibility of a text-based approach to national cinema. Here the key questions become: what are these films about? Do they share a common style or world view? What sort of projections of the national character do they offer? To what extent are they engaged in 'exploring, questioning and constructing a notion of nationhood in the films themselves and in the consciousness of the viewer?'[2]

Third, there is the possibility of an exhibition-led, or consumption-based, approach to national cinema. Here the major concern has always been to do with the question of which films audiences are watching, and particularly the number of foreign, and usually American films which have high-profile distribution within a particular nation state – a concern which is generally formulated in terms of an anxiety about cultural imperialism. Fourth, there is what may be called a criticism-led approach to national cinema, which tends to reduce national cinema to the terms of a quality art cinema, a culturally worthy cinema steeped in the high-cultural and/or modernist heritage of a particular nation state, rather than one which appeals to the desires and fantasies of the popular audiences.

In other words, very often the concept of national cinema is used prescriptively rather than descriptively, citing what *ought* to be the national cinema, rather than describing the actual cinematic experience of popular audiences. As Geoffrey Nowell-Smith has noted, it has always been something of a struggle to enable 'the recognition of popular forms as a legitimate part of national cultural life'.[3]

If these are some of the ways in which the term national cinema has been used, what are the processes by which, or what are the conditions under which, a particular mode of film practice, or a specific range of textual practices, or a particular set of industrial practices comes to be named a national cinema? Indeed, what is involved in calling forth the idea of a national anything, cultural or otherwise. In other words, what is involved in positing the idea of nationhood or national identity?

To identify a national cinema is first of all to specify a coherence and a unity; it is to proclaim a unique identity and a stable set of meanings. The process of identification is thus invariably a hegemonising, mythologising process, involving both the production and assignation of a particular set of meanings, and the attempt to contain, or prevent the potential proliferation of other meanings. At the same time, the concept of a national cinema has almost invariably been mobilised as a strategy of cultural (and economic) resistance; a means of asserting national autonomy in the face of (usually) Hollywood's international domination.

The process of nationalist myth-making is not simply an insidious (or celebratory) work of ideological production, but is also at the same time a means of setting one body of images and values against another, which will very often threaten to overwhelm the first. The search for a unique and stable identity, the assertion of national specificity does then have some meaning, some usefulness. It is not just an ideological sleight of hand, although it must always also be recognised as that. Histories of national cinema can only therefore really be understood as histories of crisis and conflict, of resistance and negotiation. But also, in another way, they are histories of a business seeking a secure footing in the market-place, enabling the maximisation of an industry's profits while at the same time bolstering a nation's cultural standing. At this level, the politics of national cinema can be reduced to a marketing strategy, an attempt to market the diverse as, in fact, offering a coherent and singular experience. As Thomas Elsaesser has suggested, 'internationally, national cinemas used to have a generic function: a French, Italian or a Swedish film sets different horizons of expectation for the general audience – a prerequisite for marketing purposes',[4] and it is this attempt to establish a generic narrative image, a particular horizon of expectation, which is at stake.

There are perhaps two central methods, conceptually, of establishing or identifying the imaginary coherence, the specificity, of a national cinema. First, there is the method of comparing and contrasting one cinema to another, thereby establishing varying degrees of otherness. Second, there is what might be termed a more inward-looking process, exploring the cinema of a nation in relation to other already existing economies and cultures of that nation state.

The first of these means of defining a national cinema is premised upon the semiotic principle of the production of meaning and identity through difference. The task is to try to establish the identity of one national cinema by its relationship to and differentiation from other national cinemas: British cinema is what it is by virtue of what it is not – American cinema, or French cinema, or German cinema, etc . . . Elsaesser again: 'Other countries try to maintain themselves on a terrain staked out by the competition. West Germany is one example, but the implications affect all developed countries whose sense of cultural identity is based on a need to maintain markers – and markets – of difference vis-à-vis the products of the international entertainment business.'[5] To some extent, then, the process of defining a national cinema, and thereby establishing some sort of unique and self-contained identity, takes meaning in the context of a conceptual play of differences and identities. And, as Benedict Anderson has argued, 'nations . . . cannot be imagined except in the midst of an irremediable plurality of other nations'.[6]

Within this discourse cinema itself is almost taken for granted, and the task becomes one of differentiating between a variety of apparently nationally constituted modes of cinematic practice and filmically produced signs and meanings. Such an operation becomes increasingly problematic as cinema develops in an economy characterised by the international ownership and circulation of images and sounds. It is therefore necessary to examine the overdetermination of Hollywood in the international arena. By Hollywood, I mean the international institutionalisation of certain standards and values of cinema, in terms of both audience expectations, professional ideologies and practices and the establishment of infrastructures of production, distribution, exhibition, and marketing, to accommodate, regulate and reproduce these standards and values. While Hollywood's classical period and its studio system may have disappeared, whatever the prophecies about the end of cinema in the late 1970s and early 1980s, cinema – and Hollywood – are, in the late 1980s, still very much alive and key components in the international mass entertainment business. This is the era of the multiplex, the package deal, the blockbuster, but also the revival of genre cinema and the serial film, even if the site and system of delivery are no longer primarily theatrical.

Hollywood never functions as simply one term within a system of equally weighted differences. Hollywood is not only the most internationally powerful cinema – it has also, of course, for many years been an integral and naturalised part of the national culture, or the popular imagination, of most countries in which cinema is an established entertainment form. In other words, Hollywood has become one of those cultural traditions which feed into the so-called national cinemas of, for instance, the western European nations. 'Hollywood can hardly be conceived . . . as totally other, since so much of any nation's film culture is implicitly "Hollywood"'.[7] Being both a naturalised part of national culture, and also, visibly different, even exotic,[8] Hollywood thus functions as a double mode of popular fantasy, hence its propensity to be dismissed as escapism.

Geoffrey Nowell-Smith has attempted to account for the appeal of American films in the British market as follows – and his account would seem at least to be partially applicable to other national cinemas as well:

> The hidden history of cinema in British culture, and in popular culture in particular, has been the history of American films popular with the British public. The strength of American cinema was never just economic . . . [and] the basic reason for Hollywood's dominance was artistic and cultural. The American cinema set out in the first place to be popular in America where it served an extremely diverse and largely immigrant public. What made it popular at home also helped make it popular abroad. The ideology of American cinema has tended to be far more democratic than that of the cinema of other countries. This in part reflects the actual openness of American society, but it is above all a rhetorical strategy to convince the audiences of the virtues and pleasures of being American. Translated into the export arena, this meant a projection of America as intensely – if distantly – appealing. When matched against American films of the same period, their British counterparts come across all too often as restrictive and stifling, subservient to middle class artistic models and to middle and upper-class values.[9]

At times, Nowell-Smith's claims seem overstated.[10] To suggest, for instance, that 'British cinema ; has never been truly popular in Britain'[11] is to ignore the box-office success over the years of numerous British stars, films, genres and cycles of films. And to argue in terms of a generalised, monolithic 'British public' is to ignore class, race, gender and regional differences. Even so, Nowell-Smith's revaluation of American films in terms of the appeal of apparently democratic aspirations seems useful. For a start, it displaces the idea that American box-office success in foreign markets is due solely to manipulative marketing and aggressive economic control. Furthermore, it challenges the conventional attacks, both conservative and radical, on American culture by noting the way in which its integration into the British cultural formation broadens the cultural repertoire available to audiences. As Tony Bennett has suggested, the argument that America is involved in a form of cultural imperialism 'although not without point . . . misses much of the essential ambivalence of the impact of American popular culture in Britain which, in many respects, has been more positive, particularly in making available a repertoire of cultural styles and resources . . . which, in various ways, have undercut and been consciously mobilised against the cultural hegemony of Britain's traditional élites'.[12]

The rhetoric of democracy and populism is built into the formal organisation of the American film, with its classically strong and dynamic narrative drive towards individual achievement – although this also points to the limitations of the rhetoric, since problems and their resolutions are invariably articulated only in relation to the *individual* within a substantially unchanged capitalist patriarchy. Further, classical

Hollywood cinema conventionally ties this narrative structure of achievement to the romantic appeal of the formation of the heterosexual couple, and situates the narrative both within a visual form whose *mise-en-scène* and organisation of spectacle and spectating has proved intensely pleasurable, and within a physical context of film-watching which emphasises the process of fantasising. Overall, this form has a propensity to engage the spectator thoroughly in a complex series of identifications, with an almost ruthless disregard of the nationality (as well as class and gender) of the spectator, and it is often the figure of the star which holds together these various formal strategies, narrative, visual and identificatory.

This is not to suggest that many British films, for instance, do not also work within the same formal system. But it is generally accepted that American film-makers innovated, applied, and exploited this form of film-making much earlier and more consistently than their British counterparts who operate with a much more mixed, and so-called 'primitive', variety of modes compared to Hollywood where this mode of representation had become institutionalised by 1917. It is also generally accepted that Hollywood has had the resources, which British film producers have lacked, to exploit the potential appeals of the institutional mode of representation.[13] Thus, for instance, British cinema has never been able to sustain a star system on the same glamorous scale as Hollywood for long periods of time – not least since Hollywood tends to consume British stars for its own films, thereby increasing the stake which British audiences have in those films.

If we confine discussion to film production, it makes sense in this context to speak of national cinema as non-standard and marginal activities. Part of the problem, of course, is the paradox that for a cinema to be nationally popular it must also be international in scope. That is to say, it must achieve the international (Hollywood) standard. For, by and large, it is the films of the major American distributors which achieve national box-office success, so that film-makers who aspire to the same level of box-office popularity must attempt to reproduce the standard, which in practice means colluding with Hollywood's systems of funding, production control, distribution and marketing. Any alternative means of achieving national *popular* success must if it is to be economically viable, be conceived on an international scale, which is virtually impossible for a national film industry, unless it has a particularly large domestic market, as in the case of the Bombay film industry. The difficulty is to establish some sort of balance between the 'apparently incompatible objectives of a national cinema – to be economically viable but culturally motivated', 'to be "national" in what is essentially an international industry'.[14]

Historically, at least within the Western European countries, there has been one major solution to this problem, one central strategy for attempting to reconcile the irreconcilable and maintain both some form of national cultural specificity and achieve a relative degree of international visibility and economic viability: the production of an art cinema, a nationally-based (and in various ways state-subsidised) cinema of quality. As Steve Neale has argued, art cinema has played a central role 'in the attempts made by a number of European countries both to counter American domination of their indigenous markets in film and also to foster a film industry and a film culture of their own.'[15] The discourses of 'art', 'culture' and 'quality', and of 'national identity' and 'nationhood', have historically been mobilised against Hollywood's mass entertainment film, and used to justify various nationally specific economic systems of support and protection. But there are two further points to note here. First, that this is yet another instance of 'the peculiarity of a national film production within an international market-place',[16] since the market for art cinema is indeed decidedly international, as is the network of film festivals and reviewing practices, and other means of achieving a critical reputation and both a national and an international cultural space for such films.[17] And second, that perhaps the situation isn't quite so peculiar after all, given the increasing tendency for international co-productions (invariably with the involvement of one or other of the still-extant national television networks), and the development of transnational forms of industry support and protection within the European Community.

However, the various international art cinemas have rarely achieved a national popular success, partly because of their modes of address, and partly because of the international hegemony of Hollywood at the level of distribution, exhibition and marketing. Indeed, in the case of the British film industry at least, the distribution and exhibition arms of that industry have primarily been organised to foster, extend and consolidate the domination of the British market by American popular films. Thus for some time the major American studios have had their own distribution companies operating in Britain, while the major British companies have built up close relationships with American producers and distributors, who often also have substantial financial interests in British companies. British companies have found this sort of co-operation necessary, since, in capitalist terms, the American film industry was much better organised before the British film industry, and was able to pursue imperialist policies with some vigour, undercutting the charges of local distributors, since they could go into the British market in the knowledge that costs had already been recovered from the huge American domestic market.[18]

In other words, the influence of Hollywood on domestic markets is always much more than simply a question of the poverty or élitism of domestic film-making. This suggests that national cinema needs to be explored not only in relation to production, but also in relation to the question of distribution and exhibition, audiences and consumption, within each nation-state. The idea that Hollywood – and now, of course, television – has become a part of the popular imagination of British cinema audiences needs to be taken seriously.

As such, it becomes insufficient to define national cinema solely by contrasting one national cinema to another, and we need also to take into account the other key way of defining a national cinema – what I have suggested is a more *inward-looking* means, constituting a national cinema not so much in terms of its difference from other cinemas, but in terms of its relationship to an already existing national political, economic and cultural identity (in so far as a single coherent identity can be established) and set of traditions. In this way, British cinema would be defined in terms of already established discourses of Britishness, by turning in on itself, on its own history and cultural formation, and the defining ideologies of national identity and nationhood, rather than by reference to other national cinemas – bearing in mind always that Hollywood may itself be an integral part of that cultural formation.

At one level, in terms of political economy, a national cinema is a particular industrial structure; a particular pattern of ownership and control of plant, real estate, human resources and capital, and a system of state legislation which circumscribes the nationality of that ownership – primarily in relation to production. The relative economic power of a national film industry will depend upon the degree to which production, distribution and exhibition are integrated, regulated, technically equipped and capitalised; the size of the home market and the degree of penetration of overseas markets. At the level of production, we need to take into account both the means and modes of production employed (the organisation of work, in terms of systems of management, division of labour, professional organisations and ideologies, availability of technology, etc) and the access that producers have to both domestic and overseas markets. It is important to recognise also that even the domestic market is not homogeneous, and that production companies often deliberately limit themselves to specific areas of exploitation, especially when faced with the mainstream box-office supremacy of the major American distributors overseas. These limited areas of exploitation will, in many cases, be areas considered marginal (that is, marginally profitable) by Hollywood (low-budget films, B movies, films made primarily for the domestic market rather than for export, art cinema, and so on).

It is worth underlining again the role of the state, and the terms of its intervention in the practices of a film industry, in determining the parameters and possibilities of a national cinema (as both an economically viable and a culturally motivated institution) – at least since the mid 1910s, when governments began to recognise the potential ideological power of cinema, and cinema itself could seem to be something like a national cultural form, an institution with a nationalising function. But it is also important to recognise that the state intervenes only when there is a felt fear of the potential power of a foreign cinema, and particularly when the products – and therefore the ideologies and values – of a foreign cinema are widely circulated within a nation state, and assumed to be having also a detrimental effect on that nation state's economy. In other words, while it is conceptually useful to isolate a single national cinema, it is necessary also that it is seen in relation to other cinemas.

The same of course is true when we come to examine the cultural identity of a particular national cinema. The areas that need to be examined here are, first, the content or subject matter of a particular body of films – that which is represented (and particularly the construction of 'the national character'), the dominant narrative discourses and dramatic themes, and the narrative traditions and other source material on which they draw (and particularly the degree to which they draw on what has been constructed as the national heritage, literary, theatrical or otherwise) – in other words, the ways in which cinema inserts itself alongside other cultural practices, and the ways in which it draws on the existing cultural histories and cultural traditions of the producing nation, reformulating them in cinematic terms, appropriating them to build up its own generic conventions. Second, there is the question of the sensibility, or structure of feeling, or world-view expressed in those films. And third, there is the area of the style of those films, their formal systems of representation (the forms of narration and motivation which they employ, their construction of space and staging of action, the ways in which they structure narrative and time, the modes of performance which they employ and the types of visual pleasure, spectacle and display with which they engage), and their modes of address and construction of subjectivity (and particularly the degree to which they engage in the construction of fantasy and the regulation of audience knowledge).

In considering cinema in terms of cultural identity, it is necessary also to pay attention to the process by which cultural hegemony is achieved within each nation-state; to examine the internal relations of diversification and unification, and the power to institute one particular aspect of a pluralistic cultural formation as politically dominant and to standardise or naturalise it. Historical accounts of national cinema have too often been premised on unproblematised notions of nationhood and its production. The search for a stable and coherent national identity can only be successful at the expense of repressing internal differences, tensions and contradictions – differences of class, race, gender, region, etc. It is important also to pay attention to historical shifts in the construction of nationhood and national identity: nationhood is always an image constructed under particular conditions, and indeed nationalism itself, as a concept in the modern sense, can only be traced back to the late 18th century.[19] 'History', as Benedict Anderson puts it, 'is the necessary basis of the national narrative.'[20]

As Stephen Heath has suggested, 'nationhood is not a given, it is always something to be gained'[21] – and cinema needs to be understood as one of the means by which it is 'gained'. Thus, definitions of British cinema, for instance, almost always involve, on the one hand, the construction of an imaginary homogeneity of identity and culture, an already achieved national identity, apparently shared by all British subjects; and on the other hand, the valorisation of a very particular conception of 'British cinema', which involves ignoring whole areas of British cinema history. In each case, a process of inclusion and exclusion is enacted, a process whereby one thing is centralised, at the same time necessarily marginalising another, a process wherein the interests of one particular social group are represented as in the collective or national interest, producing what Anderson has called 'the imagined community of the nation'.[22]

Proclamations of national cinema are thus in part one form of 'internal cultural colonialism': it is, of course, the function of institutions – and in this case national cinemas – to pull together diverse and contradictory discourses, to articulate a contradictory unity, to play a part in the hegemonic process of achieving consensus, and containing difference and contradiction.[23] It is this state of contradictoriness which must always be born in mind in any discussion of national cinema. Cinema never simply reflects or expresses an already fully formed and homogeneous national culture and identity, as if it were the undeniable property of all national subjects; certainly, it privileges only a limited range of subject positions which thereby become naturalised or reproduced as the only legitimate positions of the national subject. But it needs also to be seen as actively working to construct subjectivity as well as simply expressing a pre-given industry.

National cinema is, then, a complex issue, and I would argue that it is inadequate to reduce the study of national cinemas only to consideration of the films produced by and within a particular nation state. It is important to take into account the film culture as a whole, and the overall institution of cinema, and to address the following issues:

- the range of films in circulation within a nation state – including American and other foreign films – and how they are taken up at the level of exhibition; in the present era, of course, films are 'in circulation' and 'exhibited' or on display in a variety of ways, and not just to be physically projected at cinemas (multiplexes, city-centre cinemas, art-house cinemas, etc): they are available on video and via the various forms of broadcast and cable television as *films*, but they are also present and re-cycled in popular culture *intertextually*, as icons, reference points, standards and pastiches;
- the range of sociologically specific audiences for different types of film, and how these audiences *use* these films in particular exhibition circumstances; that is to say, we need to take into account not only the historically constituted reading practices and modes of spectatorship and subjectivity, the mental machinery and relative cultural power or readerly competences of different audiences – but also the experience of cinema(s) in a more general cultural sense: the role of marketing and audience expectation, the reasons why particular audiences go to the cinema, the pleasures they derive from this activity, the specific nature of the shared social and communal experience of cinema-going, differentiated according to class, race, gender, age, etc, the role of television (and video) in mediating and tranforming the experience of cinema, the different experiences offered by the various types of theatrical exhibition spaces. It is worth remembering that, from the point of view of economic historians such as Douglas Gomery, film industries marked by a high degree of horizontal and vertical integration can be seen as no more nor less than highly diversified cinema circuits, where production is a necessary high-risk service industry, and where cinemas are as much luxurious sites for the consumption of or advertising for commodities other than films, as they are sites for the fantasy experience of watching films;[24]
- the range of and relation between discourses about film circulating within that cultural and social formation, and their relative accessibility to different audiences. Crucial among these discourses is the tension between, on the one hand, those intellectual discourses which insist that a proper national cinema must be one which aspires to the status of art (and therefore adheres to the current dominant definitions of cinema as an art form), discourses which, from a particular class perspective, dismiss Hollywood's popular cinema as culturally debilitating; and on the other hand, those more populist discourses where, in effect, the idea of 'good entertainment' overrides questions of 'art' or 'nationality'. This latter discourse suggests that a cinema can only be national, and command a national-popular audience if it is a mass-production genre cinema, capable of constructing, reproducing, and re-cycling popular myths on a broad scale, with an elaborate, well capitalised and well resourced system of market exploitation. Again, the role of television must be taken into account as one of agents which generates, sustains and regulates film cultures and renders discourses about the cinema more or less accessible.

To explore national cinema in these terms means laying much greater stress on the point of consumption, and on the *use* of films (sounds, images, narratives, fantasies), than on the point of production. It involves a shift in emphasis away from the analysis of film texts as vehicles for the articulation of nationalist sentiment and the interpellation of the implied national spectator, to an analysis of how actual audiences construct their cultural identity in relation to the various products of the national and international film and television industries, and the conditions under which this is achieved.

The current state of film studies is characterised by a tension between those who are working on the political economies of cinema and those who analyse and investigate textuality and the putative spectator, and by the corresponding absence of much work on actual audiences, beyond the examination of critical discourses. Bordwell, Staiger and Thompson have proposed the most acceptable form of relationship or mediation between political economy and textuality in terms of a sort of sociology of organisations and professional ideologies.[25] Clearly, this is something that could be fruitfully explored in relation to other national cinemas. But it doesn't at present help to bridge the gap between textual analysis, the analysis of critical discourses in print-form, and the vast continent of the popular audiences for film – and the question of audiences has to be crucial for the study of national cinema. For what is a national cinema if it doesn't have a national audience?

Notes

1 This article is based on a chapter from a PhD thesis which I am currently preparing. I would like to acknowledge the work of Thomas Elsaesser in enabling me to develop some of the arguments advanced here.

2 Susan Barrowclough, 'Introduction: the dilemmas of a national cinema', in Barrowclough, ed, *Jean-Pierre Lefebvre: The Quebec Connection*, BFI Dossier no 13, 1981, p. 3.

3 'Popular culture', *New Formations*, no 2, Summer 1987, p. 80.

4 'Chronicle of a death retold: hyper, retro or counter-cinema', *Monthly Film Bulletin*, vol 54, no 641, June 1987, p. 167.

5 *New German Cinema: A History*, London, BFI/Macmillan, 1989, pp. 6–7.

6 'Narrating the nation', *Times Literary Supplement*, June 13, 1986, p. 659; see also Benedict Anderson, *Imagined Communities: reflections on the origin and spread of nationalism*, London, Verso, 1983.

7 Elsaesser, 'Chronicle of a death retold', p. 166.

8 See Nowell-Smith, *New Formations*, op. cit., p. 81.

9 'But do we need it?', in Martin Auty and Nick Roddick, eds, *British Cinema Now*, London, BFI, 1985, p. 152. For other writers advancing a similar argument, see also Paul Swann, *The Hollywood Feature Film in Post-War Britain*, London, Croom Helm, 1987; Paul Willemen, 'In search of an alternative perspective: an interview with Armand and Michelle Mattelart', *Framework*, nos 26–27, 1985, p. 56; Geoffrey Nowell-Smith, 'Gramsci and the national-popular', *Screen Education*, no 22, Spring 1977; Don MacPherson, 'The Labour Movement and oppositional Cinema: introduction', in *Traditions of Independence*, London, BFI, 1980, pp. 127–128; Peter Miles and Malcolm Smith, *Cinema, Literature and Society: élite and mass culture in inter-war Britain*, London, Croom Helm, 1987, pp. 170–178; Robert Murphy, 'A rival to Hollywood? The British film industry in the thirties', *Screen*, vol 24, nos 4–5, July–October 1983.

10 See Tony Aldgate, 'Comedy, class and containment: the British domestic cinema of the 1930s', in James Curran and Vincent Porter, eds, *British Cinema History*, London, Weidenfeld and Nicholson, 1983. See also my 'Saturday night or Sunday morning? British cinema in the fifties', in *Ideas and Production*, issue IX–X, 1989, pp. 146–149.

11 Nowell-Smith, 'But do we need it?', p. 152.

12 'Popular culture and hegemony in post-war Britain', in *Politics, Ideology and Popular Culture*, Unit 18 of Open University Popular Culture course (U203), p. 13.

13 See eg David Bordwell, Janet Staiger and Kristin Thompson, *The Classical Hollywood Cinema*, London, RKP, 1985; Barry Salt, *Film Style and Technology: History and Analysis*, London, Starword, 1983; Kristin Thompson, *Exporting Entertainment*, London, BFI, 1986; Charles Barr, ed, *All Our Yesterdays: 90 Years of British Cinema*, London, BFI, 1986; Roy Armes, *A Critical History of British Cinema*, London, Secker and Warburg, 1978.

14 Elseasser, *New German Cinema*, p. 3 and p. 39.

15 'Art cinema as institution', *Screen*, vol 22, no 1, 1981, p. 11.

16 Elseasser, *New German Cinema*, p. 49.

17 See Neale, op. cit., pp. 34–35.

18 See chapters on the film industry in Curran and Porter, eds, op. cit.; and Barr, ed, op. cit.; and Margaret Dickinson and Sarah Street, *Cinema and State*, London, BFI, 1985.

19 See eg Eugene Kamenka, 'Political nationalism: the evolution of the idea', in Kamenka, ed, *Nationalism*, London, Edward Arnold, 1976, pp. 3–20; and Tom Nairn, *The Break-up of Britain*, London, Verso, 1981, pp. 329–341.

20 Op cit, p. 659.

21 Questions of property: film and nationhood', *Cine-tracts* vol 1, no 4, Spring/Summer 1978, p. 10.

22 Op cit, p. 659.

23 See Paul Willemen, 'Remarks on *Screen*: introductory notes for a history of contexts', *Southern Review* vol 16 no 2, July 1983, p. 296.

24 See Douglas Gomery, *The Hollywood Studio System*, London, BFI/Macmillan, 1986.

25 Op cit.

Chapter 15

David Gillespie

IDENTITY AND THE PAST IN RECENT RUSSIAN CINEMA

CINEMA IN POST-GLASNOST RUSSIA, like every other field of cultural endeavour, has undergone a profound and probably irreversible revolution. With the disappearance of the old certainties, across the countries of Eastern Europe nationalism of various hues and extremes fills the gap left by the collapse of ideology. It would, however, be wrong to assume that the emerging search for national self-consciousness is a new phenomenon. In Soviet cinema, as in literature, the search for new forms of expression and new ideas of belonging and destiny began with the death of Stalin in 1953, and assumed certain shapes in the 1960s. Particularly since the 1960s writers and film-makers in Russia and the USSR have turned their attention to the historical past in an attempt to find out the truth, and also to reflect on the events and personalities that have shaped the present. This paper will examine some films of the post-Stalin period that deal with the past in an attempt to give a picture of the emerging ideas of national self-awareness and the historical destiny of Russia.

What do we mean by Russian nationalism? In other countries, national identity is framed through the cultural consciousness, political and social institutions and an awareness of the historical forces that have shaped the nation. Russia is a country that before 1992 did not exist. Before 1917, the Russian Empire embraced many peoples and lands that have since 1991 declared themselves independent, such as Georgia, Ukraine and Armenia. Russia stretches from the Baltic to the Pacific, from the Arctic Circle to the sub-tropical reaches of the Caspian, and the search for Russian identity goes on at a time when political institutions have been discredited and the historical past is being rediscovered after decades of falsehood and ignorance. Only the cultural consciousness remains, and this is being constantly enriched and changed as 'new' (i.e. forgotten or repressed) names and works (re-)enter the canon.

Thus, the search for identity is plagued by uncertainties, which themselves give way to extremist positions and polarities (until very recently, the Russian language had no word for 'identity'; now it is a calque: 'identichnost'). For centuries Russia has toyed with its relationship with the West, with its intellectual elite torn between the pull of the Slavophiles, emphasizing Russia's uniqueness and moral superiority over the West, and the Westerners, who see Russia's only path to the future through adoption of Western social-democratic structures and institutions. We find these polarities, and these same parameters, prevalent in Russian culture, and in particular film, of the past few decades.

Before looking at film, however, it is necessary to discuss ideology. For decades socialist realism was the only acceptable artistic method in Soviet culture, and this method applied equally to music, art, cinema, literature and even architecture. Socialist realism basically required the artist to show how all conflicts can be resolved with the aid of the Party, and that the future was being built according to the wise doctrine of the Party. In pratice it meant that anything that suggested that the Party was not in control, or, worse, corrupt, or that actual situations did not conform to their ideological projections, was deemed unacceptable. In cinema the screenplay was thus of vital importance, as it was the main means of conveying the propagandistic method. The screenplay would be completed before filming, having been supervised by the Party, and could not subsequently be developed or changed without Party permission. The finished product would then be viewed by Party and film officials.[1] Films which were deemed unsuitable, for whatever reason, were put on the shelf and not made available to the public. Thus in cinema, as in literature, the years 1986-88 largely saw the release of films that had been on the shelf, perhaps for up to twenty years.

The supervision of the cinema industry was carried out by Goskino, who had the sole responsibility to finance and distribute films. Goskino also had the power to prevent films from being shown if they did not conform. The persecution of Andrei Tarkovskii in the 1970s and 1980s is ample evidence of the abilities of this organization to enforce its will on Soviet film-makers. That is, he was allowed to make films, but these films were given only a restricted showing, if at all, and Goskino even argued against the award of prizes to Tarkovskii at major international festivals.[2]

Socialist realism also promulgated the idea of the socialist fraternity, the coming together of all peoples under the Soviet banner of internationalism. Individual nationhood was therefore subordinated to the idea of the greater Soviet 'family'. The opening of the floodgates in 1986-87, not surprisingly, saw a release of pent-up anger, frustration and bile that has done much to shape the emerging social and civic consciousness in the Russian cinema. One of the major themes, not surprisingly, in these years has been the sense of historical injustice, especially crimes committed in the name of the Party under Stalin. The age-old Russian questions are asked: how did this happen? Who is to blame? What are we to do now? What does the future hold? Such questions are at the heart of recent films that confront such seemingly divergent subjects as problems of youth, the investigation of the past, and the soap-opera-like pictures of spiritual and moral conflicts set in a recognizably drab and desolate urban present.

It is instructive at this point to look at the example of literature, as its links with cinema will become increasingly more obvious. Certainly, observers of the literary scene in Russia over the last thirty years have commented on the emergence of several groups professing to 'rediscover' Russia, its literature and its cultural identity. These groups, originating in the mid-1960s, have usually been based around literary journals such as *Young Guard* and *Our Contemporary*, and now not only affirm the greatness and uniqueness of Russian literature, but also espouse hardline attitudes towards other nations (especially the West), strong autocratic leadership and an accompanying contempt for democracy and parliamentarism. There are heated arguments between so-called 'patriots' and 'democrats' on what is Russian literature and what makes a Russian writer. Russian nationalist writers and critics of varying hues attempt to define a particularly 'Russian' literature, excluding from its canon such established and respected authors as the Jewish Isaak Babel', Osip Mandel'shtam, and even Boris Pasternak, or the Kirghiz Chingiz Aitmatov. The search for national identity has taken place not only in the critical press, but also in fiction, especially in the works of the so-called 'village writers': Vasilii Belov, Vladimir Soloukhin, Boris Mozhaev, Viktor Astaf'ev and Valentin Rasputin are the main representatives of this trend still alive, all representing various points of the compass of nationalist thought.[3]

There is a clear link between 'village prose' and nationalism in film, for some of the major successes of 'village prose' were made into equally (if not more) successful films: Elem Klimov's 1983 film *Farewell,* an adaptation of Rasputin's 1976 novella *Farewell to Matera,* and Vasilii Shukshin's 1973 novella *Snowball Berry Red*, written especially for the cinema and which Shukshin not only directed himself, but in which he also played the leading role, are two outstanding examples. In *Farewell,* a three-hundred-year-old island community on the river Angara in Siberia is threatened with destruction as a hydro-electric dam is built upriver. The dam requires a huge reservoir, of which the river will form part, and, as the water level is to be raised, the village Matera is to be flooded, its culture, traditions and history consigned to oblivion. Both the author of the original novella Rasputin, and the film-maker Klimov, invest the story-line with considerable lyricism and symbolism, to create an elegy not only for a disappearing rural way of life, but also as a statement on the fate of Russia in the industrial age. There is also considerable anger at the way in which decisions are taken thousands of miles away in Moscow that affect the lives of people whose views are not even sought. In the novella, the bureaucracy, and the so-called 'sanitary engineers' who come to 'cleanse' the island of its trees and houses (so that they do not protrude above the water level after the flooding) are seen in negative, inhuman terms, outsiders destroying the homes of others; in the film, the depiction of them is ambivalent, as they are seen as 'necessary'. Both film and novella nevertheless offer an Apocalyptic picture, as Matera is to be razed by fire before being flooded by the rising waters of the dam. Consequently, man's link with the land, and his cherished link with the past and with his ancestors, is lost.[4]

In *Snowball Berry Red* we are introduced to Egor Prokudin, a thief and ex-con, on his release from prison. He tries to be re-integrated into his former gang, but is soon disillusioned and attempts instead to get a job on a farm and settle down. He goes to live in a village near where he was born. Prokudin, it transpires, was separated from his parents while a teenager, one of the millions of Russians uprooted and torn from their rural origins through Stalin's disastrous policy of collectivization in the late 1920s. Just as Prokudin appears at last to have found his place – as a tractor driver, symbolically re-establishing his links with the land – his gang come to reclaim him as one of their own, and in the ensuing fight, Prokudin is killed. The film asserts the moral superiority of the village over the town, where the village is populated by essentially good and wholesome folk, and danger lurks only when it is threatened by outsiders. The town, on the other hand, is the home of criminals and a place of debauchery. Undeniably a powerful and compelling film, *Snowball Berry Red* was phenomenally popular in Russia in the 1970s exactly because millions of ordinary Russians, similarly uprooted and alienated, identified with it.

More fundamentally, in both films (as well as the literary works on which they are based), urban lifestyles are consistently contrasted with the lives of simple people from the village. The village and the countryside are more wholesome, morally pure, than the city; people from the city have sold their souls in exchange for spurious material benefits. Moreover, the village is the repository of age-old customs and values, it is where the national character itself is rooted. In short, the village is Russia, and the move to urbanization leads to disaster. In the village prose movement, and the films that proceeded from it, there is the affirmation of a mythical picture of Russia, a Russia whose heritage lies in the countryside, and where corruption and ultimately death accompany urban ways and industrialization.

To be sure, the so-called uniquely Russian values of kindness, humility and capacity for honest toil, and the saintliness associated with it, are not the preserve of Russian nationalism. Rather, these are the mythical values associated with living on the land and next to the natural rhythms of life, and part and parcel of what the urban population in all industrialized countries would call 'the good old days'. Russian claims for a hegemony of spiritual goodness belie their discomfort with the modern world and their place in it.

Compare this idealization to Andrei Mikhalkov-Konchalovskii's *Asya's Happiness*, a simple and unadorned picture of collective farmers gathering in the harvest over a palpably hot and sweaty summer, and the private life of the Asya of the title. In this film there is no idealization of rural life or the rock-solid values that purportedly emerge from it. Furthermore, there is no cinematic stylization: there is little background music, the action is filmed almost in a documentary, fly-on-the-wall fashion, and there are few professional actors. The director allows his villagers to speak in their natural idiom, retelling stories of the War and the Stalinist purges in a natural and straightforward way, without any sensationalism or sentimentality. The overall effect of the film is to give a picture of a strongly bonded community who share the same faith, beliefs and outlook on life, and expect little from life other than what they receive through the fruits of their labour. They are at one with their environment (as the camerawork stresses, catching individuals against the backdrop of fields, river and rolling hills). It is a raw and naturalistic picture, of ordinary people at work and relaxing, speaking about their own lives in their own language, and consciously rejecting any nationalist or so-called 'patriotic' uplifting interpretation of Russia's hardships. It is perhaps exactly because of the absence of any ideological underpinning that this film was withdrawn from circulation in the USSR for twenty years.[5]

The films of Andrei Tarkovskii, perhaps the best-known Russian film-maker of his generation, are also relevant here. In such films as *Nostalgia* (1983) and *Sacrifice* (1986), both made in the West, he, too, reflects on Russia's national identity in the form of its relationship with the West. Throughout Tarkovskii's work (and he made only seven films in twenty-five years), the image of the border is predominant, as Tarkovskii's heroes try to define themselves and their country through 'the other'. Very often in Russian culture, self-definition is attempted not on the basis of what I am, but what I am not. Whereas in earlier films made in the Soviet Union, such as *Andrei Rublev* (1965) and *Mirror* (1974), Tarkovskii had pondered the Russia-West relationship and found scope for cooperation and accommodation between Russia and the West, when he actually arrives and works in the West he rejects any communication. In true Slavophile tradition, a homesick and despondent Tarkovskii saw the West as morally bankrupt and devoid of spirituality, and heading for catastrophe. In *Nostalgia* he rejects the idea of mutual understanding, as he, the *auteur,* tries to transform an Italian landscape into something resembling Russia, just as Gorchakov, the erstwhile hero, tries to see Russia all around him. Thus, he sees a mad Italian hermit as a Russian 'holy fool' foretelling the end of the world, and finds it impossible to achieve any real communication with his beautiful Italian guide. She, in particular, is made to look superficial, a Russian speaker who cannot penetrate beyond the surface meaning of the words in the poems she reads (significantly, poems written by Tarkovskii's own father). The end of the film sees the gradual merging of a Russian and Italian landscape, with Russian folk music blending with Verdi's *Requiem* in the background. External landscapes are confused, juxtaposed, but inner, psychological landscapes remain distinct, separate. In *Sacrifice* Tarkovskii's predicted catastrophe happens, as nothing less than nuclear war is the theme.[6]

In this context it is instructive to turn to a documentary film, *The Russia We Have Lost* (1992), by Stanislav Govorukhin. This film offers a kind of socialist realism in reverse, where the Tsarist past and in particular the Tsarist family are presented in glowing colours, with hardly a mention of the repression, poverty, institutionalized anti-semitism or chronic civil backwardness historians tell us were prevalent. The destruction of the monarchy is said to have been an unmitigated catastrophe for Russia. Furthermore, the director, who also narrates and presents the film, is intent to impress upon the viewer not only a nostalgic and rose-tinted picture of Russia as a nation with a glorious heritage, but also as a great power. Throughout the film the point of reference is 1913, the year before the outbreak of the First World War, which led to the abdication of the Tsar and the Bolshevik seizure of power in 1917. Although Govorukhin admits the weakness of the Tsar, he is enamoured of the pageantry and majesty of the royal family, its links with European monarchs, and spares us no details in his blow-by-blow account of the brutal murder and disposal of the bodies of the entire Romanov family in 1918. Significantly, the major circumstance that destroyed the credibility and legitimacy of the Romanov dynasty – the influence of Grigorii Rasputin at court in the last years of the monarchy – is totally ignored in this film.

Govorukhin is also at pains to paint a black picture of Lenin as a cynical opportunist with a pathological hatred of the monarchy, and also spends considerable time exploring Lenin's Jewish ancestry. All in all, the glorification of the Tsarist past is not that far removed from the idealization of a mythic Russia in the films by Klimov and Shukshin, and it is not surprising, therefore, that in the closing credits Govorukhin acknowledges in particular his debt to the writings of Alexander Solzhenitsyn. Solzhenitsyn, too, has much in common with the 'village prose' movement – indeed, with his novella *Matryona's Home* in 1963, he started it – but the film *The Russia We Have Lost* follows exactly Solzhenitsyn's interpretation of Russian history in the early years of this century, including his advocacy of Stolypin, the reformist Tsarist minister whose efforts to modernize agriculture and the rural community are seen by Solzhenitsyn as offering the way forward for Russia in the years before the First World War. Stolypin was assassinated in 1911, and with him, according to the Solzhenitsyn/Govorukhin variant, went Russia's chances of averting revolution and catastrophe.

A word perhaps could be added here on another film by Klimov, *Agony*, released only in 1985, about the last days of the Romanov Empire, and in particular the baleful and ultimately disastrous influence of Rasputin at court. The film became controversial by nature of its very subject-matter, and is remarkable perhaps only in that it presents a far-from negative picture of the Tsar, shown here as weak and indecisive, but with positive traits. This film has also become something of a landmark in that it has willy-nilly become part of the post-Soviet Russian search for an idealized and glorious past.

While discussing nationalism in the Russian context, we must inevitably touch on the question of anti-semitism. The anti-semitic brand of nationalism has obviously been prevalent in official circles in Soviet culture throughout the Brezhev period. Aleksandr Askol'dov's *The Commissar* was banned for twenty years, ostensibly for its sympathetic portrayal of a Jewish family looking after a Russian female commissar during the Civil War. Gleb Panfilov's *The Theme* was banned until 1987, as it featured a long discussion on the Jewish emigration to Israel in the 1970s (a taboo subject in the official media).

The preoccupation with the past, in particular Stalinism, has been a major feature of the culture of the past thirty years or so. The investigation of the crimes and injustices of the past, begun in earnest since *glasnost* but tentatively initiated by Khrushchev in 1956, is an attempt to identify the painful areas of national and collective experience, and is, in films to be discussed below, fundamentally different from the elegiac nationalist preoccupations of Klimov, Shukshin, and others. The attempt to put right the wrongs of the past is a concentration on the facts of history, and not on mirages or myths of some idealized past 'golden age'.

The reappraisal of the more recent past, especially the Stalin years, is to my mind the most important aspect of the search for identity and justice in post-glasnost cinema. For these directors, just like writers and journalists, are interested not in the sufferings of the Russian soul, the idea that to be Russian is to 'feel' Russia and the Russian soul, but rather concentrate on actual facts, events and personalities. The first major film to explore the impact of Stalin's terror on family life was not a Russian film at all. The Georgian Tengiz Abuladze's 1987 *Repentence*, through a mixture of religious symbolism, allegory and fantasy offers a relentless picture of the destruction of a family in a police state run by a ruthless dictator, Varlam. But more fundamentally, the dictator's own family are unable to live down the consequences of his tyranny, after his death, and Varlam's grandson commits suicide.[7] The relationship of the individual to tyranny has also been explored in *The Servant*, made in 1988 by Mindadze and

Abdrashitov. Here the relationship of two men, one an important official, the other his driver, is turned into an allegory of power and submission to it, for it is not so much the official who imposes his will on his driver (and others); rather the driver has an inner need to be subservient. Is this an explanation for the domination of the Russian people by one man for over quarter of a century?

Another film that explores the psychological and social effects of Stalinism, but in a recognizably Western format, is Alexander Proshkin's 1987 film *The Cold Summer of 1953,* where political prisoners do battle with criminals who take over a village following Beria's amnesty of prisoners in 1953 (shortly after Stalin's death). It is not, however, the (admittedly exciting) shoot-out that is important, but rather the psychological aftermath for the hero. This is Sergei, a former political prisoner who overcomes his cynicism to realise the value of relationships and human inter-action. Indeed, the violence serves as Sergei's catharsis, after which he, like his times, becomes settled and balanced.

Another film that combines the elements of the traditional detective story with historical enquiry is Aleksei German's *My Friend Ivan Lapshin* (1985), a film based on the literary works of Iurii German, the director's father. The plot deals with the local policeman, Lapshin, and his eventual tracking down of a local band of violent criminals, but the film also evokes the atmosphere of provincial Russian life in the 1930s, when the action is set. There is no explicit mention of the historical background, such as collectivization, purges, mass starvation in the countryside (save for a portrait of Stalin glimpsed towards the end of the film), but the ordinary life of people is portrayed as hard and sometimes brutal. Here people live together in communal apartments, have little or no privacy, and criminals are shot in cold blood by the police. With its candid portrayal of life in 1935, the film undoubtedly has a nostalgic appeal for many Russians, but on a deeper level the director is subverting the socialist realist depiction of reality that his father gives in his stories. Set just before the onset of the Great Terror, the film offers hints at what is to come. Furthermore, the film's plot is narrated retrospectively from the vantage point of the present, thus establishing a broad temporal perspective. Thus, the times live on in the present through memory.[8]

A major documentary film in this vein is *Solovki Power* (1988), directed by Marina Gol'dovskaia. Solovki used to be a monastery in the White Sea, founded in the fifteenth century, that became under the Bolsheviks one of the most infamous and brutal camps for political prisoners. Gol'dovskaia's film goes to Solovki, tells of its terrible regime, but, and most tellingly, brings into the narrative the first-hand accounts of those who spent time there and survived. Interestingly, it also includes footage of former guards, and shows how they have prospered in the post-Stalin period. It is indeed a harrowing film, and all the more powerful for not overstating its case (or overstaying its welcome).

In the 1970s and 1980s there have been several popular and respected films dealing with life in Russia before the Revolution. What is of interest in these films is the absence of any explicit ideology condemning the iniquities of that time. Moreover, films based on works by Russian authors, such as *Unfinished Piece for Mechanical Piano,* directed by Nikita Mikhalkov in 1977, *Vassa,* directed by Gleb Panfilov in 1983, and

Cruel Romance, directed by El'dar Riazanov in 1984, are based, respectively, on pre-revolutionary literary works by Anton Chekhov, Maksim Gor'kii and Aleksei Tolstoi. Each of the directors displays a reverence for the literary source, both in characterization and fidelity to the original plotline, but each film has a contemporary resonance. Mikhalkov's film, in particular, is purportedly about the inner torments and self-doubt of a failed radical at the turn of the century, but it also contains many passages that can be interpreted as an explicit comment on the capitulation of the Soviet intelligentsia in the 1970s. In all of these films it is as if the problems of collective and individual morality, emotional vacuity and spiritual malaise, prevalent in Tsarist society, are equally true of the modern age. Individual morality is measured against the touchstone of Russian literature of the nineteenth century; these film-makers demonstrate above all a cultural continuity between past and present.

In a different context an important film is *The Garage,* directed in 1979 by El'dar Riazanov, with a script by himself and Emil Braginskii. It is a satire, a genre very difficult to practice in Brezhnev's Russia, and its target is the selfish materialism of modern Muscovites. The plot revolves around a meeting called in a research institute to decide who is to lose their allocated garage space because of a planned motorway route. In fact, the institute's leadership has already decided on the four people who will lose out, and the meeting is intended merely as a rubber stamp exercise. However, in the course of the evening – and then the night and the following morning, as those present are locked in – not only are the greedy and self-serving instincts of today's intelligentsia laid bare, in varying degrees, but the collective overturns the decisions laid down from on high and asserts its own priorities. Those who lose out, in the end, are the highly-connected and those in positions of power, and a new order is born. Amid chaos and anarchy (some of it extremely funny), the old elite is overthrown. Thus the film can be seen as an allegory, and a remarkably perceptive and prophetic one, about the revolt of the masses against their leaders, and the removal of the social hierarchy. At the end of the film, the last garage space to be lost is decided by drawing lots. In other words, democracy replaces autocracy. It is remarkable that this film was allowed to appear in Brezhnev's time, for it offers a subversive picture of what can be achieved with 'people power'. The world was to be witness to a much greater illustration of this in 1991.

Russians today grope their way towards an as yet uncertain identity, an unknown destiny. This is an identity not as yet based, as in Western Europe, on political institutions, but above all on culture, and the cultural consciousness is one which 1917 did not break. Russian culture has always been deeply religious, and it is perhaps worth pointing out here some films with a clear Christian subtext. Larisa Shepit'ko's war film *The Ascent,* made in 1976, offers a picture of a Soviet partisan tortured and eventually executed by the Germans, and whose death scene is framed in hallowed light as he assumes a Christ-like aura. *Scarecrow,* directed in 1987 by Rolan Bykov, is the story of the persecution of a girl by her classmates, and her suffering is increasingly seen as a martyrdom.[9]

To conclude: in the years since Gorbachev came to power and effectively ushered in the end of totalitarianism, national identity has been based on the concept of the Russian soul, the cultural heritage and the belief in the strength and spirit of Russia. This latter concept is particularly evident in Nikita Mikhalkov's *The Barber of Siberia*

(1999). For Russians, the collective identity is based on the national experience and the people's culture. Given the cataclysms of twentieth century Russian history, the assault on its culture by Bolshevik ideology, and the decimation of its people, it is no wonder that the current search for identity and purpose is beset by bitter argument and division. For some national identity becomes associated with a glorification of the past, the assertion of a mythic, golden age of order, stability and above all faith in the destiny of Russia. Gleb Panfilov, in *The Romanov Family* (2000), effectively rehabilitates the Royal Family and portrays them as tragic martyrs, victims of the Provisional Government, the Bolsheviks and above all their own duplicitous generals. The Russia of glory and pageantry disappears with them.

On the other hand, there are film-makers intent on exploring the actual events and personalities of the past in order to put right historical injustices, and to understand the people who made such momentous decisions. Alexander Sokurov's *Taurus* (2000) takes a cold, harsh look at the final days of Lenin, lying helpless after his stroke, an empty shell of a man who only just realises how useless he now is. Russian cinema, like Russian culture in the broadest sense of the term, is still torn between its twin attractions: insularity and the affirmation of all things truly 'Russian', and the quest for historical justice. However, the exorcism of the past and the search for new meanings and identities continues apace. Above all, these strivings offer direction and a sense of purpose for the future.[10]

Notes

1 For a concise and illuminating account of socialist realism in Soviet film, and the stranglehold the Party managed to exert on film production under Stalin, see Peter Kenez, *Cinema and Soviet Society, 1917–1953*, Cambridge Univesity Press, 1992, especially pp. 101–85.
2 In particular, the conservative Soviet director Sergei Bondarchuk, Goskino representative and member of the Jury, opposed the award of the Palme d'Or for *Nostalgia* at the 1983 Cannes film Festival. Tarkovskii writes in detail about his troubles with Goskino throughout his career in his diaries: Andrei Tarkovskii, *Time Within Time: The Diaries 1970–1986,* translated by Kitty Hunter-Blair, Seagull Publishers, Calcutta, 1991.
3 For information on the 'new right' and nationalism, I am indebted to Kathleen Parthé, in particular her paper 'The Empire Strikes Back: How Right-Wing Nationalists Tried to Recapture Russian Literature', presented at the 26th Annual Convention of the American Association for the Advancement of Slavic Studies, Philadelphia, November 1994.
4 The most comprehensive account of Russian village prose can be found in Kathleen Parthé, *Russian Village Prose: The Radiant Past,* Princeton University Press, 1992.
5 In 1994 Konchalovskii released *Kurochka-riaba,* a sequel to *Asya's Happiness,* which brings the story up to date, and explores the demoralization and poverty in the countryside in the immediate post-Soviet years.
6 I have written at more length on Tarkovskii's neo-Slavophilism in my paper 'Russia and the West in the Films of Andrey Tarkovsky', *New Zealand Slavonic Journal*, 1993, pp. 49–61.
7 For a full discussion of this important Soviet film, see Elizabeth Walters, 'The Politics of *Repentance:* History, Nationalism and Tengiz Abuladze', *Australian Slavonic and East European Studies,* vol. 2, no. 1 (1988), pp. 113–42.

8 For a fuller discussion of this film, see Benjamin Rifkin, 'The Reinterpretation of History in German's Film *My Friend Ivan Lapshin:* Shifts in Center and Periphery', *Slavic Review,* vol. 51, no. 3 (Autumn 1992), pp. 431–47.

9 For a fuller discussion of this film, see Benjamin Rifkin, 'The Christian Subtext in Bykov's *Cucelo*', *Slavic and East European Journal,* vol. 37, no. 2 (Summer 1993), pp. 178–93.

10 For further discussion of cinema in Russia today, see the following: Anna Lawton, *Kinoglasnost: Soviet Cinema in Our Time,* Cambridge University Press, 1992; Andrew Horton and Michael Brashinsky, *The Zero Hour: Glasnost and Soviet Cinema in Transition,* Princeton University Press, 1992; Julian Graffy, 'Unshelving Stalin: After the Period of Stagnation', in Richard Taylor and Derek Spring (eds), *Stalinism and Soviet Cinema,* Routledge, London and New York, 1993, pp. 212–27; Birgit Beumers, *Russia on Reels: The Russian Idea in Post-Soviet Cinema,* I. B. Tauris, London and New York, 1999.

Filmography

Proshchanie: Farewell, dir. Elem Klimov, 1983

Kalina krasnaia: Snowball Berry Red, dir. Vasilii Shukshin, 1973

Zerkalo: Mirror, dir. Andrei Tarkovskii, 1975

Asino shast'e: Asya's Happiness, dir. Andrei Mikhalkov-Konchalovskii, 1967

Nostal'giia: Nostalgia, dir. Andrei Tarkovskii, 1983

Offret: Sacrifice, dir. Andrei Tarkovskii, 1986

Agoniia: Agony: dir. Elem Klimov, 1985

Rossiia,, kotoruiu my poteriali: The Russia We Have Lost, dir. Stanislav Govorukhin, 1992

Komissar: The Commissar, dir. Aleksandr Askol'dov, 1967

Tema: The Theme, dir. Gleb Panfilov, 1979

Pokaianie: Repentence, dir. Tengiz Abuladze, 1987

Sluga: The Servant, dir. Vadim Abdrashitov, screenplay by Alexander Mindadze, 1988

Kholodnoe leto 53-ego: The Cold Summer of 1953, dir. Alexander Proshkin, 1988

Moi drug Ivan Lapshin: My Friend Ivan Lapshin, dir. Alexei German, 1985

Solovetskaia vlast': Solovki Power, dir. Marina Goldovskaia, 1988

Neokonchennaia pesnia dlia mexaniheskogo pianino: Unfinished Song for Mechanical Piano, dir. Nikita Mikhalkov, 1977

Vassa: Vassa, dir. Gleb Panfilov, 1981

Zhestokii romans: A Cruel Romance, dir. El'dar Riazanov, 1984

Garazh: The Garage, dir. El'dar Riazanov, 1979

Voskhozhdenie: The Ascent, dir. Larisa Shepit'ko, 1976

Chuchelo: Scarecrow, dir. Rolan Bykov, 1987

Sibirskii tsiriul'nik: The Barber of Siberia, dir. Nikita Mikhalkov, 1999

Romanovy – ventsenosnaia sem'ia: The Romanov Family, dir. Gleb Panfilov, 2000

Telets: Taurus, dir. Alexander Sokurov, 2000

Chapter 16

Barton Byg

DEFA AND THE TRADITIONS OF INTERNATIONAL CINEMA

A T THE HEIGHT OF THE COLD WAR, shortly before the landmark conference on Kafka at Liblice near Prague, Jean-Paul Sartre compared Kafka to a railway carriage loaded with dynamite which each Cold War camp kept trying to push to the other side.[1] Now that the Cold War era is over, the cultural legacies of socialist states may well serve a similarly stimulating if unwelcome function. Indeed GDR culture has long been the repressed 'other' within the culture of the Federal Republic; since unification, this is now also true in a geographical sense. In the East, its critical, creative potential constantly had to be tamed, as Deleuze and Guattari said of Kafka in the West.[2] The potential now is for another Liblice, in which this productive and problematic legacy – no less contradictory than Kafka's identity as a canonical, German author – can be discovered by new audiences.

In the West so far, the reception of DEFA has generally been blocked by ignorance about the films and lack of access to them. Such a starting point, however, is not unusual in the context of popular culture. Many generally educated Americans have never seen *Citizen Kane* (1940) or a John Ford Western or a Douglas Sirk melodrama. As each generation has to create its own relation to film history, then, a rediscovery of DEFA can belong to the next generation. The method of taking this new look at DEFA might also parallel the development of women's history out of the women's movement. Just as feminism has not merely consisted of adding the 'great women' to the histories of 'great men', it is also not enough now to add DEFA to the books already written on German film that excluded this aspect. The subject must also address the question why these books were written to exclude DEFA in the first place.

1945: rupture or continuity?

A starting-point in the discussion of DEFA is the question, 'What significance does it have that DEFA happened to be located in the German Democratic Republic?' One particularity is that there was less of a rupture in cultural identity in 1945 in the East than in the West, despite the socialist rhetoric of the 'New Germany'. As Christiane Mückenberger and Günter Jordan's book has made clear, to a great degree both the facilities and the personnel were the same.[3] The popular front policy of the German Communist Party (KPD), Socialist Unity Party (SED) and the Soviet Union meant that for a long period, extending into the 1960s, DEFA was meant to be a German studio, and not just the East German studio. The number of people who kept their jobs after Nazi Germany may even have exceeded the number who have kept their jobs since 1989. And the mode of production, which has only recently given way to more emphasis on project-based subsidy, was also more continuous with the rather centralised studio system that had developed since World War I.

The official anti-fascism of the GDR played a role in this tolerance for continuity with Nazi instructions. Regardless of the degree of complicity of its citizens with Nazism, the official self-definition of the GDR as an anti-fascist state freed them from many of the conflicts regarding German cultural symbols and practices that otherwise may have been tainted by Nazi Germany. Appeals to such concepts as folk, nation, *Heimat* and even the term *Kultur*, could eventually be given socialist content. The GDR thus could preserve some institutions and forms from earlier states without the admission that the form of these institutions necessarily was tainted by National Socialist content. A prominent example would be the Free German Youth (FDJ), a national youth organisation developed out of the Communist youth groups of the 1920s and 1930s. In the West, such a group is unthinkable due to its similarity to the Hitler Youth; in the socialist context, it was logically the victorious, and thus justified, alternative. Other examples could be named here, from the uniform of the National People's Army (NVA) to the word *Reichsbahn*, an 'Imperial Railway' operated by a little people's republic.

This feeling of guiltlessness for the crimes of German culture, whether justified or not, supports the assertion that GDR cinema was almost always more of a 'national cinema' than the cinema of the West. Philip Rosen has defined a 'national cinema' as arising at the intersection of multiple narrative discourses of nationhood.[4] [. . .]

The cinema of the GDR was also more 'German' and 'National' than that in the West partly because it did not feel the need to make such a radical break with the past. Along with the lack of guilt-driven break there is the fact of the more 'foreign' occupation by the Soviets, not the Western allies dominated by the USA. Thus the debate over American popular culture that plagued the West from the late 1940s on and became one of the defining qualities of the national cinema called the 'New German Cinema', was not the same issue in the East. Whereas in the West, identification with the occupiers became fundamental to identity, in the East, to the extent that the USSR influenced the cinema of the GDR, it did not – or could not – successfully represent an alternative, popular-culture identity.[5] The 'popular culture' forms that did develop in GDR film thus mediate in a unique way between Western, Eastern

European and Soviet models. The historian Uta Poiger has demonstrated how central the cinema was to struggles over youth culture in the early phases of the Cold War, and study of youth film from an Eastern point of view demonstrates its importance to GDR film culture generally.[6] The deservedly paradigmatic banned films of 1965 are thus not an exception, but the culmination of at least a decade of creative development.

Beyond the influence of Western popular culture in the East, however, a rather unproblematic acceptance of 'Germanness' still allowed for cultural continuities that were much more controversial or even taboo in the West. One genre that benefited from this dispensation of innocence was comedy, which in the West has almost always had either a regional or slapstick quality, or has referred to American forms such as the screwball comedies of Doris Dorrie. The DEFA comedies, however, were relaxed enough to laugh to a degree at their own Germanness – with such examples as Wolfgang Staudte's *Der Untertan* (*The Kaiser's Lackey*, 1951) and Frank Beyer's *Karbid und Sauerampfer* (*Carbide and Sorrel*, 1963) most prominent. [. . .]

Cinema and national identity

What is 'German cinema' is an old question, like Adorno's 'What is German?'.[7] With the opportunity to ask the question anew in regard to DEFA and the cinema of the GDR comes the obligation to ask questions in regard to West Germany too, lest we perpetuate the common assumption that the Federal Republic is synonymous with 'Deutschland'.

Future study of the cinema of the GDR, which is already not synonymous with the cinema of DEFA, could profit from a continuation of the work already begun by Cultural Studies. In doing so, the subject is not only DEFA or the GDR, but how the Cold War has structured an entire apparatus of intellectual history. Anna Szemere has written about this challenge, noting that Cultural Studies has mainly concentrated on advanced capitalist society or the Third World, i.e. 'the dominated or colonised "Other"'. 'Yet,' she goes on, 'those societies which until quite recently have been the site of "existing socialism" have been left virtually unexplored by cultural studies.'[8]

In considering the various cultural contexts of DEFA and DEFA scholarship, then, the kind of social history of cinema pioneered by Thomas Elsaesser in regard to New German Cinema provides an excellent model. This approach does not treat history as a narrative, but examines the intersection of various cultural realms, from politics and cultural policy to technical, financing and reception conditions to literary, artistic creativity and personal fantasies and desires. All this is at work in the cinema of DEFA, and has often been neglected by the polarities of Cold War concepts.

The following will thus look at some of the films of DEFA in contexts other than the linear historical narrative of the GDR, and interrogate their Germanness, their Euopeanness and their resonances with international film history from a 'third point of view', to borrow Peter Weiss's phrase. After all, it is more liberating to think of Germany not as synonymous with the Federal Republic or either state that existed before 1990 but as that entity described by Hans Koning in a 1987 article, 'Where money has little currency'. Koning writes that 'the Red Michelin Guide titled "Germany" does not even mention the existence of East Germany. My Webster's *New World Dictionary* quite properly says under "Germany": "Former Country in North Central Europe, divided . . .".'[9]

The challenge is to look at the history of DEFA without forcing it into a narrative that merely leads to the outcome we now know since 1989. It is unlikely that any system of government has either succeeded or failed because of the films that were made under its auspices. But looking at the cinema of DEFA can tell us some things we cannot learn anywhere else – about the possibilities and limitations of both cinema and socialism, about particular German practices in regard to European film traditions, and about the interrelations of East and West German cinemas which now make up what presently confronts us as 'The German Cinema'.

[. . .] This essay will consider DEFA not primarily as an expression of GDR national culture, but as a space where film styles, movements and traditions were or could have been pursued.

The expressionist legacy

If one thinks of the situation of 1945–6, with film artists returning from exile, some as members of occupying forces, and joining with others who had worked in the Nazi cinema, one asks what would have been the most likely traditions to pursue. The first strain that comes to mind is Expressionism, and it would be interesting to trace the Expressionist traditions in postwar German cinema both East and West up to the present. One legacy of this German tradition took the form of *film noir*, gangster and horror films – especially in the United States. Horror films seem to have been virtually eliminated from the German tradition by the real horrors of Nazism and the state's wish to deny the existence of monstrous or evil forces in society, for fear of turning them loose in political form once again. But Expressionist styles were indeed used in early DEFA films to look backward at the horrors of the past, in a rather *noir* style in Staudte's *Die Mörder sind unter uns* (*The Murderers Are Among Us*, 1946) and in the gangster genre of Erich Engle's *Affaire Blum* (*The Blum Affair*, 1948). The tactic of using the Expressionist-gangster genre as a popular way to depict the Nazi enemy of course goes back at least to Fritz Lang's 1943 Hollywood film *Hangmen also Die* (with a script by Lang, John Wexley and Bertolt Brecht). The formalism debates of the early 1950s, led by SED cultural functionaries such as Alexander Abusch and Alfred Kurella, attempted to bring such stylised film-making to an end. This aversion to Expressionist film in official GDR cultural policy must also be understood in the context of the problematic relation of the GDR to German Romanticism. Romanticism's implication in the irrational seductiveness of Nazi imagery (indirectly by way of Expressionist film) has made many film people averse to this German tradition of meretricious spectacle (if not narrative pleasure), and not only in the East. This also accounts in part for the relative reticence of West German cinema where spectacle and narrative are concerned.[10]

Looking at a film such as *Die Mörder sind unter uns* in the context of *film noir*, we see both the common postwar theme of threatened masculinity and a strong woman. But in the socialist context, the woman is not and cannot be seen as the threat to masculinity but instead must offer a civilising solution to the crisis. It is telling that Staudte at first wanted his male lead to murder the villain in a final scene, and removing the murder was the only change insisted on by the Soviet film officer Alexander Dymschitz. In a *film noir*, the revenge might as often as not have included the murder of the emasculating, aggressive woman (as in George Marshall's *The Blue Dahlia* (1946), written by Raymond Chandler, or John Huston's *The Maltese Falcon* (1941)). The rather indirect relation to the true horrors of the Nazis' destruction of the Jews in GDR anti-fascist films could also be productively contrasted with American films of the era. The realist drama *Gentleman's Agreement* (directed by Elia Kazan in 1947), for instance, ostensibly attacks anti-Semitism head-on, but manages to avoid all mention of either Nazism or World War II. Edward Dmytryk's *Crossfire*, a *film noir* from the year 1947, similarly limits anti-Semitism to a personal villainy, but manages to use a *noir* compromise to the dilemma of *Die Mörder sind unter uns*: like the voice of Susanne Wallner at the end of the Staudte film, Robert Young's fatherly civilian authority figure tames the unruly soldiers among whom the murder of a Jew has been committed; here, however, the murderer is not brought to trial, but is gunned down in 'satisfying' *noir* fashion as he tries to escape down a dark city street.

Another strain of Expressionism's legacy can be found, however, in the stylised socialist realism that replaced the gangster or *noir* thriller in the GDR. Here the most apt Hollywood comparison may be the Western. The socialist realist epics produced by DEFA in the 1950s share with their earlier Soviet counterparts a grand scale, a stark dramatic conflict between good and evil, the visual pleasure of spectacular and stylised cinematic qualities, and a viscerally engaging narrative characterised by suspense as well as a satisfying climax and resolution. [. . .]

Melodrama

The other great tradition of Weimar cinema seen in the early years after the war, along with the Expressionist legacy, is the melodrama. Here, too, like the gangster style, it was necessary in the early GDR context to confine melodrama largely to the fascist/anti-fascist problematic. This is no doubt related to the connection often made in German culture of this century between women, consumer pleasures, and fascism.[11] The 1920s equation between the cinema itself as sensual commodity and a female prostitute has perhaps never been completely absent from views of melodrama, and may account for its general absence as a separate genre from DEFA production. Like the myth-making Western, however, such a 'pleasurable' form could not be totally eliminated from a film industry, but was also partly replaced by a particularly socialist form, the anti-fascist film.

Seeing DEFA's anti-fascist films as melodramas may be one among many explanations for the fact that so many such films have female protagonists and are structured around a heterosexual love affair. The drama of the Wielands in Kurt Maetzig's *Ehe im*

Schatten (*Marriage in the Shadow*, 1947), with the love triangle almost grotesquely juxtaposed with the rise of Nazism, is the clearest, and perhaps trend-setting, example. [. . .]

Other anti-fascist films could also be seen as melodramatic love stories, however, from Wolf's *Lissy* (1957) to Günther Rücker and Günter Reisch's *Die Verlobte* (*The Fiancée*, 1980) and even one of the latest DEFA Films, Siegfried Kühn's *Die Schauspielerin* (*The Actress*, 1988). The protagonists of these films suffer for the man they love, and in the case of Lissy, Wolf makes explicit the link between female desire (both for her Nazi husband and the commodities he provides) and the seductions of Nazi Germany. A woman seduced by pleasure is a theme consistent with melodramas from Hollywood in the same period (those by Douglas Sirk have been most exhaustively studied in this respect).[12] Wolf's *Lissy*, however, takes an explicit stand against the evil represented by these seductive Nazi commodity pleasures, but, in a manner not unlike that of the morally upright Hollywood, this at the same time allows the audience to briefly revel in them in the form of spectacular film production values.

The message of Western melodramas regarding gender roles seems to have been consistent with the urging of postwar women to abandon their war-time 'masculinised' roles as independent workers and return to the role of house-wife and consumer. Although this sacrifice of independence is one form of renunciation, it is compensated by both the pleasure of the film and the commodities offered to women in the market-place. In the DEFA version, the renunciation is more complete and is seldom compensated by the heroine ending up with the good man after all. On the contrary, her compensation for renouncing the seductions of commodities and fascism is mainly the role of producer/worker and socialist citizen. For that reason, a woman alone (partly due to her confidence in the support of socialism) is the final image of numerous DEFA films – including the Konrad Wolf films *Lissy*, *Sonnensucher* and even *Der Geteilte Himmel* (*The Divided Heaven*, 1964) – anything but a melodrama in formal terms, but less clearly so in regard to its love story.[13]

[. . .]

DEFA and modernism

Less visible after 1946 are the prewar traditions of the leftist avant-garde and the New Sobriety ('Neue Sachlichkeit'). After Stalinism rejected the left avant-garde tradition about 1929 and the Nazis destroyed the rest in 1933, its presence in German cinema and in DEFA has been submerged but never entirely absent. This could not be the case for biographical reasons alone, since many artists who were important for 1920s modernism – Slatan Dudow and Hanns Eisler, for example – were involved with DEFA as well. Even the logo of the DEFA studio has its origins in the graphic arts innovations of the Weimar Republic. The word modernism alone suggests that virtually all aspects of DEFA cinema, except perhaps for certain nineteenth-century narrative styles, belong to European modernism. As such, they grew out of the movements responding to the social realities and material possibilities presented by urban, mass, industrial society. DEFA in particular participates in this modernism in part merely by its location in Babelsberg, with its industrial studio tradition and its proximity to Berlin, a city virtually synonymous with modernity. Modernism is quite evident in the consistent support for documentary film as a cultural product, and in the role that cinema played in GDR society, whatever its political significance. Even the stylised socialist realism of the Stalin era and after has to be classified as a form of modernism, functionalised as it may have been. There is no other term to describe it.

But the strongest modernist legacy in feature films of DEFA is a submerged one – the hidden and embattled influence of the leftist avant-gardes that had so much influence between the wars. If we look at the legacy of those leftist movements internationally, we see both that DEFA was not exceptional, and also that it represents a specific interaction with that portion of film history. Doubtless the most significant and sustained dialogue with another modernist, leftist film tradition was DEFA's relation to Italian neo-realism. It should not be forgotten, first of all, that DEFA provided production facilities for one of the landmarks of Italian neo-realism in Germany, Roberto Rossellini's *Germania anno zero* (1947). It is no surprise that the first DEFA film, and the first 'rubble-film' ('Trümmerfilm'), also has at times a neo-realist look – Staudte's *Die Mörder sind unter uns*. The neo-realists had an impact on a few other films of the postwar years, but, as Klaus Kreimeier has argued, their direct influence at the time was relatively limited.[14]

The relation of DEFA to neo-realism does not stop there, however. Neo-realist films remained central to discussions among DEFA artists throughout the 1950s, ranging from both Friedrich Wolf and Konrad Wolf to Heiner Carow, Wolfgang Kohlhaase, and Gerhard Klein. [. . .]

A politically and chronologically parallel development in cinema to neo-realism, perhaps the dominant type among all of DEFA productions, is what has been called the 'social-realist' film. Although usually linked to the 1970s cultural liberalisation in the GDR, this type arises from *Neue Sachlichkeit* in the 1920s and the social problem films that include the worker milieu films *Kuhle Wampe* (1932) directed by Slatan Dudow and *Cynakali* (1929) directed by Hans Titner (and based on Friedrich Wolf's play), Piel Jutzi's *Mutter Krausens' Fahrt ins Glück* (*Mother Krause's Journey to Happiness*, 1929) and aspects of such films as G.W. Pabst's *Kameradschaft* (*Comradeship*, 1931).

Social realism was also found in Hollywood, as a recent videotape called *Red Hollywood* (1995), by Noël Burch and Thom Andersen, so clearly documented. [. . .]

DEFA thus connects to international movements both in terms of the youth films influenced by Italian neo-realism and the persistent attempts to make 'social problem films' that treated controversial subjects.

Film and literature

Another international aspect of film culture relevant to GDR film studies is the relation of films to literature. In many countries, especially those with subsidy systems, literature makes film bureaucratically possible. But, as Karsten Witte has pointed out, canonical works of German literature are often criticised by GDR films.[15] This again is part of the GDR's unique *Erbe-Diskussion* – the debate over its relation to the

German cultural heritage. Also specific to the GDR, and perhaps another example of continuity with pre1945 studios, is the prominent status of the screenwriter. [. . .] The role of literature and the writer in DEFA also could be productively studied in the context both of German Romantic views of the artist and the bureaucratic structures of subsidised culture, as Thomas Elsaesser has done for West Germany. Elsaesser writes, 'The subsidised artist, I have argued, has thrust upon him his role of representative: a middle ground where originality is compromised by speaking on behalf of others. The label of author thus becomes a dubious value. Conferred by committees, in advance filled with social meaning, his status is, by an ironic twist, a subtle form of revenge society extracts for his privilege.'[16] [. . .]

DEFA beyond the GDR

A final assumption to be challenged is that DEFA was completely confined by the border represented by the Berlin Wall. DEFA does not belong to the GDR alone, and cannot bear sole 'blame' for the GDR, if for no other reason than its continuous relationship with FRG cinema. In the beginning this was true in practical terms, since it was not until 1961 and the Berlin Wall that DEFA had an exclusively Eastern identity. And from a Western point of view, where convenient, early DEFA films are even treated as simply German. Later there was an explicit campaign to keep Western talent out of DEFA and keep DEFA films out of the West. But DEFA contributions exist in many Western films, including Roberto Rossellini's *Germania anno zero* (1947), Straub/Huillet's *Chronik der Anna Magdalena Bach* (*The Chronicle of Anna Magdalena Bach*, 1967), Wenders's *Der Himmel über Berlin* (*Wings of Desire*, 1987). Numerous actors prominent in both theatre and film in the West also had started out with DEFA, often leaving from political reasons. [. . .]

Mapping the metaphorical journeys of these actors would provide an interesting intertextual account of DEFA's place in the imaginary geography of contemporary Germany: Hilmar Thate from the troubled youth of the 1950s to the reliable factory director of *Der geteilte Himmel* to the troubled newspaperman in Fassbinder's *Veronika Voss* (1981); Manfred Krug from the irrepressible worker heroes of *Spur der Steine* or *Fünf Patronenhülsen* to *Liebling – Kreuzberg*; Armin Mueller Stahl from the blind violinist in *Der Dritte* to the comic taxi-driver in Jim Jarmusch's *Night on Earth*. This kind of intertextuality has recently been studied in regard to Marlene Dietrich and allusions to persona by Hanna Schygulla, Marianne Sägebrecht, Barbara Sukow and even Madonna, for instance in an article entitled 'The Marshall Plan at the movies'[17] The 'Stalin Plan' has yet to be chronicled.

DEFA's location among a complex and shifting network of state institutions, film movements, historical and aesthetic periods, and production arrangements beyond the GDR could be exemplified by the career of the composer Hanns Eisler.[18] In 1923 Eisler composed music for Walter Ruttmann's *Opus III*, a part of the international avant-garde extending across Europe. From this rather abstract and formalist beginning, Eisler's film work moved to Alexis Granowsky's working-class film *Das Lied vom Leben* (*The Song of Life*, 1931), with songs sung by Ernst Busch. On the other hand, one of Eisler's collaborators on the film was Friedrich Hollaender, author of several of Marlene Dietrich's most famous siren songs. After the pathbreaking work *Kuhle Wampe*, Eisler worked on leftist documentaries such as those by Joris Ivens, and eventually ended up in the USA, writing music for a Joseph Losey film commissioned by the oil industry, *Pete Roleum and His Cousins* (1939). Hollywood also gave Eisler the chance to work with John Ford on *The Grapes of Wrath* (1940) and Fritz Lang on *Hangmen also Die* (1943), on leftist works by Harold Clurman and Clifford Odets as well as films by Douglas Sirk, Jean Renoir, and Edward Dmytryk. In Hollywood he also wrote the important book *Composing for the Films* with T. W. Adorno, an author not usually associated with the GDR. And lest the Cold War be forgotten, in the light of McCarthyist attacks on Eisler and others, Adorno concealed his co-authorship of that book until the 1960s.

Thus Eisler's career – like many at DEFA – begins in the Weimar cinema and touches the leftist avant-garde as well as socially-engaged Hollywood. [. . .] For DEFA he worked on Dudow's *Frauenschicksale* (*Fates of Women*, 1952) and *Unser täglich Brot* (1949), Maetzig's *Der Rat der Götter* (*Council of the Gods*, 1950) and Andrew Thorndike's *Wilhelm Pieck* (1950). His modernism was banned as decadent and formalistic in the form of the opera *Johann Faustus*, but was part of the French New Wave in the form of *Nuit et brouillard*.[19] He ended his career writing for DEFA and GDR television, in such productions as Erich Engel's *Geschwader Fledermaus* (*Bat Squadron*, 1958) and Walter Heynowski's *Aktion J* (*Operation J*, 1961). Clearly, on the basis of one example, the historical, political and aesthetic boundaries are very fluid, and deserve a renewed reception and study.

Part of the excitement of this time is to anticipate a rediscovery by young Europeans of such aspects of their cultural heritage the Cold War either hid from them or presented in an oversimplified and unproductive view. [. . .]

One of the truisms of the German cinema has it that to be carefree is to be dull. To be tormented is to be interesting.[20] The torment of DEFA's history is a tradition to be explored and built on, and a tradition to be resisted. For these reasons, DEFA will always be interesting.

Notes

1 See Paul Reimann (ed.), *Kafka aus Prager Sicht 1963*, Prague, 1965 and Jean-Paul Sartre, 'Die Abrüstung der Kultur: Rede auf dem Weltfriedenskongreß in Moskau' (trans. Stephan Hermlin), *Sinn und Form* 14, 1962: 805–15.

2 See Gilles Deleuze and Félix Guattari, *Franz Kafka: toward a Minor Literature* (Trans. Dana Polan), Minneapolis, 1986.

3 Christiane Mückenberger and Günter Jordan, 'Sie sehen selbst, Sie hören selbst . . .': Die DEFA von ihren Anfängen bis 1949, Marburg, 1994.

4 See Philip Rosen, 'History, Textuality, Nation: Kracauer, Burch, and Some Problems in the Study of National Cinemas', *Iris* 2, no. 2, 1984: 69–84.

5 Wolf Biermann underscores this difference in 'Reden über das eigene Land: Deutschland', *Klartexte im Getümmel: 13 Jahre im Westen. Von der Ausbürgerung bis zur November-Revolution*, Cologne, 1990, pp. 235–57 (p. 247).

6 Uta Poiger, *Taming the Wild West: American Popular Culture and the Cold War Battles over East and West German Identities, 1949–1961* (Phd Diss., Brown University, 1995). See also Hannelore König, Dieter Wiedemann and Lothar Wolf (eds), *Zwischen Bluejeans und Blauhemden: Jugendfilm in Ost und West*, Berlin, 1995.

7 Theodor W. Adorno, 'On the question "What is German?"', *New German Critique* 36, 1985: 121–31.

8 Szemere goes on to place the question in the context of Western leftist intellectuals' Cold War situation: 'I have wondered whether this apparent lack of interest might be due to Western leftists' ambivalence towards these societies: are they perceived as sites of a compromised, abused, and now defeated utopia? Could there have been a fear that a critical stance towards these political systems (while they were still socialist) would threaten the distinctive political edge of cultural studies and Western leftism *vis-à-vis* the dominant discourse on socialism in their own society?' See Anna Szemere, 'Bandits, Heroes, the Honest, and the Misled: Exploring the Politics of Representation in the Hungarian Uprising of 1956', in *Cultural Studies*, ed. Lawrence Grossberg, Cary Nelson, Paula Treichler, New York, 1992, pp. 623–39 (p. 623).

9 Hans Koning, 'Where Money Has Little Currency: Travels in East Germany', *Harper's Magazine*, November 1987: 71.

10 See Anton Kaes, *From Hitler to Heimat: The Return of History as Film*, Cambridge, MA, 1989, p. 8.

11 See Poiger, *Taming the Wild West*, p. 5 and p. 11.

12 On Hollywood melodrama see Christine Gledhill (ed.), *Home Is where the Heart Is: Studies in Melodrama and the Women's Film*, London, 1987.

13 On Konrad Wolf's female characters, see Marc Silberman, 'Remembering History: the film-maker Konrad Wolf', *New German Critique* 49, 1990: 163–91.

14 Klaus Kreimeier, '*Germania, anno zero: eine Momentaufnahme*', *epd film* 12, no. 6, 1995: 17–25 (22).

15 See Karsten Witte, 'Geteilte Filme: einige Erfahrungen mit Literatur und Politik im DEFA-Film', *Film und Fernsehen* 23, no. 1, 1995: 17–19.

16 Thomas Elsaesser, *New German Cinema: A History*. New Brunswick, NJ, 1989, p. 74.

17 Joseph Lowewenstein and Lynne Tatlock, 'The Marshall Plan at the Movies: Marlene Dietrich and Her Incarnations', *The German Quarterly* 65, nos. 3–4, 1992: 429–42.

18 This information relies on the entry on Eisler in Hans-Michael Bock (ed.), *Cinegraph: Lexikon zum deutschsprachigen Film*, Hamburg, Munich, 1984.

19 Tellingly, the cover of the video version of *Night and Fog* distributed in the USA makes no mention of Eisler's music.

20 Vlado Kristl: 'German films are by far the most accurate reflections of the Europe of our time. For film history they are more important as failures than where they were successful . . .' Cited in: Elsaesser, *New German Cinema*, p. 79.

Chapter 17

Marvin D'Lugo

CATALAN CINEMA
Historical experience and cinematic practice

Something like a national cinema

JAIME CAMINO'S 1986 DOCUMENTARY DRAMA, *Dragón Rapide*, is a striking example of the little understood development of Catalan film that has emerged in recent years to challenge the more generally accepted conception of a unified Spanish national cinema.[1] In addition to attempting to recuperate the long-suppressed sense of a regional cultural identity for Catalonia, Camino's film also questions the cultural constructions of nationhood that have stabilized the idea of a homogeneous Spanish nation at the expense of its distinctive regional cultures.

On the surface, the film looks like yet another historical reconstruction of aspects of the Civil War period, not unlike the spate of such films that, for more than a decade now, Spanish filmmakers have been churning out as a form of national Catharsis through which to expose for their countrymen many of the interdicted images and perspectives on the war that the iron hand of Francoist censorship had long prohibited. In chronicling the plotting by right-wing politicians and army officers in the summer of 1936 to overthrow the Spanish Republican government, however, Camino appears less interested in historical vindications than in finding a way to mobilize his audience's involvement in their own interrogation of political and cultural history. He finds that strategy by first presenting the narrative of the plan to transport the young General Franco from the Canary Islands to the Spanish mainland in a private airplane, the Dragón Rapide of the film's title, to head the insurrection, and then punctuating that narrative with a series of five brief scenes that have nothing to do with the military and political intrigues but are important indicators of the film's underlying political allegiance. The noted Catalan cellist, Pablo Casals, appears in each segment, first preparing and then rehearsing an orchestra and chorus in Barcelona's Palace of Music for a performance of Beethoven's Ninth Symphony.

What draws out attention to this micro-narrative embedded into the larger plot is not only its apparent lack of connection with the main action, but also the fact that during these scenes, Casals addresses his performers in the Catalan language. In the last sequence, the fateful eighteenth of July, he speaks to the orchestra and chorus for one final time to announce that the concert for which they have rehearsed has been cancelled because the army has risen up against the Republic. In a gesture of hope and 'fraternity,' Casals asks the group to play and sing Beethoven's 'Ode to Joy.' The singing fades as the final image of the film shows the airplane landing in Tetuán delivering Franco to lead the invasion of the peninsula.

As some critics have argued, Camino's presumed *Catalanidad*, his 'Catalanism,' leads him to insert this eccentric and irrelevant chain of scenes into his historical drama. Yet, far from being irrelevant, the Casals scenes which culminate in the 'Ode to Joy' sum up in narrative terms an underlying enunciative strategy that seeks to identify and develop a unique form of Catalan spectatorship. Juxtaposing the tradition of Catalan cultural achievement in arts and letters as embodied by Casals with the venality and ruthlessness of the Castilian-speaking military officers and politicians, *Dragón Rapide* invites its audience to reflect upon the historical events that imposed the Francoist hegemony on the Spanish nation while marginalizing and suppressing all other forms of popular cultural expression.

Camino is not alone in his effort to move his audience to a meditation/inquiry about the nature of the cultural identity that has been constructed for it by the dominant ideology of the Francoist state. *Dragón Rapide* connects in a logical way with a body of films by other Catalan directors, films which since the early 1960s have insistently challenged not only the dominant Spanish film productions coming out of Madrid, but, as well, the very notion of Spanishness to which such cultural production subscribes. These films do not easily fit into our conventional notions of autonomous national cinema, nor do they adhere to the folkloric prescriptions of regional, ethnographic film. Rather, they reflect the larger historical problematic of a number of marginal cinemas, that is, the filmic production of 'sub-national' cultural or ethnic groups whose self-realization as cultures threatens the coherence and possibly even the integrity of the political units within which they exist. In this respect, the experience of Catalan cinema can prove highly instructive to the understanding of the cultural dynamic of any emerging national cinema, as it does to the more immediate question that cinematic Catalanism raises about the nature of Spanish film itself.

Raymond Carr and Juan Pablo Fusi argued that 'the Catalan view of Spanish history was [that] Spain was a plural society of different peoples artificially hammered into the straitjacket of unity by Castilians.'[2] Like Catalonia itself, Catalan cinema challenges the assumption of Spain as a unified cultural unit by mobilizing a variety of discourses of regional identity in opposition to that cultural otherness. Though not a national cinema in the conventional sense that one speaks of Italian or German cinemas, for instance, the multiple expressions of Catalanism in film nonetheless suggest to us something like a national cinema. While lacking a formal state apparatus through which to authenticate its 'nationhood,' Catalan cinema is marked by a pattern of conceptualizations – shared cultural-historical traditions and textual coherencies across a significant body of different filmic texts over time – that in other contexts would lead us to consider it as a national cinema.[3] The pivot of these 'coherencies' lies in the deployment of certain issues of history into a chain of discursive practices that inscribe the historical trace of Catalan identity into the enunciative structure of a variety of films. Such strategies are understandable as a response to the sustained practices of the Franco regime to eradicate all overt signs of regional cultural identity from public life and gradually to erase even their memory. For that reason the conceptulaization of history and the intertextual construction of a Catalan historical referent will play a pivotal role in the development and evolution of modern Catalan cinema.

Catalanism and cinema

At its root, the problematic status of Catalan cinema derives from the disjunction between Catalonia as a historically-rooted cultural community and the imposed constructions of political authority of the Spanish state that over centuries have sought to subsume all regional differences under the rubric of Castilianized, Spanish culture. 'Catalanism' is the term that has traditionally been applied to any one of the variety of political and cultural positions that focus on the notion of Catalonia as a community separate and unique from the Castilian culture that dominates most of the rest of Spain. Situated on Spain's eastern Mediterranean shores, Catalonia historically comprised the provinces surrounding the city of Barcelona and the adjacent province of Valencia, as well as the Balearic islands. Throughout its history, however, this region claimed to be more than simply a geographic entity. It boasted a distinct language dating back to the ninth century and a strong literary heritage that, in the medieval period at least, rivaled that of Castilian literature. Catalonia has been politically associated with the Castilian monarchy of the central plateau since 1469. What remnants of political autonomy it enjoyed ended in 1715 when it was officially incorporated into the monarchy of Philip V. Nevertheless, there is ample evidence in eighteenth and nineteenth century writings to suggest that Catalans continued to think of themselves as a nation apart, bolstered as they were by their linguistic and cultural differences, and by their closer identification with the rest of Europe, an identification nurtured by the region's coastal location and Barcelona's strength as a mercantile center.

The mid-nineteenth century *Renaixença* or renaissance of Catalan literature brought a rebirth of nationalist spirit as it awakened interest in earlier Catalan culture as a source of distinctive regional identity.[4] Though understandably restricted to a cultural elite, the *Renaixença*'s emphasis on the rich heritage of Catalan letters was to contribute to the more generalized view in later decades of a profound Catalan difference from the rest of Spain. [. . .] The ideal of a politically independent state, freed from the domination of Castilian Spain, inspired at least two popular uprisings against the Spanish monarchy, in 1909 and 1917, both of which were quickly suppressed by the central government.

Catalan demands for some form of home rule were a constant of Spanish parliamentary politics during the first decades of the twentieth century, but not until 1931, with the fall of the monarchy and the formation of the Second Republic, did the regional aspirations of self-governance become a realistic political possibility. Under a series of agreements with the Republican government, Catalonia was given semi-autonomous legal status, with the right to its own parliament, administration, law courts, budget, and the development of its own culture.[5] [. . .]

Catalonia's allegiance to the Republican government during the Civil War was unswerving, for survival of the Republic clearly meant hope for the continuation of a semi-independent Catalan state. As the war dragged on and the fortunes of the Republic waned, Catalonia became progressively more autonomous, experiencing what amounted to a degree of political nationhood during the final months of the war. With the Republican defeat, and as a bitterly ironic twist to their nationalist aspirations, Catalans were treated by the triumphant Francoist armies as a defeated enemy nation. Francoist policies in the immediate postwar period suggested that the goal of the fascist victors was the intentional extinction of Catalan culture. The Catalan language was banned in public, and a new law prohibited the use of any language but Spanish in films shown in Spain.

The massive blockage of all public displays of Catalan culture persisted well into the 1960s, and only under the gradual redirection of the Franco dictatorship did the possibility of some sort of cultural and cinematic revival of the Catalan difference take form. The period of 1963–1969 was the era of the first major liberalization of the censorship system in Spain. Under the direction of Manuel Fraga Iribarne, as Minister of Information and Tourism, and his director of the ministry's film division, José María García Escudero, the country experienced a relaxation of the rigid patterns of permissible representation in film. This liberalization coincided with the first open manifestations of cultural nationalism in the region since the war's end. In this context, and against the historical backdrop of the Catalan struggle for some form of cultural self-definition and self-realization, we see the emergence of a new generation of filmmakers. The maintenance of the official film censorship apparatus, however, assured that there would be no overtly pro-Catalanist films for many years to come. Yet, as the decade progressed, it gradually became obvious that the recent history of political autonomy and the ferocious suppression of Catalan cultural identity were the important historical intertexts out of which these young filmmakers were shaping their own sense of cinematic Catalanism.

Perhaps the most problematic aspect of this early group of Catalanist films is the apparent lack of any overt signs of common textual or political referents that might constitute a coherent and unified body of filmic works. Not merely films made in Catalonia, nor films that espouse the usual themes of a patriotic Catalanist culture, these were works that mobilized the concept of Catalan identity in a variety of ways in order to rewrite and ideally to displace the Francoist ideal of a Castilianized Spanishness. The conceptual gesture most common to the young Catalanist filmmakers was their subtle exploitation of the old Manicheanism that pitted Europeanized and culturally developed Catalonia against provincial and backwater Castile. Though their strategies vary, their common stance was to conceive of their own cultural activity as filmmakers against the specter of Spanish national cinema as defined by the body of filmic and political practices as well as the cultural ideology that historically has sought to suppress and marginalize the Catalan difference.

Yet as much as these were works born of cultural opposition, it is often difficult to read into them the kind of political message that is most often associated with traditional Catalanist rhetoric. For instance, the conceptual opposition between Catalonia and Francoist Spain that inspires a number of these films reveals a gradual slippage of the idea of the Catalan 'difference,' not towards the identification of Catalonia with the political and artistic avant-garde of Europe, as Catalan nationalists had long argued, but precisely as the creative frontier or 'supplement' of liberated culture and modernity capable of revitalizing the rest of Spain. In the sense that it emerges in Catalan films of the last decade and a half before Franco's death, Catalanism focuses on the image of Catalonia as a creative margin within a larger national consciousness extending beyond the limits of its geographically defined region.

Consistent with that conceptual tendency we find these films taking their common inspiration from a notion of Catalonia in general and Barcelona in particular as the bastion of pluralistic Spain and the haven of tolerance. Though not overtly historical, such a characterization carries with it the power of allusion, specifically the evocation of a Utopian Catalonia as the defender of the values of toleration and pluralism commonly associated with the political philosophy of the Republican government. Out of this conceptual move comes the earliest serious efforts by filmmakers to prolematize cultural history around a series of interrogations of contemporary Catalanism in ways that, perhaps surprisingly for many Spaniards, transcend mere regionalism and are linked with the larger question of a Spanish national identity.

Textualizing difference

During the early 1960s, and under the aura of the regime's liberalization of its censorship norms, we find the first films made in Catalonia which focus on Catalan cultural images, although most of these are embedded in secondary plot elements or merely provide local color. Following the inspiration of the *Nova Cançó* movement, Jaime Camino's first film, *Los felices sesenta* (1964: *The Happy Sixties*), is the first, for example, to use a song interpreted in Catalan (by the popular folk singer Raimón), in its credit sequence. Of more substantive import are three films, Josep María Forn's *La piel quemada* (1964: *Burnt Skin*), Camino's *España, otra vez* (1968: *Spain, Again*), and Vicent Aranda's *Fata Morgana* (1966: *Mirage*), which represent serious efforts to rechannel into aesthetic structures the idea of Catalonia's cultural and political identity.

Burnt Skin is perhaps the first film in Francoist Spain to center explicitly on a wholly Catalan theme. The government's promotion of economic expansion on the Catalan Costa Brava, in large measure through the development of tourism, had led to the large-scale migration of workers from Andalusia to the coastal areas of northeastern Spain. The film traces one fateful day in the life of José, a migrant worker. By the use of radical juxtaposition of simultaneous actions, we follow José's last day of bachelorhood before his wife's arrival, and Ana's travel from her stark Andalusian village to the train station, then the long trip to Barcelona, and finally, to the coastal town where José will meet her. These juxtapositions are, in turn, punctuated by a series of silent flashbacks of José's memories of the economic hardships that led him to go to Catalonia, temporarily breaking up his family.

Forn's script underscores the popular notions still held in many quarters, of Catalonia as a frontier for Spaniards who have been economically and socially marginalized by the regime's failed economic policies, and also of Catalonia as a 'melting pot.' The individual's struggle, therefore, appears to transcend the horizons of purely proletarian narrative and borders on the mythic narrative of foundation. Tellingly, Forn joins the theme of economic hardship with the question of cultural and national identity by introducing at certain points reference to the new settlers' linguistic difference. The treatment of old-guard Catalans who refuse to speak Castilian to José, for instance, are made to seem like the Francoists of earlier decades who mocked the language and customs of their fellow Spaniards.[6] If there are those who taunt José, however, there are also more generous, giving Catalans who treat him with warmth and Camaraderie.

Juxtaposed against José's experiences are moments showing Ana and her children on their pilgrimage to Catalonia that evoke the iconography of the war years, particularly the images of whole families fleeing to safety beyond the reach of the Francoist armies. While only a single verbal reference to the war is made (by an old man Ana meets on the train who tells her about how it was when he first arrived in Barcelona), the indelible memory of the war and of the Catalonian haven clearly informs the film's narrative structure. The emphasis in *Burnt Skin* is clearly contemporary, but the elements of Forn's script cast the film's action into the figuration of recognizable national history.

[. . .]

In the films of the so-called 'Barcelona School' of the mid-1960s we find perhaps the most radical approach to the question of cultural identity to surface in that decade. The Barcelona School was a group of young filmmakers, most of them from upper middle-class backgrounds, who organized a cooperative of film productions which, as they theorized, would repudiate nearly everything dominant Spanish cinema stood for. Their rejection of the realist penchant of the Castilian-language opposition cinema – which included the established filmmakers such as Juan Antonio Bardem and Luis Berlanga, as well as the recently promoted 'New Spanish cinema' of Carlos Saura, Mario Camus and Basilio Martín Patino – was a way of rejecting the provincialism of the Spain that those films reflected. Instead, the cooperative embraced a more cosmopolitan Europeanism whose modernity was evident as much in the settings and characters they depicted as in the thematic foci, inspired by the recent works of Antonioni, Godard, and Resnais. One particular feature of the modernity the group embraced was the emulation of a glossy, fashion magazine style and chic television advertising techniques. Even in terms of production, the group repudiated the Castilian style of filmmaking by arguing that experience, rather than academic training of the sort the National Film School (*Escuela Oficial de Cine*) provided, was what counted in filmmaking. To that end they established their own production cooperative, with directors collaborating on both the technical and directorial aspects of each other's films.

At its core, these 'positions' voiced by members of the Barcelona School represented a critique of everything dominant Spanish cinema stood for. The essence of that critique was the ideological cleavage between cosmopolitan, universalist culture in Barcelona, strongly identified with the intellectual and artistic currents of the rest of Europe, and the Francoist Castilianism of Spanish culture and film which was, in their eyes, provincial and anachronistic.[7]

Visually, the films of the Barcelona School did not even look Spanish. When they were not modernist, constructed landscapes, their settings were shot precisely in those areas of Barcelona that would give a futuristic feel to the films. As one sympathetic Catalan film historian would later write, this was 'an aristocratic, left-thinking intelligentsia, but their films were all variations on personal myths and disconnected from anything even a liberal Catalan audience might identify with.'[8] Had they at least been spoken in Catalan, which was by the late 1960s a legal option, these films might have been more easily identifiable as a repudiation of Madrid. But, in fact, the Barcelona School seemed disengaged from its potential audiences by virtue of its strong commitment to a reconceptualization of the visual aesthetics of cinema.

Of the various film makers associated with the Barcelona School,[9] the only one to achieve wide attention after the dissolution of the group in 1968 was Vicente Aranda. Of Aranda's work in the sixties, perhaps the most significant film was his *Fata morgana* (1966: *Mirage*), actually made prior to the formation of the Barcelona School, but often cited as the perfect embodiment of the group's aesthetic. Aranda recalls that when writing *Mirage*, he and fellow filmmaker, Gonzalo Suárez, sacrificed 'conventional coherence' for the cinematic and phenomenological possibilities of each action. This was, he claims, a move to distract the censors' attention from the covert political implications of the film by use of the stock genres of detective and science fiction films.[10]

Mirage recounts the story of Gim (Terest Gimpera), a highly successful and famous fashion model, who receives a mysterious message informing her that she will be assassinated. The warning arrives on the very day that the city is being abandoned by its population, impelled by some inexplicable fear. Gim chooses to remain but is agitated by continual anxiety caused by the death threat. She comes into contact with three mysterious figures: a professor, who has made the prophecy of Gim's assassination in a lecture on the nature of victims; J. J., a secret agent charged with finding Gim and saving her; and Miriam, the assassin who is in search of her victims. J. J. never finds Gim, but Miriam does assassinate J. J. The model finally manages to escape from the city accompanied by a group of youths. As this brief plot suggests, in *Mirage* Aranda seeks to define an aesthetic texture to his film devoid of the topicality of provincial, Francoized Spain. By its very narrative and cultural insufficiency, the plot of *Mirage* becomes an aesthetic enigma, problematizing for its audience the question of its own identity. The flaunting of a structured absence (What city is this? What is the fear that grips the populace?) initiates a hermeneutic chain, the decipherment of which should motivate the spectator to read the entire film as the allegory of suppressed Catalan identity.

Such questions lead us back into the social and historical geography of Francoist Spain and are textualized within the narrative space, as personal and collective identity are continually put under a mark of interrogation. Combining a blockage of concrete national, geographical, or even historical specificity with suggestive dialogue, the film dramatizes the persecution and annihilation of the urbane, cultured identity seen but never verbally identified as Catalan. That historical-political intertext is suggested in the professor's lecture on the theory of the victim in which he tells his audience that 'only a desired fatality can truncate an existence and that fatality is the daughter of fear, fear the authentic whip, the true epidemic, so contagious that all of the city, all of the country change into its victim.'[11]

The twin questions of identity and identification are at the source of the film's various enigmas. J. J.'s efforts to find Gim and help her, Miriam's parallel effort to find Gim and kill her, even the professor's claim that some individuals were born to be victims are all part of a register of the struggle to identify and thereby 'fix' the identity of the other. *Mirage* begins with Gim's disavowal of the group by her insistence on remaining in the city when everyone else leaves; it ends as she departs in the company of the youths. Discursively, the film follows a similar shifting trajectory, for it begins with a refusal to root itself in a specific cultural milieu, but then gradually situates its axis of meaning within the narrow specificy of a political allegory of the cultural subjugation of Catalonia by the forces of Francoism.

Mirage is an undeniably complex work, and, given its flaunting of popular detective and science fiction genres, it stands as a rare example of cryptic narrative in the constrained cinematic production of Spain in the 1960s. Yet, finally, it is not as unfathomable as Spanish critics have made it out to be. Like Saura's *La Caza* (1965: *The Hunt*), it employs a political intertext to expose suppressed historical memories. But whereas Saura elected to posit the explicit historical referent of the Civil War, Aranda and Saurez follow the implicit model of Kafka's *The Trial*, actively involving their audience in the questioning of suppressed cultural identity by staging the past as a suppressed *mise-en-scène* in which the spectator's active interrogation of the symbolic blockage of that past leads to a form of historical reflexivity.

Recuperations

The decade following Franco's death in November, 1975, saw the dismantlement of the repressive apparatus of state censorship and the establishment in Barcelona of a regional government administration that, in accordance with the new federal constitution of 1978, sought to normalize the existence of Catalan culture by, among other measures, developing film as a form of expression of regional cultural identity. [. . .]

Of the more than one-hundred productions that the Catalan regional government, the *Generalitat*, has claimed as Catalan films since 1979, two sub-genres emerge which rigorously stablize a notion of Catalan identity in light of the thinking of the films of the Sixties. The first is an apparent continuation of the theme of historical recuperation, but unlike Ribas's films, these works sustain their focus on the thematics of the Civil War as the single historical epoch which transcends parochial local themes. Perhaps playing on the general view of Barcelona throughout Spain as a place of liberal and liberated culture, the second sub-genre narrativizes that liberation thematics, particularly in terms of sexual liberation, a theme that connects with the Civil War ethos of Barcelona. A closer examination of representative examples of these genres suggests that they are more than a random grouping of films, but actually cohere with the historical poetics of Catalan cultural identity established in earlier films.

Films by Catalan directors dealing with the theme of the Civil War abound in the years after Franco's death. Camino's *Las largas vacaciones del '36* (1975: *The Long Vacation of '36*), Francesco Bertriu's *La Plaça del Diamant* (1982: *Diamond Square*) and *Requiem por un Campesino español* (1983: *Requiem for a Spanish Farmer*), Gonzalo Heralde's *Raza, el espíritu de Franco* (1977: *Raza: The Spirit of Franco*), Forn's *Companys: Procesco a Cataluña* (1979: *Companys: Catalonia On Trial*), and José Luis Madrid's *Memorias del General Escobar* (1984: *The Memoirs of General Escobar*) are only some of the dozen or so films which attempt historical reconstructions of events of the Civil War with a specific anchoring in the Catalan experience. In truth, however, a large number of these seem inspired by a notion of historical vindication for the Francoist excesses rather than by an effort to sustain the vision of contemporary Catalan identity forged in the noble and generous vision of the past.

By far, the most significant of these works of meaningful recuperation and, to many critics, the most significant Spanish film dealing with the Civil War is Jaime Camino's third treatment of the Civil War theme, *La vieja memoria* (1977: *The Old Memory*) a documentary film consisting of a series of interviews with eighteen people who played prominent roles on either side of the fighting, people such as Enrique Lister, the communist commander of the Republican 'People's' Army in Barcelona, Dolores Ibarruri, better known as *La Pasionaria*, and the anarchist, José María Gil Robles, the leader of the right-wing deputies in the pre-Civil War Republican parliament. While asking each informant to recall specific events during the war, Camino employs a technique of testimonial engagement, including in each interview shots of the other interviewees reacting to the speaker's descriptions, often shaking their heads in disagreement or derision at a given interpretation. The cross-cutting technique produces a continuous chain of *faux raccords* as it appears that these individuals are 'sitting around the table' in conversation when, in fact, they are merely being filmed viewing and reacting to other filmed interviews. [. . .]

By means of their persistent address to their audience through an often intricate system of historical allusion, Catalan filmmakers have insistently constructed a concept of their cultural heritage that opposes the narrowness of the old Francoist mythology and displaces it with a notion of Catalonia as the spiritual complement to that other Spain. The conception of Catalan identity inscribed in this body of filmic texts is, as we have seen, a persistent impulse that seeks not only to demarginalize the Catalan cultural community within Spain, but perhaps more importantly, to challenge the traditional Castilian monolithic view of a single and unitary definition of Spanish culture itself. As such films insistently demonstrate, Catalan cinema does not attempt to draw barriers, but instead, to address all Spaniards in ways that both history and geography have conspired through the years to frustrate.

Notes

1 The research for this essay was conducted in Spain during the 1986–87 academic year under the auspices of a grant from the US-Spanish Joint Committee for Cultural and Education Exchange.

2 Raymond Carr and Juan Pablo Fusi, *Spain: Dictatorship in Democracy*, Second Edition (London: Allen and Unwin, 1981), p. 11.

3 In making the case for the consideration of Catalanist film as approximating the category of a national cinema, I am indebted to Philip Rosen's reading of the methodological implications of the concept of national cinema as it is used in the classical works on the subject by Siegfried Kracauer and Noel Burch. Rosen identifies three areas of conceptualization as central to the rigorous formulation of a national cinema:

   (1) not just a conceptulaization of textuality, but one which describes how a large number of superficially differentiated texts can be associated in a regularized, relatively limited intertextuality in order to form a coherency, a 'national cinema'; (2) a conceptualization of a nation as a kind of minimally coherent entity which it makes sense to analyze in relation with (1); (3) some conception of what is traditionally called 'history' or 'historiography.'

   See Philip Rosen, 'History, Textuality, Nation: Kracauer, Burch, and Some Problems in the study of National Cinemas,' *Iris* 2, no. 2 (1984): 70–71.

4 Benjamín Otra, Francesc Mercadè, Francesc Hernández, *La ideologia nacional Catalana* (Barcelona: Editorial Anagrama, 1981), pp. 19–20.

5 Pierre Vilar, *Spain: A Brief History* (Oxford: Pergamon Press, 1967), p. 93.

6 There is a curious underplaying of the Catalan language as a critical mark of cultural identity in films of this period. While language is used at times to evoke some feature of Catalan culture, it is never seen as *the* exclusive mark of identity. In a country in which, for nearly fifty years, all foreign-language films were regularly dubbed into Castilian, and where, even today, audiences still prefer Castilian-dubbed to subtitled films, language has ceased to be a stabile signifier of cultural identity.

7 The frequent identification of Catalan cinema with European rather than Spanish artistic movements should not be read as a mark of a colonized film culture, but instead as a sign of a powerful strategy of resistance against Castilian culture.

8 Domenèc Font, *Del Azul a verde: el cine español durante el franquismo* (Barcelona: Editorial Avance, 1976), p. 270.

9 Critics often dispute exactly who were the actual members of the group. Of those most frequently cited, Jacinto Esteva, Gonzalo Suárez, and Carlos Durán were, according to Juan Antonio Martínez-Bretón, the 'nucleus' of the group. During the two-year life of the School (1967–68), various others became closely identified with that core. These included: Vincente Aranda, José María Nunes, Jorge Grau, Pedro Portabello, and

Joaquín Jorda. See Juan Antonio Martínez-Bretón, *La doenominada Escuela de Barcelona* (Madrid: Universidad Complutense, Facultad de Ciencias de Información, 1984), pp. 609–610.

10 John Hopewell, *Out of the Past: Spanish Cinema After Franco* (London: BFI Books, 1986), p. 69.

11 Hopewell, p. 70.

The boundaries of European film criticism

Im Laufe Der Zeit: BFI collections

INTRODUCTION TO PART FOUR

THIS FOURTH SECTION CONSIDERS two aspects of European cinema which have only recently been the subject of critical debate: the audience and the industry. It also considers European–American and intra-European relations. Whilst we have used the term 'film industry' in relation to Europe, it is one with which several writers would argue:

> when moving in Spanish film circles, use of the expression 'the Spanish film industry' tends to bring a wry smile to the lips of those producers hoary with experience and savvy to all the intrigues and vagaries of production.
>
> (Besas Chapter 21)

Here, there is the opportunity to compare how the film industries of several nations have been organised and then to review what kinds of films have therefore been produced. David Gillespie touches in Part 3 on the subject of the state apparatus in Russia which 'allowed' a particular form of cinema to exist; whilst none of the examples here are quite so evidently regulated, there is still evidence that state policies are brought in to allow a certain type of cinema and that they do indeed shape output. Perhaps the strongest example of this is given by Peter Besas when he cites the role of Pilar Miló, a film maker herself, who, when made director general of cinematography brought in measures which promoted only 'quality' – read *auteur* and art – cinema.

Though Miló's rule was an extreme moment, it is in keeping with Spanish strategy in general, which has in various ways left the audience out of the equation. Indeed, this would seem to be a tendency of all the national industries discussed here: German, British, French and Spanish, in which policy and funding seem to be driven by the beliefs of committees, ministers or powerful producers. The first observation of this section, then, is that whereas American cinema is known for its audience-pleasing tactics and its market-led approach to film production, European cinemas have paid far less lip-service to their audiences. National film policy has pronounced on the 'national culture'; however, whilst speaking *for* the people, European films do not seem to have *listened to* them.

It is just such a dilemma which is presented by Janet Thumim's attempt (see Chapter 19) to discern what films were popular with British audiences during a certain period, and then to examine those films for what they might tell us about 'conditions of social formation' and the 'language and attitudes of social groups'. Thumim, then, is keen to listen to the audience about what they like and dislike, her problem is that these tastes have never been recorded, and in order to reconstruct this she has to find her way through the complex web of literature which surrounds the films shown at that time. Clearly, Thumim is responding to Higson's call in the previous section for a national cinema to be constructed at the site of consumption, and her starting point is aligned with his proposal of those films to which national audiences are exposed.

Maltby and Vasey (Chapter 18) have a similar focus here with their analysis of the place of American culture in the European film industry. The popularity of American films and stars which is explored by Thumim is re-configured by Maltby and Vasey into a narrative of 'Americanisation' to which audiences were happy to succumb, but which 'the bourgeois nationalists' attempted to resist by emphasising the threat American mass culture posed to European culture. Hollywood, Maltby and Vasey point out, does not present itself as a national culture, instead it wants to appeal to everyone, and in the period which they study the suggestion is that it succeeds.

Maltby and Vasey's discussion of in what ways Hollywood managed to retain its hegemonic presence despite the coming of sound – which obviously destroyed some of the universal qualities of silent cinema – is interesting to compare to Martine Danan's argument (see Chapter 22) about English-language production in France from the late 1980s onwards. The different versions Hollywood prepared for different language groups meant the transition to sound cinema was gentle and American cinema retained many of the qualities that had made it so popular in the silent era. What these writers describe is a process of 'translation', which is very different from the policy described by Danan which is rather one of 'dilution'.

As both of these essays point out, the 'Film Europe' period of the 1920s, whilst trying to beat Hollywood at its own game, only managed to make super-productions with little sense of cultural specificity or worth. The same may be true of those productions described by Danan as part of the most recent attempt to address the 'globalisation' of cinema product. Again, in both the 1920s version and the present, the issue is raised that whenever a pan-European, big-budget cinema is proposed, the end result turns out as an emulation of the Hollywood model, thus minimising national cultural specificity. Reading between the lines, Danan's objection seems to be not that France makes these films, but that they are allowed to fall within the boundaries of French national cinema, thus diluting its Frenchness. Here, Danan seems to be echoing the film maker Louis Delluc, who is said to have proclaimed: 'Let French cinema be real, let French cinema be really French.'

Amid these discussions of the influence of American cinema and culture on European film industries we need to insert the important point – made in one way or another by most writers here – that part of the problems Europe has suffered with

America have come about because of the difficulties involved in any collective form of 'European' cinema. We might look to Finney's comparative article for evidence of national differences in film support; however, though his discussion upholds the lack of co-operation between nations (thus he observes that only 10 per cent of Europe's films are ever shown in cinema theatres in another country), it also shows the harmony between national film policies, most of which have a cultural and commercial remit. Concurring with the view of disharmony though are Danan, who points out that France's film policy is purely national, and Maltby and Vasey: 'the tensions between European nationals in the 1930s inhibited the development of any coherent strategy for resisting the American invasion'.

As Danan's essay lucidly shows, the difficulty in co-operating that European countries have had in the past has not changed in the present. The differences of approach, opinion, style and subject are those things which mitigate against the all-encompassing term 'European cinema' to instead lead us towards talking of 'cinemas in Europe'. Whilst in the first three sections of the Reader some notion of the 'European' seemed to exist (as shared culture, history or mode of practice), in this final section the 'European' is splintered and we are forced to face up to the differences between cinemas in Europe.

References and further reading

Hayward, Susan. (1993) 'State, Culture and the cinema: Jack Lang's strategies for the French film industry 1981–93', *Screen* vol. 34, no. 4 Winter, pp. 380–91.

Hill, John, Martin McLoone and Paul Hainsworth. (eds) (1994) *Border Crossing: Film in Ireland, Britain and Europe*, London: BFI

Holmes, Diana and Alison Smith. (eds) (2000) *100 years of European Cinema – Entertainment or Ideology*, Manchester: Manchester University Press.

Finney, Angus. (1996) *The State of European Cinema: A New Dose of Reality*, London: Cassell.

Jeancolas, Jean-Pierre. (1996) 'From the blum-Byrnes Agreement to the GATT Affair', in Nowell-Smith and Ricci (eds), (1998), pp. 47–62.

Petrie, Duncan. (ed.) (1992) *New Questions of British Cinema*, London: BFI.

Strode, Louise. (2000) 'France and EU Policy-Making on Visual Culture: New Opportunities for National Identity?', in Ezra and Harris (eds), pp. 61–75.

Chapter 18

Richard Maltby and Ruth Vasey

'TEMPORARY AMERICAN CITIZENS'

Cultural anxieties and industrial strategies in the Americanisation of European cinema

> The film has often been called 'an international language.' Even though the coming of the sound film may have weakened the force of this statement, the film still remains an international problem.[1]

IF THE FILM WAS EVER TO SPEAK in 'an international language' after the First World War, the industrialists of American cinema were determined that it would speak in the equivalent of American English. From 1916 onwards, the American film business was internationalised far more extensively than any other national cinema, so that by 1932, when the British report on *The Film of National Life* declared the film to be 'an international problem,' it hardly needed to identify the problem as being Hollywood's pervasive Americanisation of other national cinemas and the national cultures in which they were rooted. [. . .] The American film industry made attempts to maintain its hegemony in the 1920s and 1930s, and the European film industries attempted to challenge that hegemony. This struggle between Film America and Film Europe was primarily an industrial contest, but it was paralleled by another set of concerns which were much more ideological in complexion. Bourgeois commentators frequently worried over the displacement of indigenous cultural, and especially national, identities and these concerns were at times mobilised by European film spokesmen in their efforts to promote resistive economic strategies or by politicians defending trade restrictions. This chapter explores the terms of these debates, especially where they touch on questions of morality and cultural identity, in order to provide a context in which to place the struggle between Film Europe and Film America. In the latter part of the essay, we shall focus particularly on the conversion to sound, [to briefly explore] [. . .] the specific problems that synchronised dialogue and the spoken language posed for the international exchange of films.

The coming of sound sharpened the issue of cultural identity raised by the international trade in moving pictures, and led producers, audiences and governments alike to reassess their relation to the medium and to the fact of American dominance.

During the 1920s, quota legislation and international co-productions had raised questions about what constituted the product of a national culture, but the introduction of sound made these questions much more pressing. The addition of sound to the movies was a cause of cultural anxiety everywhere, including in the United States, where the question of the regulation of the industry was under active debate for most of the 1930s. To American anxieties about whether Hollywood conformed to what one of the Payne Fund Studies called 'Standards of Morality,' Europeans added a concern over the appropriateness of American standards of cultural conformity. In a directly material sense sound standardised the movies, making them less malleable and restricting their cultural adaptability.[2] Hollywood's American identity became audible, and when its fans imitated its speech patterns, so did its effect. Sound forced Hollywood to confront the cultural and linguistic diversity of its international audience; to those members of European cultural elites already alienated from cinema by its mechanical mode of reproduction, sound comprised an additional *Verfremdungseffekt*.

The 'Americanisation of the world,' however, was an intricately bilateral process. Legislative definitions of the 'national' were vulnerable to commercial manoeuvre: the British Cinematograph Act of 1927, for instance, determined whether a movie counted as 'British' not on the basis of cultural considerations, but on the proportion of labour costs paid to British nationals. Equally, commercial manoeuvres that sought to evade a movie's national identity did not always produce the intended effect, as the history of both European international co-productions and Hollywood's investment in multiple-language versions reveal. Perhaps most importantly of all, Hollywood did not appear to its audiences as a national cinema. Summarising arguments made by producers B.P. Schulberg and Joseph Schenck in the mid-1920s, Nataša Ďurovičová argues that they presented Americanness not as a specific national phenomenon but 'as the very signifier of universal human evolution, subsuming under it all the local currencies of cultural exchange, a limitless melting pot of mores, nations and classes.'[3] The America of the movies presented itself less as a geographical territory than an imaginative one, which deliberately made itself available for assimilation in a variety of cultural contexts. Hollywood's geographical location has always been elusive: the America of American movies was as imaginary to the residents of Des Moines or Atlanta as it was to the citizens of Brussels or Budapest.[4]

[. . .]

Arguments about the cultural influence of Hollywood were part of a pervasive, pan-European discourse of anti-Americanism among European cultural elites; what André Visson called 'the fundamental prejudice of the European intellectual élite toward the American conception of the "Common Man."'[5] Or possibly Common Woman: in a House of Commons debate on film industry legislation in 1927, one Conservative Member of Parliament quoted a *Daily Express* article claiming that British viewers 'talk America, think America, and dream America. We have several million people, mostly women, who, to all intent and purpose are temporary American citizens.' [. . .]

According to its detractors, mass culture also possessed two other properties: it was seen as feminine and, in a narrowly nationalistic sense, as 'American.'[6] The British report on *The Film in National Life* [. . .] described 'the cinema public' as a pyramid.[7]

At its base, making up 'nine-tenths of its volume' was 'the general public.' At its apex were members of film societies. But it was most concerned to appeal to a third group, which it identified as the 'stratum of educated opinion (largely in the provinces) which will see good films if good films are brought to it, but which will not seek them out.' Persuading this critical bourgeois audience that 'the film is a serious form of art, worthy of respectful consideration,' would heal the breach between national culture and film activity.[8] Quite typically, *The Film in National Life* understood the idea of a national cinema exclusively in terms of production, looking forward 'to the time when the film industry in Great Britain has gathered power and is producing films which are an unequivocal expression of British life and thought, deriving character and inspiration from our national inheritance, and have an honoured international currency.'[9] But as Andrew Higson has pointed out, if the parameters of a national cinema were to be drawn at the site of consumption rather than the site of production, questions of national and cultural identity would become considerably more complex.[10]

The success of the American product generated conflict between the sectors of other national film industries, since producers and exhibitors had markedly different interests. European exhibitors were almost invariably opposed to any restrictions on American imports, since they were their most consistently successful product. [. . .]

Producers, on the other hand, were in direct competition with Hollywood for access to those exhibition sites in their home market as well as elsewhere. Noting that it was 'local domestic producers' who were 'behind the agitation for contingents, quotas and other restrictive measures,' Col. Edward G. Lowry expressed their case succinctly:

> We (in Austria or France or Germany or England, as the case may be) cannot make pictures on equal terms with the Americans. Because of their great supply of capital and great resources accumulated during the war while we were fighting for our lives, they dominate our country. They can make and do make many more pictures than all of us together. They recover the negative cost and a profit from their rich and huge home market. They can sell their pictures to us at any price because it is all or nearly all pure profit. If measures are not taken for our protection in our own country, soon you will see nothing but American pictures . . . We have a right to make our own national pictures but we can't have them unless this powerful foreigner is held in check . . . If we are to see our own national life in pictures, the American imports must be held down.[11]

However, European governments pursuing policies protecting domestic production industries through the imposition of quotas on American imports found themselves lining up against the economically dominant exhibition sector of their domestic industry. Given the popularity and market dominance of the American product and the general disdain in which cinema was held by cultural elites, only arguments which emphasised the damage done to the country's social and moral fabric by Hollywood were likely to convince governments to take action.

The threat that American mass culture posed to European cultural nationalism was insidious. Underlying concerns about the mechanical in mass culture were broader political issues, resulting from shifts in cultural authority attendant on the development of consumerism. Cultural elites worried less about the movies themselves than about what was happening to the culturally subject classes as a result of their seeing movies. In particular they worried about what Paul Swann has called 'their supposed homogenizing effect,' by which 'external differences in dress, speech and demeanor, which had previously been clear demarcators of class and background' became increasingly ambiguous.[12] Hollywood, identified as the key industry of mass culture, was scapegoated in a process of displacement of responsibility for social change. Even the American argument that film was an industrial commodity rather than a cultural form seemed to provide evidence of a debased American sensibility. Bourgeois defenders of the status quo [. . .] constructed the consumers of American culture as being simpler than they were, not only in the sense of being comparatively intellectually retarded, but also as monolithic in their adoption of American culture. In the process, the rejection of cinema as a cultural form denied European cultural elites a hegemonic role in the formation of popular culture, and inadvertently encouraged the more thorough Americanisation of European mass culture.[13]

Although cultural arguments were undoubtedly based on sincerely held anti-American prejudices, at the level of legislation governing Hollywood's access to European national markets they functioned rather as a rhetorical justification for policies of economic protectionism. Given the minor role that film production played in a national economy, a special case had to be made for its receiving preferential treatment by emphasising Hollywood's pervasive cultural influence. Arguments about the cultural importance of film were used to justify quotas in policy statements, which therefore expressed a mixture of commercial and cultural motives. [. . .]

But in practice, as Margaret Dickinson and Sarah Street have argued in relation to Britain, 'little account was taken of the claim that film was an "educational and cultural medium."'[14] The British government accepted the truth of one of Will Hays's many dictums, that trade no longer followed the flag, but instead 'trade follows the film,' and justified their protectionist policy on those grounds. A broad consensus of European industrialists, represented by the industrial and banking consortium supporting Ufa in Germany or in Britain by the Federation of British Industries (FBI), developed an interest in questions of cinema because of the threat posed to their own commercial interests by Hollywood's allegedly pervasive power to advertise goods.

Hardly surprisingly, the American motion picture industry invariably denied the validity of culturally based arguments. In 1927 the American commercial attaché at Berlin told representatives of the major companies that a principal source of opposition to American movies in Germany was 'the professional newspaper critics, who represented a press which is also engaged in the motion picture business and desires to free itself from competition.' Fortunately, 'this opposition may be discounted because the general public fails either to read or to observe the advice of the critics.'[15] Major F.L. Herron, head of the MPPDA's Foreign Department, insisted that:

> the cultural argument is merely another alibi. Conceding their idea that films do have a cultural effect on the community, every one of those countries that

are now passing laws against us has national censorship boards. Every motion picture that goes into that country from a foreign country must pass that board before it can be released. If there is anything harmful from a cultural standpoint in such films, there is the place that they can be stopped.[16]

Herron's argument sought to separate cultural and economic questions, and in the process to deny the importance of cultural issues, by suggesting that it was all a matter of detail. Despite the public support the industry received from successive US administrations, however, some State Department officials privately acknowledged the validity of the European cultural argument.

The United States had first achieved its domination of the world's movie screens during the First World War, when its European rivals were largely debilitated. It had consolidated its hold during the 1920s with aggressive marketing procedures. In 1922 the major vertically integrated companies formed a trade association, the Motion Pictures Producers and Distributors of America Inc. (MPPDA, to advance their mutual, non-competitive interests, and appointed Postmaster-General Will H. Hays as its President. As Jens Ulff-Møller details[17] many aspects of foreign trade fell under this category, and the MPPDA was extremely effective in soliciting State Department support, in part because of the movies' widely recognised role in increasing the demand for American consumer goods abroad. When bartering for State Department co-operation in the late 1920s, the MPPDA repeatedly cited the Commerce Department's undemonstrable statistic that every foot of film exported from the United States brought back a dollar's worth of trade.[18]

Beyond these contingent commercial factors, however, the problem that American motion pictures presented to European governments and producers was their apparently universal appeal. Why was Hollywood's output so popular? Certainly it was more highly capitalised than any other motion picture industry, and audiences, then as now, were encouraged by the American industry's publicity machine to associate lavish production values with a superior product. For a German or French exhibitor, Hollywood's economic miracle was that it spent much more on the movies it made than domestic producers could, and sold them much more cheaply. In that fact alone, Hollywood projected an image of American material abundance that was of considerable importance to its appeal.

In the 1920s, Hollywood promoted the idea that the movies constituted an 'international language' that could communicate ideas and values across national and linguistic boundaries.[19] Silent movies were peculiarly well-suited to consumption in a wide range of different cultural contexts, but this was probably due less to their capacity to impart a single universal message than to the fact that they were amenable to a wide range of different interpretations. As 'texts,' silent movies were inherently unstable: titled in different languages, projected at varying speeds, tinted or toned differently, and presented with a wide variety of different musical accompaniments. [. . .] More generally, it was the nature of the medium that metaphor and allusion should predominate. Intertitles could be used to 'fix' the meaning of a scene, but the titles themselves could remain vague and euphemistic, and audiences formed a construction of the narrative mainly from visual cues.

At the same time, silent movies were also easily modified, and could therefore be adapted to a wide variety of cultural contexts. [. . .] By 1927 intertitles, which constituted the principal site of international adaptability, were routinely translated into thirty-six languages. Visuals were subject to excision or rearrangement, but titles could be creatively modified to cater to diverse national and cultural groups.[20] Hollywood characters could speak any language or dialect; indeed, in the case of the Baltic States they spoke three languages at once, since historical and political circumstances required the intertitles to be rendered in German and Russian as well as the local language. Theoretically, at least, the process of translation allowed anything inappropriate or potentially offensive to be changed. [. . .]

Intelligibility was not the only matter at issue. By 'naturalising' movies, distributors were encouraging audiences to adopt the imaginative content of the movies as part of their own cultural territory. The Hollywood universe was not a foreign country to its *aficionados*, whatever their nationality. As active interpreters, audiences made sense of Hollywood in their own cultural terms. The movie-going habit was a familiar, domestic ritual around the world, and American movies and their stars were a significant part of everyday experience for millions of non-American people. Foreign audiences constituted a market not only for the movies themselves, but also for fan magazines, which encouraged personal identification with American stars. [. . .] In 1926 a State Department official observed that:

> If it were not for the barrier we have established, there is no doubt that the American movies would be bringing us a flood of the immigrants. As it is, in vast instances, the desire to come to this country is thwarted, and the longing to emigrate is changed into a desire to imitate.

As a consequence, he argued, 'the peoples of Europe now consider America as the arbiter of manners, fashion, sports customs and standards of living.'[21] But it was in their own cultures that these audiences imagined America, imitated Hollywood, and irritated their native bourgeois nationalists. Literal instances of the domestication of Hollywood's influence occurred, for example, when British working-class parents in the 1930s named their children Shirley, Marlene, Norma or Gary.[22]

One of the ironies of American cultural imperialism in the inter-war period was that, just as European elite critics perversely intensified the influence of American culture, so it was in the interests of American producers to encourage the idea that Hollywood belonged to the world, rather than to the United States alone. By obscuring the American origins of the movies in sensitive markets, the producers enabled them to take on some of the cultural colouring of their customer nations, subtly combating any consumer resistance that might have been inspired by overt instances of flag-waving. [. . .]

If the technical and semantic malleability of the silent medium contributed to the success of American movies abroad, the question then arises as to how Hollywood managed to retain its grip on its overseas markets after the introduction of sound at the end of the 1920s. Even when sound tracks were largely limited to synchronised sound effects and music, the new technology meant that the motion picture medium was much less adaptable to diverse cultural contexts than it had been previously. It was no longer possible to rearrange or excise sequences without ruining entire reels. Recorded music could itself cause problems: Italian and German exhibitors, accustomed to providing their own musical accompaniments, complained that the new sound tracks sounded 'too American' for the taste of their customers.[23] When 'sound' came to mean 'talking,' the problem of language specificity and the loss of ambiguity in the treatment of sensitive subjects only compounded the difficulties associated with distributing the new medium abroad. But although American producers admitted that there were some problems to be overcome, most expressed little fear that sound would cause them to lose their grip upon their non-English-speaking markets. To understand their sanguine attitude, it is necessary to take into account several factors affecting the economic performance of the industry outside the United States.

Although the timing of the conversion to sound was largely dictated by factors affecting the domestic market, it also happened at a relatively fortuitous time for the American export trade, and when other European production industries were poorly prepared for the disruptions of such a substantial technical advance. For several years prior to 1929 Hollywood's foreign market had been glutted with pictures, creating a buyer's market, especially in Europe.[24] The introduction of quota legislation in the late 1920s obliged American distributors to be more selective in choosing which Hollywood movies they distributed. In order to meet quota requirements for the distribution of domestically produced pictures, the American companies replaced their own cheaper productions with what were known in Britain as 'quota quickies,' cheap, locally produced movies made largely as ballast to meet quota requirements.[25] As a result, the prestige and attractiveness of the American product was enhanced. Under these circumstances, the increased visibility of the local product was a mixed blessing.

The arrival of sound raised the stakes involved in the motion picture business at every level. The introduction of the new sound technology reduced the number of films available, increasing the value of each picture to the distributor. The changes to exhibition were even more marked. Silent movies had been shown virtually anywhere there was a flat space, including small back-country halls that masqueraded as cinemas one or two nights a week. These tiny operations in foreign territories were of little or no value to the American producers and distributors, who earned the vast majority of their profits from key cinemas situated in the large cities. In the United States approximately 85 per cent of total revenue was obtained from a third of the theatres, and overseas the differential between first-run and subsequent-run theatres was just as dramatic. [. . .]

The Americans had always seen the large numbers of small and medium-sized cinemas in Europe as a blight upon the territory.[26] In the sound era many of these smaller theatres closed, unable to afford the new technology and unable to obtain silent products. They were replaced by new, larger and more centralised establishments purposely built for sound.[27] Fewer, more carefully selected movies played in more expensive cinemas, with longer runs. In general, the changes wrought by sound seemed to point to bigger and better business for American companies abroad, notwithstanding the specific problems associated with sound technology.

The main factor working against the Americans in Europe in the late 1920s was government legislation specifically designed to restrict the Hollywood product. Quota and contingent legislation was either in place or pending in many European countries, including Germany, Britain, Austria, France and Hungary. However, in as much as these laws were intended to limit the volume of American imports, they reinforced the tendency of the sound era toward a more careful selection of products for export, and hastened the elimination of the bottom of the range. Reacting to the British initiative to increase the proportion of domestic product seen on British screens, the US Department of Commerce commented:

> Conservative estimates place the American share of the annual [British] feature import market henceforth at practically 70 per cent. This figure is healthier than previous larger percentages, since increased British and Continental competition, forcing the American contribution down to this figure, has only eliminated the poorer output of the American companies, pictures which in the past have been used principally in so-called block-booking transactions.[28]

A similar pattern prevailed in many of the other quota-regulated countries in Europe. Germany, where contingent legislation genuinely eroded American profits, was the exception rather than the rule, primarily because the German industry had a more fully vertically-integrated structure than that of France or Britain, and a production sector strong enough to supply 50 per cent of its domestic exhibition needs. From the American point of view, the real problem with most quotas was not that they were restrictive but that they were subject to change without notice, which made long-range planning for the foreign field a marketing nightmare.[29]

For a while in 1929 the American companies were hopeful that the development of sound might cause quota legislation to be universally abandoned.[30] They reasoned that if public demand for sound pictures continued, most foreign industries would lack the necessary capital and expertise to be able to fulfil their side of quota agreements.[31] In fact restrictive legislation did continue to survive in various forms. But the conversion to sound did in an important sense thwart plans to restrict the circulation of American product in Europe – not at the national level, but across the continent as a whole. The various pan-national industrial initiatives that constituted the 'Film Europe' movement were ambitious even in the silent era, not least because in order to compete with the Americans on their own economic terms the Europeans needed to gain a proportion of the wider global market, as well as achieving dominance in their own territories. As Richard Abel has suggested, in at least one respect the European 'international' co-productions promoted through the Film Europe initiatives only confirmed American dominance, since they increasingly imitated Hollywood in their appearance, 'reflecting a modern style of life whose characteristics of material well-being and conspicuous consumption were basically American.'[32] Nevertheless [. . .] by 1928 a number of coalitions for European co-production had been made, treaties forged, and displays of European solidarity achieved. [. . .] Ultimately, however, the effect of talking pictures was to splinter any incipient European unity into its component language groups. Any sense of cohesion that had arisen from the shared determination to resist the American industry was undermined by the local cultural imperative of hearing the accents of one's own language. In Italy, for example, the Italian Commission for Censorship suppressed the dialogue of American and other foreign sound films after 1929, arguing that they would encourage Italians to learn languages other than their own. A 1931 decree required all foreign films to be dubbed, and in 1933 a tariff was imposed on films dubbed outside Italy. Similar strictures were temporarily instituted in Portugal and Spain.[32]

[. . .]

The problem of talking a different language, however, remained an obstacle to the success of American sound films abroad even as it was an important factor in the failure of the European trading bloc [. . .]. By late 1929, the non-English-speaking world was getting tired of patched-up synchronised versions and unintelligible dialogue.[34] [. . .]

During this period of experiment, as Hollywood discovered the relative unpopularity of its multiple language versions (MLVs), the American industry seemed, ironically, to be caught in the same set of circumstances that had frustrated its foreign competitors since the First World War. American MLVs always seemed compromised, neither genuinely expressive of a local sentiment nor adequate to the prestige of Hollywood. High capitalisation was impossible for these pictures, since their intended markets were too small to recoup large investments, but less expensive productions lacked the drawing power to justify their relatively modest costs.

Subtitled movies found a satisfactory response in several markets, particularly in Latin America, where they were often preferred to those dubbed, or indeed produced, in standard Castilian Spanish. For similar reasons, audiences in Portugal found the Brazilian Portuguese of the casts employed by American companies to be unendurable, and pleaded for subtitled versions instead.[35] As these instances illustrate, subtitles in some cases could not only solve problems of translation, but also ameliorate some of the problems produced by the cultural specificity that characterised sound production, re-introducing some of the advantages of semantic flexibility provided by silent intertitles. [. . .] In Europe, however, the performance of titled prints was patchy, especially in the larger markets where there was more competition from local productions. It was with a view to the European market that the American companies continued to experiment with dubbing.

The original problem with dubbing had been that the existing technology had not been capable of mixing or accurately synchronising sound tracks. By late 1930s the invention of the multiple-track Moviola had overcome these limitations, enabling music and effects to be mixed with separately recorded vocal tracks. Dubbing an individual print was not particularly expensive – United Artists estimate the cost of dubbing a picture into Spanish as $3,500 in 1933 – but it depended upon the maintenance or rental of a dubbing plant and associated personnel.[36] This was only economically feasible for the major language groups – Spanish, German and French – and for Italian, which constituted a special case due to the governmental restrictions on the use of foreign languages in the cinema. Germany and France introduced regulations requiring that dubbing into their native languages be carried out on their home soil, in an effort to secure at least part of Hollywood's business, and presumably to keep some control over the application of their languages.[37] Even for these markets, by no means all of Hollywood's products were dubbed, since the process was only considered appropriate for action pictures with little dialogue. The reasons for this were not merely technical. As Ginette Vincendeau has argued [. . .],[38] if non-English-speaking audiences eventually accommodate themselves to the dislocation of voice and body, its potential for alienation was nevertheless always present. Hollywood's solution lay in a mode of production characterised by action-oriented aesthetics: it was an influential truism of foreign distribution that movies reliant on dialogue to explain their plot and develop their story, known in the industry as 'walk and talk' pictures, fared substantially less well in the non-English-speaking market than did action pictures.[39] Hollywood's preference for a cinema of action was at least in part the result of its obligations to its foreign market.

Dubbed versions were culturally and semantically more inflexible than subtitled ones, but they, too, allowed latitude for adaptation during the movie's progress from studio to audience. Small-scale causes of offence could be eliminated in the process of translation, and in Europe the use of a population's first language often helped to localise the action and obscure the foreign origins of the product. Audiences could continue to consume a product that was delicately poised between the 'authentic' world of Hollywood, with its international connotations of glamour and fantasy, and a more domestic and personal realm consonant with the culture and experience of the spectator. Although dubbing and subtitles were only partial solutions to the alienating effects of foreign voices, these adaptations of dialogue continued to present the Hollywood original as international, and the negotiated version, which in one way or another divided sound and image tracks, as a local variant. The bifurcation of sound and image localised the act of consumption, not Hollywood's act of production.

Ironically, then, by the early 1930s the necessity of preparing different versions for different language groups actually worked in favour of Hollywood's global trade rather than against it: firstly by undermining the cohesion of Film Europe, and secondly by restoring some of the flexibility in form and meaning that had facilitated the acceptance of the silents around the world. For the rest of the decade Hollywood's biggest production problem arising from the introduction of sound was probably associated with its English-speaking territory. This collective market, mainly comprising the British Empire and accounting for more than 50 per cent of foreign income, had to be serviced with the American domestic product, preferably with a minimum of cultural intervention. This posed so many difficulties that the MPPDA mooted the possibility of making special British versions of 'all pictures that would normally be construed as being contrary to their policies . . . in order to take advantage of the profits to be made there'; and indeed, the same mixing technology that had facilitated dubbing made possible the 'reconstruction' of sound movies for non-American English-language markets.[40] However, this expensive option was only tenable as a last resort; and the English-speaking market, more than any other, had to be taken into consideration during the routine scripting and production of Hollywood's movies.

[. . .] Much of the hegemonic anxiety about the influence of American culture lay in its particular appeal to working-class audiences, but the elite critiques of mass culture as American in conception and feminine and working-class in consumption succeeded only in confirming that part of its appeal lay in its ideologically disruptive presumptions of democracy. The movies offered European working-class audiences an escape into an imagined Utopian society called 'Hollywood,' in which the inflexibility of class distinction either did not exist or was not recognisably coded. The use of American idioms and semiotic systems in general offered European audiences the imaginary possibility of an evasion of class distinction, rather than a repudiation of it. Although the barrier of language operated to some extent as a site of resistance, Hollywood's Utopianism was also intensified by the distance of foreign audiences from the specific forms of American social coding inscribed within Hollywood movies. Thus James Cagney's accent lost its specific class coding and became generalised as 'American,' not to be distinguished from, say, William Powell's. By contrast, for every European cinema, the coming of sound brought accents into play as unavoidable signifiers of social class. British working-class audiences notoriously objected to British films as being, as *World Film News* called them, 'frenziedly upper class'.[41]

> The expectation that audiences would prefer to hear British rather than American voices was rudely disappointed as working-class audiences, particularly in Scotland and the North, showed their hostility to and derision for the accents and mannerisms of the London stage. Ironically, they found more to identify with and relate to in the films of what was seen in the 1930s as an alien culture.[42]

Hollywood's Utopianism was part of what made it complexly part of European cultures and separated from them, a familiar foreign country in the environs of European imaginations. Insidiously, then, 'American' culture – at least as represented by Hollywood, American popular music and American-styled consumer goods – became 'naturalised' within the host cultures. Few French people wanted to be Germans, few Italians wanted to be British, but almost everybody wanted to be Gary Cooper, or James Cagney, and Greta Garbo and Marlene Dietrich showed that you could be, and be so despite your nationality and even your accent. If Hollywood was a foreign country it was also the imaginative home of everybody to whom it appealed. And if that appeal was concentrated, as it was, among women and the working class, then that represented a further threat to bourgeois nationalism. [. . .] Philip Schlesinger has argued that national or ethnic identity is as much about exclusion as about inclusion, and that 'the critical factor for defining the ethnic group therefore becomes the social *boundary* which defines the group with respect to other groups . . . not the cultural reality within those borders.'[43] Seen in these terms, identity is 'a system of relations and representations' with difference and distinction at the heart of the issue. As James Donald has suggested: 'Manifest in racism, its violent misogyny, and its phobias about alien culture, alien ideologies and 'enemies within' is the terror that without the known boundaries, everything will collapse into undifferentiated, miasmic chaos; that identity will disintegrate.'[44] Bourgeois cultural nationalism defined mass culture as American in order to define itself against other national cultures. In their assertion of the idea of boundaries, these nationalisms required an Other against which to define themselves. 'American culture' served that purpose for different European elites during the 1920s and 1930s as at other times. But the tensions between European nations in the 1930s inhibited the development of any coherent strategy for resisting 'the American invasion.' If the emerging European cultural nationalisms of the period were defined in significant part in conscious opposition to 'American culture,' they were also defined separately from each other, and their nationalistic antagonisms were in the event directed more toward each other than to the American model used as counter-definition.

Notes

1 *The Film in National Life: Being the Report of an Enquiry Conducted by the Commission on Educational and Cultural Films in the Service which the Cinematograph May Render to Education and Social Progress* (London: Allen and Unwin, 1932), p. 26.

2 Alan Williams, 'Historical and Theoretical Issues in the Coming of Recorded Sound to the Cinema,' in Rick Altman, ed., *Sound Theory, Sound Practice* (New York: Routledge, 1992), pp. 128–9.

3 Nataša Ďurovičová, 'Translating America: The Hollywood Multilinguals 1929–1933,' in Altman, ed., *Sound Theory*, p. 11.

4 For a more extended discussion of this topic, see Ruth Vasey, *The World According to Hollywood, 1918–1939* (Exeter: University of Exeter Press, 1997).

5 André Visson, *As Others See Us* (Garden City, NJ: Doubleday, 1948), pp. 232–3, quoted in Paul Swann, *The Hollywood Feature Film in Postwar Britain* (London: Croom Helm, 1987), p. 3.

6 Andreas Huyssen, 'Mass Culture as Woman: Modernism's Other,' in *Studies in Entertainment: Critical Approaches to Mass Culture* (Bloomington: Indiana University Press, 1986), pp. 188–207.

7 *The Film in National Life*, pp. 4, 41.

8 *The Film in National Life*, p. 83.

9 *The Film in National Life*, pp. 142–3.

10 Andrew Higson, 'The Concept of National Cinema,' *Screen*, vol. 30, no. 4, Autumn 1989, p. 36.

11 Ibid., p. 39.

12 Swann, *Hollywood Feature Film*, p. 22.

13 Peter Miles and Malcolm Smith, *Cinema, Literature and Society: Élite and Mass Culture in Interwar Britain* (London: Croom Helm, 1987), p. 165.

14 Margaret Dickinson and Sarah Street, *Cinema and State: The Film Industry and the British Government, 1927–84* (London: British Film Institute, 1985), p. 2.

15 Douglas Miller, addressing a meeting of the Studio Relations Committee, 25 November 1927, MPA.

16 Herron to Hays, 13 March 1929, Will H. Hays Papers, Department of Special Collections, Indiana State Library, Indianapolis (hereafter Hays Papers).

17 Jens Ulff Møller, 'Hollywood's "Foreign War": The Effect of National Commercial Policy on the Emergence of the American Film Hegemony in France, 1920–29', in Richard

Maltby and Ruth Vasey, eds, *Film Europe and Film America: Cinema Commerce and Cultural Exchange* (Exeter: Exeter University Press, 1999), pp. 181–206.

18 See, for example, Julius Klein, 'What are Motion Pictures Doing for Industry?,' Frank A. Tichenor, 'Motion Pictures as Trade Getters,' and C.J. North, 'Our Foreign Trade in Motion Pictures,' in *The Motion Picture in its Economic and Social Aspects, Annals of the American Academy of Political and Social Science*, vol. 128, November 1926, pp. 79–93, 100–108. Klein was the Director of the United States Bureau of Foreign and Domestic Commerce, and North was the Chief of the Motion Picture Section of the Department of Commerce, established in 1926 to 'keep the Department, and through it the motion picture industry, in the closest touch with foreign market possibilities, and also the activities of our competitors in their endeavors to limit the showing of American films within their borders.' *Film Daily Yearbook*, 1926, p. 854.

19 See, for example, Lamar Trotti, 'The Motion Picture as a Business,' Address Delivered by Carl Milliken, Secretary of the MPPDA, 3 April 1928, MPA. Trotti was the MPPDA's chief publicist.

20 Edwin W. Hullinger, 'Free Speech for the Talkies?' pamphlet, n.p.: June 1929, reprinted from *North American Review*.

21 James True, *Printer's Ink*, 4 February 1926, quoted in Charles Eckert, 'The Carole Lombard in Macy's Window,' *Quarterly Review of Film Studies*, vol. 3, Winter 1978, pp. 4–5.

22 Jeffrey Richards, *The Age of the Dream Palace: Cinema and Society in Britain, 1930–1939* (London: Routledge and Kegan Paul, 1984), p. 57.

23 Guy Croswell Smith to Arthur Kelly, 16 May 1930, O'Brien Legal File, Box 6, Folder 1, United Artists Archive, Wisconsin Center for Theater and Film Research, Madison (hereafter UA): 'The European Motion-Picture Industry in 1929,' *Trade Information Bulletin*, no. 694, p. 26.

24 George R. Canty, 'The European Motion-Picture Industry in 1927,' *Trade Information Bulletin*, no. 542, 1928, p. 15.

25 Equivalent productions in Germany were known as *Kontingent Filme*; some were never given public exhibition. The Germans abandoned this system in 1928 and substituted a system of import permits.

26 Britain, where even suburban cinemas were often lavishly proportioned and appointed, was an exception to the general European pattern.

27 'The Motion-Picture Industry in Continental Europe in 1931,' *Trade Information Bulletin*, no. 797, p. 4.

28 *Trade Information Bulletin*, no. 617, p. 19.

29 *Trade Information Bulletin*, no. 694, p. 4.

30 *Trade Information Bulletin*, no. 694, p. 7.

31 Harold Smith to MPPDA, 14 February 1930. O'Brien Legal File, Box 97, File 5, UA.

32 Richard Abel, *French Cinema: The First Wave 1915–1929* (Princeton: Princeton University Press, 1984), p. 38.

33 James Hay, *Popular Film Culture in Fascist Italy: The Passing of the Rex* (Bloomington: Indiana University Press, 1987), p. 86.

34 There were even reports of Polish and French audiences rioting at the shoddy adaptation of American films. See Ginette Vincendeau, 'Hollywood Babel: The Coming of Sound and The Multiple Language Version,' *Screen*, vol. 29, no. 2, Spring 1988, p. 28; see also the essays by Martine Danan, Joseph Garncarz and Mike Walsh in Maltby and Vasey, eds, *Film Europe and Film America*.

35 *Trade Information Bulletin*, no. 797, 1932, p. 56.

36 G.F. Morgan to Arthur Kelly, 21 July 1933, W. P. Philips file, Box 2, Folder 3, UA.

37 This did not always have the desired effect, since Harold L. Smith observed in 1935 that none of the people directing the dubbing operations in Paris were in fact French. MGM came the nearest, with a woman of Polish origin whom Smith thought to have been naturalised. Smith to Herron, 7 February 1935, W.P. Philips file, Box 2, Folder 3, UA.

38 Ginette Vincendeau, 'Hollywood Babel', op. cit.

39 Sam Morris to Jack Warner, 12 November 1937, JLW Correspondence, Box 59, Folder 8, Warner Bros Archive, Department of Special Collections, University of Southern California.

40 Jason Joy to E.A. Howe, 16 June 1931, *Milly* Case File, Production Code Administration Archive, Academy of Motion Picture Arts and Sciences, Los Angeles.

41 *World Film News*, vol. 2, no. 2 May 1937, p. 13, quoted in Richards, *Age of the Dream Palace*, p. 32.

42 Robert Murphy, 'Coming of Sound to the Cinema in Britain,' *Historical Journal of Film, Radio and Television*, vol. 4. no. 2, 1984, p. 158.

43 Philip Schlesinger, 'On National Identity: Some Conceptions and Misconceptions Criticised,' *Social Science Information*, vol. 26, no. 2, 1987, p. 235.

44 James Donald, 'How English Is It? Popular Literature and National Culture,' *New Formations* 6, (1988), p. 32.

Chapter 19

Janet Thumim

THE 'POPULAR', CASH AND CULTURE IN THE POSTWAR BRITISH CINEMA INDUSTRY

IN 1946 THE 'BIGGEST BOX OFFICE ATTRACTION' in the UK, according to *Kinematograph Weekly's* (*KW*) annual review, was *The Wicked Lady*. It was also the 'Best British Film', featuring two of the 'Most Popular and Consistent Stars', James Mason and Margaret Lockwood; it had one of the 'Best British Directors', Leslie Arliss; and was made by the 'Most Successful Studio', Gainsborough. What does this string of superlatives tell us, though, about the film or its audience? Josh Billings, in his introduction to *KW's* review, had no doubts about the solidity of the film's value:

> their success was no fluke. They had the stars, the stories and the necessary production glamour and not even an indifferent Press could halt so persistent and shrewd a box-office combination.[1]

In *Tribune*, the 'indifferent press', in the form of Simon Harcourt-Smith reviewing the same film, clearly operated according to quite a different set of values:

> This, on the whole, is a time when the new films can claim no privilege as works of art . . .
> *The Wicked Lady* arouses in me a nausea out of all proportion to the subject . . .
> Six months hence one of my friends in the industry will announce that this portentous piece of shabbiness has broken all records in, let us say, Middlesbrough. My argument will, however, remain valid.[2]

Now this film was the box-office hit of 1946, and thus in quantitative terms an immense popular success. This very popular object, however, gave rise to Harcourt-Smith's admittedly disproportionate nausea: it was not well liked by him. His choice of the term 'nausea' indeed suggests such extreme revulsion that we might well wonder what it was about the film that so disturbed him. It is hard to believe, as he claimed elsewhere in his review, that it was simply a question of his historical sensibilities being offended. The most interesting question about the contemporary popularity of this film – what was it about 'this portentous piece of shabbiness' that was so well liked? – is one that Harcourt-Smith was incapable of answering, simply because it had not occurred to him that it was worth asking. For the cultural historian it is the very success of this film which provokes questions about its content: what pleasures did it offer, what widespread desires did it satisfy, in short, how was it *used* by its audiences? In other words the ascertainable fact of *The Wicked Lady*'s popularity in quantitative terms makes it an ideal candidate for an exploration of the qualitative aspects of popularity: despite Harcourt-Smith's nausea, large numbers of people chose to view this film: why *this* film?

The study of popular culture in any given period offers insights into both the conditions of social formation and also the language and attitudes of the various social groups competing with each other for dominance – in hegemonic struggle – at the time. This paper is concerned with the qualifications which must be borne in mind while engaging in such an exploration of cinema popular in Britain in the immediate postwar period (between 1945 and 1960). There are complex problems to be faced in the course of such an exploration of the discursive field within which meanings were produced by the industry, the critics and the audience. Though all three groups both contributed to and drew upon this discursive field, it is no simple matter to discover the details of specific interventions. My concern here is to map some points in the field, to draw attention to tendencies rather than attempt categorical assertions about the substantive interactions of these interrelated historical groups. My remarks are therefore necessarily general – and this may be their weakness: their strength rests on the systematic methods used to generate a sample of films for analysis[3] and on a scrupulous insistence on the correlation of data from disparate sources as the foundation for any proposition.

A notable feature of popular cinema during this period, for example, is the striking change in the typical heroine: the transgressive adult woman portrayed by Margaret Lockwood in *The Wicked Lady* gave way by 1964 to the troubled child-woman played by Tippi Hedren in *Marnie*. But can this observation offer any insights about the evolution of gender politics in the postwar period, and how can we understand these representations to have been read by their contemporary audiences? Not only were the internal features, as it were, of popular films, subject to change: the context of the cinematic institution itself altered dramatically between 1945 and 1960. Billings's ebullient optimism, in his review of 1946 –

> More than anything else the Box-Office balance sheet of 1946 shows that this has been the best year on record for the British film industry. Of the estimated yearly takings of £110,000,000, contributed by the 25,000,000 British filmgoers who regularly attend their 'local', a substantial sum in now 'stopping at home'. This is good news.[4]

– had by 1960 given way to a more circumspect tone:

Let's face it, 1960 hasn't exactly been a vintage film year, but what it lacked in quality it gained in variety. Moreover it was a comparatively prosperous year and for these reasons: one, the lifting of the Entertainments Tax, which has made a tremendous difference to gross takings in West End and key provincial halls; two, the aforementioned variety of the pictures, particularly those made by British producers, who have again stolen a march on the Yanks; and three, the masses' growing discontent with television programmes. They not only want a change of fare, but an excuse to retire from the parlour.[5]

Over these fifteen years, the 'struggle' between the trade itself and the film critics responsible, through their reviews, for the discourse surrounding films, was conducted against a background of major social changes: postwar austerity and reconstruction gave way to the consumer boom and apparently increased affluence of the fifties, of which one feature was the widening of leisure choices and the overall decline of cinema as the dominant cultural form. In this context it is legitimate to ask what 'the popular' connotes, and whether indeed it is possible to discover what was widely enjoyed at various moments.

The fan magazine *Picturegoer* carried out an annual poll of its readers and awarded its 'gold medal' to the most popular male and female actors in respect of their performances in a particular film; they also published the top ten names in each category yielded by their poll. From the 1930s until 1958, when the magazine ceased publication, the *Picturegoer* poll provides a consistent and useful summary of audience preferences, albeit confined to those cinemagoers who regularly subscribed to the magazine. On its own, this would be an inadequate guarantor of the contemporary success of individual actors or films; but it does offer a useful corrective to film distributors' annual assessments, which were more directly concerned with the profitability of films or the future market potential of stars.

The most frequently quoted distributors' assessment is that published in the *Motion Picture Almanac*: this was an American publication summarizing the activities of the US film industry at home and abroad, in which a simple list of the ten most popular films and stars at the British box office during the preceding year was given, apparently based on returns from distributors in Britain and presumably intended for the benefit of the US industry. The entry for the British box office occupies less than one of the one thousand pages in the publication. This is nevertheless a useful – and relatively accessible – rough guide to the dominant trends in popular cinema; though what it offers is limited by its derivation from the experience of distributors routinely dealing with the US industry (if not owned by US interests) and by its address primarily to interests which were in direct, and often bitter, competition with the British film industry during the period.

The periodic evaluations conducted within industry trade papers such as *KW* and *Motion Picture Herald* were addressed to those involved in the business of selling films to audiences, and accordingly aimed to inform their readers about the degree of success achieved by various products. For the historian, the problem in dealing with these assessments lies in their inconsistency and variety and, most difficult of all, in the lack of information about how given judgements were formed. *Kinematograph Weekly*, the major British trade paper during the period, used over forty different categories in its assessments published in December each year: only four of these, however, appeared consistently. Several factors account for the lack of simple data about box-office receipts for particular films, and for the often eccentric proliferation of categories in *KW*'s annual awards.

During the latter part of the 1940s, cinema was undoubtedly the dominant form of popular culture in the UK, and seemed, to optimists at any rate, to be an expanding industry. Economic relations between Britain and the dominant US film industry in the austere postwar years were complicated by the British government's sporadic and ill-judged attempts to protect the home industry. Plotting the fiscal performance of individual products must have been an accountant's nightmare; and this, combined with the hope that the market would become more buoyant, might explain the lack of reliable data. But cinema audiences peaked in Britain in the late 1940s, with 1600 million admissions per year, thereafter declining continuously through the 1950s, the most dramatic fall occurring between 1955 (1182 million) and 1960 (501 million).[6] By 1965 they were down to 327 million; and the relentless fall continued, until by the late 1980s cinema admissions were a mere five per cent of what they had been in 1946.[7] Therefore, while the British economy as a whole appeared healthier during the consumer boom of the 1950s, the cinema industry had no respite. The major competitor in the field of entertainment was, of course, broadcast television; and references to this competition litter the cinema trade papers throughout the 1950s.

A correlation of films and stars cited in various sources can offer a more trustworthy picture of 'popularity', at least in its quantitative dimension, than can dependence on any one source alone. A discussion of individual films selected according to such a correlation offers interesting historical insights to set alongside those available in studies whose *raisons d'être* and starting points are more firmly located in questions about particular genres, directors, stars or production strategies. The problem with studies of the latter sort has always been their tendency to overemphasize film texts whose actual exposure to the mass audience was relatively marginal, because of their intrinsic interest for critics and scholars. This overemphasis, and the concomitant marginalization of films which might have enjoyed greater success at the box office, becomes problematic to the degree that the canons by which critics and scholars have evaluated films are different from those by which it is legitimate to understand either the predilections or the 'reading activities' of the mass audience.

The vicissitudes of the various branches of the film industry are germane to a discussion of popularity because these relate to both the number and the types of film offered to audiences. As far as audiences themselves are concerned, we might speculate that although cinemas had substantially diminished in number by the mid-1960s while typical admission prices had risen appreciably, the overall range of leisure choices open to audience members had not changed as much as these facts might imply. Going to the cinema, from the 1960s onwards, was just one amongst a range of entertainment options. What this qualitative social change does suggest, however, is that the concept of popularity in relation to cinema has a different meaning in the period after the sixties than it did in the forties. This must be taken into account in assessments of the social consequences of cinematic representations towards the end of the postwar period. Popular cinematic imagery was far less widely consumed in the sixties than it was in the forties; and it should also be remembered that correlations of various assessments of popularity in any given year are conducted against a background of overall and absolute decline in the popularity of the institution of cinema. The demise of the fan magazine in the late fifties is a reminder of this.

If the distinguished feature of British society in the forties was a stoical collectivism, by the sixties there was instead an impatient fragmentation. Is there any evidence of this in the content of films achieving large-scale box-office success? It is certainly true to say that characteristic themes treated in popular films underwent marked changes through the period, and that at any given moment all of the most popular films tended to share some common concerns. However, unless we are to subscribe to the idea that films in some way reflect the society in which they circulate, understanding the significance of such changes is a complex matter. Given that the meanings of a film are the product of active negotiation between reader and film text operating within a discursive field constructed via the activities of the industry and its critics, how did audience members 'read' the images they were offered?

Here we are immediately plunged into the realm of speculation. Although the answer to this question can never be known, its determinants maybe considered; for example by means of detailed analysis of box-office successes yielded through a correlation of different sources, considering not only overall narrative themes, structures and resolutions, but also details of representations of characters and the nuances of their relation to narrative development. So far, so good: but this only attends to the film itself. What of the audience? What forms of evidence are available here? It is possible to envisage an oral history enquiry which would attempt to reconstruct, through interviews and questionnaires, some traces of the audience. But aside from the logistical difficulties of such an undertaking, any conclusions would be subject to all the limitations inherent in its methods: hindsight, faulty memory and unrepresentative samples of respondents, for example; though such conclusions would still offer fascinating correlative material along the lines of the Mass-Observation survey of cinema audiences in Bolton in1938.[8] More satisfactory might be an examination of contemporary published material: if we cannot resurrect the audiences themselves, we do have access to discursive materials routinely circulating among them: in this form evidence does exist of the terms in which various films, characters, plots and stars were discussed. We can discover which representations were acceptable, which were the subject of controversy. In short, if we cannot meet with the audience, we can reconstruct the discursive contexts of their cinemagoing and their readings of films.

Trade discourses

A cursory glance at the list of films popular at the British box office between 1945 and 1965 (see the table on pp. 204–6), compiled from a correlation of the sources outlined above, shows that overall the British market was dominated by the US (Hollywood) product[9] – which explains the anxieties of the British industry concerning what they perceived as major threats to their livelihood: US 'investment' in British films, and the perennial competition with the US industry for box-office revenue. In the late forties the share was more even, and the continuing success of Hollywood films with British audiences was masked by the fact that the smaller number of top box-office hits was dominated by British titles: hence the celebration, in many histories of cinema, of British film production at this time. During the fifties, however, the US product was dominant, both in numbers of popular successes and within the handful of top selling titles in each year. Towards the end of the fifties and in the early sixties, British films once again figure significantly both in overall market share and in the top hits listings – though given the contribution of US finance to these productions we should perhaps be wary of the claims about the 'revival' of the British cinema abounding in the press of the period: if the term is justified in cultural terms, it is certainly questionable in fiscal terms. By the mid-1960s, in any case, the situation was back to 'normal': a market dominated by imported material, with a nonetheless significant minority of popular box-office successes emerging from the home industry.

   Kinematograph Weekly was the main forum for the distribution and exhibition branches of the British industry. Josh Billings's annual review was clearly intended as a kind of survey of work in progress addressed to distributors and exhibitors. His references to the conditions in which the work was carried out – 'in spite of rain, snow, slush, fuel cuts, unprecedented months of sunshine and the chaotic economic conditions of 1947 . . .'[10] – allude to the shared experiences of exhibitors, as does his assessment of the value of the review to the trade:

> Originally the 'Kine Review of the Year' was called the 'Kine Book of Form', but when the survey caught on and renter and exhibitor alike found it provocative and stimulating, even if they did not always agree with the findings, it was decided to adopt a more dignified title. Nevertheless, there is a strong analogy between 'the review' and 'the racing manual'. Both cover twelve months and assess value on performance.[11]

Billings's analogy with the uncertainties of the racecourse and his reference to 'dignity' show how chancy the business was perceived to be by those engaged in it, and also that, the impatience of some film critics notwithstanding, there was no question for distributors and exhibitors about where cinema should be placed on the art-industry axis: 'art and the box office are seldom synonymous'.[12]

The function of Billings's annual reviews, besides reinforcing the industry's sense of collectivity, was to attempt predictions of future performance in order to ensure profits, and hence survival. This attempt would have had implications for the range of titles available to audiences in succeeding years; for it is distributors and exhibitors who make the initial selections from which audiences choice produces the box-office hit. Thus the politics of distribution, after those of production, constrain and order the very possibility of any particular film becoming a box-office hit. The large number – over forty in all – of different and changing categories employed during the period provides evidence of the industry's unease: attention to the details of these categories, to the day-to-day terminology of product classification, allows the historian insight into the various attempts to stabilize it. It also allows consideration of the rather more elusive question of what a 'popular' film meant, in the terms of the trade, and how this meaning was subject to change as cinema audiences declined through the fifties. These categories fall into three distinct groups: those directly concerning the all-important issue of monies received; those responding to the imperative to define the product as closely as possible; and those concerning the box-office drawing power of particular performers.

Of these, the latter group is the most stable: the importance of actors to the marketing of films and the subsequent assessment of their success was apparently uncontested. Three categories citing an actor's name in respect of a particular film appeared consistently throughout the period. 'Best Individual Performance', 'Most Popular and Consistent Star', and 'Most Promising Newcomer'. 'Best Individual Performance' is the category for which Billings appears to draw most heavily on conventional notions of quality: on the values of 'art' as opposed to the more quantitative values – those of 'commerce' – implied in his use of the term 'popularity', where he habitually referred to the numbers of tickets sold, the length of queues or the perceived demand for films featuring a particular performer.

[. . .]

In 1946 Billings cited only one actor in his category 'Best Individual Performer' – Celia Johnson for her performance in *Brief Encounter*. In 1951 he listed Michael Redgrave in *The Browning Version*, Alec Guinness in *The Mudlark*, Judy Holliday in *Born Yesterday* and Bette Davis in *All About Eve*, referring in particular to Redgrave's 'superlative straight acting', his 'gentle tour de force'. By 1957 the number of 'Best Performances' had risen to ten.[13] However, although Billings did occasionally refer to individual performance in his prose accompaniments to the annual review, this practice was on the whole unusual. Most of his text is concerned with an assessment of distributors' output and with the contours of the successful film. Again and again he stressed that individual performance, stars, technological innovations and the like can never compensate for a poor script:

> The wide-screen and colour can unquestionably make a good film even more attractive, but, like many a so-called star, these embellishments are no compensation for an indifferent script. There never has been and there never will be a substitute for a strong story.[14]

As far as individual actors are concerned, Billings was undoubtedly most at ease with the category 'Most Popular Stars'; though it is interesting to note the relatively poor correlation between his assessment of who these were and that of *Picturegoer*'s annual readership poll. *Picturegoer* cited ten male and ten female actors each year in its annual 'Best Actor' and 'Best Actress' awards, whereas Billings was more erratic, giving forty-three names in 1948 and only five in 1953 and 1959. In general the number was between ten and twenty-five. The correlation between these and the *Picturegoer* assessments was never more than fifty per cent, and frequently much less. In 1946, when Billings cited Celia Johnson for 'Best Individual Performance', he was actually far more enthusiastic about James Mason and Margaret Lockwood, who were among *KW*'s sixteen 'Most Popular and Consistent Stars':

> We have no hesitation in placing James Mason first. Although he has only appeared in one film this year, *The Wicked Lady*, his popularity has enormously increased. Evidence of this is the constant demand for his old films and the furore he has created in the States. He is clever enough to keep in the news, without making too many pictures. The studio which eventually gets him – and may it be British – will definitely be on velvet.
>
> Margaret Lockwood, of *The Wicked Lady* and *Bedelia* fame, is easily Britain's Number One feminine star.[15]

[. . .] Despite his regular attention to actors, however, by the late fifties Billings clearly had reservations about the scope of their power at the box office:

> I've mentioned who I believe to be the most popular stars, but, with the exception of Kenneth More, who is unquestionably a big draw here, I know of no actor who can turn an ordinary film into a box office success mainly on the strength of his name.[16]

The category 'Most Popular British Star' appeared only once, in 1945. 'Most Popular and Consistent Young Star' appeared in 1945[17] and in 1954–5.[18] Although it is clear both from film reviews and from letters from fans published in the two fanzines of the period, *Picturegoer* and *Pictureshow*, that stars were often identified with particular film genres, there is no reference to this aspect of their performances in the annual popularity assessments, except in the case of comedians. [. . .]

The 'glorious uncertainties' of the business in the period between 1945 and 1960, and the concomitant innovations in marketing strategies in the late fifties, are also in evidence in the third group of categories, those relating to the primary function of film as perceived by exhibitors and distributors – namely to generate profit at the box office. The categories which appeared consistently throughout the period were 'Biggest Box Office Attraction', with a separate listing of 'Runners-Up', and 'Best Output', which cited a distribution company. These were the two most important items of information for exhibitors: which films made the most money, and which distribution company routinely offered the best booking opportunities. There was considerable attention, most marked in the late forties, to specifically British operations; and during the fifties attention was paid to novel marketing strategies with such categories as 'Best Double Bill', 'Best British Double Bill', 'Best Re-Issue Double Bill' (1951, 1953–60), or the colourfully named 'Super Special Long Run Propositions at Special Prices' (1958) and 'Hard Ticket Giants', 'Block Busting Exploitation Offerings' (1959–60), which, like 3-D and CinemaScope in the earlier fifties, drew attention to films which could not be fairly accounted for in the overall national box-office picture. The 'Super Special Propositions' in 1958 were *The Ten Commandments*, *South Pacific* and *Around The World in 80 Days*; and the same titles reappear as 'Hard Ticket Giants' in 1959, accompanied by *Gigi* and *The Nun's Story*. In 1960 the term was

'Block Busting Exploitation', and the film was *Hercules Unchained*. Billings's remarks about the latter are interesting both for their insight into contemporary marketing practices and for their clear separation between the 'good' (the well made, engaging film) and the 'good' (the health of the industry):

> The fabulous spectacle starring Steve Reeves was exploited in this country by Joe Levine who wears Barnum's cloak with astonishing and brilliant aplomb, and his skilfully timed saturation campaign in newspapers and magazines and on TV paid off and showed that box office success can be bought. There is of course a tendency to condemn pressurised salesmanship, but don't let us be pompous. *Hercules Unchained* was, admittedly, not half as good as it was cracked up to be by Joe Levine, but it went out during the August holidays and helped by a U-certificate and inclement weather brought into the cinema many young children who had never seen 'the flicks'.
>
> The experience unquestionably gave them a taste for hokum but as their education advances there is no reason why they shouldn't acquire a liking for really first class films and become regular picturegoers.[19]

Although most of these titles attracted considerable razzmatazz and long queues in urban centres, none appeared in the 'Biggest Box Office Attraction' listings: these categories, then, appear to embody a suggestion to exhibitors about new strategies for filling (or saving) their cinemas. By the end of the fifties it had become inescapably clear that cinema was no longer the dominant form of mass entertainment, and that in order to survive at all outside the 'art house' it would have to reorganize itself radically. These raucous categories represent an attempt to do this; and the films themselves, with their lavish production values and grand-scale panoramas, recall the struggles in the USA between the MPPC cartel and the 'independents' in the early years of the century, as the cinema institution engaged in a formative contortion similar to that which was to characterize the late 1950s.

In this exploration of the changing meanings of the notion of 'the popular' as it referred to the relation between films and their audiences (a relation always mediated by the box office, the object of Billings's and *KW*'s scrutiny), it is the category which measures successive films' drawing power at the box office which is of greatest interest. In the succession of 'Biggest Box Office Attractions' between 1945 and 1960, there is evidence of the gradual shift in audience preferences: for *KW* 'the popular' is simply that which the most people prefer and will pay to see. Any sociologically motivated interpretation of such preferences, though, must also take into account the overall and absolute decline in audiences during the period and the related politics of distribution.

Popular themes

The simultaneous popularity of different genres and stars, not to mention the vagaries of release dates, make it difficult to claim with certainty that any single film was the 'top hit' of its year. Nevertheless this correlative method is sound enough to offer groups of titles which, taken together, can be analysed to reveal common themes. Discovering thematic unities amongst groups of films whose only common feature, at first glance, is a temporal one, requires an analytic method which can be employed over a range of different genres. I selected (on the basis of their 'popularity' at the British box office) groups of six films from 1946–6, 1950–1, and 1955–6, and performed a careful textual analysis of each film. These analyses involved a dual enquiry into the status and narrative experience of characters; taking into account firstly their fundamental contribution to the unfolding of the narrative, and secondly the degree to which the character allowed (or invited) audience insight into the diegesis. This method entailed a schema whereby all characters in any film could be classified in one of four groups (central, major, minor, figures); and the schema allowed comparisons between films contemporary with each other, and between films separated by a temporal interval. Having analysed each film in isolation according to this method, I was then in a position to consider individual films and groups of films in terms of thematic and structural similarities and dissimilarities. In this approach in which film texts are privileged, dictating questions or observations about their social and/or political contexts, I hope to have avoided the pitfalls of a reflectionist analysis. The elaborate correlation of sources employed to generate sample films for analysis is fundamental to this mode of enquiry, since it is contemporary success at the box office, or contemporary audience choice, which determines the selection of film objects in the first place and therefore allows the following question: what changes are discernible in the content and narrative structure of films found to be 'popular' at different moments?

In the mid 1940s a common theme in the majority of the most successful films at the box office concerned the status and behaviours of women. Time and again, films offered a central female protagonist who transgressed the implied social order either wilfully, as Barbara (Margaret Lockwood) did in *The Wicked Lady*, or as a consequence of 'tragic' circumstances, such as those suffered by Diana (Anna Neagle) in *Piccadilly Incident* (1946). Frequently, the films focused on the psychic makeup of the character in an attempt to explain her troubles by reference to her past experience: Francesca (Ann Todd) in *The Seventh Veil* (1945) and Maddalena (Phyllis Calvert) in *Madonna of the Seven Moons* (1944) are examples of characters whose narrative path is constructed in this way. The case of Laura (Celia Johnson) in *Brief Encounter* is exemplary of this narrative method at its most uncompromising, since the entire film is structured in the form of her 'silent' – given in voice over to the audience alone – address to her husband, in which she details the agonies and delights of her extramarital liaison. The consequence of this narrative method is that problems which might, from a more distanced point of view, reasonably appear to be general social concerns – in this case the attempt at reestablishment of prewar conventions of family life following the disruptions of the war period – are suggested to be the discrete and private concerns of a lone (female) individual. Even when the subject matter of the film does not overtly concern an individual heroine, there is a clear tendency for the thematics to be personalized in this way: in *The Bells of St Mary's* (1945), for example, the central enigma concerning the fate of the convent school is delineated primarily in terms of the developing relationship between the head teacher, Sister Mary Benedict (Ingrid Bergman), and the school's new padre Father O'Malley (Bing Crosby).

Most popular films at the British box office 1945–1960

1945   *Madonna of the Seven Moons* (UK) 5*
Mr Skeffington (UK) 4
The Seventh Veil (UK) 5
Henry V (UK) 2
The Way to the Stars (UK) 2
A Song to Remember (US) 2
Valley of Decision (US) 3
The Affairs of Susan (US) 3
I Live in Grosvenor Square (UK) 2
Old Acquaintance (US) 2
Frenchman's Creek (US) 2
Mrs Parkington (US) 2
Here Come the Waves (US) 2
They Were Sisters (UK) 3
Perfect Strangers (UK) 2
Conflict (US) 2
Duffy's Tavern (US) 2
A Place of One's Own (UK) 2

1946   *The Wicked Lady* (UK) 5
The Corn is Green (US) 4
Piccadilly Incident (UK) 4
Ceasar and Cleopatra (UK) 4
Brief Encounter (UK) 4
Spellbound (US) 3
The Captive Heart (UK) 2
The Bells of St Mary's (US) 3
Mildred Pierce (US) 2
Leave Her to Heaven (US) 2
Road to Utopia (US) 3
Kitty (US) 2
Caravan (UK) 2
Blue Dahlia (US) 2
Bedelia (UK) 2
O.S.S. (US) 2

1947   Great Expectations (UK) 5
Odd Man Out (UK) 5
The Courtneys of Curzon Street (UK) 4
The Jolson Story (US) 3
Deception (US) 2
They Made Me a Fugitive (UK) 2
The Razor's Edge (US) 2
Frieda (UK) 3
Black Narcissus (UK) 3

Duel in the Sun (US) 2
So Well Remembered (UK) 2
October Man (UK) 2
The Upturned Glass (UK) 2
Two Mrs Carrolls (US) 2

1948   Spring in Park Lane (UK) 5
Oliver Twist (UK) 5
The Red Shoes (UK) 5
Miranda (UK) 5
Hamlet (UK) 4
The Winslow Boy (UK) 2
My Brother Jonathan (UK) 2
The Fallen Idol (UK) 2
Saigon (US) 2
The Best Years of Our Lives (US) 3
I Remember Mama (US) 2
Homecoming (UK) 2
It Always Rains on Sunday (UK) 3
Road to Rio (US) 2
An Ideal Husband (UK) 2
Green Dolphin Street (US) 2
Forever Amber (US) 2
Life With Father (US) 3
The Weaker Sex (UK) 2
If Winter Comes (US) 2

1949   Maytime in Mayfair (UK) 5
Johnny Belinda (US) 3
Whispering Smith (US) 2
Jolson Sings Again (US) 3
Scott of the Antarctic (UK) 3
Red River (US) 2
Madness of the Heart (UK) 2
Adam and Evelyn (UK) 2
The Secret Life of Walter Mitty (US) 2
Paleface (US) 2
The Blue Lagoon (UK) 2
Easter Parade (US) 3
The Barkleys of Broadway (US) 2
Three Came Home (US) 2
The Forsyte Sage (US) 2

1950   *Odette* (UK) 5
Annie Get Your Gun (US) 5

Father of the Bride (US) 3
Sunset Boulevard (US) 2
Morning Departure (UK) 2
The Wooden Horse (UK) 3
Samson and Delilah (US) 4
Pandora and the Flying Dutchman
(UK) 2
All About Eve (US) 4
The Blue Lamp (UK) 2
The Happiest Days of Your Life
(UK) 2
Treasure Island (UK) 2
Fancy Pants (US) 2

1951   The Lavender Hill Mob (UK) 2
The Great Caruso (US) 4
Born Yesterday (US) 2
The Browning Version (UK) 2
No Highway (UK) 2
The Lady with the Lamp (UK) 2
Encore (UK) 2
Detective Story (US) 2
Captain Horatio Hornblower (UK) 4
White Corridors (UK) 2
Laughter in Paradise (UK) 2
Worm's Eye View (UK) 2
Cinderella (US) 2
King Solomon's Mines (US) 2
The Mudlark (UK) 2
Scrooge (UK) 2

1952   The African Queen (UK) 4
The Sound Barrier (UK) 4
The Greatest Show on Earth (US) 3
The Planter's Wife (UK) 3
A Streetcar Named Desire (US) 2
Where No Vultures Fly (UK) 2
The Quiet Man (US) 2
Ivanhoe (UK) 2
Angels One Five (UK) 2
Reluctant Heroes (UK) 2
Mandy (UK) 3

1953   The Cruel Sea (UK) 4
Shane (US) 2
Roman Holiday (US) 2
Moulin Rouge (UK) 3
Quo Vadis (US) 2

Limelight (US) 2
Come Back Little Sheba (US) 2
The Snows of Kilimanjaro (US) 2
Genevieve (UK) 2
Call Me Madam (US) 2
A Queen is Crowned (UK) 2
Road to Bali (US) 2

1954   The Glenn Miller Story (US) 5
Calamity Jane (US) 4
The Purple Plain (UK) 3
On The Waterfront (US) 3
Magnificent Obsession (US) 2
The Caine Mutiny (US) 3
Doctor in the House (UK) 3
The Robe (US) 2
Hobson's Choice (UK) 3
Sabrina Fair (US) 2
Rear Window (US) 2
Trouble in Store (UK) 2
The Belles of St Trinians (UK) 3
Knock on Wood (US) 2
From Here to Eternity (US) 3

1955   *The Dam Busters* (UK) 5
Doctor at Sea (UK) 3
Marty (US) 3
The Country Girl (US) 3
East of Eden (US) 2
A Man Called Peter (US) 2
All That Heaven Allows (US) 2
A Star is Born (US) 2
Love Me or Leave Me (US) 2
I Am a Camera (UK) 2
Young at Heart (US) 2
White Christmas (US) 2
One Good Turn (UK) 2
Raising a Riot (UK) 2
20 000 Leagues Under the Sea (US) 2

1956   *Reach for the Sky* (UK) 5
The King and I (US) 4
The Man with the Golden Arm
(US) 2
Rebel Without a Cause (US) 2
It's Great to be Young (UK) 3
Guys and Dolls (US) 3
A Town Like Alice (UK) 2

The Man Who Knew Too Much (US) 2
The Rose Tattoo (US) 2
Picnic (US) 2
Trapeze (US) 2
Private's Progress (UK) 2
The Baby and the Battleship (UK) 2
The Searchers (US) 2

1957** Anastasia (US) 5
Doctor at Large (UK) 3
Yangtse Incident (UK) 3
Campbell's Kingdom (UK) 2
Giant (US) 3
The Teahouse of the August Moon (US) 2
The Spanish Gardener (UK) 2
The Story of Esther Costello (UK) 2
Woman in a Dressing Gown (UK) 2
Heaven Knows, Mr Allison (US) 2
High Society (US) 2
Tea and Sympathy (US) 2

1958** The Wind Cannot Read (UK) 3
The Bridge on the River Kwai (UK) 3
The Young Lions (US) 2
Pal Joey (US) 2
Indiscreet (UK) 2
The Defiant Ones (US) 2
Carve Her Name With Pride (UK) 2
Ice Cold in Alex (UK) 2
Peyton Place (US) 2

1959** Room at the Top (UK) 2
***   The Inn of the Sixth Happiness (UK) 2
I'm All Right Jack (UK) 2

1960** Sink the Bismarck (UK) 2
***   The Millionairess (UK) 2
Inherit the Wind (US) 3

Films analysed in detail are given in italics.
*The 'score' figure given for each film refers to the number of mentions it received in the following annual award categories: *Picturegoer* 'Best Actor'; *Picturegoer* 'Best Actress'; *Kinematograph Weekly* 'Top Box Office Film'; *Kinematograph Weekly* 'Best Individual Performance'; *Kinematograph Weekly* 'Most Popular Star'; *Motion Picture Herald* 'Top Ten Films'.
** There are no *Motion Picture Herald* citations for the British Box Office in this year.
*** There are no *Picturegoer* awards for this year.

By the mid-1950s, by contrast, the thematics of popular films are concerned more with men than with women, with narrative structures tending to be a generalization from the particular, as opposed to the 1940s personification of social – generally expressed as female – concerns. Here we have a mythologizing process at work: the narrative experience of central characters (by now usually male) exemplifies contemporary ideals, is idealized, rather than being relegated to the realm of the private where, whether tragic or fortunate, characters' experience is not inevitably seen in symbiotic relation with that of the wider social group.

Thus the angst-laden performances of James Dean in *Rebel Without a Cause* (1955) and *East of Eden* (1954) are made to stand for the general problem of socializing the young in middle-class America and, in the case of the latter, for an even more generalized interrogation of American values. Both films implicitly pose the question 'what is the American way of life?' exploring it through a dramatic construction in which the central character is posed as embodying wider concerns. This is true of such apparently diverse films as *Rebel Without a Cause*, *East of Eden* and *The Searchers* (1956), as well as of the British pictures *The Dam Busters* (1954), *Reach for the Sky* (1956) and *Doctor at*

Sea, in which the question relates to Britain and the British way of life. The point which concerns us here is that all these films enjoyed outstanding success at the British box office in the mid-1950s. [. . .]

Critical discourses

This major change in the thematics of 'the popular' over a ten-year period provokes further questions about the critical discourse surrounding these films. My textual analyses were followed by collecting critical responses to the sample films from a variety of sources, both British and American: trade journals, film journals, fan magazines, and national press and more general papers which sometimes reviewed, or referred to, new films.[20] In general, the less specialized the source the more likely it was that a radically oversimplified reading of a film would be presented. Nevertheless, this set of sources remains, for the historian, the best contemporary evidence of audience understandings of the films. Clearly the caveat underlying my remarks about changes in the thematics of the popular – that only generalized propositions based on a plurality of instances have any validation – is also operative in the case of these published responses to films.

What is immediately of interest here is that, rather than the striking change in the thematics of the popular noted in the films themselves, there appears to be a striking consistency: critics and reviewers seem to be virtually unanimous in the sociological and aesthetic models on which they implicitly draw in their summary judgements. Moreover these models, unlike the thematics of films, did not change appreciably between the mid-1940s and the mid-1950s. The majority of critics affirm, in their responses to films, the conventional status quo as typically confirmed in narrative resolutions, referring additionally to the canons of 'high' art as these were understood in postwar Britain[21] in their applause for a particular performance – Redgrave in *The Browning Version* and *The Dam Busters*, Johnson in *Brief Encounter* – or in their denigration of a particular film whose 'popular' tone reveals, to the critic, a lamentable absence of such an aesthetic. It is in practice often difficult to separate aesthetic references from those pertaining to social mores: this confusion between cultural and ethical values has, I suspect, substantive consequences for the maintenance of middle-class hegemony during the so-called 'classless' fifties. *Tribune* noted approvingly the 'Beautifully sincere and natural playing of Celia Johnson' in *Brief Encounter*, endorsing her eventual repudiation of the 'affair' with Alec (Trevor Howard) by referring to the 'guilt, humiliation and [a] heroic integrity at the centre'. It is tempting to infer that Johnson's 'playing' could be considered 'natural' precisely *because* of her 'heroic integrity' revealed in her appropriately felt 'guilt and humiliation'. Margaret Lockwood's performance as the ebullient, unashamedly transgressive heroine in *The Wicked Lady* was, on the other hand, 'inept to the point of exasperation'; though for this evidently misogynist critic, James Mason in the same film 'aroused both admiration and sympathy'.[22] The implicit opposition between (high) drama and (low) melodrama which underlies reviews throughout the period surfaced clearly in the *News Chronicle* review of *The Dam Busters*:

Drama . . . never once degenerates into melodrama, nor the humour into the irrelevant flippancy of comic relief.[23]

In addition, many reviews in the forties reveal an alignment between 'high art' values and French cinema, which had given way by the end of the fifties to a repudiation of the sexual explicitness of French (by now 'Continental') films. B*rief Encounter* was equated by many with both 'art' cinema and, in what seemed a self-evident corollary, 'French' cinema.

> . . . it would be difficult to find a more profound study of love outside the French cinema.
> . . . this is a poet's film, harsh, cruel and lovely.
> Four people remarked separately to me after its preview that *Brief Encounter* was more like a French film, finding about the highest praise they could for it.
> What they meant is that the film, among other things, is emotionally grown up . . .
> It is because of this sincerity and its infallible evocation of Haute Suburbia that I rank this as the best of the Noel Coward/David Lean/Havelock Allen/Ronald Neame productions, and forgive its disturbing patches of violent light relief.[24]

We should also note, however, the context of these critical judgements. Since much of the British trade and critical press during the fifties was deeply concerned about the survival of the home industry, there is always an imperative in their writing to encourage – to search for indications, however insubstantial or tenuous, of future success, as well as to exhort audiences to attend. This tendency took a positively jingoistic turn as the decade progressed and the British industry crumbled before its critics' very eyes.

Running through the shifting alliances and discords which characterized the British film industry from 1945 onwards there is a thread of agreement: an anxiety shared by all, though expressed and understood in implacably different ways, about the growing cultural dominance of Britain by the USA. Stafford Cripps at the Board of Trade in 1945, for example, saw the problem in terms of imports and exports: 'I am anxious', he said, 'to leave the strong Rank combine effective for meeting and possibly dealing with American competition.'[25] Whereas Ralph Bond, a leading member of the film technicians' union ACT, offered a rather different perception of the dual imperatives of Rank's export drive in the USA and his investment in distribution and exhibition in Britain:

> It is a curious but evident fact that the more cinemas Mr Rank owns the more he is dependent on America to provide films to fill them.[26]

Lord Reith, appointed in April 1949 as the first chairman of the National Film Finance Corporation, the body set up to administer funds acquired through the Eady Levy, certainly felt his task to be at least as much a cultural as an industrial one:

Let us be clear as to the issues at stake . . . The most compelling are of the moral order – evidenced in the influence which the industry can exercise over so considerable a proportion of the population – interests, outlook and behaviour; in the projection of England and the English way of life to the Dominions and foreign countries; in the enhancement of the prestige and worth of England.[27]

And Harold Wilson, then President of the Board of Trade, to whom this memorandum was addressed, had dealt with the point in more detail during a parliamentary debate on the film industry in June 1948:

We are getting tired of some of the gangster, sadistic and psychological films of which we seem to have so many, of diseased minds, schizophrenia, amnesia and diseases which occupy so much of our screen time. I should like to see more films which genuinely show our way of life, and I am not aware . . . that amnesia and schizophrenia are stock parts of our social life.[28]

The antipathy towards America which lurks beneath these remarks, as well as in the more specific responses to films by critics and reviewers, also surfaces as a thematic element in many British productions during the fifties, as well as in the implicit chauvinism of *KW*'s blithe division of the world into 'British', 'American' and 'Continental' in its annual review categories. A general sense that British cinema audiences were receiving a diet inappropriately dominated by Hollywood pervaded both critical writing and trade reviews, as well as informing the various governmental interventions in the regulation of the trade. British critics' alignment of the Hollywood film with the aesthetics of 'low'/mass/industrial culture and their attempts to find in the British film the values of 'high' culture can perhaps be understood as a solidly based suspicion of US infiltration of the UK market, couched in the terms of intellectual snobbery.

[. . .]

All these issues – the changes in the thematics of the popular between the mid-1940s and the mid-1950s: the consistent critical support for the conventional status quo (in sociological terms) and the routine dependence on the values of high art (in aesthetic terms); the increasing defensiveness on the part of the British industry and its critical support towards popular successes produced in Hollywood rather than Elstree – are condensed in the case of the 1951 George Cukor film, *Born Yesterday*. This film, released on the cusp of the new decade (its UK release date was 6 June 1951), was one of the top box-office hits of 1950–1.

The interesting thing is that whereas in 1951 in *Born Yesterday* the audience is invited to empathize with Paul Verral's/William Holden's conception of the almost sacred nature of American 'democracy' and the centrality of high culture to this ideal, later in the decade this position is revealed (in popular cinema, at least) to be a hopelessly impractical one. In *East of Eden* it is Cal's materialistic pragmatism which wins the day. British reviewers, while continuing to subscribe to the dominant social discourses concerning morality, the family, citizenship and so on, also betray an increasing unease about the aesthetics of popular culture:

> Steinbeck has provided an old-fashioned heavy sentimental drama, and Kazan has slickly tailored it in the modern, neurotic manner to suit a sick society.
>
> . . . a film dedicated to display, that mistakes mannerisms for style, artifice for art.
>
> Inflation is not only a headache with politicians and augurers of the stock markets: it hits one with a sickening thud from the screen. Before even the lights went down on *East of Eden*, I knew that it was inflated. One of those glossy melodramatic folders, all big names and hideously tinted photographs, had been handed to me, and at the top of it were the words: 'GREAT BOOKS, GREAT PLAYS, GREAT TALENT MAKE GREAT PICTURES (signed) Jack L. Warner.' Do They? What about GREAT GUFF? *East of Eden* is that.[29]

But this thinly veiled distaste of the middle-class British aesthete for the melodramatic form itself, as well as for the unseemly American habit of loudly proclaiming one's virtues in the marketplace, conceals, it seems to me, a more deepseated unease about what was clearly understood, by the middle of the 1950s, to be the threatening invasion of American cultural influence in Britain.

Notes

1 *Kinematograph Weekly* (*KW*), 19 December 1946, p. 46.

2 *Tribune*, 23 November 1945.

3 The annual assessments of 'popularity' published by three difference sources – the British fan magazine *Picturegoer*, the British trade paper *KW*, the American trade paper *Motion Picture Herald* – were correlated: only films which appeared in two or more out of six possible citation categories being considered 'popular' for the purpose of my sample. A table showing the full list of these titles appears on pp. 204–6 below.

4 *KW*, 19 December 1946, p. 46.

5 *KW*, 15 December 1960, p. 8.

6 James Curran and Vicent Porter (eds), *British Cinema History* (London: Weidenfeld and Nicolson, 1983), p. 372.

7 Geoffrey Nowell-Smith, 'On history and the cinema', *Screen*, vol. 31, no. 2 (1990), pp. 160–71.

8 Jeffrey Richards and Dorothy Sheridan (eds), *Mass-Observation at the Movies* (London: Routledge & Kegan Paul, 1987).

9 The table lists 105 US and 101 British films. Only titles with a 'score' of 2 or more have been included here. The remainder, with 1 citation each, is heavily dominated by the US product – thus the picture overall shows the British industry dominated by US imports. In addition many of the British pictures were financed by US companies.

10 *KW*, 18 December 1947, p. 18.

11 *KW*, 20 December 1951, p. 9.

12 *KW*, 18 December 1952, p. 146.

13 They were: Heather Sears in *The Story of Esther Costello*, Yvonne Mitchell in *Woman in a Dressing Gown*, Ingrid Bergman and Yul Bryner in *Anastasia*, Deborah Kerr in *Tea and Sympathy*, Carrol Baker in *Baby Doll*, Richard Todd in *Yangtse Incident*, Andy Griffith in *A Face in the Crowd,* Ben Gazzara in *End as a Man*, and Anthony Perkins in *Fear Strikes Out*.

14 *KW*, 12 December 1957, p. 9.

15 *KW*, 19 December 1946, p. 47.

16 *KW*, 12 December 1957, p. 9.

17 This was Margaret O'Brien.

18 Vincent Winter in 1954, Jonathan Ashmore, Colin Gibson, Lesley Dudley and Peter Asher in 1955 were referred to as 'Most Promising Youngsters'.

19 *KW*, 15 December 1960, pp. 8–9.

20 Such as: *Picture Post*, *New Musical Express* (formerly *The Accordion Times*), and some women's magazines – *Woman*, *Woman's Illustrated*, *Woman and Beauty*, *Woman's Own*.

21 John Ellis 'Art, culture, quality: terms for a cinema in the forties and seventies', *Screen*, vol. 19, no. 3 (1978), pp. 9–50.

22 *Tribune*, 23 November 1945.

23 *News Chronicle*, 17 May 1955.

24 *Britain Today*, February 1946; *Monthly Film Bulletin*, December 1945; *Chronicle*, 24 January 1946.

25 Public Record Office, Board of Trade 64/2188 (November 1945); quoted in Margaret Dickinson and Sarah Street, *Cinema and State: The Film Industry and the British Government 1927–84* (London: British Film Institute, 1985), p. 170.

26 Ralph Bond, *Monopoly, the Future of British Films* (London, ACT, 1946): quoted in Dickinson and Street, *Cinema and State*, p. 172.

27 Public Record Office, Board of Trade 64/4519 (February 1949): quoted in Dickinson and Street, *Cinema and State*, p. 216.

28 Hansard, 5th series, vol. 452, column 775, 17 June 1948: quoted in Charles Barr (ed.), *All Our Yesterdays: 90 Years of British Cinema* (London: British Film Institute, 1996), p. 14.

29 *Daily Worker*, 9 July 1955: *Sunday Times*, 10 July 1955; *New Statesman*, 16 July 1955.

Chapter 20

Angus Finney

SUPPORT MECHANISMS ACROSS EUROPE

> Cinematographic production in Europe is in an extremely critical
> position, and unless major efforts are made, the twentieth century –
> i.e. the first century of the existence of cinema – is going to end on a
> near failure of the European cinema.
>
> The Treaty of Maastricht

> We can either become dinosaurs, locked in a cultural theme-park of
> our own making, fed on a diet of pre-cooked subsidies – or we can use
> our talents and imagination to get back into the real game – commu-
> nicating or better still, delighting a viable audience.
>
> David Puttnam, film producer

MORE THAN $500 MILLION of national and European Union public money
is spent every year in propping up the production of European films. Some
600 films are produced in Europe annually, although fewer than 250 actually find
their way through distribution and successfully onto a cinema screen. A vast majority of the remaining 350 films end up on television, played late at night and never
to see the light of day.

The $500-million investment constitutes regional and national support systems, and
pan-European support in the form of MEDIA II (albeit not directly a production subsidy) and the Council of Europe's Eurimages fund. When public television, new
technology and distribution support is added to the production subsidy, the figure rises
well beyond $1 billion. It should be stressed, however, that Europe's film industry is
not necessarily receiving special treatment. Other European-based industries, including manufacturing, transport, telecommunications and new technologies, receive
huge European subsidies on a regular basis. [. . .]

This chapter examines the different approaches to film support in Europe, and
analyses how effective different public-subsidy systems are at encouraging a competitive and vibrant film industry. It also considers the new MEDIA programme and
certain tax incentives that are available to film-makers in Europe.

Illusions of subsidy support

Typically, few European professionals can even agree on the precise wording and interpretation used to describe film support. When four key European film industry personalities were interviewed in 1993 for an analysis of European national subsidy systems, they shared one common viewpoint: none of them liked the word 'subsidy'. Producer David Puttnam called subsidies 'production investment credits'; administrator Dieter Kosslick preferred 'conditionally repayable loans'; British Screen's Simon Perry argued that he operates an 'intervention mechanism'; and the French producer Rene Cleitman insisted that France has no straight subsidies: 'The system is audience-driven and the French producer is totally free.'

The growing antipathy to the word 'subsidy' is a result of it too often being equated with 'free money'. In turn, this artificially protects feature films from the demands and commercial realities of the international market-place. As film expert Terry Ilott argues, 'It may be a useful and even essential thing to subsidize local production. But subsidies provide the film-maker with a phantom audience, whose "attendance" can boost the revenues of a film as if by magic. Far from addressing the needs of this "audience", the European film-maker, naturally, treats it with contempt.'

The point is that television and straight subsidy money is not at risk, and hence recoupment of it is not a requirement. Ilott concludes that 'If Europe is to raise the average level of success and reduce the incidence of failure, it must restore the link between production and performance. Far from eliminating risk, Europe should place it as the keystone of its audiovisual production system.'[1]

Other critics of Europe's subsidy structures argue that there are inherent problems that stem from the establishment of culturally-orientated funds. These in turn become dominated by the director, who in turn produced his or her own work or used a producer simply to fill in forms for public finance. No real links are created with sales companies or distributors, the tough areas of the market which take into consideration whether a film has an intended audience or not. 'We can't talk about a film industry in Europe,' says Danish producer Mads Egmont. 'This is partly because state support emphasized the creation of art over an industrial product, and did away with the producer. The challenge of the entertainment business has always been to fuse culture and industry together, and create an industrial package that keeps the audience in mind.'

[. . .]

A heated subject

The level of debate over European subsidy support has certainly grown more heated over the past three years, on both a domestic and pan-European scale. Europe's national and regional subsidy systems have come under increasing scrutiny and attack, as efforts to create a single market for European films have clashed with local rules, criteria and local funding bodies. Meanwhile, the MEDIA II programme has had a spectacularly uncertain start, caught between bureaucratic mismanagement and policy squabbles between the member states.

On the other hand, the ensuing debate has grown slightly more open and hence more healthy when compared to the protective slanging matches during the early 1990s. As a special working paper for the 100 Years of Cinema colloquium in Strasbourg (October 1995) stressed 'How can intervention be made most effective in ensuring that the films supported are able to be taken out of the cupboard and shown to the audience?'

The paper went on to criticize grants organized and selected by committees: 'However good the committee, it takes no risks and hardly bears any responsibility for its decisions. Unfortunately, the decision to make a film nowadays depends less on the producer's willingness than on a committee's view. Producers sometimes spend their time chasing public funds. There is a complex web of procedures open only to the few in the know. Ought they not be reorganized, or perhaps new thought given to them, with a view to a pan-European cinema policy?'

True to form, the Strasbourg colloquium did nothing of the kind. Instead, a muddled, rambling conference highlighted how little politicians understand of the workings of the international film industry. The most common threat in any argument was a call for more money for marketing European films to combat Hollywood's muscle, with little thought for development strategy, constructive subsidy structures, or why we should be making the films in the first place. [. . .]

The different approaches

Mechanisms for raising and distributing money for film vary greatly across Europe. National and regional governments set aside sums of money for film which are raised either through a levy, such as in France, or a tax, as in the German Laender system. The terms on which the money is passed to the producer determines the subsidy's 'weight'. For example, the more a producer returns on an investment, the closer the subsidy comes to being a commercial investment. At present, Europe's national systems can be crudely broken down into seven or so different mechanisms, five for production support[2] and two (selective and automatic) for distribution (see Chapter 9). The five production types are as follows:

1 Soft, culture-orientated subsidy systems. This money is rarely recouped, and normally applies to smaller countries where their minority language and size of market makes commercial recoupment almost impossible. Most national film 'institutes' tend to work on a culture-driven basis, alongside national broadcasters. However, this kind of funding is critical for the discovery and development of new writing and directing talent. There are many examples of directors who started their careers with 'soft' support, including Ridley Scott, Peter Greenaway, Bille August and Lasse Halstrom. Territories that have soft, culture-orientated funding systems include smaller territories like the Nordic territories, Benelux, Portugal and Greece. Germany's federal source of public funding, including Federal Ministry of the Interior (BMI) and the Federal Subsidy Fund (FFA), also follow soft grant systems. For example, between 6 and 7 per cent was repaid to FFA on average between 1985 and 1992.

2 Regional, economic loans. This system drives the main German 'economic'

Laenders, where interest-free loans are awarded in return for a production obligation to spend about 50 per cent of that loan in the relevant region. The system
is flexible, with sometimes two Laender or more supporting the same production
although the return is mainly to one region. Their recoupment level is just 10 per
cent, but as Nordrhein-Westfalen Filmstiftung's (NRWF) Dieter Kosslick points
out, the key aim is to build and establish successful film activity in the region, so
the funds should not just be judged on recoupment alone. Other systems have
copied the economic model, including most recently, the Rotterdam Film Fund,
managed by former SOURCES head, Dick Willemsen.

3   The 'tough' repayable-loan mechanism, which more closely matches an equity
investment than a subsidy loan. This is the system championed by British Screen
Finance and the European Co-Production Fund, and imitated in part by Scotland's
regional funds and the Irish Film Board. The approach is not easy to balance, as
it requires both a cultural remit to support new talent and projects that otherwise
would not reach the market-place, and to take a tough enough position to see
some of its funds recouped on a regular basis. It is this model that the pan-
Scandinavian fund, the Nordic Film and TV Fund, run by Dag Alveberg, has
taken a keen interest in examining. However, while the system looks attractive to
professionals concerned about the new breed of 'overhead' producers, who do
little more than fill in forms and cover their costs; culture and language are
sometimes raised as obstacles to such a strident, commercial approach.

4   One of the leading kinds of production support, known as 'automatic' aid, is best
explained by the French system. Producers registered with the Centre National de
la Cinématographie (CNC) can apply for CNC funds annually. The level of annual
subsidy is calculated as a percentage of a CNC levy on the gross theatrical receipts
on all films (including imports) released during the year. Receipts from films made
by each French producer and released in the previous year are added up and the producer gets a share of the levy in proportion to those receipts. The subsidy is only
paid if it is to go straight back into film – either to pay off debts on former projects,
or the more likely case of re-investment in new productions. A bonus is paid for the
latter. The 'automatic' system has been heralded as constructive 'recycling' of profits from the industry back into domestic production. Spain has recently introduced
an automatic system to its industry with striking results (see below).

5   The last system, known as 'selective' aid, is also best represented by the French
system, and is applied in a strictly cultural sense. Selective aid in France is mainly
distributed by a system known as the Advances on Receipts. Grants are handed
out to projects normally on the basis of a screenplay, and are deliberately given to
first-time or new directors, and to challenging or interesting cultural work. (This
is much closer to the culturally soft system described in 1.) While the above
descriptions are useful for explaining the basic premises of the two types of aid,
it should be noted that the French system is currently under review. See the
analysis later in this chapter for further details.

6   Tax incentives, as introduced by the Irish and French governments, have been
used to attract private finance for production. The Italian government is now considering such an approach.

What kinds of films are we making?

Before examining in further detail the UK, German, Spanish and French systems, it is important to establish the relative scale and market that European films are aimed at, if aimed is indeed the operative word. Film expert Neil Watson carried out a study to assist with the setting up of ACE, the Paris-based European Film Studio. He broke European film production down into three broad types:

1   Films that are expected to recoup in a single national market; embracing low-budget (under $4 million to $5 million) arthouse pictures usually financed, at least in part, through national film subsidy mechanisms. This sector tends to perpetuate the need for 'subsidy' rather than forming a springboard for broader commercial acceptance. It also includes domestically orientated comedies (such as Germany's 'Otto' series, or Belgium's 'Hector'), characteristic of almost every European territory, that have substantial popular appear but only within national borders. Indeed, Germany has recently produced a string of successful comedies which have performed very well at the domestic box office but failed to travel.

2   Films, shot in any European language, which are expected to recoup across Europe as a whole. The industry consensus is that the current budgetary ceiling for such pictures is in the region of between £5 million and $6 million, although Farinelli [. . .] showed that a $13 million film can recoup from Europe. This category includes higher-budget national productions, but largely comprises projects co-produced or co-financed with at least one European partner. A North American distribution deal is an attractive bonus but is not essential to the financing of such films.

3   Films expected to recoup from the worldwide market. A North American distribution deal is essential to the financing of movies of this scale. Such films are usually shot in English – with obvious recent examples including *1492: Conquest of Paradise*, and *The House of the Spirits* – but occasionally a large-scale foreign-language film can succeed in recouping. The example Watson cites is *Cyrano De Bergerac*, whose 'excellence' managed to 'transcend linguistic barriers'.[3]

Given that only around 10 per cent of Europe's films are currently ever shown in cinema theatres in another country, it is quite clear that our national and regional subsidies are mainly used up in the effort to keep heads above water rather than crossing borders. Part of the problem that compounds this trend is that historically, many European subsidy systems were organised with the aim of supporting national, and only national production. Hence these systems don't fit into co-production models. Internal rules, points systems and the protectiveness of national language inhibits multilateral support.

The Spanish upswing

The current upswing of Spanish film production and a turnaround in the fortunes of Spanish films at the local box office during 1995 is partly due to recent changes in the industry's financing infrastructure. The new incentives were announced by the Spanish government at the San Sebastian Film Festival in September 1994 and introduced at the start of 1995.

The key piece of legislation is an automatic subsidy scheme. The Spanish Film Institute (ICAA) now awards a grant of 33 per cent of a film's budget to any Spanish film that takes more than pta30 million ($230,000) at the box office, up to a maximum value of pta100 million ($773,000) per film. The strategy is to encourage producers to make more commercial films. According to top Spanish producer Andres Vicente Gomez, in practice it means that 'producers can also start their own films without having to go through committees', a major burden to speedy and sensible decisions under the old selective system. [. . .]

The new subsidy mechanism has coincided with some supportive co-operations between Spain's private bankers and its major broadcasters. The Federation of Spanish Producers' Associations (FAPAE) has been building on the landmark deal that it struck with the Official Credit Institute (ICO) and state broadcaster RTVE in late 1994. [. . .]

Meanwhile, in January 1995 the Banco Exterior de Espana (BFX) renewed its agreement with the Spanish Ministry of Culture, increasing its credit lines for feature film production to pta4.5 million ($36 million) per annum. FAPAE is working on another film financing agreement that would see terrestrial pay-TV operator Canal Plus Spain link up with ICO or Spain's Banco Central.

In addition to public broadcasting and banking support, it is important to note how Spain's private sector has become far more active in film financing since 1994. The main player is GRUPO Prisa, which has considerable media assets and production ambitions.

The German scenario

Over the past five years, and despite recent high-level domestic success stories, national films have continued to take between 8–12 per cent of the German box office. The entire German support system has risen since 1993 from around DM200 million ($115 million) to DM250 million ($160 million), partly due to the arrival of the Berlin-Brandenburg Filmboard and also due to a restructured Hamburg Filmfund and new Baden-Wuerttemberg fund.[4]

As a 1994 report by London Economics stressed (and further expanded upon in the February 1995 report),[5] regional support from the Laenders has become so numerous as to have been described as 'a jungle of subsidies'. There has been a certain amount of leap-frogging by the government to provide more and more attractive aid packages for producers willing to locate production in a Laender. Indeed, according to one senior source, German producers would encourage writer-directors to 'become gypsies, and write road movies all over Germany so that they could access each fund accordingly.'

To limit these and other alarming tendencies, the Laenders decided in 1994 onwards to pool some part of their funds. However, calls for even further centralization have been consistently rejected by the regions.

If there was no regional competition and effort to build up infrastructures in different areas, then the money would not be there for film-makers to use.

It's crazy to suggest that the regional fund system should 'go national' when
effectively that would destroy much of the help available now.

Dieter Kosslick, head of the
NordRhine-Westfalen Filmstiftung (NRWF)

Rather than centralize, the main Laenders have tried to co-operate with one
another. [. . .]

Berlin-Brandenburg Filmboard

When Keil joined the Berlin-Brandenburg Filmboard in October 1994, his plans surprised large sectors of the industry. Not only were his plans hugely ambitious –
including the aim to 'double the German theatrical market share from 8 per cent to
16 per cent within ten years' – but he also wanted to achieve that goal by doing away
with the 'watering can' approach of other regional funds and following a more
market-orientated direction. He has placed a strong emphasis on development and
packaging, telling *Screen International*: 'In Germany, the screenplay equals literature,
which is a piece of art and may only be altered by the creator. This is a scandalous attitude. All the millions piled up in the film funds are a waste of money if the script isn't
up to scratch.'[6] In addition, Berlin-Brandenburg's selection mechanism differs from
the other funds by not working by committee, and Keil is himself free to green-light
projects. And it operates as a private company, not a government-run bureaucracy.

[. . .]

One of the areas which Keil has toughed up on is the requirement to have a domestic theatrical distribution agreement in place before any project receives production
monies. While this approach makes sense in theory, in practice many German distributors already have production interests, and are far less interested in backing
other, rival producers' projects for support. 'It's a major problem, because most of the
distributors simply aren't interested in giving productions a pre-sale minimum guarantee, especially when they are competing for funds,' says one Berlin-based producer.

The other two problems that face Keil are the amount of time it takes to service
applicants and get decisions made; and the budget difficulties he has faced between late
1995 and 1996. [. . .]

The production support available from the NordRhine-Westfalen Filmstiftung
(NRWF) is second to France's CNC in terms of size and power. Established in 1991,
NRWF operates as a limited company, two-thirds owned by the regional broadcaster
WDR, and one-third owned by the local Laender government. Consequently, two
separate funds are operated – one fully funded by the region, and one 50 per cent
financed by WDR and 50 per cent from the regions. Conditionally repayable loans are
paid into a special account which can then be used for the producer's next project with
the Filmstiftung, a system that Kosslick describes as 'recycling success', and one that
made the fund initially very attractive to producers.

[. . .]

While NRWF's track record of successful films has been distinctly varied, and has come in for strident criticism over the past three years, the level of regional support towards the film industry appears to be working. Figures produced by the fund and the region back claims that production houses, facilities and media activities have all increased considerably since 1991. [. . .]

What is wrong with Germany?

Ask most German film producers about the state of their industry, and they will normally point to the subsidy system as a key problem. However, having slammed it, when it is actually suggested that the system is removed completely, they throw their hands up in horror. 'It may not work, but it's the only thing we've got,' says one defensive and very senior producer. 'Without it we'd have nothing.'

More specifically, criticisms claim that, firstly, more time and energy is put into applications for funding than the projects themselves; and secondly, projects lose their focus by trying to please committees and public broadcasters, rather than considering audiences.

The new UK film world

Although Britain has very little direct government intervention towards film production, those bodies that do have money are surprisingly competitive and effective. The main source of film finance via subsidized/government sources are British Screen Finance, which incorporates the European Co-Production Fund; and the British Film Institute.

The key definition when discussing UK film support is the difference between 'financial intervention' and 'subsidy finance'. Even the BFI invests money as a 'leverage' to attract either other public support and/or private money. BFI Production exists both to back new talent and partly to compensate for the market's structural inadequacies and difficulties, and unlike many softer funds has a very active sales operation.

The production department had a production budget of around £650,000 ($975,000) for 1993, which was expanded in 1994/95 to support three films per year at a maximum budget level of £450,000 ($675,000). BFI finance is designed to encourage creative talent to make films with the freedom to experiment with new ideas rather than those aimed at the market. Many of the crews, directors and producers involved in these productions enter the wider market following their induction with BFI films. For example, Stephen Frears, Karel Reisz, Lindsay Anderson, Peter Greenaway, Terence Davies and Derek Jarman all benefited from BFI support in the making of their first films.

British Screen Finance and the European Co-Production Fund (which is administered by BSF) are the most important sources of government intervention to stimulating production in the UK. It should be noted that recent commercially and culturally successful films, including *Land and Freedom*, *Jack and Sarah*, *Before the Rain*, *The Crying Game*, *Orlando*, *Tom and Viv*, and *Damage* have made British Screen's financial position relatively healthy as a result of its tough position on its investments. In 1994 and 1995, British Screen had £2 million ($3 million) in the form of direct government grant, and £2 million for the European Co-Production Fund (ECF). In addition, it had returns from its investments at healthy rates, plus an additional £2m from a BSkyB satellite TV output deal. According to British Screen chief executive Simon Perry, British Screen makes good returns on its investments by European 'subsidy' standards. This is mainly because it puts in the minimum investment required to help a UK film get made, and its loans are not soft. 'Our economic and cultural strategy is to put into the market films that would not otherwise be there. If enough of those films work, then the example will stimulate the making of more such films, with and without the support of British Screen,' Perry explained.

The other key factor behind British Screen and the BFI is the clear growth of genuine co-production finance for UK films. Most of this rise in activity stems less from choice, and more from financial imperatives. The fact is that in a relatively small country like Britain, which enjoys a low level of government support, co-finance is the *only* means of getting films made. Given than more than 70 films are now being made per year in the UK, in contrast to the lows of the early 1990s (with fewer than 30 films being made in 1989), production has improved considerably. However, of the 73 films made during 1994 and 1995 respectively, fewer than half were totally British financed, reflecting the difficult market-place.

Ironically, after many years of complaining about lack of government support, the British industry has recently received an unexpected shot in the arm. This new 'drug' package originates from the National Lottery, and is worth around £30 million ($45 million) per annum for all film-related activities, including film production (and development), exhibition, training, and distributions support in the form of prints and advertising support. Of that figure, the Producers Alliance for Cinema and Television anticipates that about £24.5 million ($36.75 million) will be available for production investment during the years up to 2000.

While on one level the support looks miraculous in terms of its size when compared to pre-existing funds for UK film support, the lottery money has not come without its drawbacks. The Arts Council of England (ACE), the largest body dispersing the funds alongside its regional partners, has tended to fall into the trap of running film-production funding decisions by committee. Single applications have suffered from some of the idiosyncrasies that go hand-in-hand with such a system. [. . .]

One of the new strategies in the Greenlight Fund, administered by British Screen and aimed at halting the move to Hollywood by so many UK directors after they have completed their first feature film. The plan is to invest about £5 million ($7.5 million) a year in bigger-budgeted films on commercial terms, and a pilot year was carried out as this book was published. The Greenlight Fund also raised the problem inherent with its administration. Simon Perry, BSF's chief executive, already has considerable executive control over funding decisions at BSF and the European Co-Production Fund. If the Greenlight Fund is successful in its bid to continue, then a third fund run under his aegis may be too much for some to handle. That's not to suggest that his track record has been poor. On the contrary, BSF has not only enjoyed notable successes, but has over the last six years managed to reorientate UK producers towards Europe.

Nevertheless, such power and individual taste concentrated in the hands of one public executive would be resisted by certain quarters of the industry.

[. . .]

'Getting to grips with the market' was also supposed to be the guiding principle behind the Arts Council's own lottery plans for film. The Arts Council is hoping to use Lottery funds to back eight or nine companies (called 'franchises') made up of groups of film-makers and distributors who will work together to each make two or three films a year. Over time, it is hoped that these companies will build up good track records and become attractive to City and international investors. [. . .]

Overall, there are considerable problems as well as pluses that come with the Lottery money. For a start, the money was never actually expected by an industry that has long canvassed for tax incentives rather than straight subsidy support. The key will be to hold on to what the government *already* invests in British film, rather than allowing Lottery money to sweep all previous support from the British film industry's door.

[. . .]

The French tax system

[. . .] France's tax shelter investment scheme, SOFICAs (Sociétés pour le Financement du Cinéma et de l'Audiovisuel) provide the best-documented example of the opportunities and problems generated by tax initiatives in the European film industry.

The SOFICA attracts mostly higher earning individual tax payers looking to limit the amount of their income tax liability in France's higher income bracket of 56.8 per cent. These individuals may write off the whole of their investment in a SOFICA share capital, providing they do not sell those shares for five years (formerly eight years).

Under similar conditions, there is no tax owing on capital gain after the investor's exit from the SOFICA. For companies, the corporation tax relief is significantly less attractive, with a write off of just 50 per cent.

The SOFICAs were first launched in 1985–86, amid great hopes that they would provide a significant boost to the financing of independent films in France. By 1991 however, it had become apparent that the tax shelter investment provided a marginally better yield than straightforward bank loans. Over eight years, SOFICAs were able to return between 75 per cent and 80 per cent of their nominal capital sum to investors. For FFr100 ($19) invested, the immediate relief was FFr56.8 ($10.84). After deduction of the capital sum not recovered however – around FFr25 – the total yield was only about 4.5 per cent tax free per annum.

In 1992 the law was changed to accommodate pressures by SOFICAs to improve the return to investors. The banks managing the SOFICAs were allowed to offer investors a guarantee that they would buy back the entirety of their initial capital sum after eight years. Overnight, those SOFICAs were therefore able to offer a risk-free investment which – after the minimum duration of the investment was brought down to five years – offered an impressive tax-free return on investment of around 15 per cent.

The measure has fostered concentrations in the SOFICA market, which is now threatening to make access by independents increasingly difficult. In order to cover their risk, those SOFICAs offering to purchase the entirety of the initial capital put in by investors tend to work exclusively with the French 'Majors' such as Gaumont or UGC.

While the SOFICA guarantees its shareholders that it will re-purchase 100 per cent of what they put in, the Major to which the SOFICA is associated guarantees the SOFICA that it will reimburse all of those sums. As a condition of providing such a guarantee however, the Major will insist that the SOFICA funds, and only SOFICA funds, be used exclusively as production finance. In doing so, the Major has effectively access to an interest-free credit system.

The SOFICAs that are unable to align themselves with a powerful production studio, by contrast, are finding it increasingly difficult to survive. Independents are concerned that they will find access to SOFICA finance increasingly arduous. In an attempt to prevent a lockout, the government amended the rules, making it obligatory for SOFICAs to dedicate at least 35 per cent of their funds to film projects that do not emanate from the group with which they are aligned.

The problem with tax breaks

According to Bertrand Moullier, PACT's head of European affairs, the disadvantage of current tax incentives in Europe is that they are exclusively national in character and are very cumbersome to use. [. . .]

Tax incentives are primarily entered into by domestic governments as a means of generating value for the local economy. These conditions force European producers to enter into complex compromises which may range from the impractical to the downright counter-productive, in order to ensure that they make use of the statutory proportion of local craft and skills.

The conversion of all these national schemes into a single European Union tax relief mechanism is not for the European Commission to propose, as fiscal issues have been clearly identified by the Treaty as a national responsibility. Even if it were legally possible to unify such measures, no member state would see the benefit of it, as the principal attraction is precisely to be able to offer more attractive conditions than your neighbours.

Notes

1 Media Business File, *MBS*, Summer 1996, p. 15.
2 For much more detailed information and contact numbers of the national funding systems, see *Developing Films in Europe: A Practical Guide*, Routledge/MBS, Angus Finney (ed.), 1996. Also see *Sources of European Feature Film Funding*, PACT booklet, September 1995.
3 European Film Studio Feasibility Study MBS, Neil Watson, 1992, p. 10.
4 Contact as 2 above.
5 'Film subsidies in Germany', *London Economics*, September 1994.
6 *Screen International*, 5 April 1996, p. 12.

Chapter 21

Peter Besas

THE FINANCIAL STRUCTURE OF SPANISH CINEMA

THE ECONOMICS OF FILM PRODUCTION in Spain and, indeed, in most countries outside the United States, must seem baffling to those accustomed to thinking of filmmaking as essentially a process wherein a picture is produced at a given cost and either makes or breaks it depending on subsequent revenue received from box-office receipts and sales in ancillary markets such as television, cable, and home video, as well as in offshore outlets.

How can it be that a small country such as Spain can continuously produce over fifty features a year, 90 percent of which prove to be duds upon release or never even see the light of the screen? How is it that producer/director/scripters who fail dismally time and again nonetheless continue to burden cinemas with new aberrations? How can it be that in 1991, $87.7 million was spent on making films, but only $37 million was recouped at the box office (of which the producers received only one-third) and the following year another $82 million was poured into production, with a piddling $32 million return, and so on, year after year?[1] Even the local solons I consulted were hard pressed to shed more than partial light on this conundrum. Certainly, no two films are financed in quite the same manner; the formulas are as varied as schemes on how to get rich quick.

Generally, however, the answer lies in the financing structure of cinema in Spain and in a varied system of subsidies and pre-sales, mostly within Spain, which enable many filmmakers to limit the risk factor to a minimum, if not to nil. The secret, in many cases, is that profits are assured at the *financing* stage and not at the box office.

Only after all concerned have tucked away their profits does production begin. Then, the film is shot as best as one can with whatever remains of the budget. Of course, not all films use this fail-safe system, and the trails of debts left every year from unsuccessful productions testify to the pitfalls of the method and the folly of those providing services to such ventures. Yet this modus operandi certainly prevails for many films made in Spain and elsewhere in Europe, though admittedly there are also producers who put their own money on the line and run financial risks.

This economic cushioning and minimal-risk financing, in turn, conditions the genre and quality of the films made. With audience acceptance treated as an afterthought, the films all too often turn out to be insular, self-indulgent, uninspiredly experimental, pretentious, and, on occasions, hopelessly amateurish. These are the films rarely seen outside Spain and barely within Spain, though occasionally one does surface at a film festival if it is quirky enough. But mostly, they ignominiously end their aborted careers as a government statistic. For example, Title: *La fiebre del oro* (Gold Fever). Budget: $3.16 million. Subsidy from Madrid government: $850,000. (Other subsidies from the Catalan regional government.) Box-office gross $130,000. Or, Title: *Una estación de paso* (A Passing Season). Budget: $2.36 million. Subsidy: $650,000. Box office: $40,000. These are not rare exceptions. They tend to be the rule for the bulk of production.[2]

Hence, when moving in Spanish film circles, use of the expression 'the Spanish film industry' tends to bring a wry, indulgent smile to the lips of those producers hoary with experience and savvy to all the intrigues and vagaries of production. For 'industry' is a rather grand term to describe what is often more akin to artisanry.

[. . .]

The mainstay of financing in Spain for the past fifty years has been the subsidy system, which continues to provide the wherewithal that enables most Spanish films to be made. Without public funding, Spanish cinema, like that of virtually all countries outside the United States, would have long since withered and disappeared, barring perhaps half a dozen features each year.

With the advent of television in Spain in 1956, a massive influx of tourism in the late 1950s and 1960s, and growing international and political and economic pressure on the Franco government to ease up and be less restrictive, a new kind of film structure came to supersede the old 'classic' studio-type film.

Enter on the one hand new, committed, earnest filmmakers and 'auteurs' such as Luis García Berlanga and Juan Antonio Bardem, some producing their own films, others seeking out a new generation of producers who denounced the naive simplicities of earlier productions and embraced the earthy verities of Italian neorealism.[3]

Simultaneously, on the other hand, a phalanx of producers cranking out simplistic schlock appeared, purveyors of boulevard comedies starring sexy principals and new funnymen. Much of this trite domestic fodder, as thought-provoking as a tortilla, was tremendously popular and successful. It titillated and teased a generation of Spaniards who had been barred from seeing so much as a kiss on the screen. [. . .] These were the films never seen at film festivals or written about in 'serious' books on Spanish cinema, though perhaps they better reflect the reality of Spain in those days than the films made by the auteurs.

This spate of comedies was supplemented by dozens of Italian-co-produced spaghetti westerns shot in Almería, and cheaply made horror films suitable for export after being dubbed into English – pictures a few notches below the Hammer films made in England.[4]

Through the 1960s and 1970s, both the serious films and the boulevard pap vied for government subsidies and received them. For a number of years, in addition to the automatic 15 percent of box-office subsidy, an additional 25 percent of box office was heaped on for high-budget films. Still another subsidy was awarded for the nebulous 'special quality' category.

The criteria for giving subsidies have always been murky, vague enough so that political and private favoritism could be exercised. Nepotism and influence-pulling overshadowed the system and continue to be a key factor in the subsidy system, whether under Franco or under the Socialists. [. . .]

The outcome was that production boomed. In the Uniespaña (official Spanish film-promotion organization of the time) catalogue of 1968, 134 features are listed. The films ranged from Carlos Saura's *Peppermint Frappé* to the singing nun *Sor Yé Yé* to *The Return of the Magnificent Seven* with Yul Brynner and Warren Oates.[5] By 1977, Spanish films culled 29.76 percent of the domestic Spanish market.[6]

The administration's dilemma has always been how to encourage more ambitious films that might stand a chance of chalking up foreign sales and thus not only bring in revenue to Spain but also provide prestige to the *madre patria*. The scales have alternately tilted towards more 'commercial' and more 'artistic' films. Thus, it is not surprising that during the 1960s and early 1970s the auteurs and schlockmasters were always at daggers drawn. In their personal political attitudes they tended to polarize into Left and Right. The auteurs were staunch opponents to the dictatorship and tried to push the contents of their films to the brink of censorship limits; the 'commerce-floggers' were happy to crank out their comedies and teasing sex films and rake in the profits.

When Franco died in 1975, the panorama changed radically. The auteurs suddenly had the upper hand and could now openly excoriate and vilify the producers and directors of the boulevard pap. New legislation increasingly favored the auteurs in detriment to the comedy, gore, boulevard schlock, and 'lower' genres that had proved popular mass entertainments.

But neither 'auteurs' nor schlockmasters could produce if the subsidies weren't forthcoming. Those Ministry of Culture officials involved in film matters began, at the behest of vociferous arthouse producers and directors, pushing 'quality' films by reputable writers/directors such as José Luis Borau, Jaime de Armiñán, Manuel Gutiérrez Aragón, Vicente Aranda, Mario Camus, Pilar Miró, Gonzalo Suárez, Víctor Erice, and Carlos Saura. The nods went towards those producers with an affinity to the new Socialist political spectrum such as Elías Querejeta, Andrés Vicente Gómez, Emiliano Piedra, José Luis Borau, Luis Megino, and others.

In 1983, with the Socialist Party in power, a significant filip was given to this policy of encouraging 'quality' fare when film director Pilar Miró was appointed director general of cinematography. Miró, a staunch liberal who had confronted the Guardia Civil in her film *El crimen du Cuenca* (The Cuenca Crime, 1979) and who knew the quirks of the film business and everyone in it, pushed through a new film law, known locally as the Miró Law, which lavished funds upon 'serious' filmmakers and virtually turned its back on the traditional 'commercial' directors and producers [. . .]. The law provided hefty advance subsidies aimed at encouraging 'quality films, the projects of new directors, those directed towards a children's audience or those of an experimental character.'[7] In effect, the Miró Law decimated the ranks of those not within the inner circle of 'serious' production. It lavished money on new 'talent' and on the by-now aging anti-Franco centurions with their penchants for politics, the Spanish Civil War, and 'educating' audiences.

The results were not long in manifesting themselves, not terribly different from those in other countries where the commercial targets of films are not adequately taken into account, where an attitude of high-minded didacticism eclipses 'crass' business objectives, where, in short, 'entertainment' and 'commercial' become dirty words. The agelong and perhaps a trifle puerile controversy about whether film should be 'art' or 'commerce,' hotly argued and debated in innumerable smoke filled cafés and in film festivals and symposiums, was peremptorily decided in favor of the former.

The Miró Law, in retrospect, proved nigh disastrous, which is not to say that some excellent films were not made. But then two or three excellent films have *always* come out of Spain each year, no matter what the subsidy system used or the government in power. Well-intentioned perhaps as are so many idealistic ventures that produce nefarious results, the Miró Law in fact proved so crippling that Spanish cinema is still reeling from it. Miró's coterie has largely faded into obscurity, leaving in their wake dozens of films that simply didn't interest modern audiences. (She herself still directs commercial duds such as the recent *Tu nombre envenena mis sueños* [Your Name Poisons My Dreams] and *El perro del Hortelano* [The Gardener's Dog], both 1996.) Not only did production plummet to about fifty features a year, but, far worse, local audiences were turned off by the majority of Spanish films. The share culled by local pictures in their own market dropped to 10.80 percent in 1991, 9.32 percent in 1992, and 8.52 percent in 1993.[8] Repeatedly disappointed by pictures that had been hyped by film critics, many of whom were often in cahoots with the filmmakers, Spanish audiences started to shun local fare.

[. . .]

[T]he three financial crutches that have enabled the Spanish 'industry' to survive are subsidies, exhibit quotas, and dubbing licenses for foreign films issued only when Spanish films are also released. Obviously, the producers' very existences are at stake should any of the three elements slacken. The subsidies alone are not enough to assure their survival because, even if a producer succeeds in completing a film, he must then find a distributor who will adequately push his or her film, promote it, and obtain a good release date. However, because most Spanish films perform poorly at the box office, more often than not the distributor releases the film in order to obtain the dubbing license rather than for the revenue expected from its release. As for the exhibitors, they usually consider Spanish product to be their bane, since the average Spanish film draws about 40 percent less audience than the average American one.[9] The best play dates are usually reserved for Yank blockbusters.

The three legal dispositions have only been partially complied with. Subsidies were often as late as a year or two in being paid to producers; exhibition quotas were frequently winked at by theater owners; and dubbing licenses, until recently, were 'sold' from one distributor to another, which is to say arrangements were made for a distributor with a surplus of licenses to release films from one who lacked them.

With all their imperfections, the subsidies and quotas nonetheless form the cornerstone for financing and sometimes amortizing most Spanish films. However, other sources of revenue are needed before a producer can arrive at that felicitous state in which he has brought the risk factor down as close as possible to zero. There are thousands of variations, twists, exceptions, intrigues, swindles, and heartbreaks involved in the arcane methods of raising production money, both in Spain and in every country in the world. The following rundown covers the most common finance sources in Spain.

1. *Government subsidies.* Many films receive their initial impetus when the producer/director/writer sends a screenplay and production and financing plan to the film department of the Ministry of Culture (ICAA) applying for a subsidy to make a film. If this is approved, the film maker is guaranteed, say, anywhere between $200,000 and $600,000, though there are cases where far more was given [. . .].

In 1993, about $14.1 million were earmarked for subsidies to Spanish films. The ICAA's budget for subsidies in 1994 was 3,174 million pesetas (about $25 million at that year's exchange rate), of which 2,788 million were for features. Of this amount, 1,606 million were destined for advanced subsidies to projects and 1,022 million to *ayudas a la amortización*, that is, to Spanish films made without prior subsidies, but payable upon commercial release. [. . .]

In any case, all producers at present continue to receive the automatic 15 percent-of-box-office subsidy for their films. Those not requesting advance subsidies receive the additional 25 percent, that is, a total of 40 percent of box office. Moreover, in 1994 those who presented three films within a two-year period got 60 percent-of-box-office subsidy for each film. There are also subsidies for scripts (about $25,000), and 'special quality' subsidies ($250,000) once the film has been released. Subsidies are usually awarded three times a year.

About two-thirds of films receive advance subsidies [. . .] no advance subsidies are usually awarded to horror genre films or overt pornographic films; hence, these are rarely produced, though extreme violence is considered okay.

2. *Television.* You can then apply to one of the local television networks for financing. Previously that meant Radiotelevisión Española (RTVE), the government network; as of five years ago, it could also be one of the private channels, mainly Antena 3 TV. RTVE had been especially profligate in providing financing for cinema, and until its recent financial debacle would foot sums of $400,000 to $600,000 per project. In return, the network kept the domestic TV screening rights for the film, in addition to the foreign sales rights. But the latter tended to be negligible because RTVE sold off the bulk of Spain's most prestigious films at a pittance in 'packages.' RTVE usually helped finance about twenty films a year.

If losses were incurred, no feathers were ruffled, for as a state-owned network RTVE was expected to support local production and, until the private networks came in, was making fortunes in spot advertising, it being the only game in town. [. . .]

According to official figures, in 1990, 22.6 percent of the average film's budget came from TV advances. In 1994, it was 24 percent and in 1995, 17 percent. In 1991, thirteen films obtained TV advances, ranging from 8 to 200 million pesetas ($80,000 to $2 million).[10]

Further financing may come from Spain's private pay-TV channel Canal Plus España, which acquired 93 percent of all Spanish films produced in 1993. The pay scale usually runs between $50,000 and $100,000.

3. *Autonomous regions*. The producer will next try to get further financing from provincial authorities. If the film was shot in Aragon, or the Basque provinces, or in Catalonia, for example, an additional $100,000 or $200,000 might be obtained from local sources eager to have their regions promoted. Officially, 6.4 percent of financing came from the regional authorities in 1991. That year ten films received subsidies from regional sources, ranging from $50,000 to $400,000.[11]

4. *Distribution advances and home video*. A relatively minor sum might be obtained as an advance from the distributor of the film in Spain, say $100,000 (5.1 percent of budget, per official sources). However, in 1991, only 42.9 percent of films received distribution advances. Home video rights are usually negligible for most Spanish films, but for a while, before private TV channels came into Spain, there was a big home video boom, making Spain the fourth largest market in the world. At that time some advance money might be obtained from the home video sector as well. In 1991, after the video boom ended, only 0.8 percent of the average film's budget came from home video advances. [. . .]

5. *Co-productions*. Further financing might be sought by setting up a co-production, usually with France, Germany, Italy or Portugal, in which case funds could also be obtained from government subsidies in the co-producing country or countries, provided some token actors or technicians were employed. Each of the participating countries might then apply for local subsidies and benefits.

6. *European Union*. Financing may also come from the EU mechanisms, known as the Media Programme, which had a budget of $300 million over a five-year period (1990–1995) to promote the European audiovisual industry. In 1990 4.2 percent of the average film's budget came from these sources. However, in 1991 only two Spanish films obtained financing from this fund, one $30,000, the other $420,000.[12]

7. *Eurimages*. Another source of money is the Eurimages organization. This pan-European fund was set up by the Council of Europe in 1989 and has supported the co-production of 144 films between 1989 and 1992, providing about $60 million. In order to obtain Eurimages subsidies, producers from three participating countries must apply jointly.

8. *In-house financing*. According to the official Film Institute statistics, in 1990 only 23.3 percent of financing came from the producers themselves. The real percentage is probably much lower. The turnover in production companies is tremendous and few master the intricacies of survival.[13]

[. . .]

Private funding can include anything from a generous father who believes in his son's genius as a filmmaker to a rich financier in Bilbao who can be conned into investing in the world of glamour and show business. But mostly, in-house financing is kept to a minimum, and producers are loath to sink their own resources into their films. Better to use other people's money.

9. *Pre-sales.* In rare cases, producers may pre-sell their films to distributors in other countries. Today, about the only producers with enough clout to do this are El Deseo (the Almodóvar brothers) and Iberoamericana Films (Andrés Vicente Gómez), the latter via Sogepaq, the sales arm of Sogetel, Goméz's current corporate sugar daddy.

10. *Official bank loans.* The government's BEX bank in 1991 provided about $600,000 in low-interest loans, but 76.2 percent of producers did not apply because the bank usually asks for personal guarantees and collateral.[14]

11. *Private financing.* At present there are virtually no tax shelters for Spanish producers. A small write-off of from 20 to 25 percent of a film's profit may be obtained, but with a low limit. Otherwise, financing from private venture capital in Spain is negligible, since filmmakers are still considered suspect and the commercial results of most Spanish films are discouraging.[15]

12. *Other sources.* From 1988 to 1992 another important source of financing was the Quinto Centenario organization, which lavished funds on a wide range of Spanish and Latin American projects, in conjunction with the 500th anniversary celebrations of the discovery of America. [. . .]

Financing has also been raised in the past from everything from religious orders (*El hombre que supo amar* [*The Man Who Knew How to Love*, 1976]) to dubious sources laundering money – but that is a twilight area too touchy to expand upon.

In 1991, sources of financing for Spanish films were officially declared as follows:[16]

ICAA subsidy	26.0%
Regional subsidies	6.4%
European funding	1.4%
Private bank loans	5.8%
Public bank loans	9.3%
Producer's own finance	25.8%
Distribution advance	5.2%
TV advances	16.5%
Pre-sales	2.8%
Home video advances	0.8%

Thus – and this, perhaps, is the critical reason for the failure of so many non-US films – if financing from a part or all of the aforementioned sources is obtained before production begins, the commercial success or failure of the film becomes of secondary interest, since everyone involved in making the film has already raked off his or her money. Should the film prove successful upon release, should the producer be able to sell it outside Spain, that is further icing on the cake. But even if the film is a disaster, runs only one week, and dies a quick death, the producer can often go on and start the next project, especially if the producer has a track record that has provided him or her with some prestige. In short, the financial return is often not made at the box office but in the financing stage. And this is why fifty films or more continue to be made in Spain year after year. This system has provided Spain over the past two decades with a handful of exquisite, provocative, brilliantly limned films. But also with a huge number of stinkers that Spanish audiences have turned their backs on.

[. . .]

This financing legerdemain and investment penury inevitably condition the nature of the films made in Spain. Even though the average *declared* budget in 1995 almost doubled to 247 million pesetos, or about $2 million,[17] Spanish producers clearly must stick close to home. Not for them the film boasting flashy special effects; banish the thought of lavish historical reconstructions; eschew expensive stunts or exotic locations or films based on pricey international literary properties or those requiring high-paid foreign actors and actresses. Also strike off those that will receive no subsidies for being too crassly 'commercial.'

Usually the safest economic bet will prevail: a local comedy or a violent youth picture. Dozens such are cranked out each year. Some of them are big moneymakers, at least in Spain. For here are genres where Spain can hold its own ground: local humor, local celebrities, local slang, local situations that titillate an eye-winking audience, with the current crop of locally popular thespians Javier Bardem, Aitana Sánchez-Gijón, Penelope Cruz, Antonio Resines, Maribel Verdú, Jorge Sanz, Ariadna Gil, Carmelo Gómez, María Barranco, and Juan Echanove. Rather like the comedies of yore, so vilified at the time by critics and highbrows, these films can sometimes be very funny and well scripted. But they are usually dead ducks outside the country. However, if the production costs are kept down as much as possible, they can be gold mines – well . . . copper mines.

[. . .]

In an altogether unique category, almost unrelated and certainly not representative of other films made in Spain, are the comic melodramas of Pedro Almodóvar, which of late have risen to the $4 million budget range and are pre-sold worldwide. The last few have been co-financed by the wealthy Ciby 2000 group in France. Almodóvar's *Mujeres al borde de un ataque de nervois* (Women on the Verge of a Nervous Breakdown) was shot in 1988 on a shoestring and in Spain alone grossed an astounding $11 million. Add to that the TV, home video, and foreign sales of the film. Almodóvar now does not need subsidies. Even when not as successful as *Mujeres*, his films do well. Indeed, in Spain Almodóvar has been the butt of envy and dislike in the 'industry' and now pretty much goes his own way.

[. . .]

In 1994, a few new twists were given to film financing when the subsidy system was modified by the government in an effort to abolish some of the ills heretofore outlined. Advance subsidies, the cornerstone of the Miró Law, have in many cases been replaced by subsidies geared to the commercial results of films, a measure that clearly favors Spain's largest producers. Thus a law passed on June 10, 1994, and amended on October 5, 1994, provides for subsidies of one-third of the money put up by a film's producer up to a limit of 100 million pesetas if and when, upon release, it grosses 30 million pesetas (presently about $250,000). For films of new directors making their first two features, the threshold is 20 million. In addition, if the film is made in a regional tongue (e.g., Basque or Catalan), the amount drops to only 10 million pesetas. That subsidy is in addition to the automatic 15 percent of box office.

But as I write this article, and with a new conservative party government in power, it very much seems again that *plus ça change, plus c'est la même chose*. Quotas and dubbing licenses were to be abolished, subsidies decimated . . . The twelve years of Socialist film policies were branded as 'nefarious' by the new government. But soon the reaction from the vested interests of the film community were heard, the government had second thoughts, and things have more or less returned to what they have been in the past.

Notes

1 Equipo de Investigación de Fundesco, *La industria cinematográfica en España (1980–1991)* (Madrid: ICAA, 1993), 162–63.

2 *Quadre Pel. licules espanyoles per ordre de recaptaciones, segons LICCA*, Barcelona, August 10, 1994. List provided to author by Pérez Coinar.

3 See Peter Besas, *Behind the Spanish Lens: Spanish Cinema under Fascism and Democracy* (Denver: Arden, 1985).

4 Uniespaña catalogues (Madrid: Uniespaña), e.g., 1969 through 1975.

5 The Spanish Cinema. Uniespaña catalogue (Madrid: Uniespaña, 1968).

6 ICAA, *Avances cinematográficos* (Madrid: ICAA, 1977).

7 Royal decree of December 28, 9183, and Preamble thereof, Madrid.

8 ICAA, *Avances cinematográficos* (Madrid: ICAA, 1991, 1992, and 1993).

9 Jaime Tarrazón, interview by author, ACEC (Catalan exhibitors group), Barcelona, July 1993.

10 Santiago Pozo, *La Industria del cine en España* (Barcelona: Publicacions i Edicions de la Universsitat de Barcelona, 1984), 138, 140.

11 Ibid., 132.

12 Ibid., 140.

13 Ibid., 136.

14 Ibid., 154.

15 J. M. Cunillés, interview by author, November 3, 1995.

16 Pozo, 140.

17 José Angel Esteban and Carlos López, 'El trabajo del año,' *Revista Academia*, January 1996.

Chapter 22

Martine Danan

FROM A 'PRENATIONAL' TO A 'POSTNATIONAL' FRENCH CINEMA

[F]ilm is not, is no longer, a national product. Film today is by definition a transnational product.[1]

T HE 'CULTURAL EXCEPTION' AGREED UPON in the recent GATT agree-
ments, as the result of the pressure exerted by French negotiators on their American
counterparts, suggests that the French Government appears to be as committed as it has
been for the last half a century to the protection of its national cinema and to the defense
of culture over purely economic interests. But in spite of this apparent continuity, a closer
examination of recent French cinematographic policies reveals that the French State's
attitude towards its national cinema may in fact be changing to the point of affecting the
prevalent mode of film practice among French filmmakers. In particular, the State is now
openly encouraging the making of English-language superproductions (usually coproduced by two or more countries) in the hope of capturing a larger share of the global
market. Surprisingly, a similar search for successful international formulas was under-
taken by European film industrialists in the 1920s, at a time when the State had little
interest in cinema affairs. These changes, I would like to suggest, correspond to two
turning points in the relationship of the French State to cinema. A first transformation
led to the disappearance of the 1920s 'prenational' cinema and to the creation of a
'national' cinema; and a second transformation since the late 1980s may be leading to the
emergence of a 'postnational' cinema, which shares some (but not all) of the features of
the 'prenational' model. After a brief description of the prenational model, contrasting
the national with the postnational stages may ultimately enable us to gain a better understanding of the changing 'cultural logic,' linked to the development of capitalism, which
has most influenced film production in the French nation-state.

'Prenational' search for an international model in the 1920s

World War One left the French film industry in disarray and unable to resist the massive influx of films – primarily American ones – , which by 1918 represented 75 per

cent of the films marketed in France.[2] This first French cinema 'crisis' prompted
French film industrialists to search for new strategies that would allow them to survive in an economic environment which was no longer favorable to them. After the
failure of the first French-American joint ventures in the late 1910s came a number of
American-style, high-budget superproductions by French Majors and independents,
such as Nalpas's exotic tale *La Sultane de l'amour* (1919), Gance's war epic *J'accuse*
(1919), Feyder's colonial story *L'Atlantide* (1921), and Pathé-Consortium's serial *Les
Trois Mousquetaires* (1921–22). However, French companies were too financially frag-
ile and technically unmodernized to sustain such large investments, especially since
most of these superproductions, with the exception of *L'Atlantide*, failed to penetrate
the American market; and, in spite of their great popular success domestically, these
films did not curb American imports sufficiently either. Consequently, this strategy
was also largely abandoned by 1922.[3]

   These failures encouraged several important French film industrialists to seek another
strategy able to challenge Hollywood's control of world markets. By forming alliances
with other European producers, especially Germany, these industrialists hoped to produce 'international' films that could appeal to a European or even an American audience.
The creation of a united European industry, whose goal was to override the specificity
of national cultures (at a time when national schools in other art forms were paradoxi-
cally strongly defined), was judged necessary to reach markets larger than national ones
and amortize the huge costs of movie-making. As early as in 1924, upon the signing of
a reciprocal distribution agreement between Louis Aubert, the head of a powerful
French film company, and Erich Pommer, the leader of the German cartel UFA,
Pommer expressed the urgent need for close cooperation among European producers.
The ultimate goal of this cooperation, from Pommer's perspective, was to produce
competitive film commodities that could be marketed throughout Europe.

> One must manage to produce European films which will no longer be
> French, English, Italian, or German films, but true 'continental' films, able
> to find an outlet in the entire Europe, and the amortization of costs, which
> are enormous everywhere, will occur easily.[4]

   Although Aubert was not as openly willing to sacrifice cultural identity for the sake
of economic competitiveness, he nevertheless declared upon his return from the
meeting with Pommer that he had high expectations from a pan-European cinema
capable of competing with American cinema:

> I expect that the future will bring European Films, which will maintain and
> highlight national individuality while forming a homogeneous production
> worthy of facing America's excessive competition. We are not against
> America, but we want our place in the sun.[5]

If the means to create such a European cinema appear unclear and slightly contradictory in Pommer's and Aubert's statements, the goals, on the other hand, are clear:
uniting European cinemas in order to resist Hollywood's economic hegemony.

European film industrialists were learning from their American competitors that cinema required greater concentration of capital and significant market expansion to remain economically successful. Practical proposals to set up a 'Film Europe' were even made in 1926 at the First International Film Congress, held in Paris, and at the 1928 International Exhibitors' Congress in Berlin. At these meetings, in particular, recommendations were made for the creation of an international economic film bureau collecting and disseminating reliable statistical information on the entire film industry to prepare for joint productions, film exchange contracts, and comparable legislative restrictions.[6]

Furthermore, to be on par with American cinema, films had to acquire an essentially international character, not only on the financial level but also from an artistic point of view, in order to become commodities appealing to a world audience. The coproduction policy for prestige international films was perhaps facilitated in the latter half of the 1920s by the development of a new genre, 'the modern studio spectacular', whose popularity soon surpassed that of another profitable genre – the 1920s historical epics.[7] The studio spectaculars sought to emulate American films by representing characters in a stylized European decor that seemed to symbolize the material well-being of an emerging class of urban consumers. They conspicuously depicted affluent younger men and women (often played by an international cast), indulging in the good life, on an ultramodern and neutral backdrop of nightclubs, resorts, and art deco mansions. Therefore, they relied on a 'fantasy of internationalism' which negated the past and the specificity of national cultures.[8] The movie which helped most establish the genre may have been the Ciné-France/Westi production directed by Germaine Dulac, *Ame d'artiste* (1925). It was a coproduction based on a contemporary Danish play, financed by French, German, and Russian émigré investments, played by French, German, and Russian artists whose cultural differences were neutralized by the deliberately uniform style of acting; and although the action was set in London, it could have easily taken place in any industrialized country. By 1927, Cinéromans, Aubert, and even Paramount had invested heavily in this type of spectaculars, and the genre was so popular that it became the main model for commercial filmmaking until the advent of sound.[9]

The success of these European superproductions and the attempt to create European alliances striving to control economic competition on an international scale led to a note of concern on the American side, afraid that a truly united Europe could challenge the American hegemony.[10] However, it was not this emerging European cinema that really came to challenge Hollywood, but the drastically changed conditions that arose with the coming of sound.

Government obstacles to the internationalization of cinema: the creation of a 'national' cinema

The initial turning point in the French State's attitude towards cinema affairs can be traced back to 1928 when, as a result of two years of pressure by some of the same industrialists who were seeking European alliances and demanded protectionist measures against American imports, the French Government passed the first cinema statute. Thanks to this statute, cinema was proclaimed a 'protected national institution', and the principle of state intervention into the affairs of the film industry was finally established. The first task assigned the Control Commission, representing most government ministries and the main cinema professions, was to protect French cinema by defining it, differentiating it from foreign films, and attempting to impose import quotas – a measure strongly opposed by proprietors of motion-picture theaters.[11] The presence of industry representatives in the Control Commission indicated the Government's willingness to seek consensus in a divisive matter of national importance since not all film industrialists, divided by diverging interests, agreed on direct state intervention in the film industry. Even within the Government itself, those who believed that purely economic considerations should prevail opposed those who felt that national economic and cultural goals should not be dissociated.

The advent of sound less than a year later most decisively altered the relationship of cinema to the national public and to the State. Sound introduced a realistic dimension to cinematographic expression, which significantly increased its appeal as a form of entertainment for the mass audience.[12] Part of this appeal in France derived from the French spectators' nationalistic pride in images and dialogues which, grounded in their own culture, strengthened their sense of identity.[13] The French public's enthusiastic reactions to national films, in turn, made political leaders more fully aware of the social impact of cinema. Unlike the prenational stage, when the French State had refused to take an active interest in the film industry because it viewed cinema as a weak and disorganized industry of negligible cultural significance for the nation, by the late 1920s Government officials became determined to prevent private industrialists or foreigners from entirely controlling national cinema affairs.[14] The turmoil occasioned by a series of legislative measures also triggered a passionate long-lasting debate in the patriotic and literary press on the necessity to take the cultural dimension of cinema into account. In a tone that is reminiscent of today's discourse on the 'cultural exception', René Jeanne, for example, reminded the 1931 readers of the *Revue des Deux Mondes* that cinema had intellectual, moral, artistic, as well as economic repercussions because 'film is not a merchandise identical to a sack of flour, a length of cloth, or a pair of shoes.'[15]

By the early 1930s, it had become clear to many intellectuals and politicians that reconciling the cultural and economic aspects of cinema was a national necessity which required direct governmental involvement to achieve a profound reorganization of the film industry. As a result of the newly perceived significance of movies, the State endeavored to transform cinema into a true 'national' institution, namely an institution defined in relation to the larger cultural, economic, and political system of the nation in which it functioned. Thus, cinema was progressively integrated into the structure of the nation-state, which in its strongest, nationalistic forms, relies on centralized power in the hands of the ruling classes, on differentiation from external elements likely to threaten national sovereignty, and on internal unification to achieve consensus among competing interest groups. However, it finally took a coercive power, the Vichy Government, to impose widespread State intervention in the film profession and the creation of a national cinema center, which in 1946 took the name of *Centre National de la Cinématographie* (CNC).

Through the CNC, every single industrial practice has been codified by the State in order to control the film industry, defend it against external attacks, and turn it into an agent of transmission of national culture. With the CNC responsible for control and implementation, the French State has established guidelines for every aspect of the French film industry, provided financial incentives, and set up protectionist measures. For over 50 years, this mixed economy system, in which economic and cultural objectives, private and public interests are intertwined, has allowed French cinema to combat internal crises, withstand strong external competition, and contribute to the cultural unity needed to strengthen the capitalist nation-state.[16] The main measures, which were elaborated in the 1950s and early 1960s, have essentially remained unchanged ever since. A support fund, subsidized by a tax on all ticket sales from French and foreign films (and increasingly since 1985 by a tax on television earnings), has financed and regulated the film industry by redistributing internal resources within the various branches of the French film industry. Revenues from the fund, supplied by profits from commercially viable films, have been primarily redistributed in the form of 'automatic' subsidies for national production and exhibition.

To remedy the cultural limitations of the automatic aid schemes, the State set up additional measures ensuring that cinema also fulfill its high cultural mandate by allocating part of the fund resources on a 'selective' basis. The selective subsidies, attributed on the basis of 'quality' criteria determined by the CNC, have permitted more direct State emphasis on cultural objectives, carried out since the early 1960s by two main measures: the *avance sur recettes* (production advances on takings) and the *Art et essai* theater network. The advance mechanism has freed State-approved filmmakers from the need to seek short-term commercial success. Therefore, it has been influential in helping innovative *auteurs* like the *Nouvelle Vague* directors, and it is still giving unknown young talents a chance to contribute to the renewal of a national high culture, clearly differentiated from mass-appeal Hollywood movies.[17] These high cultural productions can reach a public of cinephiles thanks to the *Art et essai* theaters, which receive special tax incentives for supporting 'quality' or 'artistic' filmmaking, unlikely to meet with widespread interest.[18] However, encouragement to both national mass culture through automatic subsidies, and to high culture through selective aid schemes should not be viewed as a contradiction but rather as the necessary means to maintain the vitality of a closed national system. If only high culture is encouraged, it runs the risk of becoming artificially cut off from mainstream culture, losing its potential for self-renewal and its impact on the majority of the citizens. And mass culture which does not find a source of inspiration in the official culture is likely to escape the State's control.[19] Thus, until recently, the strength of French cinema may have largely derived from a perpetual symbiosis between high and mass culture, a symbiosis necessary to the vitality of the 'national popular' culture (as theorized by Gramsci).

Although State-approved 'art' films have enjoyed relative economic autonomy, the cultural and economic aspects of cinema should not be truly dissociated. By appealing to an elite national and international public and by playing a 'research and development role,' even art films have contributed to the overall economic success of the national film industry, which, in turn, has supported the Government's cultural initiatives.[20]

Towards a 'postnational' model?

The Government's interventionist and protectionist approach, which successfully transformed the French film industry into a quasi-closed system, was based on the primacy of a national over a global policy since the logic of the cinema support fund corresponded to a redistribution of resources within a protected economy with a sufficient domestic market. Globalizing counter-forces, such as the strong presence of Hollywood imports or the search for international markets through coproduction agreements since the 1950s did exist but never prevented French cinema from functioning as an important national institution. However, the thrust towards globalization has become so strong since the late 1980s that France's previous emphasis on a nationally-oriented film policy may have finally been superseded, giving way to a 'postnational' cinema promoted by an increasing number of film professionals and Government officials (although it is still being contested by many others).

The globalizing forces to which the national cinema system is now confronted result in part from the intensified pressure of international competition and the increased interdependence of capitalist economies. For instance, the merging of Hollywood film studios within enormous media conglomerates able to orchestrate massive marketing campaigns on a world scale has helped American blockbusters win a majority of the French box office since 1989.[21] Similarly, the most powerful French multimedia groups (Havas, Hachette, les Editions Mondiales, and CLT-RTL) operate far beyond national boundaries, although these giant conglomerates are based in France. Their ambitions are bound to clash with a traditional protected economic system subject to state-imposed cultural objectives.[22] Even the semi-public television channel, Canal Plus, which pre-purchases the vast majority of the French film production, has also invested in American films through its production company Studio Canal Plus, while the two French Majors, Gaumont and UGC signed agreements with Buena Vista and Twentieth Century Fox respectively.[23]

In an effort to join in the movement towards worldwide economic expansion, the French State has now embraced a film policy resembling the efforts towards the internationalization of cinema which were initiated by film industrialists in the 1920s. This movement towards internationalization, once again, requires encouraging new modes of film practice centered around the production and promotion of coproductions intended for mainstream consumption by foreign and domestic publics alike. But unlike the 1920s, the State is directly supporting the development of this new internationally-oriented cinema, which requires dissociating cinema's cultural and economic functions according to Government officials. To fulfill cinema's direct economic mission, the Government is more openly encouraging the making of films adapted to the global market and attempting to compete with Hollywood on its own terms, since Hollywood has most successfully produced a film culture able to transcend national boundaries. At the same time, the French Government is still supporting the production of films which primarily fulfill a 'cultural' function for the elite national (as well as international) audience and protect France's image as the land of Culture.

To achieve these new expansionist goals, a 1988 report to the Minister of Culture advocated adopting a more pragmatic approach to filmmaking, and, in particular, encouraging the making of superproductions shot in English. The recommended use of English by French filmmakers reinforced the perception of English as the foremost prestige language and the accepted international business norm in the global market.[24] Moreover, English-language filmmaking appeared as the necessary step to overcome the resistance of the American public – supposedly intolerant of both dubbing and sub-titling[25] – considered the most important target audience and the key to global success. Purely cultural considerations, the author of the report argued, had to be left to less commercially ambitious films.

> The language issue is, of course, essential to a country and to its culture. Cinema is a vehicle of culture, undoubtedly. However, it seems necessary to put things in perspective. . . .
>
> English-language filming is a question that essentially arises when the return from the American market constitutes, from the onset, an important part of the expected amortization. It mainly applies, then, to ambitious big-budget projects.
>
> Cinema is a vehicle of language and language must be defended. But this defense should be pragmatic and not turned into a religious war.[26]

In the late 1980s , such experts' recommendations resulted in a major policy shift stressing that the correlation between commercial success, English, and big-budgets was unavoidable. In particular, a 1989 decree made it possible for English-language films to receive the *agrément* that confers French nationality to a film, thus entitling its producer to an aid from the national support fund.[27] Jack Lang announced the recognition of English-language films by the CNC together with new state-aid mechanisms that would facilitate the packaging of ambitious large-budget pictures.[28] Lang's initiative reflected the rapidly escalating cost of filmmaking in France and the desire to narrow the gap with the cost of production in the United States.[29] Furthermore, in order to help finance increasingly costly and numerous superproductions, the Government initiated new European projects, such as Eurimages or Audiovisual Eureka, designed to boost coproductions, while actively pursuing bilateral agreements with other countries.

But the change initiated by these policies has not been simply quantitative. Most important, the perceived need to shoot high-budget films in English might only be the most blatant strategy for emulating the hegemonic Hollywood model while minimizing national cultural specificities, which often appear to have become obstacles to global success. English-language films, like a number of French-language films, reflect a significant effort to adapt the French mode of film production to the demands of the global market.[30] The 'postnational' mode of production erases most of the distinctive elements which have traditionally helped define the (maybe) imaginary coherence of a national cinema against other cinematographic traditions or against Hollywood at a given point in time: for example, an implicit or explicit worldview, the construction of national character and subjectivity, certain narrative discourses and modes of address, or intertextual references.[31] A closer examination of *Valmont* (1989), *L'Amant*

(The Lover, 1992), and *1492 Christophe Colomb* (1492, Conquest of Paradise, 1992), which have been among the most successful English-language French exports, should illustrate how these 'New Holly-Wave' films attempt to downplay their 'Frenchness' as they depart from Hollywood productions only through the choice of subject matter or the presence of iconic French stars.

As the result of the newly-acquired importance of subject matter as the main differentiating element, French producers have recently turned their attention to numerous lavish costume productions, often drawing on canonical literary culture and revisiting the nation's past – especially selected periods of French history brought to the fore by contemporary events.[32] Since the late 1980s much of these 'heritage films' have focused, in particular, on the French Revolution and its aftermath, the nation's colonial past, and some glorious moments of European history, which have all attracted the attention of the media. For example, *Valmont*, a colorful depiction of late eighteenth-century France based on the famous epistolary novel *Les Liaisons dangereuses* by Choderlos de Laclos, was part of a trend to capitalize on the bicentennial of the French Revolution. At least nine other productions begun in 1988 had already taken advantage of this historical interest, including *The French Revolution* (1989), a particularly ambitious $50 million epic financed by four European nations and Canada, shot in English and French with a multinational cast from all over Europe.[33] As for *L'Amant*, based on the Marguerite Duras's best-seller taking place in French Indochina, its release in the first quarter of 1992 coincided with the release of two other French-language films (with budgets of up to 150 million francs) dealing with French Indochina (Régis Wargnier's *Indochine* and Pierre Schoèndorffer's *Dien Bien Phu*). France's interest in its colonial past had surfaced in the early 1990s, after the Vietnamese Government announced the reopening of its borders, and the three films on Indochina generated unprecedented media coverage and American-style promotional campaigns. Similarly, *1492* was released in a timely fashion in 1992 (like its Warner Bros.'s counterpart, *Christopher Columbus: The Discovery*) when the 500th anniversary of the discovery of America was well publicized by the European and American mass media.

Successful heritage films, therefore, generate media coverage that resembles the extensive marketing campaigns surrounding the release of Hollywood blockbusters. Furthermore, like Hollywood superproductions, they are intended for both domestic and international consumption, in spite of the apparent importance of national culture or famous European historical figures. Not surprisingly, as in the Hollywood system, high-budget heritage films are backed by prestige producers and entrusted to well-established directors who have mastered the art of well-crafted, technologically perfect, traditional narratives. Claude Berri coproduced the $30 million *Valmont*, directed by Milos Forman, and the $18 million *L'Amant*, directed by Jean-Jacques Annaud; and *1492*, a British/Spanish/French coproduction directed by Ridley Scott, was the most lavish 'French' production of 1991. Oftentimes, the main character is played by a famous star which functions as a national icon; he or she must be easily recognized abroad as a signature identifying an exotic luxury product, much like fashion or champagne brand names. Catherine Deneuve, the star of *Indochine*, symbolizes the beauty and sophistication of French femininity, while Gérard Depardieu, starring in

1492, appears as the epitome of male Frenchness, a mixture of romantic audacity and down-to-earth common sense, which his theatrical yet naturalistic acting style emphasizes.[34]

These stars are turned into images of themselves, just as French history itself is turned into a series of beautiful images in these internationally-oriented French films. The past is recounted through glossy, aesthetized representations which do not compel spectators to challenge stereotypes, reexamine the past, and make actual connections with their present experience. It becomes one more spectacle or media event in our 'media society'.

The use of English in some of these French superproductions further points to the desire to court an international audience and ensure that reference to national history does not detract from the international potential of such films. But English also reinforces the depthlessness of the quasi-mythical character-types whose language does not need reflect individual complexities. Such an artificial use of the language helps remove characters from their social context and turn them into commodified abstractions detached from experience. This may be particularly apparent in *1492*, in which Depardieu and other non-anglophone European actors transformed English, spoken with disparate accents, into a sort of contemporary Esperanto. The acceptance of this all-purpose Esperanto English, deprived of any coherence and cultural authenticity, may also point to the very process by which a new stateless, globalizing culture may be eroding sensitivity to cultural differences.

Unlike realistic films with a claim to 'authenticity', or avant-garde films seeking some psychological 'truth,' films like *Valmont, L'Amant*, and *1492* are 'nostalgia films' which confirm easily recognizable stereotypes or turn representations of national culture into faintly exotic images.[35] In *Valmont*, for example, an aristocratic soap opera of sort, the costumes, the French names of the characters, and the habit of addressing each other as *Monsieur* or *Madame* by the native English-speaking actors functioned as simplistic signifiers for eighteenth century France. In *L'Amant*, the French heritage was reduced to Duras' name, prominently displayed at the beginning of the movie, the name of the local company and schools, a French literature lesson, and, oddly enough, a group of schoolchildren singing in French. In the words of one reviewer, the movie was turned into 'a best-selling artifact, in which the most important element is the look of the girl', with 'many blurrings of lines and boundaries by which identities become increasingly indistinct.'[36] Thus, the film director attempted to give the illusion of tapping authentic cultural roots while in fact creating 'visual mirages'[37] (as well as occasional 'auditory mirages') of the past, transforming them into exotic details which might appeal to a global audience.[38] In this manner, world consumers eager to accumulate some 'cultural capital' may be given an impression of sophisticated diversity. Indeed, these luxury glossy superproductions are intended for middle-class national and international consumers sensitive to production values, technological progress, and pleasurable cultural representations which are socially acceptable.[39] Perhaps the acceptance of a postnational cinema also signals the emergence of a new 'middle culture,' equally detached from the nation's popular and high culture, and spreading among a 'techno-bourgeoisie' lured by the promises of globalization.

In the most extreme cases, there may be nothing French at all in an English-language coproduction considered 'French', according to CNC regulations, provided French financial participation met the minimum legally required. Former CNC director Dominique Wallon indeed recognized the danger of encouraging investments in such coproductions because France, which can provide the greatest financial support for filmmaking through its cinema fund, could be simply used as source of financing by French and foreign businesspeople:

> There is a risk of a slide toward more films that are less French, in which case France would then become merely a kind of financing center for coproductions that no longer reflect its creativity and culture.[40]

This danger, and perhaps the greater than expected number of English-language coproductions in the wake of the 1989 measures, forced the Government to issue new decrees in 1992 and 1993 to slow the trend towards the use of English. But the latest (1999) legislation reversed the trend once more, by making optimal subsidies available to English-language coproductions.[41]

It is still too early to gage the full impact of such shifting and somewhat contradictory policies. Government officials contend that all the measures aim at ensuring the survival of French cinema in a very competitive environment. Even globally-oriented films, it is argued, make it possible to continue supporting the State's traditional cultural policy because the taxes and profits which they originate can be used to fund the works of filmmakers dedicated to the pursuit of 'quality' cinema and keep open the necessary network of theaters to show their films. And, indeed in France, which for many appears as the last champion of film culture, *auteur* cinema still plays an active role (if one judges by the annual number of films by new directors not integrated into the commercial network, for example[42]). Thus, France will probably continue to produce prestigious 'masters of cinema' who will go on challenging commercial modes of film production.[43]

Perhaps a new generation of filmmakers eager to have their own voices heard by a more heterogeneous national public has even started to come forth. One of the most commercially successful examples of such renewal in film production may be Mathieu Kassovitz's *La Haine* [1995], which has been critically praised for its 'force,' 'truth,' and the spontaneous inventiveness of its characters' language. By staging three young underprivileged youths – a Jew, an Arab, and a Black –, the film not only illustrates France's social malaise but also creates original characters governed by their own codes.[44] Although *La Haine* was co-produced by Studio Canal[+], France's largest film producer, other films which have similarly revealed unique characters and modes of narration challenging conventional representations, have been produced outside the mainstream production system. Among others, *Hexagone* [1994], by Malik Chibane, and *Etats des lieux* [1995], by Jean-François Richet, were produced with little money by groups of individuals or associations.[45] One could hope that through such alternative films, stressing heterogeneity *within* the nation rather than difference with outside cultures, cinema may survive in the twenty-first century as a creative and popular form of expression, beyond the mere reproduction of commodified images.

But however encouraging it may be, this pocket of heterogeneity is not very likely to prevent the postnational mode of film practice from prevailing since the French Government still strongly supports an expansionist approach. In fact, a 1994 official report on the exportation of French cinema stressed again the need to continue producing globally-oriented films in order for French cinema to survive:

> . . . Productions which, from their inception, take international stakes into account, strive and are intrinsically meant to impose themselves on foreign markets are obviously the driving force behind the other French films.[46]

The report further pointed out that the use of English in films designed to conquer international markets, combined with careful planning at the pre-production stage, had been pre-conditions for wide-scale commercial success. In 1989 and 1992, only two films shot in English (*Valmont* and *L'Amant*) brought overall exportation returns of over 50 million francs, or over 10 per cent of the total exportation receipts. In addition, in 1992, 71 per cent of the gross receipts generated by French films in the United States originated from only three movies – *L'Amant*, *1492*, and *The City of Joy*. *1492* and *L'Amant* succeeded in leading all other French films at the box office in France in 1992, which indicates the French public's overwhelming acceptance of many postnational films.[47] Most recently, a third English-language film has met with exceptional international and domestic success: Luc Besson's *The Fifth Element* became the top-grossing film at the French boxoffice in 1997, was linked to 75% of the French exportation receipts in the United States, and brought in an unprecedented 460 million francs (about $65 million dollars) in exportation revenue.[48]

Given the exportation success of these English-speaking films, and in light of statements emphasizing short-term economic goals rather than cultural considerations, one may speculate that governmental support for similar types of productions will actually increase, even if they are in English. If France fully embraces the latest stage of capitalist development that has been called global capitalism, it will continue to encourage modes of cultural production based on the erosion of cultural differences and further a 'global culture' directly subject to the logic of the global market.[49] And as long as belief in global capitalism prevails, postnational films, even if they coexist with alternative modes of production, will remain the dominant mode of film practice.

Conclusion

The national cinema system put in place after World War Two has served the interests of the traditional nation-state, whose capitalist organization relied on boundaries reinforced by culture. This nation-centered cinema framework prevented film industrialists from further pursuing the internationalization of cinema started in the 1920s and, in a sense, forced the film industry back into an already outmoded form of production, which delayed the integration of cinema into a more advanced capitalist system. However, as a result of the growing pressure of economic globalization in recent years, the French State has begun to actively encourage the development of an international cinema capable of competing equitably with Hollywood for a share of global markets. The strong emphasis on global pursuits explains the emergence of commodified postnational productions which transform national culture into a pleasurable spectacle for both domestic and foreign audiences. Nevertheless, this emerging postnational cinema still coexists today with other modes of film practice (such as auteur cinema), which suggests that French cinema remains in a state of transition and the site of an intense struggle among film industrialists, artists, and Government officials. But if the French Government follows through with the logic of global capitalism, to which it now appears to be adhering in order to remain a leading economic force in the world and keep up with capitalist expansion, even seemingly heterogeneous forms of cultural expression may indirectly support France's pursuit of global markets. With the emergence of a film culture meant to succeed in a global economic system, the overall nature of national culture may be in the process of being altered.

Notes

1 [My own translation from the French, as all other translations, unless noted otherwise] Jean Dondelinger (EC Commissioner responsible for audiovisual and cultural affairs) in *Les rencontres cinématographiques de Beaune* (17–20 Oct. 1991). Unpublished proceedings, 87.
   An earlier version of this paper was presented at the 15th Annual Ohio University Film Conference ('National Cinemas Revisited', 21–23 Oct. 1993) under the title 'The New 'Holly-Wave': France's Post-National Cinema.'
2 Richard Abel, *French Cinema. The First Wave, 1915–1929* (Princeton: Princeton University Press, 1984), 40.
3 Abel 15–23, 27.
4 In Georges Sadoul, *Histoire générale du cinéma, Vol. 5: L'art muet 1919–1929, 1er volume: L'après-guerre en Europe* (Denoël, Paris, 1975), 434.
5 In Sadoul 37.
6 *The European Motion Picture Industry in 1928,* Trade Information Bulletin 617 (Washington: US Printing Press), 11.
7 Abel 38.
8 Abel 71, 205–206.
9 Abel 210–214, 216.
10 *The European Motion Picture Industry* 11–2.
11 Paul Léglise, *Histoire de la politique du cinéma français*, Vol. 1, *Le cinéma et la IIIe République* (Paris: Lherminier, 1969), 70, 262.
12 Jameson, 'The existence of Italy', *Signatures of the Visible* (New York: Routledge, 1990), 174–175; Walter Benjamin, 'The Work of Art in the Age of Mechanical Reproductibility', *Illuminations* (trans. Harry Zohn, New York, Schocken Books, 1969), 244.
13 Martine Danan, 'A la recherche d'une stratégie internationale: Hollywood et le marché français des années trente,' Y. Gambier (ed), *Les Transferts linguistiques dans les médias audio-visuels* (Lille: Presses Universitaires du Septentrion, 1996), 112–113.
14 Sadoul 35–38, 41; Douglas Gomery, 'Economic Struggle and Hollywood Imperialism: Europe Converts to Sound', *Yale French Studies* 60 (1980): 81–82; Abel 38.
15 'La France et le film parlant', *Revue des Deux Mondes*, 1 June 1931: 550.
   There is a striking analogy between Jeanne's words and the 1989 speech by Jacques

Delors, President of the European Commission, at the European Audiovisual Conference in Paris, 2 Oct. 1989: '[C]ulture is not just another type of merchandise . . . we cannot treat culture as we would treat refrigerators or even motor cars.' Quoted and translated in Matteo Maggiore, *Audiovisual Production in the Single Market* (Luxembourg: Office for Official Publications of the European Communities, 1990), 197.

16 Bernard Miège and Jean-Michel Salaun, 'France: a Mixed System. Renovation of an Old Concept', *Media, Culture and Society* 11 (1989): 55–57.

17 Steve Neale 'Art Cinema as Institution', *Screen* 22.1 (1982): 14, 37.

18 René Bonnell, *La vingt-cinquième image: une économie de l'audiovisuel* (Paris: Gallimard/ FEMIS, 1989), 602–605; François Rouet et Xavier Dupin, *Le soutien public aux industries culturelles* (Paris: Documentation française, Ministère de la Culture et de la Communication, 1991), 89–93.

19 Itamar Even-Zohar, 'Polysystem Theory', *Poetics Today* 1.1–2 (1979): 295–296.

20 Neale 14, 37; Bonnell 576, 578, 602, 605–606.

21 *CNC info* 246, Bilan 1992 (Ap.–May 1993): 24.

22 Miège and Salaun 59.

23 Dominique Wallon, *Pour une stratégie d'exportation et de diffusion du cinéma français*, Rapport à Monsieur Jacques Toubon, Ministre de la Culture et de la Francophonie, June 1994 (internal documentation supplied by Jean-Marc Vernet, Director of the Study and Information Service at the CNC); *SACD* (Journal de la Société des Auteurs et Compositeurs dramatiques) 18 (Mar–Ap. 1995): 8.

24 Jean-Michel Djian, 'Faut-il tourner en anglais', *Après-demain* 329 (Dec. 1990): 32.

25 *Programmer des films européens dans les salles européennes*, Premiers Plans, Colloque public, 24 and 25 Jan. 1992, unpublished proceedings, 11, 13; Peter Fleischmannn (German film-maker) in *Les rencontres cinématographiques de Beaune*, 77.

26 Jean-François Court, *Le cinéma français face à son avenir,* Rapport au Ministre de la Culture et de la Communication (Paris: La Documentation française, 1988), 54–55.

27 Lenny Borger, 'Anglo filmers Find New Angles as CNC Tears Down the Language Barrier', *Variety* 22 Oct. 1989: 115.

28 Toby Rose, 'French Producing More and Bigger Pics', *Variety* 18 March 1991: 42.

29 'Le développement des coproductions: quels partenaires préférer?' *Ciné Finances Info* 36, 29 July 1991; 'Légère hausse de la production des films français', *Le Monde* 16 Jan. 1993: 18.

30 The effect of globalization on national cinemas has recently attracted the attention of many scholars. See, for example, the special issue on 'Mediating the National' in the *Quarterly Review of Film & Video* 14.3 (1993).

31 Andrew Higson, 'The Concept of National Cinema,' 'Introduction: Over the Borderlines.' *Over the Borderlines: Questioning National Identities.* Spec. issue of *Screen* 30.4 (1989): 36, 38, 43, 44; Philip Rosen, 'History, Textuality, Nation: Kracauer, Burch, and Some Problems in the Study of National Cinemas,' *Iris* 2.2 (1984): 83.

32 Ginette Vincendeau, 'Unsettling Memories' *Sight and Sound* July 1995: 31.

33 'French Make Bicentennial Pix As Big As Revolution Itself,' *Variety* 19 Oct. 1988: 453, 460.

34 Vincendeau 32.

35 Fredric Jameson, 'The Existence of Italy,' *Signatures of the Visible* 157, 223.

36 Molly Haskell, 'You saw nothing in Indochina', *Film Comment* 29.1 (Jan.–Feb. 1993): 32.

37 Fredric Jameson's phrase in *Postmodernism or, the Cultural Logic of Late Capitalism* (Durham: Duke University Press, 1991), 46.

38 The movie achieved relative success in the United States, but met with unprecedented success in Japan, according to Unifrance, Sept. 1994 (internal documentation supplied by Laurent Valière, Service économique).

39 Vincendeau 30.

40 Quoted and translated in Borger 115.

41 See France (1998) *Rapport au parlement sur l'application de la loi du 4 août 1994 relative à l'emploi de la langue française.* <*www.culture.gouv.fr/culture/dglf/rapport/1998/rapport98–28.htm*>

42 *CNC info* 256: 11.

43 Dudley Andrew's phrase in 'Appraising French Images', *Wide Angle* 16.3, 'National Cinemas Revisited: Selections from the 15th Annual Ohio University Film Conference' (1995): 63.

44 Thierry Jousse, 'Prose de Combat,' *Cahiers du Cinéma* June 1995: 34–35.

45 Thierry Jousse, 'Le Banlieue-film existe-t-il?' *Cahiers du cinéma* June 1995: 37–39.

46 Wallon, 19.

47 Wallon, 7, 13, 19; *CNC Info* 246: 29.

48 *CNC info* 280, bilan 2000 (May 2001): 27 and *CNC info* 276, bilan 1999 (May 2000): 28.

49 Jameson *Postmodernism* 48, 366, 412.

Bibliography

General

Aitken, Ian. (2001) *European Film Theory and Cinema*, Edinburgh: Edinburgh University Press.

Bazin, André. (1967) *What is Cinema? Vol. 1* (trans. H. Gray) Berkeley: University of California Press.

—— (1972) *What Is Cinema? Vol. 2*, Berkeley: University of California Press.

Cook, Pam and Mieke Bernink. (eds) (1999) (2nd edition) *The Cinema Book*, London: BFI Publishing.

Dyer, Richard and Ginette Vincendeau. (eds) (1992) *Popular European Cinema*, London and New York: Routledge.

Everett, Wendy. (ed.) (1996) *European Identity in Cinema*, Exeter: Intellect Books.

Finney, Angus. (ed.) (1993) *A Dose of Reality: The State of European Cinema*, European Film Academy and Screen International.

—— (1996) *The State of European Cinema: A New Dose of Reality* London: Cassell.

Forbes, Jill and Sarah Street. (eds) (2000) *European Cinema – An Introduction*, Basingstoke: Palgrave.

Hjort, Mette and Scott Mackenzie. (eds) (2000) *Cinema and Nation*, London and New York: Routledge.

Konstantarakos, Myrto. (ed.) (2000) *Spaces in European Cinema*, Exeter: Intellect Books.

Maltby, Richard and Andrew Higson. (eds) (1999) *'Film Europe' and 'Film America' – Cinema, Commerce and Cultural Exchange 1920–39*, Exeter: Exeter University Press.

Morley, David and Kevin Robbins. (1989) 'Spaces of identity: communications technologies and the reconfiguration of Europe', *Screen* Vol. 30, no. 4, Autumn.

—— (1990) 'No Place Like *Heimat*: Images of home(land) in European culture', *New Formations* no. 12, Winter pp. 1–23.

Orr, John. (1993) *Cinema and Modernity*, Cambridge: Polity Press.

—— and Olga Taxidou. (eds) (2000) *Post-War Cinema and Modernity – A Film Reader*, Edinburgh: Edinburgh University Press.

Petrie, Duncan. (1992) *Screening Europe: Image and Identity in Contemporary European Cinema*, London: BFI.

Pieterse, Jan Nedeveen. (1991) 'Fictions of Europe', *Race and Class : A Journal for Black and Third World Liberation*. Vol. 32, no. 3, January–March.

Sorlin, Pierre. (1991) *European Cinemas, European Societies 1939–1990*, London: Routledge.

Stollery, Martin. (2000) *Alternative Empires: Modernist Cinema and the Culture of Imperialism*, Exeter: University of Exeter Press.

Vincendeau, Ginette. (ed.) (1995) *The Encyclopedia of European Cinema*, London: BFI/Cassell.

—— and Richard Dyer. (eds) (1992) *Popular European Cinema*, London: Routledge.

Wollen, Peter. (1993) 'Films: why do some survive and others disappear?', *Sight and Sound*.

British cinema

Aldgate, Anthony and Jeffrey Richards. (1994) (2nd edition) *Britain Can Take It: The British Cinema in the Second World War*, Edinburgh: Edinburgh University Press.

—— (1999) *Best of British: Cinema and Society from 1930 to the Present*, London: I. B. Tauris.

Armes, Roy. (1978) *A Critical History of British Cinema*, London: Secker and Warburg.

Ashby, Justine and Andrew Higson. (eds) (2000) *British Cinema, Past and Present*, London: Routledge.

Auty, Martin and Nick Roddick. (eds) (1985) *British Cinema Now*, London: BFI.

Bamford, Kenton. (1999) *Distorted Images: British National Identity and Film in the 1920s*, London and New York: I. B. Tauris.

Barr, Charles. (ed.) (1986) *All our Yesterdays: 90 Years of British Cinema*, London: BFI.

Burton, Alan and Laraine Porter. (eds) (2000) *Pimple, Pranks and Pratfalls – British Film Comedy before 1930*, Trowbridge: Flicks Books.

—— (eds) (1999) *The Showman, the Spectacle and the Two-Minute Silence – Performing British Cinema before 1930*, Trowbridge: Flicks Books.

Chanan, Michael. (1996) *The Dream that Kicks – the Pre-History and Early Years of Cinema in Britain*, London and New York: Routledge.

Chapman, James. (1998) *The British at War: Cinema, State and Propaganda 1939–45*, London and New York: I. B. Tauris.

Cook, Pam. (1996) *Fashioning the Nation: Costume and Identity in British Cinema*, London: BFI.

—— (ed.) (1997) *Gainsborough Pictures*, London and Washington: Cassell.

Dickinson, Margaret and Sarah Street. (1985) *Cinema and State – the Film Industry and the British Government 1927–84*, London: BFI.

Dixon, Wheeler Winston. (ed.) (1994) *Re-Viewing British Cinema 1900-1992 – Essays and Interviews*, Albany: State University of New York Press.

Dochery, David, David Morrison and Michael Tracey. (1987) *The Lost Picture Show Britain's Changing Audiences*, London: BFI.

Drazin, Charles. (1998) *The Finest Years: British Cinema of the 1940s*, London: Andre Deutsch

Eyles, Allen. (1996) *Gaumont British Cinemas*, London: BFI.

Fitzsimmons, Linda and Sarah Street. (eds) (2000) *Moving Performance – British Stage and Screen 1890s–1920s*, Trowbridge: Flicks Books.

Friedman, Lester. (ed.) (1993) *British Cinema and Thatcherism – Fires Were Started*, London: UCL Press.

Geraghty, Christine. (2000) *British Cinema in the Fifties – Gender, Genre and the 'New Look'*, London and New York: Routledge.

Harper, Sue. (1994) *Picturing the Past – the Rise and Fall of the British Costume Film*, London: BFI.

Higson, Andrew. (1995) *Waving the Flag: Constructing a National Cinema in Britain*, Oxford: Oxford University Press.

—— (ed.) (1996) *Dissolving Views: Key Writings on British Cinema*, London: Cassell.

Hill, John. (1986) *Sex, Class and Realism: British Cinema 1956–63*, London: BFI.

—— (1999) *British Cinema in the 1980s*, Oxford: Oxford University Press.

Hogenkamp, Bert. (2000) *Film, TV and the Left in Britain 1950–70*, London: Lawrence and Wishart.

—— (1985) *Filmmaking in 1930s Britain*, London: George Allen and Unwin.

Low, Rachel. (1997) (2nd edition) *The History of British Film, Vols I–IV*, London and New York: Routledge.

Mackenzie, S.P. (2001) *British War Films 1939–1945*, London and New York: Hambledon and London.

Macnab, Geoffrey. (1993) *J. Arthur Rank and the British Film Industry*, London and New York: Routledge.

Macpherson, Don. (ed.) (1980) *British Cinema – Traditions of Independence*, London: BFI.

—— (1989) *Realism and Tinsel, Cinema and Society in Britain 1939–49*, London and New York: Routledge.

Murphy, Robert. (1992) *Sixties British Cinema*, London: BFI.

—— (ed.) (1997) *The British Cinema Book*, London: BFI.

—— (ed.) (2000) *British Cinema of the 90s*, London: BFI.

Park, James. (1990) *British Cinema – The Lights that Failed*, London: B.T. Bastsford Ltd.

Petrie, Duncan. (1984) *The Age of the Dream Palace: Cinema and Society in Britain 1930–1939*, London and New York: Routledge.

—— (ed.) (1992) *New Questions of British Cinema*, London: BFI.

Richard, Jeffrey. (1997) *Films in Britain and National Identity – From Dickens to Dad's Army*, Manchester: Manchester University Press.

—— (ed.) (1998) *The Unknown 1930s: An Alternative History of British Cinema 1929–39*, London and New York: I.B. Tauris.

Shafer, Stephen C. (1997) *British Popular Films 1929–39: The Cinema of Reassurance*, London and New York: Routledge.

Street, Sarah. (1997) *British National Cinema*, London and New York: Routledge.

—— (2000) *British Cinema in Documents*, London and New York: Routledge.

Taylor, Philip M. (ed.) (1988) *Britain and the Cinema in the Second World War* New York: St. Martin's Press.

Walker, John. (1985) *The Once and Future Film – British Cinema in the 70s and 80s*, London: Methuen.

French cinema

Andrew, Dudley. (1995) *Mists of Regret – Culture and Sensibility in Classic French Film*, Princeton, NJ: Princeton University Press.

Austin, Guy. (1996) *Contemporary French Cinema – An Introduction*, Manchester: Manchester University Press.

Browne, Nick. (ed.) 1990) *Cahiers du Cinéma, Vol. 3: 1969–72: The Politics of Representation*, London and New York: Routledge.

Buchsbaum, Jonathon. (1988) *Cinema Engagé – Film in the Popular Front*, Urbana and Chicago: University of Illinois Press.

Buss, Robin. (1988) *The French Through Their Films*, London: B.T. Batsford

—— (1994) *French Film Noir*, London: Marion Byars.

Crisp, Colin. (1997) *The Classic French Cinema 1930–1960*, Bloomington and Indianapolis: Indiana University Press.

Ehrlich, Evelyn. (1985) *Cinema of Paradox – French Filmmaking under the German Occupation*, New York: Columbia University Press.

Ezra, Elizabeth and Sue Harris. (2000) *France in Focus – Film and National Identity*, Oxford: Berg.

Forbes, Jill. (1992) *The Cinema in France – After the New Wave*, London: BFI/Macmillan.

Graham, Peter. (ed.) (1968) *The New Wave*, London: Martin Secker and Warburg Ltd.

Green, Naomi. (1999) *Landscapes of Loss – The National Past in Postwar French Cinema*, Princeton, NJ: Princeton University Press.

Hayward, Susan. (1993) *French National Cinema*, London and New York: Routledge.

—— and Ginette Vincendeau. (eds) (2000) (2nd edition) *French Film: Texts and Contexts*, London and New York: Routledge.

Kline, T. Jefferson. (1992) *Screening the Text: Intertextuality in New Wave French Cinema*, Baltimore, MD, and London: Johns Hopkins University Press.

Powrie, Phil. (1997) *French Cinema in the 1980s – Nostalgia and the Crisis of Masculinity*, Oxford: Oxford University Press.

Sherzer, Dina. (ed.) (1996) *Cinema Colonialism Postcolonialism: Perspectives from the French and Francophone Worlds*, Austin: University of Texas Press.

Vincendeau, Ginette. (1993) 'Gérard Depardieu: the axiom of Contemporary French Cinema', *Screen*, Vol. 34, no. 4, Winter, pp. 343–1.

—— and Keith Reader. (eds) (1986) *La Vie est à nous, NFT Dossier no. 3 French Cinema of the Popular Front 1935–38*, London: BFI/NFT.

Williams, Alan. (1992) *Republic of Images – A History of French Filmmaking*, Cambridge, MA, and London: Harvard University Press.

Wilson, David. (ed.) (2000) *Cahiers du cinéma 1973–1978: History, Ideology, Cultural Struggle*, London and New York: Routledge.

Wilson, Emma. (1999) *French Cinema since 1950: Personal Histories*, London: Gerald Duckworth.

German cinema

Byg, Barton. (1995) *Landscapes of Resistance: The German Films of Danièlle Huillet and Jean-Marie Straub*, Berkeley: University of California Press.

Coates, Paul. (1991) *The Gorgon's Gaze*, Cambridge: Cambridge University Press.

Corrigan, Timothy. (1994) *New German Film: The Dis-Placed Image*, Bloomington and Indianapolis: Indiana University Press.

Diethe, Carol. (2000) 'Anxious Spaces in Expressionist Film', in Myrto Konstantarakis. (ed.) *Spaces in European Cinema*, Exeter: Intellect Books, pp. 52–63.

Eisner, Lotte H. (1952) *The Haunted Screen – Expressionism in the German Cinema and the Influence of Max Reinhardt*, London: Thames and Hudson.

Elsaesser, Thomas. (1989) *New German Cinema: A History*, London: BFI.

—— (ed.) (1996) *A Second Life: German Cinema's First Decades*, Amsterdam: Amsterdam University Press.

—— (2000) *Weimar Cinema and After – Germany's Historical Imaginary*, London and New York: Routledge

Fox, Jo. (2000) *Filming in the Third Reich*, New York and Oxford: Berg.

Ginsberg, Terri and Kirsten Moana Thompson. (eds) (1996) *Perspectives on German Cinema*, New York: G.K. Hall & Co.

Hoffman, Hilmar. (1996) *The Triumph of Propaganda: Film and National Socialism, 1933–45*, Oxford: Berghahn Books.

Jung, Uli and Walter Schatzberg. (1993) 'The invisible man behind *Caligari*', *Film History* Vol. 5, no. 1, March.

Kaes, Anton. (1989) *From Hitler to Heimat: The Return of History to Film*, Cambridge, MA, and London: Harvard University Press.

Kracauer, Siegfried. (1947) *From Caligari to Hitler: A Psychological History of German Film*, Princeton, NJ: Princeton University Press.

Manvell, Rober and Heinrich Fraenkel. (1971) *The German Cinema*, London: J. M. Dent and Sons Ltd.

Mayne, Judith. (1986) 'Dracula in the Twilight, Murnau's *Nosferatu, 1922*', in Rentschler (ed.) (see below).

Murray, Bruce. (1990) *Film and the German Left in the Weimar Republic from Caligari to Kuhle Wampe*, Austin: University of Texas Press.

Phillips, Klaus. (ed.) (1984) *New German Filmmakers*, New York: Frederick Unger Publishing Co.

Prawer, S. (1980) *Caligari's Children*, Oxford: Oxford University Press.

Robinson, David. (1997) *Das Cabinet des Dr Caligari*, London: BFI.

Rentschler, Eric. (1996) *The Ministry of Illusion: Nazi Cinema and its Afterlife*, Cambridge, MA, and London: Harvard University Press.

—— (ed.) (1986) *German Film and Literature – Adaptations and Transformations*, New York and London: Methuen.

—— (ed.) (1988) *West German Filmmakers on Film: Visions and Voices*, New York, London: Holmes and Meier.

Silberman, Marc. (1995) *German Cinema – Texts in Context*, Detroit, MI: Wayne State University Press.

Italian cinema

Allen, Beverly and Mary Russo. (eds) (1997) *Revisioning Italy: National Identity and Global Culture*, Minneapolis, MN: University of Minnesota Press.

Bondanella, Peter. (1997) *Italian Cinema – from neo-realism to the Present*, New York: Continuum.

Buss, Robin. (1989) *Italian Films*, London: B.T. Batsford Ltd.

Hay, James. (1987) *Popular Film Culture in Fascist Italy – the Passing of the Rex*, Bloomington: Indiana University Press

Jarratt, Vernon. (1951) *The Italian Cinema*, London: The Falcon Press.

Kolker, Robert Phillip. (1983) *The Altering Eye: Contemporary International Cinema*, Oxford: Oxford University Press.

Landy, Marcia.(1986) *Fascism in Film: The Italian Commercial Cinema, 1931–1943*, Princeton, NJ: Princeton University Press.

—— (1994) *Film, Politics and Gramsci*, Minneapolis and London: University of Minnesota Press.

—— (1998) *The Folklore of Consensus: Theatricality in the Italian Cinema, 1930–1943*, Albany: State University of New York Press.

—— (2000) *Italian Film*, Cambridge: Cambridge University Press.

Lephron, Pierre. (1966) *The Italian Cinema*, London: Secker and Warburg.

Liehm, Mira. (1984) *Passion and Defiance – Film in Italy from 1942 to the Present*, Berkeley and London: University of California Press.

Mancini, Elaine. (1985) *Struggles of the Italian Film Industry during Fascism, 1930–1935*, Ann Arbor, MI: UMI Press.

Marcus, Millicent. (1992) *Italian Film in the Light of neo-realism*, Princeton, NJ: Princeton University Press.

—— (1993) *Filmmaking by the Book — Italian Cinema and Literary Adaptation*, Baltimore, MD, and London: John Hopkins University Press.

Nowell-Smith, Geoffrey, James Hay and Gianni Volpi. (eds) (1996) *The BFI Companion to Italian Cinema*, London: BFI.

Sitney, P. Adams. (1995) *Vital Crises in Italian Cinema — Iconography, Stylistics, Politics*, Austin: University of Texas Press.

Sorlin, Pierre. (1996) *Italian National Cinema 1896–1996*, London: Routledge.

Wagstaff, C. (1992) 'A Forkful of Westerns: industry and audiences and the Italian Western', in Giuette Vincendeau and Richard Dyer. (eds), *Popular European Cinema*, London: Routledge, pp. 245–62.

Witcombe, R. T. (1982) *The New Italian Cinema — Studies in Dance and Despair*, London: Secker and Warburg.

Wyke, Maria. (1997) *Projecting the Past: Ancient Rome, Cinema and History*, New York: Routledge.

Russian cinema

Bordwell, David. (1993) *The Cinema of Eisenstein*, Cambridge, MA: Harvard University Press.

Bernstein, Mathew and Gaylyn Studlar. (eds) (1997) *Visons of the East — Orientalism in Film*, London and New York: I.B. Tauris.

Beumers, Birgit. (ed.) (1999) *Russia on Reels: The Russian Idea in Post-Soviet Cinema*, London and New York: I.B. Tauris.

Brashinsky, Michael, and Andrew Horton. (eds) (1994) *Russian Critics on the Cinema of Glasnost*, Cambridge: Cambridge University Press.

Faraday, George. (2000) *Revolt of the Filmmakers*, Pennsylvania: Pennsylvania State University Press.

Goodwin, James. (1993) *Eisenstein, Cinema and History*, Urbana: University of Illinois Press.

Goulding, Daniel J. (1989) *Post New Wave Cinema in the Soviet Union and Eastern Europe*, Bloomington: Indiana University Press.

—— (ed.) (1994) *Five Filmmakers: Tarkovsky, Forman, Polanski, Szabo, Makavejev*, Bloomington and Indianapoolis: Indiana University Press.

Horton, Andrew and Michael Brashinsky. *Zero Hour: Glasnost and Soviet Cinema in Transition*, Princeton, NJ: Princeton University Press.

Kenez, Peter. (1992) *Cinema and Soviet Society 1917–1953*, Cambridge: Cambridge University Press.

Lawton, Anna. (1992a) *Kinoglasnost — Soviet Cinema in Our Time*, Cambridge: Cambridge University Press.

—— (ed.) (1992b) *The Red Screen*, London: Routledge.

Mayne, Judith. (1989) *Kino and the Woman Question*, Columbus: Ohio State University Press.

Michelson, Annette. (1984) *Kino-Eye: The Writings of Dziga Vertov*, London: Pluto Press.

Paul, David W. (ed.) (1983) *Politics, Art and Commitment in the East European Cinema*, London: Macmillan

Schnitzer, Luda and Jean Schnitzer. (eds) (1973) *Cinema in Revolution — The Heroic Era of the Soviet Film*, London: Secker and Warburg.

Stites, Richard. (1989) *Revolutionary Dreams*, Oxford: Oxford University Press.

—— (1992) *Russian Popular Culture*, Cambridge: Cambridge University Press.

Taylor, Richard (ed.) (1998) *The Eisenstein Reader*, London: British Film Institute.
—— and Ian Christie (eds) (1991) *Inside the Film Factory*, London: Routledge.
—— and —— (eds) (1993) *Eisenstein Rediscovered*, London: Routledge.
—— and Derek Spring (eds) (1993) *Stalinism and Soviet Cinema*, London, Routledge.
—— (1999) *The Battleship Potemkin*, London: I.B. Tauris.
—— Nancy Wood, Julian Graffy and Dina Iordanova. (eds) (2000) *The BFI Companion to Russian Cinema*, London: BFI.
Tsivian, Yuri. (1991) *Early Cinema in Russia and its Cultural Reception*, London and New York: Routledge.
Vronskaya, Jeanne. (1972) *Young Soviet Filmmakers*, London: George Allen & Unwin.
—— (1991) *Soviet Cinema in the Silent Era 1918–1935*, Austin: University of Texas Press.
Woll, Josephine. (2000) *Real Images: Soviet Cinema and the Thaw*, London and New York: I.B. Tauris.
Youngblood, Denise. (1992) *Movies for the Masses*, Cambridge: Cambridge University Press.
—— (1999) *The Magic Mirror – Moviemaking in Russia, 1908–18,* Madison: University of Wisconsin Press.

Spanish cinema

Besaas, Peter. (1985) *Behind the Spanish Lens: Spanish Cinema under Fascism and Democracy*, Denver, CO: Arden Press Inc.
D'Lugo, Marvin. (1997) *Guide to the Cinema of Spain*, Westport, CT, and London: Greenwood Press.
Evans, Peter William. (ed.) (1999) *Spanish Cinema – the Auteurist Tradition*, Oxford: Oxford University Press.
Fidian, Robin W. and Peter W. Evans. (1988) *Challenges to Authority: Fiction and Film in Contemporary Spain*, London: Tamesis Books Ltd.
Higginbotham, Virginia. (1988) *Spanish Film Under Franco*, Austin: Univeristy of Texas Press.
Hopewell, John. (1986) *Out of the Past: Spanish Cinema after Franco*, London: BFI.
Jordan, Barry and Rikki Morgan-Tamosunas. (1998) *Contemporary Spanish Cinema*, Manchester: Manchester University Press.
Kinder, Marsha. (1993) *Blood Cinema – The Reconstruction of National Identity in Spain*, Berkeley and London: University of California Press.
—— (ed.) (1997) *Refiguring Spain: Cinema / Media / Representation*, Durham, NC, and London: Duke University Press.
Quarterly Review of Film and Video XIII/4 December 1991, 'Bibliography on Spanish Cinema', pp. 129–31.
Talens, Jenaro and Santos Zunzunegui. (eds) (1998) *Modes of Representation in Spanish Cinema*, Minneapolis: University of Minnesota Press.

Other national cinemas

Berry, David. (1994) *Wales and the Cinema – the First Hundred Years*, Swansea: University of Wales Press.
Bren, Frank. (1990) *World Cinema: Poland*, Trowbridge: Flicks Books.
Bruce, David. (1996) *Scotland the Movie*, Edinburgh: Polygon.
Burns, Brian. (1996) *World Cinema: Hungary*, Trowbridge: Flicks Books.
Byrne, Terry. (1997) *Power in the Eye – An Introduction to Contemporary Irish Film*, Lanham, MD, and London: Scarecrow Press

Cowie, Peter. (1976) *Finnish Cinema*, London: The Tantivy Press.

Dick, Eddie. (ed.) (1990) *From Limelight to Satellite – a Scottish Film Book*, London: BFI and Scottish Film Council.

Eleftheriotis, Dimitris. (1995) 'Questioning Totalities: Constructions of Masculinity in the Popular Greek Cinema of the 1960s', *Screen*, Vol. 36, no. 3, Autumn pp. 233–42.

Hardy, Forsyth. (1990) *Scotland in Film*, Edinburgh: Edinburgh University Press.

Mackillop, James. (1989) *World Cinema: Ireland*, Trowbridge: Flicks Books.

—— (ed.) (1999) *Contemporary Irish Cinema from 'The Quiet Man' to 'Dancing at Lughnasa'*, New York: Syracuse University Press.

McIllroy, Brian. (1998) *Shooting to Kill: Filmmaking and the 'Troubles' in Northern Ireland*, Trowbridge: Flicks Books.

McLoone, Martin. (2000) *Irish Film – the Emergence of a Contemporary Cinema*, London: BFI.

Moseley, Philip. (2001) *Split Screen: Belgian Cinema and Cultural Identity*, Albany: State University of New York Press.

Mottram, Ron. (1988) *The Danish Cinema before Dreyer*, Metuchen, NJ, and London: Scarecrow Press, Inc.

Petrie, Duncan. (2000) *Screening Scotland*, London: BFI.

Pettitt, Lance. (2000) *Screening Ireland – Film and Television Presentation*, Manchester: Manchester University Press.

Rockett, Kevin, Luke Gibbons and John Hill. (1987) *Cinema and Ireland*, London and New York: Routledge.

Schuster, Mel. (1979) *Contemporary Greek Cinema*, Metuchen, NJ, and London: Scarecrow Press.

Soila, Tytti, Astrid Soderburgh Widding and Gunnar Iversen. (1998) *Nordic National Cinemas* London and New York: Routledge.

Europe and America

Durham, Carolyn. (1998) *Double Takes – Culture and Gender in French Films and Their American Re-Makes*, Hanover, NH: University Press of New England.

Ellwood, David W. and Rob Kroes. (eds) (1994) *Hollywood in Europe – Experiences of a Cultural Hegemony*, Amsterdam: VU University Press.

Elsaesser, Thomas. (1998) 'American friends: Hollywood echoes in the new German cinema', in Nowell-Smith and Ricci. (eds), pp. 142–55.

Grantham, Bill. (2000) *Some Big Bourgeois Brothel – Contexts for France's Culture Wars with Hollywood*, Luton: University of Luton Press

Higson, Andrew and Richard Maltby. (eds) (1999) *'Film Europe' and 'Film America': Cinema, Commerce and Cultural Exchange 1920–1939*, Exeter: Exeter University Press.

Horton, Andrew and Stuart Y. McDougal. (eds) (1998) *Play it Again Sam*, Berkeley: University of California Press.

Lev, Peter. (1993) *The Euro-American Cinema*, Austin: University of Texas Press.

Mazdon, Lucy. (2000) *Encore Hollywood: Remaking French Cinema*, London: BFI.

Nowell-Smith, Geoffrey and Steven Ricci. (eds) (1998) *Hollywood and Europe – Economics, Culture, National Identity 1945–65*, London: BFI Publishing.

Saunders, Thomas. (1994) *Hollywood in Berlin – American Cinema and Weimar Germany*, Berkeley and London: University of California Press.

Vernon, Kathleen M. (1997) 'Scripting a social imaginary: Hollywood in/and Spanish cinema', in Kinder. (ed.), pp. 35–64.

Vincendeau, Ginette. (1992) 'France 1945–65 and Hollywood: the policier at inter-national text', *Screen* Vol. 33, no. 1, Spring pp. 50–80.

Women and European cinema

Attwood, Lynne. (1993) *Red Women on the Silver Screen – Soviet Women and Cinema from the Beginning to the End of the Communist Era*, London: Pandora Press.

Bruno, Guiliana and Maria Nadotti. (eds) (1988) *Off Screen – Women and Film in Italy*, London and New York: Routledge.

Foster, Gwendolyn Audrey. (ed.) (2000) *The Films of Chantal Akerman*, Trowbridge: Flicks Books.

Flitterman-Lewis, Sandy (1990) *To Desire Differently – Feminism and the French Cinema*, Urbana and Chicago: University of Illinois Press.

Frieden, Sandra, Richard W. McCormick, Vibeke Petersen and Laurie Melissa Vogelsanf. (eds) (1993a) *Gender and German Cinema: Vol. 1: Gender and Representation in German Cinema*, Providence, OH, and Oxford: Berg.

—— (1993b) *Gender and German Cinema: Vol. 2: German Film History / German History on Film*, Providence, OH, and Oxford: Berg.

Günther, Renate. (2002) *Marguerite Duras*, Manchester: Manchester University Press.

Harper, Sue. (2000) 'From wholesome girls to difficult dowagers – actresses in 1930s British cinema', in Ashby and Higson. (eds), pp. 137–51.

Luckett, Moya. (2000) 'Travel and mobility – femininity and national identity in swinging London films', in Ashby and Higson. (eds), pp. 233–45.

Knight, Julia. (1992) *Women and the New German Cinema*, London: Verso.

Landy, Marcia. (1991) *British Genres: Cinema and Society 1930–1960*, Princeton, NJ: Princeton University Press.

Lant, Antonia. (1991) *Reinventing Women for Wartime British Cinema*, Princeton, NJ: Princeton University Press.

Linville, Susan. (1998) *Feminism, Film and Fascism*, Austin: University of Texas Press.

Martin-Marquez, Susan. (1999) *Feminist Discourse and Spanish Cinema – Sight Unseen,* Oxford: Oxford University Press.

Mizejewski, Linda. (1992) *Divine Decadence: Fascism, Female Spectacle and the Making of Sally Bowles*, Princeton, NJ: Princeton University Press.

O'Sickey, Ingebord Majer and Ingeborg Von Zadow. (1998) *Triangulated Visions – Women in Recent German Cinema*, Albany: State University of New York.

Petro, Patrice. (1989) *Joyless Streets: Women and Melodramatic Representation in Weimar Germany*, Princeton, NJ: Princeton University Press.

Rollet, Brigitte. (1998) *Coline Serreau*, Manchester: Manchester University Press.

Sieglohr, Ulrike. (ed.) (2000) *Heroines without Heroes: Reconstructing Female and National Identities in European Cinema, 1945–51*, London and New York: Cassell.

Smith, Alison. (1998) *Agnès Varda*, Manchester: Manchester University Press.

Tarr, Carrie. (1999) *Diane Kurys*, Manchester: Manchester University Press.

—— with Brigitte Rollet. (2001) *Cinema and the Second Sex – 20 Years of Film-making in France*, London and New York: Continuum.

Thumim, Janet. (1992) *Celluloid Sisters: Women and Popular Cinema*, New York: St Martin's Press.

Index